THE UNI
WINCI

To be returned on or before the day marked above, subject to recall.

Sara Miller McCune founded SAGE Publishing in 1965 to support the dissemination of usable knowledge and educate a global community. SAGE publishes more than 1000 journals and over 800 new books each year, spanning a wide range of subject areas. Our growing selection of library products includes archives, data, case studies and video. SAGE remains majority owned by our founder and after her lifetime will become owned by a charitable trust that secures the company's continued independence.

Los Angeles | London | New Delhi | Singapore | Washington DC | Melbourne

GLOBAL POLITICS AND
VIOLENT NON-STATE ACTORS

NATASHA EZROW

Los Angeles | London | New Delhi
Singapore | Washington DC | Melbourne

Los Angeles | London | New Delhi
Singapore | Washington DC | Melbourne

SAGE Publications Ltd
1 Oliver's Yard
55 City Road
London EC1Y 1SP

SAGE Publications Inc.
2455 Teller Road
Thousand Oaks, California 91320

SAGE Publications India Pvt Ltd
B 1/I 1 Mohan Cooperative Industrial Area
Mathura Road
New Delhi 110 044

SAGE Publications Asia-Pacific Pte Ltd
3 Church Street
#10-04 Samsung Hub
Singapore 049483

Editor: Natalie Aguilera
Assistant Editor: Delayna Spencer
Production editor: Katie Forsythe
Marketing manager: Sally Ransom
Cover design: Stephanie Guyaz
Typeset by: C&M Digitals (P) Ltd, Chennai, India
Printed by: CPI Group (UK) Ltd, Croydon, CR0 4YY

Library of Congress Control Number: 2017930216

British Library Cataloguing in Publication data

A catalogue record for this book is available from
the British Library

ISBN 978-1-4739-6048-0
ISBN 978-1-4739-6049-7 (pbk)

At SAGE we take sustainability seriously. Most of our products are printed in the UK using FSC papers and boards.
When we print overseas we ensure sustainable papers are used as measured by the PREPS grading system.
We undertake an annual audit to monitor our sustainability.

TABLE OF CONTENTS

About the Author		ix
Acknowledgements		x
List of Abbreviations		xi
Part I Theories and Concepts		**1**
Introduction		3
Global Politics Today		3
Outline of the Book		4
Part I: Theories and Concepts		4
Part II: Explanations of Violent Non-state Actors		5
Part III: Types of Violent Non-state Actors		6
Part IV: Dealing with Violent Non-state Actors		8
Conclusion		9
1	Security Studies and Violent Non-state Actors	10
	What Are the Main Approaches in International Relations?	10
	Realism	11
	Criticisms of Realism	13
	Global Relations in the Third World	15
	What Is the Field of Security Studies?	18
	Cold War Security Studies during the Cold War	18
	Expanding the Concept of Security	19
	Why Are States So Different from Non-state Actors?	21
	Is Realism Still Relevant?	22
	Conclusion	22
2	Understanding Violence and Non-conventional Warfare	24
	Old and New Violence	24
	Different Types of Violence and Conflict	26
	Criminal Violence	30
	Who Are the Violent Non-state Actors?	37

Part II Explanations of Violent Non-state Actors   39

  3 Global Explanations   41

    End of the Bipolar Cold War   42
    Globalization and Violent Non-state Actors   43
    Motivational Factors   44
    Opportunity Factors   45
    Conclusion   53

  4 State-Level Explanations   55

    Motivational Factors   55
    Opportunities   62
    Conclusion   69

  5 Individual- and Societal-Level Explanations   71

    Overview of Individual-Level Theories   71
    Demographic Factors   72
    Psycho-analytical Approaches   78
    Social Psychological Approaches   80
    Conclusion   82

Part III Types of Violent Non-state Actors   85

  6 Insurgencies   87

    Definition   87
    Political Ideology and Objectives   88
    Strategy and Tactics   90
    Structure and Recruitment   91
    Funding and Support   94
    Power and Impact on the State and Society   96
    Conclusion   100

  7 Terrorist Organizations and Terror Networks   102

    Definition   102
    Political Ideology and Objectives   103
    Strategy and Tactics   104
    Structure and Recruitment   107
    Funding and Support   109
    Power and Impact on the State and Society   111
    Al-Qaeda, Terrorist Umbrella Organization   112
    The Emergence of al-Qaeda in Iraq (AQI) and the Islamic State   114
    Conclusion   116

  8 Warlords and Marauders   118

    Definition   118
    Political Ideology and Objectives   121

Structure and Recruitment   122
Strategy and Tactics   124
Funding and Support   126
Power and Impact on the State and Society   127
Conclusion   131

9 Organized Crime and Gangs   133

Definition   133
Gangs   134
Political Ideology and Objectives   137
Structure and Recruitment   138
Strategy and Tactics   141
Funding and Support   143
Power and Impact on the State and Society   144
Conclusion   146

10 Private Security Companies and Paramilitary Units   148

Definition   148
Paramilitary Forces   149
Death Squads   150
Political Ideology and Objectives   151
Structure and Recruitment   153
Strategy and Tactics   156
Funding and Support   157
Power and Impact on the State and Society   159
Conclusion   161

Part IV Dealing with Violent Non-state Actors   165

11 Moderation and Politicization   167

Political Organizations with Militant Wings   167
Definition   168
Political Objectives and Ideology   168
Strategies and Tactics   169
Organization and Recruitment   170
Funding and Support   171
Power and Impact on the State and Society   171
Theories of Parties and Violence   172
Political Parties That Spawn or Splinter into Militant Organizations 174
Violent Groups That Turn to Politics   175
Movements That Have Both Violent and Non-violent Groups   176
Politicization of Violent Groups   179
Conclusion   181

12 Counter-strategies to Violent Groups   184

How Do Violent Groups End?   184
Dealing with Violent Non-state Actors   187

Preventive Measures   187
Administrative Reform   188
Judicial Reform   190
Security Reform   190
Prison Reform   191
Counter-strategies   192
Conclusion   198

Conclusion   201

References   205
Index   233

ABOUT THE AUTHOR

Natasha Ezrow is a Senior Lecturer at the University of Essex, where she directs the International Development Program and teaches modules in international relations, terrorism, insurgencies and conflict, as well as the politics of the Middle East, Asia, Latin America and Africa. Her research focuses on violent non-state actors, authoritarian politics, institutional decay, corruption and democratization, and she has published several books on these topics.

In addition to teaching and writing, Dr Ezrow has been featured as an analyst on BBC World, BBC News, the BBC Breakfast show and Al Jazeera. She also currently works as a consultant for the United Nations Economic and Social Commission of Western Asia (UNESCWA) and the European Union External Action Service.

She holds a PhD in Political Science from the University of California at Santa Barbara (2002).

ACKNOWLEDGEMENTS

I want to thank the students in the Government Department at the University of Essex. Their enthusiasm for global politics and violent non-state groups is what initially inspired this book. Each year I have learned so much from the discussion generated during modules on global politics, violence and violent non-state groups.

I also want to thank the entire team at SAGE Publications for being incredibly easy to work with. It was a stress-free experience and one that I thoroughly enjoyed. They helped every step of the way to ensure that the final book was much improved from the original drafts.

On a personal front, I want to thank my parents Jeff and Yvette, and my sister and past co-author, Erica for being so supportive. I have to also thank my daughters, Annika and Karolina for being totally adorable. And last but not least, I want to thank René for being my best friend and partner. I don't know what I'd do without you. Ich liebe Dich über alles!

LIST OF ABBREVIATIONS

ANC	African National Congress Party
AQI	al-Qaeda in Iraq
AQIM	al Qaeda in the Islamic Maghreb
ARENA	National Republican Alliance
AUC	United Self-Defence Forces
CV	Comando Vermelho
DDS	Davao Death Sqaud
ELN	National Liberation Army
ETA	Euskadi Ta Askatasuna
FALN	Armed Forces of National Liberation
FARC	Revolutionary Armed Forces of Colombia
FLN	National Liberation Front (Algeria)
FRELIMO	Mozambique Liberation Front
FSNL	Sandinistas National Liberation Front
GAFE	Airmobile Special Forces Group
GAL	Anti-Terrorist Liberation Groups
GIA	Armed Islamic Group of Algeria
IG	Islamic Group
IS	Islamic State
IRA	Irish Republican Army
LDK	Democratic League of Kosovo
LTTE	Liberation Tigers of Tamil Eelam
MILF	Moro Islamic Liberation Front
MK	Umkhonto we Sizwe
MNLF	Moro National Liberation Front

MS-13	Mara Salvatrucha
NPFL	National Patriotic Front of Liberia
OECD	Organization for Economic Co-operation and Development
PCC	Primeiro Comando da Capital
PFLP	Popular Front for the Liberation of Palestine
PIRA	Provisional Irish Republican Army
PKK	Kurdistan Workers' Party
PLO	Palestinian Liberation Organization
PNV	Basque Nationalist Party
PRI	Institutional Revolutionary Party
PSC(S)	Private Security Companies
RUF	Revolutionary United Front
TULF	Tamil United Liberation Front
UNITA	National Union for the Total Independence of Angola

PART I
THEORIES AND CONCEPTS

The objective of Part I is to review what scholars have learned to date about security and violent groups. We first consider traditional theories of security, focusing on major paradigms in global politics. We then consider the notion of security as it is embodied in the field of international security studies. The final section of Part I reviews the concept of violence in both its conventional and non-conventional forms.

INTRODUCTION

GLOBAL POLITICS TODAY

In the 20th century, international security studies have focused on the behaviour of *states* in the international system and on the conflicts between states. What security studies have often neglected, however, is the study of *violent non-state actors*. The new threats to global security no longer solely originate from states. Furthermore, interstate conflict has become less and less common and much of the violence taking place is irregular. This irregular type of violence occupies a space between being politically motivated and economically motivated. Political violence overlaps with crime and vice versa. Understanding irregular forms of violence and violent non-state actors is becoming more and more critical to security studies.

Nevertheless, scholarly work still lacks coherent theoretical frameworks to identify the processes that lead to their emergence, growth, transformation and power. Though violent non-state actors do not have international legitimacy and recognition, at times they are on par with states in terms of wealth, military resources and territory. Compared to states, violent non-state actors are more unpredictable and volatile. Violent non-state actors defy traditional tools that states have at their disposal to manage threats. Because of this, it makes it much more difficult to generate a strategy to deal with them.

Though the book focuses on a new type of violence, the idea that there are new threats for individuals, societies and states to contend with is not a novel concept. Survey research in Western countries indicates more and more people are concerned with the growing threats posed by violent non-state actors, with many Westerners claiming that terrorist attacks are their number one security concern (Waterman, 2013). But terror groups do not generate as much violence as organized criminal groups. For example, in Brazil dying in a terrorist attack is very unlikely, but due to gang and organized criminal activity death by homicide is the fifth leading cause of death. There continues to be a host of misunderstandings about the threats that violent non-state actors pose. Yet most studies of security have omitted examining criminal groups. But if criminal groups are the most ubiquitous and pose the biggest threat to human security, how can we understand security without including these groups in our analysis?

This book aims to accomplish the following. It is important to first clarify that the book does not examine random acts of violence, but rather aims to comprehend patterns of violence by violent groups. From there, it is important to understand the different types of violence taking place, what types of actors are responsible for perpetuating this violence and how these actors threaten security and threaten states and society. To do so, this book combines the works from multiple disciplines including: international security, global studies, warfare and conflict, area studies, comparative politics, political psychology, development and criminology.

However, we start with the field of international relations and international security studies. Understanding the threats facing the world today is something that has been covered for decades by these disciplines. As a school of thought, the focus of international relations has been on *states* and *interstate relations*. By using international relations theories as a starting point, we illustrate how security was initially conceived. This background serves as a point of contrast to understand why the threats posed by violent non-state actors have been so difficult to comprehend. This also highlights why we have so badly misunderstood how to respond to threats originating from the developing world. This book focuses on violent non-state actors in order to underline the actual threats to global and human security. This helps us to better understand the political patterns of the world in general and not just those between nation states. Thus, this book is about understanding violent non-state actors and the world that they emanate from.

OUTLINE OF THE BOOK

PART I: THEORIES AND CONCEPTS

Part I offers a literature review of all of the scholarly work that has been done on security and violent groups. The first chapter outlines the traditional theories on security, beginning with the major paradigms in international relations, and then further elaborates on the concept of security as envisioned by international security studies. A subsequent chapter builds on the work done by international relations and international security studies scholars and develops the concepts of violence, both conventional forms of violence and non-conventional forms. This helps to explain the different ways in which violent non-state actors threaten security in the 21st century. This also highlights how these non-conventional forms of violence necessitate different conceptions of security, and different responses to preventing and subduing these forms of violence.

CHAPTER 1: SECURITY STUDIES AND VIOLENT NON-STATE ACTORS

Chapter 1 begins by offering an overview of the primary paradigms of realism, with a brief focus on liberalism and constructivism. This chapter provides an explanation of how these paradigms conceptualize security threats. The chapter then explains the dominance of realist thought during the Cold War and the critiques lodged at realism by other schools of thought. This chapter offers an explanation of what is meant by a state-centric view of security. The chapter then offers a challenge to traditional theories and the assumptions made about states and their hegemony, legitimacy and sovereignty. The chapter argues that traditional theories have based these assumptions from Cold War frameworks that are no longer applicable to help us understand all of the contemporary security challenges of the 21st century. To address these shortcomings, the chapter explains how international security studies has widened its agenda focusing on different types of threats and violence, different types of security and different actors, such as violent non-state actors. The chapter concludes by emphasizing the need to understand different forms of violence that may be a departure from more conventional forms of conflict in order to formulate a more comprehensive understanding of security.

CHAPTER 2: UNDERSTANDING VIOLENCE AND NON-CONVENTIONAL WARFARE

Chapter 2 first starts by explaining what is meant by interstate war and traditional forms of violence. Using this as a starting point, the chapter then offers an explanation of what is meant by unconventional violence such as terrorism, guerrilla warfare, organized criminal and gang violence and hybrid wars – and how unconventional warfare and violence differ from traditional types. The chapter then provides an overview of the literature on these different types of violence, offering clear definitions of how these types of violence have been defined and theorized, and how different types of violence may be used by the same actor. The chapter argues that there are many important factors that can help us distinguish between different violent non-state actors.

PART II: EXPLANATIONS OF VIOLENT NON-STATE ACTORS

Part II provides an overview of the literature on violent non-state actors, using three different levels of analysis, capturing all of the scholarly work that has concentrated on this topic. In doing so, Part II demonstrates what the most appropriate lenses through which to examine the key questions in this area of study, such as the structural conditions under which certain violent non-state actors emerge, the global conditions that help them thrive and the reasons why individuals may want to join such violent organizations.

CHAPTER 3: GLOBAL EXPLANATIONS

Chapter 3 provides an overview of global factors that help explain why violent non-state actors have become more important players in international and domestic security. The chapter emphasizes that in the 21st century the significance of violent non-state actors needs to be understood in the context of globalization and the end of the bipolarity of the Cold War era. Improved connectivity, communication and transportation help explain how violent non-state actors have been able to form global networks that facilitate access to arms, recruits, resources and other sources of funding. This chapter also demonstrates how globalization has expedited the spread of ideologies across borders, aggregating beliefs under a transnational umbrella organization.

CHAPTER 4: STATE-LEVEL EXPLANATIONS

Chapter 4 explores the various state-level explanations for why violent non-state actors emerge and challenge security. The chapter looks in depth into the role of state-level factors in creating an environment that is conducive to the operation of violent non-state actors, such as poverty, corruption and regime type. Additionally, the role of different forms of institutional decay will be examined, which serve as both a motive for violent non-state groups to form and also may provide opportunities. In particular, the chapter will analyse the importance of state failure and state support in assisting violent non-state actors.

CHAPTER 5: INDIVIDUAL- AND SOCIETAL-LEVEL EXPLANATIONS

Chapter 5 explores theories of violence at the individual level. These theories may investigate the role of individual socio-economic, demographic and psychological factors in the recruitment of individuals to organized crime, gangs and violent political organizations. Thus this chapter will look primarily at individuals and groups to help understand why individuals join violent organizations. The chapter will highlight some of the limitations of this level of analysis, with a particular critique on the challenges of using psychological approaches when it comes to making generalizations about why individuals turn to violence. The chapter will also highlight where individual-level explanations can add to our understanding of violent non-state actors.

PART III: TYPES OF VIOLENT NON-STATE ACTORS

Part III acknowledges that violent non-state actors have merged and mutated, using a host of different tactics and modes of funding and operation which have blurred the lines between political and economic motives. Nevertheless, there are still some distinctions that can be made that are important for better understanding the threats posed by different violent non-state actors and how they can be dealt with. First, Chapters 6–10 will explore the literature on each group and provide a clear definition to help better conceptualize the violent group. Each chapter will then provide further explanation of each violent group focusing on the following: (1) what their ideology and political objectives are, if any; (2) what their strategy and tactics are; (3) how they are typically structured; how they recruit; (4) the various funding methods used and sources of support; and (5) the power and impact that these groups have on the state and society.

CHAPTER 6: INSURGENCIES

Chapter 6 explains what is meant by insurgencies. The chapter demonstrates that the primary raison d'être of these groups is to achieve some political goal (such as more autonomy or improved socio-economic conditions) by challenging the host state through armed struggle or challenging other paramilitary groups. The chapter clarifies how these groups may differ from other politically motivated organizations, namely terrorist groups. The chapter will offer a clearer picture of why these groups turn to violence, why they thrive and what pathways they are likely to take. The chapter offers case studies of the Tamil Tigers of Sri Lanka and the Zapatistas of Mexico.

CHAPTER 7: TERRORIST ORGANIZATIONS AND TERROR NETWORKS

This chapter provides an overview of terrorist groups of the past and present, including how terrorist groups may differ based on their ideology and objectives. In addition to highlighting the differences between global terror networks and terror organizations of the past, the chapter also explains what differentiates a terror organization from an insurgency and provides a clear explanation of the ever evolving structure, tactics, recruitment and funding. Given that al-Qaeda is the best-known global terror organization of the last two decades, Chapter 7 provides an extensive discussion of al-Qaeda and how it differs from previous terror organizations. Al-Qaeda has transformed over time into an umbrella organization that is loosely linked up with lightly structured violent groups. These groups have more amorphous political and ideological goals to challenge the status quo through violent means, with a scope that extends well beyond the nation state.

CHAPTER 8: WARLORDS AND MARAUDERS

In a departure from the previous chapters, which have focused on organizations with largely political goals, the subsequent chapters focus on organizations with primarily economic goals. Chapter 8 introduces the concept of warlords, which have become notable for their role in delegitimizing and weakening the state in countries like Afghanistan, Somalia, Chechnya and Sudan. Though warlords aim to control territory and people, their motivations are primarily economic rather than political. The chapter also examines the role of some of the marauding rebel organizations that have been spontaneously formed by warlords, whose loosely defined political goals rapidly turned economic in the process of funding the organization. In other words, the political goals of the organization are almost non-existent. The chapter uses examples from West Africa and offers a case study of Afghanistan.

CHAPTER 9: ORGANIZED CRIME AND GANGS

Chapter 9 continues with the focus on actors focused primarily on economic gain and provides an overview of organized criminal groups such as drug cartels and the Mafia. Though organized criminal groups in many cases become involved in controlling the state and the politicians within them, the chapter explains that the primary motives that drive organized criminal groups are economic. The chapter gives a thorough explanation of their level of organization and extensive operations. This chapter also offers an overview of street gangs, with particular attention to the violent gangs that have emerged in the Americas.

The chapter emphasizes the environmental conditions in which organized criminal groups and gangs are likely to thrive and their global nature of organized crime. Using examples of Los Zetas of Mexico and Maras of El Salvador, the chapter demonstrates how organized crime threatens security and why organized crime and conflict often go hand-in-hand.

CHAPTER 10: PRIVATE SECURITY COMPANIES AND PARAMILITARY UNITS

Chapter 10 provides an introduction to private security companies (PSCs). More and more commonly used, particularly by the United States in the wars in Afghanistan and Iraq, these actors are motivated by profits. These actors merit attention in order to better understand how they negatively or positively contribute to security. The chapter also examines the role of paramilitary groups and death squads. We explain how they differ from PSCs but also show their similarities. Though paramilitary units and death squads may be driven by political motivations (a departure for this section that has focused on economic actors) their primary motive is economic; they are paid to serve in a conflict that helps to defend their financial interests.

The chapter defines these actors, explains their objectives, structure, funding, methods of recruitment and support, tactics and strategy, and impact on the state and society. The negative spillovers of having private armed groups that can challenge the state's monopoly over the legitimate use of force are also explained. The chapter will offer examples of US PSCs and the now defunct South African group Executive Outcomes and paramilitary groups such as the United Self-Defence Forces (AUC) of Colombia.

PART IV: DEALING WITH VIOLENT NON-STATE ACTORS

Part IV concludes the book with a focus on the best strategies for dealing with violent non-state actors, how these groups eventually end and transition, and what are the important institutional reforms that are necessary to prevent their emergence and success.

CHAPTER 11: MODERATION AND POLITICIZATION

Chapter 11 examines violent groups that engage in conventional politics, and how they should be dealt with. To do so, it explores the various political organizations that exist with militant wings. These actors have well-organized political units which are motivated by a genuine political agenda and platform and are allowed to take part in elections and do so. They are violent non-state actors however, because they possess a militant wing (either before or after they've formed) to achieve some of their objectives. These organizations may have support from a large constituency which they represent and may be involved in the distribution of public goods. But should these groups be integrated into the political system? What impact might they have on state and society? Does engagement in the conventional political process have a moderating effect? This chapter explores these questions while also offering two case studies of Hezbollah and Hamas.

CHAPTER 12: COUNTER-STRATEGIES TO VIOLENT GROUPS

Chapter 12 offers an overview of all of the literature on strategies to counter the power of the violent non-state actors mentioned in the book. Before doing so, this chapter first focuses on how groups moderate and terminate. The chapter explains what the literature has said about the exit of violent groups, detailing the reasons why they usually exit and the conditions that are the most inhospitable for violent groups to threaten security. Building on the case studies and examples presented throughout Part III, the chapter explains what is the best course of action to deal with violent groups both before they form and after. It highlights the importance of institutional reform to undermine the viability of these groups and a comprehensive strategy.

CONCLUSION

The final chapter will offer a brief conclusion of what we have learned thus far about violent non-state actors and what avenues of future research are necessary to explore.

Key Points of the Book

- Traditional paradigms of security do not understand the biggest threats to humanity.
- Threats need to be thought of in terms of how they might affect the state, society and individuals.
- There is a general misunderstanding about violent non-state actors and non-conventional warfare and the threats they pose.
- Violent non-state actors have become more powerful, necessitating further examination; their emergence is usually a symptom of other bigger problems that need to be addressed.
- Understanding politics in the developing world and an increasingly globalized world is critical to understanding the emergence of violent non-state actors.

1

SECURITY STUDIES AND VIOLENT NON-STATE ACTORS

Key Terms

- Anarchy
- Balance of power
- Bipolarity
- Constructivism
- Collective security
- Democratic peace theory
- Human security
- International institutions
- Non-state actors
- Nuclear weapons
- Polarity
- Security dilemma
- Small arms

WHAT ARE THE MAIN APPROACHES IN INTERNATIONAL RELATIONS?

International relations (IR) is a huge field that offers theories that organize generalizations about international politics. The discipline has had a long tradition of trying to explain the relationships between states. Theories of international relations examine questions such as: What are the causes of conflict? and Why is there peace? The last several decades, however, has seen the field of IR undergo a revolution in the study of conflict and violence.

For most scholars in IR, the role of the *state* is critical.[1] Most scholars still see states as the most important actors, though others acknowledge that other actors are important.

---

[1]Legally the state is supposed to have a territorial base, with a stable population that resides within its borders and a government that the population owes its allegiance to. The state also has to be recognized diplomatically by other states (see Mingst and Arreguín-Toft, 2013: Ch. 5).

The heavy focus on the state materialized in the post–World War II era (see Waltz, 1993). It was from this time onwards that the idea of state sovereignty – that states had territorial boundaries that should not be interfered with – became more commonly espoused. By 'states', scholars are referring to the governments of different countries around the world. Assumptions are then made about states and their interests, as if the state was a unified entity. Before turning to a discussion on the role of the state in global politics today, this chapter will sum up the main approaches of IR.

The field of IR has been dominated by two main paradigms: realism and liberalism. Though heavily criticized, realism has been the most dominant paradigm, guiding policymakers since World War II. Particularly during the Cold War, realist thought dominated academic and policy circles. The importance of the superpower rivalry helped place realism as the most important approach to understanding interstate relations and security. But can it still add to our understanding of the biggest threats to security today?

REALISM

Even before the Cold War, realism had had a long philosophical tradition. The works of Thucydides, Hobbes and Machiavelli formed the philosophical underpinnings of realism. Realism is also an academic approach to understanding international politics, but there are different variants of realism (something that will be explained in more depth later in the chapter). For now we focus on the key components that tie all strands of realism together.

Realists argue that they see the world as it is. They make no attempt to sugar-coat the nature of global politics. Realists see the world as inherently conflictual. States struggle to attain power in a world that is anarchic. Without a central authority to guarantee security, states rely on their own means to protect their interests (Grieco, 1988). Because of this, realists assume that states live in a self-help system where relative gains matter more than absolute ones. By this we mean that states care more about what they have in relation to other states rather than being satisfied with what they have. States are self-interested and motivated by attaining power, more so than attaining economic wealth. Scholars such as Hans Morgenthau (1904–80) focused on how states are driven by attaining power, while other realists such as Kenneth Waltz (1924–2013) focused more on states seeking power as a means to attain security. How powerful states are is usually measured by their military capacity first, followed by their economic resources. All realists also assume that states are the most important actor. It is this assumption of realism that this book will examine the most thoroughly.

While early realists may have focused more heavily on power and human nature's quest for power, neo-realism turned more attention to the international system that shaped state behaviour. Anarchy figured heavily in the approach as an explanation for why the world was so conflictual. Most neo-realists in the Waltzian tradition focused on the uniformity of state behaviour. In addition, for most neo-realists, states are all the same. The only thing that differentiates them is their capabilities. States are all self-interested, rational, unitary actors that are driven by the need to seek power for its own sake or power to attain security.

Other realists focus more on unit-level factors such as motivations. As noted before, traditional realists wrote about the role of human nature in driving behaviour. Neo-classical realists agree that anarchy causes a sense of insecurity, but note that states may vary in terms of their motivation, with some being more dissatisfied with the status quo than other states. Classical realists and neo-realists differ in terms of the source and content of state preferences. Morgenthau's work assumed that leaders of states are motivated by their need for power. Waltz never focused on leaders' motivations or state characteristics, only assuming that states' main aim is survival.

For most realists, security is achieved by making others more insecure. One state's need to attain power or security will cause other states to seek their own security. This leads to the security dilemma, which helps to explain the spiralling arms race that took place during the Cold War. Henry Kissinger illustrates the logic of the security dilemma during the Cold War: 'The superpowers often behave like two heavily armed blind men feeling their way around a room, each believing himself in mortal peril from the other, whom he assumes to have perfect vision' (quoted by Conlin, 2013: 804). Though both the US and the Soviet Union had acquired enough weapons to blow up the world ten times over, they were never satisfied with their arsenal, and the high military spending of one camp caused the other to follow suit. Demonstrating the effects of these policies, Kissinger added, 'Of course, over time, even two armed blind men can do enormous damage to each other, not to speak of the room'.

Because the system was so unstable, achieving a balance of power was essential. States assessed one another in terms of their power and capabilities. States could balance in two ways. They could balance internally by increasing their military personnel and acquiring a large arsenal of weapons (possibly even nuclear weapons), or they could balance externally by making alliances with other states. Alliances have the advantage of reducing the resources that must be devoted to defence. But the inherent problem with external balancing is that because all states are self-interested and often cannot be trusted, alliances can be short-lived. It is not uncommon to be abandoned or betrayed by a past ally. Alliances may also draw states into conflicts that they may not wish to join. Thus, though alliances may be important for helping states alleviate the burden of internal balancing, states must always work to ensure that they can survive. Though eliminating threats is impossible, there are strategies that states can employ to achieve stalemates which may offer a respite from conflict.

For neo-realists in the Waltzian tradition, threats to security are affected by the distribution of power, referred to as *polarity*. Thus, it is the polarity of the system (whether it is unipolar, bipolar or multipolar) that influences the propensity for conflict. For Waltz (in contrast to Morgenthau), the bipolar system during the Cold War was stable because a stalemate was established between the superpowers where no state was willing to risk disrupting the balance. Though the bipolar era lasted for decades, the distribution of capabilities is constantly shifting, which causes variation in balance-of-power behaviour.

Though there are various strands of realism, the overarching theme is that states are the most important actors, states are driven by the need for power in order to achieve security and the world is naturally conflictual, which necessitates that states seek to build up their military power to defend themselves from constant threats coming from other states. These views largely shaped policymakers' agendas.[2] For a summary of the realist position, see Table 1.1.

---

[2]Realism is not associated with hawkish behaviour, however. While some realists have advocated more aggressive foreign policies, others, like George Kennan, consistently criticized the United States' confrontational policies. Many other realists, such as Hans Morgenthau and John Mearsheimer, were strong critics of the US's intervention in Vietnam and Iraq, respectively.

Table 1.1 How Realists See States

Ideology and political objectives:	Do not matter; states are all the same
Strategy and tactics:	Acquire as much power as possible (offensive) or achieve a balance of power (defensive)
Organizational structure:	Does not matter; states are all the same
Funding and support:	Varies by states' economic capacity and by the polarity of the system
Power and impact:	States are the most important actors; they differ only in terms of their capabilities

Though realists should not be accused of advocating conflict, realism has been criticized for not being able to understand global politics in the post-Cold War era. The focus on states as the most important actors makes it difficult to understand the behaviour of *non-state* actors. This is a critical omission, because non-state actors in global politics abound. Many non-state actors are non-violent and focus on improving the human condition through non-violent means. There are millions of non-governmental organizations, international organizations and international agencies committed to preventing conflict, easing poverty and improving communication and cooperation in a non-violent manner. In spite of these efforts, the world has also seen a spike in the formation of organizations that have used or still use some form of violence to achieve their objectives. Their formation, motivations and impact cannot be explained by a reductionist approach that focuses on strong, capable, unitary states. In addition to this criticism, the following section elaborates on the other key criticisms of realism.

CRITICISMS OF REALISM

Though realism dominated international security circles for decades, alternative paradigms have also been influential. Prior to World War II, the *liberal* tradition attained popularity for espousing views of progress. Known sometimes as idealists, liberals acknowledge that the world is conflictual but are optimistic about the potential for peace and cooperation. Liberals focus on what needs to take place for states to coexist peacefully. In contrast to realists, early liberals' view of human nature was optimisistic that there was a capacity for optimal outcomes, that cooperation and respect for human rights could be achieved. In their view, states cared about morality and promoting a common good.

Neo-liberals adopted many of the same assumptions that neo-realists did, but came to opposite conclusions. Neo-liberals also assumed that states were important actors that acted rationally. They concluded, however, that this rational behaviour, which was constrained by institutions, would lead to peace and cooperation. States were not as concerned with power as they were with economic and political considerations, such as the desire for prosperity and possibly a commitment to liberal values (Walt, 1991). States would see it in their self-interest to cooperate and trade. States that focused on trade emphasized the benefits of trading freely and highlighted how states that traded would become interdependent, due to the mutual benefits of trade. The benefits of trade would make the costs of war extremely high.

Other scholars focused on the importance of 'democratic peace' (Russett et al., 1995). The theory holds that democracies are unlikely to fight one another due to shared norms, the institutional checks that slow down the decision to declare war, peace-loving populations and a habit of choosing negotiation and bargaining over going to war. Democracies are used to resolving conflict through rules and negotiations. Therefore, two democracies will choose diplomacy and bargaining over going to war with each other. An additional factor is that democracies are more transparent which enhances the chance for cooperation and peace. Cooperation will be a more likely option; clear communication and transparency will help to better understand the intentions of other states. Furthermore, it may be internationally unpopular to choose to go to war if diplomatic options have not been completely exhausted.

Other liberals have focused on the importance of international institutions (Keohane, 1989), such as collective security arrangements (Kupchan and Kupchan, 1995) that could mitigate the propensity for conflict by providing a collective deterrent against aggression. Institutions could also help communication and increase transparency. This helps to lower transaction costs of cooperation and to coordinate multilateral action. Institutions could also assist in creating future cooperation by acting in reciprocity with other institutions – in effect, setting up an iterated game of cooperation. Institutions may also help states create shared values and concerns, thereby helping states become interdependent. By creating mutually beneficial relationships, states would be able to concentrate on absolute, not relative, gains. Finally, in the absence of an international government, institutions can play a role of enforcing agreements and punishing defection.

In general, liberalism has worked to understand cooperation, peace and how to avoid conflict, but has not offered a theoretical framework for explaining violence. Liberals have placed attention on non-state actors, but much less on violent non-state actors. Because of this, liberals have contributed less to our understanding of security threats and more to our understanding of how to prevent these threats. Liberals acknowledge the role of non-state actors in international politics and emphasize international cooperation when facing threats from violent non-state actors. Networks of cooperating government agencies are the best response to threats from violent non-state actors, according to political scientist Joseph Nye (2003, 2004).

Realism and liberalism have been the dominant paradigms in international relations. Constructivism, peace studies, feminist studies and critical theory have aimed at uncovering the weaknesses of traditional theories. Here we focus on constructivism.

Constructivism is not a unified school of thought – it has been interpreted very differently by various scholars – but all constructivists challenge realism's assumptions about states (Finnemore and Sikkink, 2001; Hopf, 1998; Wendt, 1992; 1995). First, they challenge the notion that states are the main actors seeking survival. Constructivists argue that state behaviour cannot be assumed; it is shaped by a combination of collective norms, social identities and elite beliefs and interests. These norms, identities and interests have in turn been affected by the discourses of societies and by historical processes and interactions. Thus the construction and evolution of ideas and discourse are more important than sheer military or economic power. For example, in examining the role of threats, constructivists argue that there are processes by which individuals and states construct threats. The goal of security may change and this may depend on how the state is constituted and how security issues are framed. Different countries have different ways of defining security and threats. For example, Cuba for decades viewed the US as the biggest threat to its survival, whereas its Caribbean neighbours viewed the US as an ally. Constructivists ask what discourse has taken place to affect how one country could be viewed so differently. In contrast, realism does not address behaviour that is based on ideologically driven agendas because it sees behaviour driven by self-interest (Hyde-Price, 2009: 34).

In addition to challenging assumptions about the importance of power and security to states, constructivists also challenge the importance of anarchy. Noted constructivist Alexander Wendt argued that anarchy is what states make of it. Spirals of hostility, arms races and war are not inevitable in an anarchic system. If states fall into conflict it is due to their own behaviour which can reproduce militaristic mind-sets. For Wendt (1992), anarchy is an empty vessel with no logic. It is the interests and identities that explain behaviour. States' interests are a function of international interactions that have taken place, not due to the looming fear of anarchy. Barry Buzan (1984, 2008) argued that security communities can emerge when there are strong states. Security communities are socially constructed when knowledge can transform international structures and security politics creating conditions for a stable peace. However, though the role of knowledge is important in establishing security communities between states, establishing security communities within states is more difficult to achieve.

GLOBAL RELATIONS IN THE THIRD WORLD

Towards the end of the Cold War, more scholarship turned its attention to the international relations of states in the Third World. Issues facing the Third World were only examined in terms of how they may affect the great powers (Nye and Lynn-Jones, 1988). Now referred to more commonly as the developing world (from here on, it will be referred to as this), states that were not part of the great power circle engaged in behaviour that was very different than the great powers. This was not just a function of differences in military power, but also differences in culture, history, regime type, governance and leadership styles.

International politics is supposedly distinct from domestic politics because there is no international government to manage and mediate between disputing actors. In international politics, the world is anarchic and states must fend for themselves and provide their own security, while domestic governments are supposed to be stable and able to provide security. This leads to a binary vision where domestic orders are stable while international orders are unstable.

The security of citizens is also supposedly guaranteed by the state. Anyone outside the state represents a potential or actual threat to citizens. But this is not the case in the developing world and in some parts of the developed world as well. Traditional paradigms assume that states provide security. In the developing world, sometimes it is the states themselves that are a source of insecurity.

Further, traditional paradigms assume that the point of origin of security threats is the interstate level. In other words, the main threats to states are supposed to be external. However, conflicts and tensions between states are rare and in the developing world the main threats are often internal. Conflicts originate within states and are largely due to internal challenges facing states (Buzan, 1991: 100). Most conflicts in the developing world are intrastate, not interstate. Much of the reason for this is due to state weakness rather than the absence of a balance of power. Assumptions that were made about states in the developed world are not as applicable to the developing world. States in the developing world have not always been sovereign and lack autonomy (Ayoob, 1995). Many states emerged after independence without a clear national identity and without social cohesion.[3] Subnational identities have challenged the legitimacy of the state. States emerged without the capacity to provide for their inhabitants.

Even when states are strong and sovereign, it is important to acknowledge that there may be other actors operating in global politics that are powerful. The notion that states are the most important actors becomes even more flawed, however, when you look at the developing world, where weak states abound. In contrast to realist assumptions, states in the developing world may be much weaker than other non-state actors.[4]

Box 1.1   Omni-balancing

Omni-balancing takes place when states offer support for a violent non-state actor, as a way of balancing against internal and external threats to their security. The logic of this theory was developed by Steven David (1991). As he sees it, states in the developing world may be much weaker both domestically and internationally. Domestically they have low levels of legitimacy and high needs to maintain survival. The weaker leaders are, the more likely they are to align with violent non-state actors to distract and appeal to different domestic groups. In a world where there are also large power disparities at the international level, weak states may also see the benefits of supporting terrorist groups. Supporting these violent non-state groups does not lead to huge challenges from either the domestic or external area. There are fewer costs of offering this support and higher gains. For these reasons weaker states may find it preferable to support non-state actors over states as alliance partners. Some examples of this include Syria's support for the Kurdish Worker's Party and Iran's support for Hezbollah.

Another issue is the notion that non-military phenomena should be excluded from the security studies agenda. Realists have tended to emphasize the anarchic international system rather than domestic affairs in their treatment of security issues. Similarly, the recent tendency to label the field 'international security' rather than 'national security' is likely to make it even harder to focus attention on domestic

---

[3]Ayoob (1995) claimed that neither traditional nor post-Cold War conceptions of security captured the predicaments of states in the developing world. These predicaments are due to when state formation took place, how it took place and how new these states are.

[4]In the 1990s as many states began to 'fail', scholars turned to use their theories that had been applied to interstate relations to explain internal conflict (Posen, 1993). Some states fail and do not erupt into conflict, and other states are stronger but face security threats.

aspects of security. Moreover, the issues that cause insecurity in the developing world may be non-security issues such as resource shortages, underdevelopment, overpopulation, educational crises, drug trafficking, migration and environmental hazards. The costs of poverty, ecological deterioration and ethnic fragmentation are more greatly felt in the developing world (Väyrynen, 1991). Because of this, the military dimension of security may be of less importance in the developing world (Thomas, 2001).

Another problem with traditional paradigms is that they have not completely understood how the structure of power within states may impact outcomes. Due to insecurities about political survival, states in the developing world are led by leaders who have different calculations than states in the developed world. Elites in the developing world may prioritize leadership survival over national security issues (see Box 1.1 on 'omni-balancing'). Their preoccupation with political survival may lead elites in the developing world to pursue foreign policy decisions that do not reflect the national interest. In essence, self-preservation may take precedence over security interests.

Another challenge to traditional paradigms is the notion that bipolarity created a stable international order. This was hardly the case in the developing world. Conflicts were permitted to take place in the developing world since this served as a safety valve to avoid direct confrontation between the two superpowers. Furthermore, when interstate conflicts did develop, this was also not due to an imbalance of power but due to internal conflicts spilling over across national boundaries that fuelled discord with neighbours. State boundaries are not honoured to the same extent as they are in the developed world. Additionally, the most effective instruments of the international order are not relying on achieving a global balance of power.

Another challenge to traditional paradigms is the focus on weapons of mass destruction. Scholars of security studies and strategic studies have placed an overwhelming emphasis on weapons of mass destruction. The focus was on nuclear strategies and deterrence. According to scholarly work, once massive retaliation was achieved and first and second strike capabilities were established, arms control, not disarmament, would achieve a nuclear balance. Nuclear weapons have had very little impact on the developing world and developed world. However, small arms which are spread easily have been responsible for high numbers of casualties (for more on this, see Box 8.1 in Chapter 8).

The traditional literature has understood security in the developing world in terms of how it affected the developed world with the main objective to preserve the status quo. However, the status quo in the developing world was the major source of insecurity. Security frameworks need to have a greater understanding of a broader range of issues – not just security issues but non-security issues as well – and should involve not just states, but non-states as well. A greater integration of security issues that face the developing world will help move beyond realist orthodoxy.

What is the nature of global politics when you also take into account weak and unstable states with complex demographics? In fact, very little from the dominant theories of international relations examines the security threats emanating from within states, and how these security threats connect with other threats outside the state, further adding to the complexity.

Box 1.2   Strategic Studies

Strategic studies is a strand of security studies that examines military strategy, military technology and the use of force. As military security has often been considered more important than other forms of security, strategic studies is often conflated with security studies. As an academic discipline, however, strategic studies is fairly limited to focusing on the means by which security is pursued, and the instruments of statecraft and management of military force (Baldwin, 1995: 129). Critics claim that the field of strategic studies focuses on the use of military force without really understanding the goals of security. The field is less interested in understanding how wars can be avoided, and more interested in understanding how wars can be fought in the most efficient way possible (Farrell, 1996, 2010).

WHAT IS THE FIELD OF SECURITY STUDIES?

Security studies are often thought of as a subfield of IR. In some ways, 'security studies' is a more encompassing field than IR and has become multidisciplinary, bringing together psychology, history, sociology and organizational theories. The focus of the dominant paradigms in IR was mostly on national security. In other words, the concept of security was limited to achieving security of the nation state (Beaton, 1972). The field of security studies looks at individuals and groups of individuals who both use violence and protect themselves from violence.

Security studies examines all of the issues pertaining to security and violence, including the causes of conflict, the conduct during conflict and the how conflicts end. Security studies may also look at intelligence, information technologies and security. It may also examine the use of military force in peace operations and peacekeeping and the role of ethics in security policy. Some studies focus on micro-level factors such as strategies in crisis management, conflict strategies and motivations for conflict. Other studies may focus on macro-level factors such as military spending and doctrines, and conventional and unconventional strategies of violence. More narrow definitions claim that security studies focus on 'the threat, use, and control of military force...[that is] the conditions that make the use of force more likely, the ways that the use of force affects individuals, states and societies, and the specific policies that states adopt in order to prepare for, prevent, or engage in war' (Walt, 1991: 212; see also Mearsheimer, 1995).

COLD WAR SECURITY STUDIES DURING THE COLD WAR

Early scholars of security theories distinguished themselves from those who studied strategy and warfare. They took a broad approach to understanding security and argued that both military and non-military means could achieve security. In other words, coercive power was not the only means to attain security (Baldwin 1995: 130). The field originally grew out of debates over how to protect the state against external and internal threats.

In particular, the field was concerned with security problems facing the United States. The US focus is hardly surprising given that most specialists in security studies are American. The downside of this is that most of the conclusions made were skewed by American thinking. Assumptions that were supposed to be universal were actually reflective of American culture. Another issue is that US scholars had a heavy focus on strategic studies (which examines the military element of security studies – for more on this, see Box 1.2). It was noted that 'the Cold War not only militarized American security policy, it also militarized the study of security' (Baldwin, 1995: 125).

Thus most scholars were interested in military statecraft. If military force was relevant to the issue at hand, it was then considered a security issue. On the other hand, if military force was not relevant then that issue was considered outside of security issues, and referred to as an issue of 'low politics'.

Most theoretical work on security was dominated by the dangers of great power conflict and the effects of bipolarity. As such, power and the nation state were concentrated on. Military aspects of security were overemphasized (Buzan and Hansen, 2009). The advancements in sophisticated weaponry ushered in an era of focusing on how to deal with the threats of nuclear weapons. There was almost a universal acceptance of the realist paradigm that states needed to focus on their national interest and deter key threats to these interests. Nuclear strategies featured heavily in security studies (Walt, 1991). Works that looked at conflicts in the developing world came from practitioners rather than academics, usually examining case studies of guerrilla warfare. The Vietnam War reduced the interest in security studies, since most leading strategists knew very little about the mechanics of guerrilla warfare. The breakdown of détente and the military build-up that took place during US President Ronald Reagan's tenure in 1980s stimulated renewed interest in security studies (Fierke, 2015).

However, the domestic dimension of national security tended to be neglected during the Cold War years. A big debate emerged about whether or not the concept of security should be broadened to fit a policy agenda that was more diverse.

EXPANDING THE CONCEPT OF SECURITY

The meaning and nature of security is constantly debated (Buzan, 1991). The concept has been debated because it has remained underdeveloped and vague for both realists and liberals. For realists, security is achieved when an actor has achieved enough power. For liberals, security is the result of peace, which provides security for all. Realists tend to focus on military threats to the security of states. But security is a very broad concept, and states may vary in terms of the value that they place on military security. States may want more than just military security. Scholars are calling for conceptualizations of security that go beyond the nation state.

Barry Buzan (1997, 2008) highlighted the importance of expanding on the concept of security. Buzan emphasized that security is not just military; it is also political, economic, societal and ecological. These are not just different concepts but constitute different forms of security. Military security was concerned with the interplay between the armed capabilities of states. Buzan argued that military security could be referred to as strategic studies (for more on this, see Box 1.2). Political security focuses on the organizational stability of states and government systems. Economic security revolves around the resources, finances and markets necessary to attain a healthy economy and provide welfare. Societal security refers to the sustainability and evolution of language, religion, national identities and customs (Wæver, 1995). Finally, environmental security centres on the maintenance of the biosphere.[5]

Buzan also questions the assumption that all actors have the same values. Realists assume that security is the prime concern of states. However, security may also include economic welfare, autonomy, psychological well-being, and so on. Another question is how much security is actually needed. Waltz (1964) claims that states need enough security to ensure their survival. But how much assurance is enough? At what point can resources be put towards other things? There is also a cost to pursuing security. Some goals may be sacrificed in order to pursue other objectives. Not all resources can be devoted to security.

Buzan also questions the realist assumption that security is a zero sum concept. According to realists, more security for one actor means less security for another. However, not everything that states do to enhance their security will necessarily make other states feel more insecure. For example, states can improve their economies and environments in ways that lead to positive outcomes for other states.

Buzan also questioned the idea that security should only be concerned with the nation state. The state has traditionally been thought of as the most important thing to be secured, usually through military power and attaining sovereignty. Though Buzan acknowledges that the state is still the referent object of analysis for international security (since it is states that have to cope with most security problems), he also emphasizes the importance of 'human security'.

Though the idea of thinking in terms of human security is incredibly popular, especially in policy circles, the conception of human security is still vague. It can denote everything from physical security to psychological well-being. This makes it hard to prioritize how to achieve security when the concept is so expansive. According to the United Nations Development Programme, human security encompasses economic security, or freedom from poverty; food security, or access to food; health security, or access to health and protection from disease; environmental security, or protection from pollution and depletion; personal security, such as physical safety from all types of violence; societal security, or survival of identities; and political security, or freedom from oppression. Other governments have tried to promote more restrictive definitions of human security to focus on freedom from threats to safety, but most governments have accepted that human security may mean the achievement of some level of quality of life.

Furthermore, because security should not always be defined in terms of the state, security can be pursued and attained by a wide variety of means. Realists have a tendency to territorialize violence, seeing threats from non-conventional forms of violence as a threat to the state. Realists assume that violent non-state actors can only survive with the support of states. This leads to a response that only considers the use of force against another state. Realists also promote a view that only force will change the behaviour of an armed group (for more on the response to violent groups, see Chapter 12). However, many different policies can be adopted in the pursuit of security. Only conceiving of security in terms of the threat, control and use of military force can lead to confusion as to how security can be pursued, favouring military solutions over non-military ones.

---

[5]The UN Secretary General High Level Panel on Threats, Challenges and Change identified six clusters of threats: poverty, disease, environmental degradation, interstate conflict, internal conflict, terrorism and transnational organized crime.

WHY ARE STATES SO DIFFERENT FROM NON-STATE ACTORS?

Though assuming the state is the most important actor can lead to a misunderstanding of the complexity in global politics today, eliminating the state from the analysis would also be problematic. States are critical for understanding why non-state actors emerge. In fact, we do not dispute the notion of realists that states are important. However, it is important to underscore that states are very different from non-states – and we cannot make the assumption that they operate according to the same logic and constraints. Achieving order between states is much easier than within states.

States may respond to different tools such as diplomacy, fear of economic sanctions and threats of force. In contrast, non-states may not be influenced by diplomatic carrots and sticks. In many instances, non-state actors have little to lose. Therefore, a diplomatic offering may provide little incentive to cooperate. As there is no formal trade taking place with non-state actors, this means that economic sanctions will also fail to make an impact. In many cases threatening to use force only enhances the image of the violent non-state actor, making threats of violence another ineffective tool. States have to respond to the needs of their domestic populations, while non-state actors often do not have much of a population to answer to. In some cases, the views of the population matter but in other cases the non-state actor can just use force and coercion to exact compliance and obedience.

States also differ from non-state actors because they can formally trade with one another. Non-state actors are involved in all sorts of trade and financial transactions, but most of this trade is done illegally and without much regularity. The lack of certainty may impede the logic of economic interdependence that emerges when states are involved in mutually beneficial trading relationships. Trade restrictions may also make it difficult to generate revenues (Bahcheli et al., 2004). De facto states such as Abkhazia have been cut off from the international community and are completely isolated. For much of the 1990s there was no telephone link to the outside world and no Internet (Lynch, 2004: 93).

States are also involved in international institutions, while non-state actors are not able to take part, though some may receive an observer status. Non-state actors are not considered legitimate internationally and do not get to reap the benefits of belonging to a large institution. As a result, states have more formal channels of communication and they can communicate with one another in a regular fashion. Non-state actors must rely on informal methods of communication which may lead to lower levels of trust.

Realists assume that actors act in their national interest. They maintain that the laws of international politics remain the same regardless of actors' identity and regime type (Cederman, 1997: 17). States in theory should prefer secure environments and want to eliminate threats. But, violent non-state actors may not operate in terms of any national interest. Violent non-state actors often thrive on insecurity and instability. They may prefer to perpetuate this insecurity in order to justify their very existence or in order to operate illegal activities or control territory.

According to realists, states may want to achieve a balance of power; violent non-state actors may not have that objective. Violent non-state actors may not be involved in typical balancing behaviour. States may offer clandestine support as might other violent non-state actors, but this may be motivated by factors other than achieving a balance of power, such as the need to support like-minded ideals or norms.

IS REALISM STILL RELEVANT?

Though realist thought has been critiqued throughout the chapter, the paradigm offers important insights about the behaviour of actors in the international system. It is true that actors are often self-interested. Actors are often power-hungry and concerned with relative gains. Actors are also usually concerned with their own survival. This helps to explain why so many politically motivated actors eventually turn to organized crime to fund themselves. In fact, rational choice approaches are examined extensively throughout the book to offer explanations for why actors behave the way they do.

Additionally, states are still very important. The state has not disappeared and withered away. The key issue is that realism does not address that states face different challenges. Moreover, these challenges manifest themselves differently depending on the context. Thus, part of the solution does involve the state; building strong states is still an important step to tackling insecurity. But utilizing only a military response will not work given the new threats facing states. Given all of these new realities, realism can update itself to the 21st century. It can apply to non-states a revised version of the logic that it applies to states in order to make predictions that are more relevant to understanding security today. States are no longer only threatened by other states. Thus the balance of power logic at the international level needs to be revisited.

CONCLUSION

This chapter has illustrated how security needs to be redefined to be relevant in the contemporary era. Though traditional views of security were useful in understanding great power behaviour during the Cold War, there is general acceptance that scholars and practitioners need to re-examine the way we think about security and expand on the definition. In the world today, we have an overabundance of military power yet new types of violence threaten civilians today more than ever. Why is this the case? Who are the main actors that threaten security? How do these actors differ and why have they emerged? What is the best way of responding to these actors?

The next chapter explains what is meant by unconventional violence, such as terrorism, guerrilla warfare, organized criminal violence and hybrid wars. New types of violence are often written about but undertheorized, under-conceptualized and poorly understood. Thus, the following chapter explains how violent non-state actors should be categorized. A clear categorization helps us to better understand the threats that they pose to security and how to respond accordingly.

Summary Points

- States are still important actors in security, but non-state actors are equally important.
- Most threats are due to internal factors that have little to do with the balance of power or the international system.

- Previous theories that focus on a state-centric model misunderstand that states operate by a completely different logic than non-states.
- State boundaries are no longer as relevant in providing security as they were in the past.
- All theories of international security (especially realism) should update the logic of their arguments to include the role of non-state actors and how they threaten security of the state and society.

Key Questions

1   What have been the primary critiques launched at realists' interpretations of the causes of insecurity and how security is achieved?
2   How did the Cold War shape realist interpretations of security?
3   How is security in the developing world conceived?
4   What is security studies and how has the conception of security changed over time?
5   What are the ways in which states are different from non-states, in particular, from violent non-state actors?
6   Theory: In what ways is realism still relevant in understanding security today? How can the theory be applicable to understanding violent non-state actors?

FURTHER READING

For students of international relations, there are many good sources that can provide a useful starting point.

Jackson, R. and Sørensen, G. (2016) *Introduction to Theories and Approaches* (Oxford University Press). Clear introduction to the two dominant traditions in contemporary realism and neo-liberalism, as well as constructivism.

Keohane, R. (2011) 'Neoliberal institutionalism', in *Security Studies: A Reader*. A short overview of the benefits of neo-liberal institutions.

Mingst, K.A. and Arreguín-Toft, I.M. (2013) *Essentials of International Relations* (6th international student ed.) (Norton). A reader that offers a thorough summary of the key terms International Relations.

Steans, J., Pettiford, L., Diez, T. and El-Anis, I. (2013) *An Introduction to Theory: Perspectives and Themes* (Routledge). Overview of alternative perspectives to the dominant paradigms such as constructivism, critical theory and green and feminist perspectives.

Waltz, K.N. (2000) 'Structural realism after the Cold War'. *International Security*, 25 (1), 5–41. Important commentary on structural realism and why it is not obsolete even after the fall of bipolarity.

2

UNDERSTANDING VIOLENCE AND NON-CONVENTIONAL WARFARE

Key Terms

- Guerrilla warfare
- Grey-zone violence
- Crime-terror nexus
- Comando Vermelho (CV) and the Primeiro Comando da Capital (PCC)
- D-Company
- Transformation

As the previous chapter explained, the bulk of scholarly work on violence focused on interstate conflict (Davenport and Gates, 2014). Recently, scholars have noted, however, that internal conflicts are not only much more common, but also much longer in duration and more destructive (DeRouen and Bercovitch, 2008; Fearon, 2004; Kegley and Blanton, 2015). Increasing conflicts involving violent non-state actors have prompted a renewed interest in the study of unconventional conflict and violence (Chenoweth and Lawrence, 2010: 2). In general, long-standing assumptions about fighting conflicts have been challenged. Definitions of threats have changed, battles have changed and conflict and violence have transformed (Sullivan, 2006). This chapter examines the different types of patterned violence used by violent non-state actors. After providing an overview of the different types of violence, we introduce a way to categorize the violent non-state actors who are involved in perpetuating violence.

OLD AND NEW VIOLENCE

HOW IS VIOLENCE TODAY DISTINGUISHED FROM VIOLENCE OF THE PAST?

Our understanding of collective violence has changed tremendously.[1] When theorizing about violence in the past, many political scientists, specifically realists, focused

---

[1] Violence is defined as the use of force to harm, injure or abuse (Schinkel, 2010: 18).

heavily on interstate conflict (or conflict between states) and conventional war. Both combatants were considered sovereign over their territories. States fought either in empires or blocs, but the key actors involved were states. Most of the conflicts in the past concerned the consolidation of borders. By the 19th century national conflicts were most common and from the early 20th century more conflicts were ideological. Conventional war aimed to capture territory through military force. Battles took place between massive professionalized and well-trained armies where some kind of parity existed between both sides. Militaries were vertically and hierarchically organized. Operations were well coordinated involving several military branches (Merari, 1993). Today's conflicts involve fighting units that are *decentralized*. They are fought by actors with both regular and irregular troops, with cells that don't respond to central authority. Collective violence no longer concerns contests between the armies of major states in which soldiers are the main violent actors (Monteleone et al., 2014: 240).

The use of violence in the past concerned securing the state and its citizens against external threats by other states, with defence provided by modern armed forces. Public order was maintained by security forces of the state (Krause, 2012: 41). Any violence that involves violent non-state actors is often referred to as non-conventional. Non-conventional violence is becoming the norm. Though interstate conflict is no longer common, new forms of violence are not confined within a state's territorial borders. New conflicts are *transnational* in that they may involve actors from different states and may interact in a transnational space; the norms governing the use of violence have changed. In some cases there are not recognized war zones; operations are carried out outside of war zones. In the past, war was limited to a recognized geographical location.

New forms of conflict also blur the boundaries between 'crime' and 'violence'. Though new conflicts have involved violence between states and organized political groups, organized criminal groups have also become involved in conflicts. Private and public has been blurred. Some of those are involved in the conflict for profit and only informally (Kaldor, 2013: 1946). For this reason, new forms of violence are often referred to as 'hybrid' wars (Hoffman, 2006). They make use of conventional and non-conventional forms of violence.

Most new forms of conflict have been prolonged but are low intensity. It is the low-intensity nature of today's conflicts that prolongs them. By low intensity we mean that there are fewer casualties for the combatants. Non-state actors have launched violent challenges to the state and to citizens but have avoided direct combat with state armies. Violent non-state actors engaged in a low-intensity conflict may prefer the status quo to negotiation and mediation, since their level of power is so much lower.

However, new forms of violence have had negative effects for civilians. They have involved massive displacement. There were 2.4 million refugees in 1975. As of 2015, there are 19.5 million refugees. There were 5.4 million internally displaced persons in 1995. Twenty years later there are 38.2 million (UNHCR). Though participation in war is low, civilians are often the targets of violence, its practitioners, or both. Moreover, zones of war and peace are not clearly demarcated.[2] In contrast, older wars usually just involved military casualties as well as damage to industry and transportation infrastructure (Merari, 1993).

---

[2]Bosnia had 6.5% of the population involved in the war (Kaldor, 2013).

Another factor that prolongs conflicts is the availability of weapons. Lighter weapons are commonly used, such as small arms (rifles, machine guns, hand grenades and short-range rockets) and land mines. Light weapons amplify the number of people who can be involved in a conflict. Since light weapons are easy to use and transport, anyone can use them. They are accurate and difficult to detect. They are also readily available and cheap thanks to the massive stockpiles of weapons that have been sold on the black market after the Cold War. Kalashnikovs are cheaper than buying a chicken in Angola (Fleshman, 2001). In the past, a full range of military hardware was used, costing millions of dollars to purchase.

New conflicts exploit different forms of advanced technology (Kaldor, 2013: 1951). Modern communications enable violent groups to cooperate. Mobile phones are widely available for communication, as is the Internet (see also Chapter 3).

Another difference between new and old types of violence is how states respond. A conflict would always involve a military response while crime necessitated a response from the police. The response to conflict now blurs the role of the police and the military. Militaries are more involved in civilian policing and the police may be more involved in multilateral operations or international missions (Adamson, 2006: 42).

DIFFERENT TYPES OF VIOLENCE AND CONFLICT

The major paradigms that have focused on conflict have mostly focused on violence between two states. The primary security threat was interstate conflict. Different forms of violence were never classified as national security threats. However, there are multiple forms of violence that threaten the state, society and individuals – much more so than interstate conflict. The following sections explain the different types of patterned violence: (1) terrorism, (2) irregular conflict (including guerrilla warfare), (3) organized criminal violence and gang violence, (4) and grey-zone conflicts.[3]

TERRORISM

There are many definitions of terrorism and it is nearly impossible to find consensus on how terrorism should be defined. Overall, most definitions of terrorist activity assume that terrorism is a premeditated form of politically motivated violence. Targets are selected for their maximum propaganda and publicity value in order to influence an audience. Thus victims are chosen for their symbolic meaning. The attack is unprovoked (in that the victim did not directly harm the perpetrator) and often has some element of surprise.

One of the important components of terrorism is to terrorize. The biggest impact of the violence perpetuated by terrorist groups is psychological, not physical. For terror groups, the psychological impact will be more important than the physical

---

[3]It is important to note that the organized criminal violence and gang violence can be interpersonal in nature.

impact (Schneckener, 2006). Anthony Richards writes that the primary purpose of terrorism is to generate 'a wider psychological impact beyond the immediate victims or object of attack' (Richards, 2014, 146). Terrorist groups aim to threaten citizens' daily routines through fear and intimidation. This fear can lead some states to terrorize themselves far better than the terrorists themselves. Rebels and insurgencies pursue their goals primarily by relying on the physical dimension. Their aim is to weaken their opponent's military strength, defeat it or force it to surrender, and subsequently take its place.

Terrorism is a calculated communication strategy or a form of signalling. It conveys messages to both allies and opponents. Terrorism also aims to send a vivid message to the target audience, which is much larger than the immediate victims (Wardlaw, 1989). The goal is to be shocking, horrifying and sensationalistic in order to catalyse political change. Terrorists need international publicity, media attention and visibility to obtain leverage, influence and power (Hoffman, 1998: 4). Without being noticed, the terrorist does not exist (Juergensmeyer, 2005). The hope is to influence the target population's objective reasoning through anxiety and fear.

In contrast to terrorism, conventional military activities do not take place on a stage with an audience in mind. Military activities have military value, whereas terrorism has very little military value.[4] Terrorism is an asymmetrical form of warfare, for those with limited resources or when the actor cannot prevail against the state in a form of armed conflict. An act of terrorism helps establish a temporary superiority over the state. To illustrate, the Islamic State (IS) has increased its use of terror attacks to counter the effects of its diminishing conventional power.

Staging an act of terrorism is often meant as a form of provocation, hoping for an overreaction from the state that may help the group gain further sympathy for their cause. Terrorism aims not only to shock and intimidate society but also to mobilize sympathizers and supporters. Terrorists may be hoping to change minds and boost the morale of supporters. They may also want to undermine peace reconciliation efforts, and act as a spoiler, as was the case with Hamas and the suicide attacks that took place during the Oslo Accords.

Though the state is often targeted, the direct victims of terrorism are individuals, not the state. The state's military power is not affected by an act of terrorism as an attack on a military arsenal usually does little damage. The threat of terrorism bypasses the state (Rasmussen, 2003). Nevertheless, some attacks on government buildings and important businesses inflict serious economic costs. Not all scholars or databases agree that the target has to be civilian. Some take into account military and government targets (Richards, 2014). As we see it, terrorism primarily targets civilians, not representatives of the state. Society is affected indirectly in the sense that a culture of fear is created and the intended impact is psychological coercion.

---

[4]According to the Uppsala Conflict Data Program (2009), an armed conflict has a minimum of 25 people killed per year and the violence and associated deaths are the product of political design or strategy. A terrorist attack may have more than 25 killed, but it is most often much less than this number. For more see the interview with Professor Peter Wallensteen, International Review of the Red Cross, No. 873 , March 31, 2009, www.icrc.org/eng/assets/files/other/irrc-873-interview.pdf.

Box 2.1   Lone-Actor Terrorism

Lone-actor terrorism is becoming more common as individuals have become increasingly inspired by the actions of larger terror organizations that they connect with through the media and various websites. Once referred to as lone-wolf terrorism, this term is now discouraged because it glamorizes this type of activity (Spaaij and Hamm, 2015). Sometimes they are inspired by highly centralized groups while other times they are inspired by groups that are headless, such as some of the violence that has been inspired by the Ku Klux Klan.

With lone-actor terrorism, a terrorist operates alone and does not appear to have any accomplices. They are operating outside of a formal terrorist organizational or command structure (Phillips, 2011). They do not have assistance, funding or cooperation with a larger organization. They plan the attack completely on their own and they do not operate within an organizational command structure. Because they act on their own, they are not concerned with garnering public support (Becker, 2014). They are weak opportunists, and their relative weakness constrains where they can strike. They tend to target civilians rather than government targets (Becker, 2014).

Lone actors' attacks are motivated by some sort of ideology, and they will make it clear what group or ideology was their inspiration. Claiming their commitment to a specific group is what distinguishes lone-actor terrorism from other types of mass murder. In contrast, mass murders are not connected to a political agenda. For example, the 12 June 2016 nightclub shooting in Orlando is considered to be an act of lone-actor terrorism because the perpetrator swore allegiance to the IS.

More studies have been devoted to understanding the characteristics of lone-actor terrorists. In a study of 119 individuals who planned or engaged in lone-actor terrorism in the US and Europe, several important conclusions were reached (Gill et al., 2014). First, there was no uniform profile of a lone terrorist except that 96.6% were men. The study also showed that 41.2% had a prior criminal conviction, which is a higher percentage than for formal terrorist organizations. Another finding is that lone actors are not always isolated individuals, and in the time leading up to the event, other people usually knew about the actor's grievances, ideology and intent to engage in violence. When comparing lone-actor terrorists, right-wing offenders were more likely to be less educated and unemployed, while single-issue offenders were more likely to have a history of mental illness. In total, the study demonstrated that 31% of lone-actor terrorists had a history of mental illness. Another study supported this finding, claiming that lone-actor terrorists were 13.49 times more likely than group-actor terrorists to suffer from mental illness (Corner and Gill, 2015).

Lone-actor terrorism is garnering more attention because lone-actor attacks are the main perpetrators of terrorist activity in the West. As many as 70% of all deaths from terrorism in the West between 2006 and 2015 were due to lone-actor terrorists. In the West, 80% of deaths by lone-actor terrorists are driven by right-wing extremism, nationalism and anti-government sentiment (Global Terrorism Database, 2015). However, in spite of the dangers of lone-actor attacks, plots by lone actors are the most likely of all plots to be foiled (Strom et al., 2010).[5]

IRREGULAR CONFLICT

Irregular conflict is a type of warfare that takes place when there is military asymmetry between two sides: a weaker side and a stronger side. The basic rules of

---

[5]In a study of 86 terrorist plots, 40% of all of the terrorist plots foiled were planned by loners.

warfare are not accepted. It is usually conducted between a state that uses regular troops and a violent non-state actor. Thus, normally two states that are in conflict with one another do not engage in irregular conflict. The regular troops may control some of the urban terrain, while the peripheral terrain is challenged by the violent non-state actor, who usually relies on hiding, and the element of surprise and harassment. These types of conflicts are wars of attrition with low levels of intensity (Kalyvas, 2005: 91). They are prolonged because although the stronger side has more power, it has much less will. The weaker side almost always refuses to confront the stronger side in a head-to-head battle, as there is an absence of front lines. Irregular warfare is sometimes referred to as conflict with no 'fronts' (Kalyvas, 2015: 13).

When irregular warfare takes place between a violent non-state actor and a constituted authority, it is commonly referred to as an insurgency. There are instances, however, where both sides are on a par with one another but also choose irregular warfare. For example, if the state deteriorates it may use irregular warfare methods as well. There are other instances where two violent non-state actors use irregular war against each other. The most common type of irregular warfare is guerrilla warfare. This assumes that the combatants have political goals and are trying to win over or control the population.

GUERRILLA WARFARE

Guerrilla warfare is a protracted struggle by armed civilians or irregular warfare conducted methodically, in order to alter the pre-existing order. Guerrillas may try to undermine the integrity of the borders and composition of the nation state, the political system, the authorities in power and the policies that they disagree with (Taber, 1970). Some guerrilla movements aim for secession while others may aim to overtake the entire state. Others may focus on trying to change deeply entrenched policies, aiming mostly for reform. When guerrillas are effective, they can take control over territory.

Guerrilla warfare is armed conflict by armed civilians or irregulars. It is typically a strategy of a weaker side, and is often associated with the oppressed (Taber, 1970). Guerrillas use different types of violence than the trained, regimented forces of major wars. A range of political, psychological and economic types of intimidation is used. They may use a variety of tactics including ambushes, sabotage, raids, hit-and-run and strategic retreats.

Guerrillas can also generate more support when they use strategies to provoke an overreaction from the government. Counter-insurgency has always attempted to use conventional military forces and destroy the environment where the revolutionaries operate and live – but this caused tremendous destruction and played into the moral favour of the guerrilla trying to convince the population of the evils of the state (Galula, 2006).

Guerrilla warfare captures territory, usually in remote areas, through political control of the population rather than just through military power. Guerrillas have traditionally had a close relationship with the communities they fight for. Some guerrillas attempt to capture the hearts and minds of the population, while newer forms are more focused on destabilizing and fostering feelings of hatred and fear in the population.

The main victims of guerrilla warfare are not necessarily armed combatants from the state. Though the state is a victim of guerrilla warfare, society also faces a heavy price. Populations are expelled if necessary and mass killings may occur. Conflicts taking place today have higher numbers of refugees and internally displaced persons, and most violence has been directed against civilians (Kaldor, 2013: 1951). In World War II, 85%–90% of the casualties were military, but by the late 1990s, 80% of all casualties were civilians, though this could be higher (Davies, 2010: 107). Thus, though the state is targeted, society is deeply affected as well.

Guerrillas have at times created an inhospitable environment for people living in the crossfire. This can be done with landmines, shells, rockets against civilians and forced famines. Those individuals who cannot be controlled by guerrilla groups are eliminated. Cultures can be erased by removing physical landmarks and destroying religious buildings and monuments. Even more concerning is the use of systematic rape and sexual abuse (Wickham-Crowley, 1990). Irregular wars that have insurgencies or guerrillas are considered to be value-neutral concepts compared to terrorism, yet the destruction caused in terms of death toll to civilian life is much higher.

LOOTING AND MARAUDING

Some forms of irregular violence include conflicts that have quasi-criminal activity taking place and do not resemble guerrilla warfare (Collier, 2000). Individuals are hastily put together to form an armed band of soldiers who focus mostly on looting and indiscriminate violence (for more on this, see Chapter 8). Though the original impetus for violence was grievance-based, greed has motivated actors that initially had political rationales to prolong conflicts in order to continue to reap the benefits of looting. The violence is sporadic, disorganized and without rules. The violence may also be barbaric and undiscerning. This type of violence is more likely to occur in more impoverished countries with greater inequalities and lootable natural resources.

CRIMINAL VIOLENCE

Criminal violence is another category which includes organized criminal groups and gangs attacking each other or non-combatants, with a threshold of at least 25 killed. It is treated differently than an armed conflict because it is not always clear what is motivating the violence or how political the violence is.

Though the state is not usually directly affected by organized criminal and gang violence, it does challenge the government's legitimacy and sometimes the government's monopoly of violence. How the state responds to criminal violence is important. If the state responds indiscriminately, it can lead to an escalation of criminal violence (Grillo, 2012: 128–9).

Most organized crime does not lead to large levels of violence (Gambetta, 1996). Criminals are mostly interested in maximizing profits, and high levels of violence could affect these interests. It may be easier to resort to bribes to politicians and law enforcers.

Criminals are also more effective when their targeting is discriminate (Kalyvas, 2015). With gang warfare, violence has become much worse and may seem more random. Civilians are threatened to dissuade them from talking to the police. Fierce gun battles spill over, leading to the deaths of gang members, law enforcement officers and innocent civilians.

More recently in Latin America criminal violence has become so massive that it has been referred to as a civil war. In Mexico, cartels have used both selective and indiscriminate violence. For example, in the case of Mexico's drug war, the level of violence has escalated to a point that there have been more deaths than in Afghanistan. Data released from the Mexican government revealed that from 2007 to 2014, more than 164,000 people were victims of homicide, with 20,000 people dying in 2014 alone. In contrast, during the same period the conflicts in Iraq and Afghanistan killed slightly over 103,000 people in total (Breslow, 2015).

As stated before, to be classified as warfare, violence is supposed to be motivated by politics, not profits. In practice the two merge. The following section provides an introduction to a different type of warfare that has become more common: grey-zone violence, or violence that involves both economic and politically violent non-state actors. Conflicts have become more privatized and private enterprise has become more political (Adams, 1999; Kalyvas, 2006, 2015). Because of this, violent non-state actors have emerged that engage in overlapping types of activities. Actors are now engaged in political violence while simultaneously being engaged in crime. This is often referred to as the crime-terror nexus, or grey-zone violence.

GREY-ZONE VIOLENCE

Violent non-state actors with political motivations have typically been distinguished from actors motivated by profits. The politically violent non-state actor wants to achieve political change through violence, while the criminal is motivated by greed. As Kimberley Thachuk notes, traditionally 'organized crime groups rarely cooperated with terrorist groups, or engaged in their activities, as their goals were most often at odds' (Thachuk, 2001b: 51).

Nevertheless, it has become more and more difficult to distinguish between groups that have political motivations and groups that have economic ones. The links between criminals and violent political groups have become blurred. Interactions between these groups are increasing and the network is constantly changing (Oehme, 2008: 82). Political insurgents have become more involved in lucrative criminal activities (such as kidnapping, extortion, drugs and arms trafficking) while criminals have become more involved with violent political networks. Private security firms have been sought after by criminal and political groups alike. Sometimes warlords pretend to have a political agenda. Conflicts that involve high levels of profit-making have led to a grey area – 'hybrid' activity or 'grey-zone' violence (Cornell, 2006: 40). Hybrid groups have emerged and political and criminal activities have become intertwined; conflict has become criminalized. Though terror is not always used as a tactic, the use of both crime and political violence by violent non-state actors has been referred to as the 'crime-terror nexus' (Makarenko, 2012).

What explains the emergence of the crime-terror nexus? Most scholars have pointed to the changes that took place at the end of the Cold War (Makarenko, 2004). Most politically armed movements were funded by the superpowers and their allies. When the Cold War ended this funding was cut off and groups needed to find their own source of funding. Groups began to increasingly rely on transnational crime as a means to finance their conflicts and agendas. To obtain arms and use them effectively, many of the violent groups needed to cooperate in arms and drug trafficking, smuggling and money laundering. They needed multiple partners to achieve their goals.

In addition to the loss of funding from the superpowers, another factor that assisted hybrid activity was globalization (for more on this, see Chapter 3). The improvements in technology and transportation have facilitated transnational crime and have helped various groups collaborate, cooperate and communicate better. Communication technology makes it easier to coordinate illicit trade across large distances. Improved communication has helped terrorist groups become more lethal and learn new skills and tactics (Asal and Rethemeyer, 2008; Phillips, 2015). Cooperation helps with the mobilization and aggregation of resources. It helps groups meet their needs relating to personnel, training, weapons and other important necessities. Many violent non-state actors have collaborated in joint training exercises or on raising funds. The Irish Republican Army (IRA) has worked with other groups, such as the Revolutionary Armed Forces of Colombia (FARC) to gain access to weapons. The Red Army Faction worked with other groups in the 1980s to carry out more damaging attacks (Merkl, 1995). The more allies a violent group has, the more lethal it tends to be (Asal and Rethemeyer, 2008).

Groups were also offered unrestricted access to financial and global market structures and to diasporic communities across the globe. There is also a thriving global market for illegal products and services, and borders are no longer impediments to criminal transactions. Transnational criminal organizations are taking advantage of the jurisdictional limitations on national police forces and weak international law enforcement. Increased financial flows make it more difficult to stop money laundering and decreased border controls make transportation of goods and people much less expensive. Groups can also capitalize on the opportunities provided by economies in transition.

Another factor has been the rise in failing states (for more on this, see Chapter 4). Gaps in security facilitate the movement of violent non-state actors and make it easier for them to cooperate and merge. Related to state weakness, conflict has also played a role facilitating the nexus between crime and politically violent non-state actors. Once the conflict has begun, the conditions of conflict make it easier for organized crime to flourish, while also providing an impetus for crime. Once the state has been deeply weakened by conflict, a black-hole state emerges and is taken over by hybrid groups (Makarenko, 2004: 138). A protracted war is promoted to secure economic and political power. Wars get hijacked by criminal organizations that use terror tactics. At the same time, politically violent non-state actors start to focus mostly on criminal activity to fund their existence.

The more unstable the region, the more likely we will see interests converge. Instability, then, is in the interest of both groups because it delegitimizes the government and maximizes criminal operations (Makarenko, 2004: 132). For example, these interests clearly converged in Latin American in the 1990s. In Colombia, conflicts eventually lent themselves to more criminal activity and many of the drug cartels became more involved in politics.

Additionally, a surge in drug production provided new opportunities for profit (Cornell, 2006: 45). Drug trafficking has blurred the boundaries between politics, crime and terrorism. The Taliban and al-Qaeda used drugs to finance their operations in Afghanistan and internationally. If there is any tradition of drug cultivation, a conflict will lead to a huge increase in drug production. If there is no tradition of drug cultivation, various smuggling operations will emerge – especially if a conflict zone is located near the destination of illicit goods.

WHAT ARE THE WAYS CRIME AND TERROR CONNECT?

This nexus takes place in several different ways. At a minimum, criminal and political groups may influence each other (Makarenko, 2012). There may be some mutual learning that ensues where practices are adopted by the other and some minimal cooperation takes place.

A deeper form of cooperation takes the form of alliances. Alliances are when criminal groups align with political groups. This can be short or long term. They may seek expert knowledge of money laundering, counterfeiting or bomb-making, or operational support for access to smuggling routes. Cooperating with a political group may benefit a criminal group because it could destabilize the political structure, undermine law enforcement and limit the possibilities of international cooperation.

'Transformation' is when a criminal entity mutates into a politically motivated agent or a political organization changes into a criminal enterprise. Transformation is more common than long-term alliances, and is most likely to go in the direction of groups moving towards crime instead of the other way around.

POLITICAL GROUPS TURNING TO CRIME

Political groups that turn to criminal activities initially to fund their efforts may change their objectives to maintain the status quo and profit from illicit trade (Makarenko, 2004: 135). Opportunities for economic profit transform the motivations of the originally ideologically motivated insurgents (Kalyvas, 2015: 2–3). In other cases, the loss of a charismatic leader leads to the rise of new factions of the organization that are solely focused on crime. Internal disagreements can also lead to a change in the group's direction.

There are many cases of political groups linking up with criminal groups. The Kurdistan Workers' Party (PKK), the Euskadi Ta Askatasuna (ETA) of Spain, and the Shining Path in Peru have been accused of linking up with the drug trade and profiting from these links (Makarenko, 2004: 134). For decades, the FARC had tactical alliances with criminal organizations in Colombia, Mexico and Venezuela (Makarenko, 2004: 131). Technical capabilities of violent non-state actors limit and affect their participation in criminal activities. For example, many members of political organizations do not have the technical skills or networks to be involved in criminal activities. Many armed insurgents are peasants who have never participated in drug production, trafficking and money laundering and find it difficult to acquire these sort of skills and networks. Thus criminal organizations are also often sought after when additional support is needed. There may be a need for forged documents or for front companies to hide illicit activity. Sometimes the political organizations take advantage of the infrastructure that has already been created by the organized criminal groups. In these instances, political groups are parasitical on the organized criminal groups' profits.

Sometimes, terrorist groups are sophisticated enough to develop the capacity to perform organized criminal acts in-house, such as the Liberation Tigers of Tamil Eelam (LTTE). They were able to raise money for the organization through extortion, the drug trade, credit card fraud, social security fraud, counterfeit currency trading, piracy and people and gun smuggling. The IRA also did not seek collaborative partnerships when they began to largely focus on organized crime.[6] They ran their own smugglings rings, protection and extortion rackets and underground brothels and engaged in contractor fraud (Dishman, 2001: 48). The same can be said for Hezbollah and Hamas, which are both involved in cigarette and drug smuggling. These groups above represent hybrid groups, that have both a political and economic agenda.

Sometimes, the political group has completely transformed into a criminal group, such as the case of the Islamic Movement of Uzbekistan (IMU), which initially wanted to create an Islamic state across central Asia. After the death of its leader, it abandoned this agenda and mostly focused on trafficking drugs and weapons. The same transformation happened to Abu Sayyaf. After its leader died in 1998, factions emerged that were focused entirely on crime (Makarenko, 2012). Having lost their ideological purity, these groups might maintain a political façade to attract recruits or to keep the government and law enforcement focused on political issues and problems as opposed to initiating criminal investigations (Makarenko, 2012: 244).

---------------------- Case Study   The Islamic State ----------------------

The IS is an Islamic extremist group that emerged out of the ongoing war in Iraq. Its main aim is to create an Islamic state in the Middle East, but the group has become global. It operates or has affiliates in many other parts of the world, including northern Africa and southeast Asia. Due to its penchant for spectacular attacks on civilians, it has been designated as a terror organization.[7] But its capacity is much stronger than that. It is more accurately an *insurgency* that operates as a de facto state, controlling territory in Iraq and Syria – at one point the size of Belgium (Cronin, 2015). Much of its power is due to its extensive capacity to raise illegal revenues. (For more on the emergence of the IS, see Chapter 7.)

Though in 2015–16 the IS lost territory and appears to be waning in power, it is still the richest militant group in the world. In 2008 it had revenues of $1 million a month, but by 2014 it was generating $1 million to $3 million a day, with $2 billion in cash and assets (Rand Corporation). How has a politically motivated organization become so rich? Initially, much of its financial support came from individuals in Arab Gulf states. Today, the IS has avoided international finance and has generated funds within its own territories and porous borders mostly from criminal activity.

Its main method of generating revenue had come from selling oil on the black market to an extensive web of shadow partners and clients (Nakhle, 2015). This was the group's major source of revenues until Western airstrikes knocked out possibly as much as 50% of the group's refining capacity (Lerman, 2014). The sale of antiquities has been another major source of revenues, generating more than $100 million a year in 2014 with over 4,500 cultural sites under its control (Mavin, 2015; Swanson, 2015). It also earns revenues from selling resources such

---

[6]The IRA refers to several armed movements in Ireland. In 1969 it split in two: the Provisional Irish Republican Army (PIRA) and the Official IRA (OIRA). The Continuity IRA (CIRA) broke from the PIRA in 1986. Then the Real IRA broke from the PIRA in 1997, which is still active. The Real IRA is often referred to as the 'New IRA'. In this book, we are over-simplifying, but unless specified otherwise, we are referring to the IRA collectively.

[7]In total, some 70 terrorist attacks around the world have been committed on behalf of or by the IS in 20 countries, with over 1,200 victims (http://edition.cnn.com/2015/12/17/world/mapping-isis-attacks-around-the-world).

as phosphate, cement and sulphur at discounted prices. It also grows crops and sells them at a 50% discount on the black market. What it does not cultivate itself, it steals from other farmers.

Another source of revenue comes from robbing banks and looting (Soloman and Jones, 2015). After taking over territory in Iraq, the group looted and resold military supplies, weapons and ammunition, construction equipment, cars and other goods. It has also engaged in seizing real estate from people who have been killed or fled the area. Property has been rented out or sold for auction. Kidnapping for ransom is another source of earnings, giving the group $40 million in 2014 (Swanson, 2015). Additionally, the IS taxes electricity and water (though electricity is sometimes only provided for one hour per day). It also taxes and extorts salaries and forces trucks entering its controlled territory to pay at checkpoints.

Though some of its sources of funding are being cut off, its involvement in multiple areas of illegal activity has made the group incredibly powerful. Its criminal activity made it capable of funding a military, planning massive terror attacks and administering an entire state, albeit one that is seriously failing to provide much of anything.

CRIMINAL GROUPS TURNING TO POLITICS

Criminal groups may also involve themselves in political violence. The criminal is supposedly mostly concerned with material satiation, but they may see the benefits of involving themselves in political violence. Criminal organizations have sought out similar operational approaches as political actors in order to intimidate or gain concessions. They may resort to using terror tactics to scare off the government or to gain further control over the government to facilitate their activities. Brazil's Comando Vermelho (CV) adopted the use of terror to establish operational control. Terror is used to distract law enforcement and focus on political issues or to intimidate rival organizations.

——— Case Study   Brazil's Organized Criminal Gangs ———

Brazil faces a variety of criminal groups, both powerful drug cartels and organized gangs.

While Brazil's security services have often used violence against the poor, the state has failed to provide welfare, healthcare, education or sanitation, while also not providing any safety. As a result, favela citizens in Rio de Janeiro and Sao Paulo prefer to support drug lords because they provide better protection than the state or police. Thus, it is the tension between the security institutions and the poor that helps explain why and how these groups operate. The criminal groups in Brazil have capitalized on this insecurity to adopt a quasi-political agenda.

One of the first drug cartels to emerge in the favelas was the CV. The group became powerful in Brazil by controlling the trafficking of cocaine in Rio de Janeiro in the 1980s. CV realized that the favelas provided strategic locations to stockpile marijuana and cocaine that was destined for sale to richer clients in other parts of Rio, South America and Europe. CV provided some services in exchange for residents to turn a blind eye to their activities. By the 1990s the CV had a big social base in the favelas and the prisons, controlling about one-third of the city's favelas. Although CV did provide some services and protection, they could also be incredibly unpredictable (Penglase, 2009). Life in the favelas became even more violent, and Brazil had one of the highest homicide rates in the world.

(Continued)

(Continued)

The Brazilian state responded to its high homicide and crime rates by increasing its public security budget from $1.37 billion to $4.9 billion in Sao Paulo state. As a result, the prison population increased dramatically, more than doubling in size. Two out of five prisoners are housed in prisons in the state of Sao Paulo. There was an acute shortage of prison guards to deal with the increasing number of prisoners and the conditions in prisons became unbearable. On average, prisons in Sao Paulo state operate with 70% more inmates that the system can support (Caramante, 2014). In 1992, in response to prison riots at the Carandiru prison, police stormed in and killed 111 prisoners (Wacquant, 2008).

The 1992 massacre was the impetus behind the formation of the Primeiro Comando da Capital (PCC) in 1993, a prison gang based in Sao Paulo, which had the support of the CV. The PCC formed, claiming to be organized on behalf of prisoners' rights. The PCC claims that it is a political party, even using the slogan, 'liberty, justice and peace'. Though the group was founded with the pretext of a political agenda, the group is mainly involved in the protection and trafficking rackets within jails, as well as some outside criminal activities such as kidnapping, drug and gun trafficking, prostitution and robbery, with about $2 million being moved each month (Bailey and Taylor, 2009: 14). However, not all members are solely motivated by profits. For some, there is a sense of camaraderie and fraternity. The PCC also has the objective of shaming the police and extracting some concessions from the state regarding prison rights.

Another example of a criminal group entering politics is D-Company. D-Company is led by Dawood Ibrahim, an Indian-born businessman who is on the world's most-wanted list. D-Company started out as a smuggling operation in the late 1970s and grew into a major transnational organized criminal group running its operations out of Dubai. In the mid-1980s, it started to work with the inter-service intelligence agency in Pakistan to smuggle weapons to militant groups in Afghanistan, the Kashmir, Bangladesh and India. Ibrahim's ideology became more radically Islamic due his perception that there was increasing persecution of Muslims. By 1993, the organized criminal group started to stage its own terrorist attacks, including a series of explosions that killed 257 in Mumbai.

In other cases, criminals move to a political agenda by providing public goods and services to a host community in order to gain more subservience. They can become a parallel state with some political and social functions. Criminals may also turn to politics to control local institutions to carry on with their activities. They may also challenge state laws such as those concerning extradition, through force. Russian and Albanian crime organizations, for example, want to produce environments that break or ruin the sense of social and political calm. In order to mobilize power to resist the state, they move beyond crime which has limited appeal and bring in elements of political protest.

Though criminals are mainly concerned with maximizing profits and securing the environment in which they operate, in order to do so, they may need to rely on the assistance of political insurgencies to offer tactical support. Collaborating with political insurgents can help them destabilize political structures and undermine law enforcement (Shelley, 2014). For example, the Medellin cartel hired the National Liberation Army (ELN) of Colombia to plant car bombs in 1993 because they didn't know how to do so.

In some cases, drug traffickers have been radicalized and lured into engaging in political violence. In the case of the Madrid terror attack, drug traffickers who had been radicalized were integrated into terrorist cells – adding contacts and skill sets required to prepare for a successful attack. Much of the radicalization of criminals takes place in the prison systems (for more on this, see Chapter 12).

WHO ARE THE VIOLENT NON-STATE ACTORS?

In this book, we focus on violent non-state actors and attempt to conceptualize them. Thus far, the labels given to groups are often contested. Terrorist groups are the best example of this. It is a pejorative term that is used to delegitimize a group. The West has labelled most groups that have used violence that do not share their agenda as terrorist groups. Thus any group can be labelled a terrorist group that does not share the same values as the West. This has led to many groups being given the terrorist label as a way to discount their grievances and services that they may be providing to their publics. This is all the more problematic given that more and more violent non-state actors are using terror as a tactic. The result is that there is as an enormous list of actors who fall into this category. Not every group that uses terror is a terrorist organization. In fact, most groups today exhibit some hybrid behaviour.

In spite of these issues, it is important to make distinctions between groups or the classification of violent non-state actors becomes one large residual category that adds little to our understanding. Categories give scholars a more orderly field to study. Moreover, categorization helps us understand how different motivations and modes of behaviour can provide insights into the most typical patterns of violence (Cronin, 2002/03: 39).

Nevertheless, while we fully acknowledge that violent non-state actors have many different repertoires of actions, most groups can be distinguished by their primary motivation and most commonly used activity. We also acknowledge that a group that was once an insurgency can mutate into an organized criminal group, such as was the case with the FARC. In spite of this, there are distinguishing features of different groups. These categories provide us with a starting point to conceptualize violent non-state actors so that we can better understand what they want and how to deal with them. It is important to note that the category of a terror organization is distinct from a terror network.

The first way that groups can be distinguished is by looking at their (1) primary motivation. Is the original objective largely political or largely economic? Are they driven by a clear political ideology, or are their objectives driven by greed? Groups can have both, but what is the key motivation? Are they trying to change the status quo or maintain it? Do they want to hold territory and administrate? Do they want to engage in the pre-existing conventional political system and take part in elections? From here it is important to examine the group's (2) primary method of achieving their objectives. Is their primary strategy to attack civilians or the state's military? What are the main strategies and tactics used by the group? (3) Groups also differ by their organizational structures. How hierarchical, tightly organized and sophisticated is the group? What are the methods of recruitment used? (4) Another important question is how does this group fund itself? Where does it receive its support? (5) A final important point of distinction is the scope of the group and its potential impact. How powerful is the group? How much territory do they control, if any? How much legitimacy does the group enjoy? How much popularity does this group have with the public? Based on this, what is the overall impact of the group on the state and society? We use these five distinctions in order to better conceptualize violent non-state actors.

Summary Points

- Contemporary violence has changed significantly and involves both states and non-states, motivated by economic and political contingencies.
- Violent non-state actors are more powerful today than in the past.
- There are different types of patterned violence: (1) terrorism, (2) irregular conflict (including guerrilla warfare), (3) organized criminal violence and gang violence, (4) and grey-zone conflicts.
- The nexus of crime and political violence occurs in several ways: violent groups can influence one another, ally with one another or transform into one another.
- Violent non-state actors can be distinguished by their key motivation, strategy, structure, method of funding and impact.

Key Questions

1   How does violence today differ from violence of the past?
2   How does guerrilla warfare differ from terrorism?
3   What is meant by the 'crime-terror nexus'? What are the ways in which crime and terror intersect?
4   Why do political groups turn to crime and why do criminal groups get involved in politics? What factors have facilitated the nexus?
5   Explain the five key ways in which violent non-state actors can be differentiated. Are there other more relevant distinctions that should be taken into consideration?
6   Theory: What do realism, liberalism and constructivism conceive of the threats posed by violent non-state actors?

FURTHER READING

Aydinli, E. (2016) *Violent Non-state Actors: From Anarchists to Jihadists* (Routledge). Thorough look at violent non-state actors, particularly from the Middle East. The first chapter also offers a conceptualization of violent non-state groups.

Chenoweth, E. and Lawrence, A. (2010) *Rethinking Violence: States and Non-state Actors in Conflict* (MIT Press). Explanation of how violence has evolved over time to include both states and non-state actors. It explores why and how states and non-state actors decide to use violence against each other and whether or not this is effective.

Hoffman, F.G. (2009) *Hybrid Threats: Re-conceptualizing the Evolving Character of Modern Conflict* (Institute for National Strategic Studies). Conceptualizes all of the threats of modern conflict and the intersection between economic and political violence.

Kaldor, M. (2013) *New and Old Wars: Organised Violence in a Global Era* (Wiley). Essential overview of contemporary conflict which, Kaldor argues, is a mixture of war, organized crime and human rights violations involving both public and private actors.

Mulaj, K. (2010) *Violent Non-state Actors in World Politics* (Columbia University Press). Thoroughly edited volume offering interesting case studies on violent non-state actors. The introductory chapter is helpful for defining different violent non-state groups.

PART II
EXPLANATIONS OF VIOLENT NON-STATE ACTORS

In order to understand the complexity in world politics, international relations has used three levels of analysis (Waltz, 1959). They are the international system (global), the state (and society) and the individual. The following three chapters use these levels of analysis to better understand why and how violent non-state actors emerge and thrive. We start by looking at how global conditions provide opportunities for violent groups to succeed and also how globalization has impacted identities.

3

GLOBAL EXPLANATIONS

Key Terms

- Diasporic communities
- Global market
- Identity politics
- Kurdish diaspora
- Privatization of security
- Tri-border area
- Tamil diaspora

Global factors are important for explaining the effectiveness of violent non-state actors and to some extent why they arise. By global factors we are referring to the decline of bipolarity and the emergence of a globalized world. Most work on globalization has focused on how it impacts international trade and the activities of multinational corporations. But globalization is not just about promoting economic linkages but also about facilitating the linkages of illicit trade, shadow markets and violent non-state actors. Global factors have affected violent non-state actors' organizational structure, strategy, coherence and longevity.[1] Global factors have made violent non-state actors more efficient and harmful (Aas, 2013).

In this chapter, we first explain how changes to the polarity of the international system led to the emergence and strengthening of violent non-state actors. We then examine the ways in which violent non-state actors have been affected by globalization, looking at both motivational factors and opportunities. In essence, we explain how globalization has been both a source of grievance and how it has helped

---

[1]Global explanations have also been used to explain the development of terrorist groups (Cronin, 2002/03; Rapoport, 2001; Sedgwick, 2007). The state and individual causes are not emphasized as much as the global dynamics of a time period. Rapoport identifies four different historical waves of terrorism, each lasting about 40 years: anti-empire, anti-colonization, anti-Western, and the religious-based terrorism taking place today. Others claim that Islamic fundamentalism had been gathering steam throughout the 1980s and beyond (Charrad, 2001). Global-wave explanations tend to be criticized for their lack of historical accuracy and lack of attention to the role of governments (Gelvin, 2008).

facilitate and perpetuate political violence and crime (Ritzer, 2008; Ritzer and Atalay, 2010). This is followed by a case study of how globalization has affected the capacity of the diasporic community to support violent non-state actors, either wittingly or unwittingly.

END OF THE BIPOLAR COLD WAR

International relations scholars have spent a great deal of attention on understanding the effects of the Cold War on stability. Neo-realists such as Kenneth Waltz (1988, 1993) have theorized that the most stable period of international security was the bipolar Cold War era. Equal levels of power were acquired by the Soviet bloc and the US and its allies, resulting in a stalemate, making direct conflict between the two superpowers unlikely. The distribution of state power, or the polarity of the system, helped determine how stable the system was. Ignored from this perspective was the power of violent non-state actors. In spite of this, new non-state actors have been supplanting states in international affairs for some time now – even prior to the end of the Cold War. But the end of the Cold War caused the disintegration of the bipolar order, and the role of non-state actors became more salient. State sovereignty broke down and geographic areas of ungovernability emerged. There were increasing challenges to the state-centric system.

First, despite the claims by neo-realists, many states during the Cold War were caught up in proxy conflicts that were being funded by the US and the USSR. Economic and military assistance were given to weak and corrupt states, their adversaries and to violent non-state actors, without a clear strategy. Many of the countries in the developing world were given military aid by the superpowers in order to maintain a balance of power in the international system. Weak and corrupt regimes were propped up if they vocalized their partisanship for one superpower. Military aid was pocketed directly by kleptocratic rulers and doled out to maintain their elite support groups. Warlords, criminals and other non-state actors who claimed to be on the right side of a superpower were also supported with military aid.

Second, compounding this problem, during this period the proliferation of small arms challenged the state's ability to maintain a monopoly over the legitimate use of force. The end of the Cold War also meant that the former Soviet states had a large stockpile of weapons that could easily be acquired by different violent non-state actors, including insurgents, terrorist groups, rebels, criminals and PSCs (Kinsey, 2007). Instead of state-building efforts, violent non-state actors were gaining more and more power, enabling them to directly challenge the state. Today, violent non-state actors are better armed than ever before, and have access to more sophisticated types of weapons. As many as 60 armed groups have access to portable air-defence systems and anti-tank guided weapons (Small Arms Survey, 2012). PSCs have access to a host of different weapons such as machine guns, helicopters, tanks and even fighter jets. Compounding this problem, the end of big military spending for some countries meant that there was a pool of ex-soldiers ready to fill the needs of the market (Kinsey, 2007).

At the same time, shifts took place in the ways that violent non-state actors found their funding. During the Cold War, violent non-state actors emerged across the globe who found support from the two superpowers. Much of the support for violent non-state actors in the 1970s and 1980s came from state funding in order to fuel proxy wars. When the Cold War ended, support from states for different political movements dissipated. With the structure of the system changing, groups had to find different sources to keep their organizations afloat. Finding new sources of funding was facilitated by globalization. And while globalization made funding easier, it was also a source of grievance, fuelling the formation of new violent non-state actors.

GLOBALIZATION AND VIOLENT NON-STATE ACTORS

Globalization denotes increased mobility of people, capital, goods and ideas and information across national borders (Held and McGrew, 2007). Spurred on by improvements in technology of transportation, communication and information, globalization is a multidimensional and transnational process that allows the economy, politics and cultures of different countries to penetrate each other (Mittelman, 2010; Robertson, 1992). International networks, associations, institutions, financial markets, multinational corporations, non-government organizations, international media, academic circles and international financial institutions have all become more important in a globalizing world (Cronin, 2002/3). With globalization, the world is not only more interdependent, integrated and connected, but is also more compressed. Globalization encompasses a global market with a free flow of goods, capital services, information and people (Barbieri and Reuveny, 2005). States interact and trade at unprecedented levels, with market forces often making important decisions instead of states. Globalization has challenged states and their sovereignty.

For many scholars, globalization, migration, integration and improvements in technology have helped the world become more efficient, more democratic and more peaceful (Barnett et al., 2013; Held, 2013). It is also argued that globalization brings together a complex web of people, cultures and practices (Goldberg and Pavcnik, 2007). However, whether or not this actually takes place is debatable. Though globalization brings like-minded individuals together, it has not united the world. In fact, rifts may have become even deeper. Globalization may contribute to both fomenting resentment of certain groups and giving them access to tools to fight with and operate more freely.

In terms of how scholars conceive of the role of globalization in causing conflict, the results are mixed. On the one hand, the conflict literature claims that globalization may ease the propensity for violence and conflict. Integration within states has a limiting effect on conflict within states (Gissinger and Gleditsch, 1999; Schneider et al., 2003). Actors in more integrated economies face greater costs from conflict. Therefore, they are less likely to risk using violence. Potential violent non-state actors may be more likely to be marginally integrated into the formal economy. Thus, in cases where there are high levels of interdependence and conflict is costly to many actors, aggrieved groups may be more likely to use non-violent ways to limit disruptions (Schneider et al., 2003).

Other scholars see globalization in a much more negative light. There have been many studies done within the terrorism/insurgency and organized crime/ gang literature that have argued that globalization has been a cause of unrest and a facilitator of violence because it has expanded the range of violent non-state actors, increasing their scope and longevity (Adamson, 2005). Earlier political ideals of violent non-state actors tended to be narrower. Today's violent non-state actors are appealing to a wider set of grievances, many related to the process of globalization. Internal issues are externalized, while external issues are internalized. Politics is more local and also more global. As a result, domestic actors and their policy concerns are now prominent on global agendas, attracting sympathies and fear worldwide. The stage for attracting attention is now global as are the potential arenas for conflict. The PKK, for example, could threaten to use suicide bombing campaigns in Germany as well as Turkey as part of its struggle (Adamson, 2005: 41).

Many conflicts that appear to be internal are actually transnational, since funding draws on transnational networks (Kaldor, 2013). Political groups can operate transnationally and build up cross-border organizational structures that help foster political loyalties and mobilize resources. Criminal groups can also operate more transnationally. Globalization has also increased cross-border crime and criminal groups can operate more transnationally (Andreas and Nadelmann, 2006). While globalization creates incentives for legitimate businesses to move production overseas and operate transnationally and globally, it also creates incentives for illegitimate businesses to do the same.

Globalization has also changed the type of violence that takes place. Violence used to be more instrumental, and would take place between states and between communities. Violence is now more expressive, more ritualistic, symbolic and communicative (Cronin, 2002/03: 51). In the next sections, we explain the reasons globalization could serve as a cause of violent group formation followed by explanations of how globalization facilitates violent groups.

MOTIVATIONAL FACTORS

GLOBALIZATION AS A CAUSE OF VIOLENT GROUPS

We first examine how globalization may foster resentment. Proponents of globalization have argued that globalization offers benefits to all who integrate into the global economy and liberalize their economies. Thomas Friedman (2006) argued that globalization simply would flatten the world. On the other hand, critics claim that globalization has only increased the gaps between rich and poor. Globalization privileges those who are best positioned to gain from globalization while other groups are excluded and receive few benefits. Competition takes place over resources. Certain groups may benefit more than others (Atkinson and Brandolini 2006; Rodrik, 1997). Disadvantaged groups may be able to mobilize in response, which will then cause dominant groups to adopt exclusionary tactics (Wimmer, 2002). Deprivation then breeds resentment against dominant minorities (Bezemer and Jong-A-Pin, 2007). When globalization privileges some groups more than others, political mobilization is likely to increase. For example, urbanization and the retreat of the state have created fertile ground for gangs. Many youths feel marginalized and disconnected from the state as it fails to provide any social welfare policies (Hagedorn, 2001). Globalization leads to social dislocation. First-, second- and third-generation Muslims living in Western countries face discrimination and feel disadvantaged (Chebel d'Appollonia, 2016); Jasperse et al., 2012; Midtbøen, 2014).

Globalization has led to a new wave of identity politics. There are more groups trying to achieve political goals based on their common identity (Coate and Thiel, 2010). Globalization has also spread and reinforced the perception that this exclusion is unjust (Meyer, 2000). Globalization spreads information across borders, potentially raising awareness of resource inequalities (Wimmer, Cederman, and Min, 2009). The perception of injustice increases the likelihood that political movements will become organized into violent movements (Tilly, 2003). Thus, the demands of insurgency movements may increase with globalization (Olzak, 2011).

Globalization has created incentives for local violent crime by threatening employment, wages, and social safety nets in industrial countries. The global circulation of capital and the promulgation of neo-liberal economic policies generate an ever-growing gap between the wealthy and the poor, enhancing the attractiveness of criminal choices (Rotman, 2000).

Others claim that globalization has driven frustration against European and US-led globalization. Disgruntled populations and international movements are more likely to lash out against global forces as they are perceived to be driven by the West (Cronin, 2002/03). Scholars add that the same global processes that unite different groups can also put them on a collision course (Thornton, 2003: 205).

OPPORTUNITY FACTORS

GLOBALIZATION AS A FACILITATOR OF VIOLENT GROUPS

In addition to serving as a source of grievances, there are several ways in which globalization has served as a facilitator for violent non-state actors. Globalization and the improvement in technology that have taken place have helped to enhance communication, connectivity and information flows. Violent groups have been able to take advantage of global communication that was unavailable before, enhancing their effectiveness. The use of TV, radio, videos, the Internet and mobile phones has helped to construct and sustain political and criminal networks. Links are easier to sustain across borders. Globalization has helped violent groups coordinate activities, communicate and disseminate information, fund themselves, increase recruitment, mobilize individuals, operate freely and move around and reposition themselves (Berdal, 2003).

Global communications can help violent non-state actors spread information about their tactics and strategies (Mulaj, 2010: 14). With technological innovation, violent non-state actors can immediately spread their messages to a global audience through both the media and the Internet. The worldwide media can also give visibility to violent non-state actors and their causes and cross-border information can spread quickly (Mulaj, 2010: 15). The media can give the impression that a violent non-state actor has more support than it actually does. This is something that earlier groups aimed to do but were unable to accomplish on this scale. Now the media can help foster the transmission of ideas and political agendas. Violent groups use self-produced videotapes to broadcast over major media outlets. The media can experience higher viewership by broadcasting these clips, helping to give violent groups an international audience.

The Internet is also important in extending the global reach of violent non-state actors. The Internet has helped violent non-state actors operate clandestinely both to communicate and to undermine law enforcement. Criminals can also make use of IT professionals to help them communicate more secretly. Encrypted messages and invisible graphic codes can be used. Criminal and political groups use the Internet to send death threats. The Internet is also used to collect intelligence. Hackers hired by politically and economically violent groups can gain access to the names and addresses of law enforcers.

Box 3.1   Cyberterrorism

Cyberterrorism denotes premeditated, politically motivated attacks by subnational groups or clandestine agents, or individuals against information and computer systems, computer programs, and data that result in violence against non-combatant targets. Often physical attacks are followed by a cyberattack, such as the downing of the US plane near the coast of China after cyberattacks by both countries had taken place. Throughout the Pakistan-India conflict and the Balkan wars, a series of cyberattacks took place.

Cyberattacks aim at gaining high levels of publicity. The main targets are the top administrative and military units of a country, or the most visible and dominant multinational corporations such as Microsoft and Boeing. Cyberattacks also are intended to inflict serious loss. A seemingly innocuous hacking of the Canadian government website which announced the resignation of Finance Minister Paul Martin resulted in a devaluation of the Canadian dollar (Jarvis and Macdonald, 2015).

Cyberattacks usually aim to prevent the use of a public system by legitimate users, defacing a website that provides government or commercial information in order to either disrupt the provision of information or spread propaganda by the organization. A violent group can facilitate identity theft, inflict computer systems with viruses and destroy important data.

Cyberterrorism illustrates that states are incredibly vulnerable. These acts of cyberterrorism can be executed by violent non-state actors as a way of threatening states without huge costs, since detecting exactly who the perpetrator is, is not that straightforward. Aum Shinrikyo cult members worked as subcontractors for firms developing classified government and police communication hardware and software. This helped the cult to develop software to track police vehicles (Singh and Verma, 2015).

The Internet has also assisted in distributing political messages to an online audience. It offers ideological support for disgruntled individuals. Groups maintain user-friendly official and unofficial websites which are all accessible in English. Radicals can post and share training videos, manifestos, blogs and e-magazines to help spread propaganda. Al-Qaeda has produced a terrorist guidebook and instructional videos on explosives. Gangs use the Internet to brag about their exploits and spread propaganda to glorify their gang (Womer and Bunker, 2010). The IS also has a well-funded web and social media propaganda campaign where it posts Internet videos of brutal violence and the destruction of cultural heritage sites. It also relies on an English language e-magazine to promote its organization.

The Internet also facilitates communication and coordination for violent groups. The communication network is central to al-Qaeda. It uses the Internet to coordinate the activities of different cells on different continents, using chat rooms, websites and e-mail (Mannes, 2003: 33). Organized criminal groups use the Internet to secretly communicate as well. The Internet also helps violent groups engage in money laundering (Abadinsky, 2012: 336).

The Internet is used to facilitate self-recruitment as well for violent groups. It helps individuals gain access to extremist groups. With over thousands of Islamic militant sites in operation, messages and videos on websites target potential recruits. Chat rooms and social networking create an environment where like-minded individuals can develop supportive relationships. The Internet acts as a meeting ground where all participants are viewed as equal (Sageman, 2004). In the case of al-Qaeda in Iraq (AQI), the Internet was used to facilitate a connection between interested recruits and the organization. The Internet helps to develop mutually supportive relationships. Candidates who seemed interested in joining were contacted and given written instructions about how to join (Hegghammer, 2007). Though personal connections are still the most important ways in which individuals are prompted to action, the Internet plays an important role in fanning the flames. Adding to this, scholars note that 'virtual networks operate at their best when they are backed by real social linkages in specifically localized communities' (Della Porta and Diani, 2006: 133).

Mobile phones can facilitate violence because it is easier for violent non-state actors to coordinate attacks and operate in a coordinated fashion without a defined chain of command. Mobile phones open up a range of fusing options for improvised explosive devices. Mobile phones can be used to set up and detonate bombs. They are used to communicate between the spotters and those controlling explosives. This means that the controller no longer needs to be within the line of sight of the explosive device (Shapiro and Weidmann, 2015). Higher casualties are possible with simultaneous coordinated attacks.

Mobile phones also keep members of violent political organizations connected, something that is critical given how networked some organizations have become. Connectivity is so important that some groups offer direct support to ensure that members can communicate. Zakaria Zubaydi, former commander of the Palestinian Al-Aqsa Martyrs Brigade in Jenin, has explained that members of the organization are supplied with mobile phone credit instead of any financial remuneration (Frisch, 2012).

Mobile phones have also greatly increased the command and control capability of criminals who direct operations from inside a prison. Some corrupt guards allow visitors to bring phones into prisons. The lack of surveillance to prevent prisoners from communicating with criminals on the outside has allowed them a powerful tool to spread information and coordinate uprisings and attacks in the state. For example, the violence of the PCC, a Brazilian prison gang (see Chapter 2), was organized using mobile phones (Sullivan, 2006). Mobile phones signals have not been blocked in Central American prisons, and military personnel have been implicated in selling mobile phones to gang leaders in prison.

Improvements in transportation both in speed and costs have facilitated travel and mobility. Global transportation makes it easier for violent non-state actors to move around and take part in actions in multiple locales (Cockayne, 2010). With the revolution in transportation in the late 1950s to 1970s, violent non-state actors could strike at global targets in a few hours. Violence could become non-territorial as violent non-state actors were not engaged in conflict within a clear geographical territory (Bunker, 2014: xxii).

More porous borders also facilitate the movement of goods and people. Increases in global trade help violent groups fund their operations. Organized criminal groups and political groups find it easier to trade the goods and services that they have control over. Globalization enables groups to engage in trading relationships with entire countries. The ease of trade has elevated the power of warlords as well (Duffield, 1998: 81). Warlords, who only control a small geographical base, are able to forge linkages with the international economy. Charles Taylor of Liberia, for example, was the biggest supplier of tropical hardwoods to France (Robinson, 2001: 125). Taylor also had alliances with multinational corporations that allowed him to get hold of equipment to sustain his war economy.

Thus, globalization does not just bring large volumes of legal trade, but also an increase in the smuggling of goods, services and persons (Aas, 2013). Free-trade zones expedite the flow of illegal products. The Mafia has become more successful due to sophisticated organizational methods by being able to create economies of scale through global partnerships and opening of new markets. With fewer tariffs, there is no oversight of illegal products. Drugs can travel from Asia, through Dubai, to Europe, to North America where an Internet seller marketed them to Americans as drugs from Canada. Different types of illicit actors may be associated with this trade, facilitated by corrupt officials at such transport hubs as airports, railroad stations and ports. Many organized criminal groups operate on the basis of ethnicity or nationality and can use their personal connections across the world to help facilitate the flow of goods.

Globalization has also spurred the trade in weapons. The ease with which arms can be traded has led to the democratization of violence. Non-state actors can gain access to illegal weapons and trade them on the open market. Modern and sophisticated weapons are now available to groups that had been previously segregated from the international community. Modem technology allows for a range of weapons and explosives to be used. Some scholars caution against the trade in weapons of mass destruction or spreading information about manufacturing biological and chemical weapons (Shapiro, 2003). In particular, there has been a massive growth of containers being used in trade. This has transformed the global trading system into a smuggler's paradise. Just as containers are helpful for trading large volumes of goods, they can be just as efficient for smuggling illegal drugs and weapons, as well as human trafficking.

Violent groups can also migrate more easily (Shelley, 1999). As a result, globalization may lead to the diffusion of insurgencies and rebel groups. Due to weak borders, insurgent groups may have a sanctuary in a neighbouring state which enables the spread of the insurgency into other countries. This took place with rebel groups in Sierra Leone and Liberia during their civil wars and in Chechnya when the insurgency spread to Ingushetia and Dagestan in Russia. The freedom of movement enabled insurgents to establish interpersonal contacts and linkages (Tarrow, 2007).

Lax regulation of borders has also enabled violent groups to conduct their operations in border zones unbothered, taking advantage of the asymmetries in legal systems (such as tax rates and currency values) and different forms and levels of governance. Blurred borders enable violent groups to exploit interconnected economies. As such, border zones are magnets for illegal flows that take advantage of the lack of regulation, supervision and cooperation (Shelley, 2014). In particular, most international ports do not have clear lines of authority (Shapiro, 2003). This problem is clearly illustrated at the tri-border area of Paraguay, Brazil and Argentina, which has been the centre of illicit activity, such as drugs, piracy and small arms. Violent non-state actors have congregated here and used the unregulated area as a base for operations. Training camps run by terrorist groups have also been found near the tri-border area.[2]

---

[2]Much of the problem is due to lax law enforcement. Corruption is a problem because law enforcement and political figures can be bought off (Shelley, 2014: 151).

Globalization has led to higher levels of migration. This is mostly a positive phenomenon, but in some cases it has led to the movement of individuals associated with violent groups and helped expand these violent groups' operations. For example, the migration of Central Americans to and from the US played a role in the expansion and development of gangs (*maras*), which have become a major transnational threat to security throughout North and Central America. Gangs used to be confined to local areas in cities, but now, due to increasing migration and travel patterns, gangs have spread. Migration contributed to the reconfiguration of gangs by changing their identities, norms and symbols associated with gang membership (Cruz, 2010). This migration also contributes to marginalization of individuals and the diffusion of gang identities.

Box 3.2   Syrian Refugee Crisis

The Syrian refugee crisis has made headlines for being the worst exodus since the Rwandan genocide over two decades ago. But while Europeans feel that they are facing the brunt of the crisis, it is neighbouring countries that actually bear most of the burden. As of 2016, millions of Syrians have fled to Turkey (2.7 million), Lebanon (1 million), Jordan (657,000 officially, but the government claims there are 1 million), Egypt (117,000) and Iraq (249,000), while another 6.6 million Syrians are displaced within Syria. Comparatively, only one million Syrians have requested asylum in Europe.

Many in Western countries have voiced concerns over the effects of the refugee crisis on their countries' economies (Fotiadis, 2016). However, most studies find that there are little to no effects from immigration on the labour market position of citizens (Borjas, 2013; Dustmann, Glitz and Frattini, 2008). Even in the case of Turkey, which is hosting almost three million Syrian refugees, there has been no effect on employment of native Turks (Akgündüz et al., 2015). Moreover, for Western countries, the number of refugees needing to be resettled represents a very small percentage of the population. For example, the countries in the Organization for Economic Co-operation and Development (OECD) have a population of more than one billion. A resettlement rate of 0.2% across the OECD would be equal to more than two million refugees placed per year. But this number is larger than the typical number of asylum applications that take place each year even where there is not a crisis (Stace, 2016).

Most governments are very resistant to integrating refugees and prefer to provide temporary solutions, where refugees live in appalling conditions. Over 50% of the world's refugees have lived in exile for more than five years, with the average length in exile about 17 years (Betts and Collier, 2015). They usually do not have freedom of movement or the right to work and their lives are placed on hold. Refugee camps are also huge health hazards as people are forced to live in inhumane and crowded conditions. Thus, these temporary solutions create breeding grounds for misery (Lischer, 2006). Refugees are often equated with threats to national security due to concerns of militarization of refugee camps (Lebson, 2013). It has been argued that the miserable conditions of refugee camps in Lebanon helped some Palestinian groups solidify and arm themselves (Salehyan, 2008). Given these valid concerns about refugee camps, it's important to have an understanding of how integrated migrants can positively contribute to societies (Betts and Collier, 2015). And though there may be some concerns to security, the alternative is much worse. (For more on the concerns, see the case study on diasporic communities.)

Globalization has also facilitated funding for violent non-state actors. Insurgencies require significant funding to maintain armies and commission acts of violence. Terror organizations that are not linked to insurgencies require much less funding. But those that do necessitate massive amounts of funding have found that this is all made easier with globalization, through global financing networks (Zimmermann, 2011). Financing comes from non-profit organizations, charities and legitimate companies that divert profits. The Internet can help groups use Listservs to collect money from donors. Websites are vehicles for raising funds. Not only is it easier to generate funds, but it is also easier to hide funds. The ease of financial transactions can be used for money laundering. Fluid movement of financial resources, computer networks and information connections makes borders irrelevant (Cronin, 2002/03: 49). The global financial system allows money to rapidly transfer from one node to another network. Offshore banking and cyber-finances have enabled organized crime to create flexible global networks that can evade regulation with limited oversight. This makes it easier for violent non-state actors to conceal the origin of their assets (Mair, 2005).

Globalization does not always necessitate the use of high technology, but lax regulations and permissible borders facilitate the transfer of funds. Violent non-state actors can make use of traditional banks, Islamic banks, money changers and other forms of informal exchange, such as the hawala or hundi system (Cronin, 2002/03: 50). The movement of money through an underground banking system is more difficult to monitor (Zimmermann, 2011).

With globalization, capital has also become more mobile, which also can serve the interests of violent groups. Illegal flows of goods can move across borders more easily with the help of transnational informal economic networks which are often embedded in existing personal relations. Funds can instantly be transmitted across the globe. For example, D-Company is a hybrid political and criminal group led by Dawood Ibrahim (see Chapter 2). The group was originally heavily involved in the film industry, having a monopoly on pirated videos. However, it gained notoriety for its key role in the Mumbai terrorist attacks in 1993 in India. After doing so, it was forced to move its home base from Mumbai, India, to Karachi, Pakistan. It was able to move its production base easily and continued to market its pirated films globally (Shelley, 2014: 276).

Technology also helps violent non-state actors decentralize their activities. Actors can be transnational and establish cells across the world. They can forge international alliances. Networks are more widespread (Castells, 2011). They can emulate other groups and work by a system of franchising under a more distant command. Violent groups lack centres of gravity helping these groups to evade law enforcement, making them more resilient (Castells, 2011). Groups like al-Qaeda were able to franchise and spawn many clones. Decentralization can also connect political groups with criminal networks. Organizations can be more complex – members can be more dispersed. These groups can outsource support functions and keep themselves distinct from the internal structure. They can keep regulations to a minimum in order to maximize adaptability (Knorr Cetina, 2005: 215). Increased technological sophistication gives more power to splinter amateurish groups (Rotman, 2000: 22). Globalization enables an organizational structure that is more immune to the application of conventional military force (Robb, 2007: 4).

Globalization has also reinforced the drive towards privatization of security (see Chapter 10). With the end of the Cold War, political constraints dissipated and there was a greater demand for private soldiers to challenge insurgent movements.

Globalization created an environment where international interests can use private militaries to provide security. As a result, there are more private militaries, and force has become more informal. These actors may provide temporary stability but add little to long-term public stability (Taulbee, 2002).

———————— Case Study   Diasporic Communities ————————

Political scientists are only beginning to understand the importance of transnational forms of social organization (Salehyan, 2007). Ethnic groups, religious communities and activist networks often span national boundaries, making it difficult for any one state to regulate their activities. Though these diasporic communities are important to facilitating trade, investment, and skills and knowledge to their home communities (Newland and Plaza, 2013), scholarly research has also examined the role of these communities in supporting violent groups (Brynen, 2002; Brinkerhoff, 2008).

Diasporic communities are dispersed persons of various countries who share the same ethnic and national origin of the cause that they are supporting. They are integrated but not assimilated into their host societies. They usually retain and want to perpetuate some elements of their original identity and maintain contacts with their homelands (Omeje, 2007).

The interaction between the diasporic community and globalization illustrates two important points. First, in an age of unprecedented mobility of goods, persons and finances, support for violent networks may be distributed across the globe (Kaldor, 2013: 139). Second, this support for violent networks may be driven by the alienation that the community feels from their host states (Hoffman 2007: viii). There is no doubt that globalization has facilitated the migration of people but also their estrangement.

In a world where many individuals feel socially dislocated, globalization has also helped the hundreds of millions of the worldwide diaspora to communicate and connect with other migrant groups as well as with populations in their home states (Sheffer, 2006: 124). The diasporic communities can maintain strong social networks that stretch across borders to assist with political mobilization and funding (Adamson, 2005: 34; Rotman, 2000). Satellite TV means that immigrants can remain linked to a virtual identity community that transcends geographic locale (Adamson, 2005: 36). Groups can also use TV to mobilize their ideas and identities. For example, in the 1990s, independently run Kurdish TV stations were broadcasting in Kurdish, which was banned in Turkey. These programmes included Kurdish language lessons that were broadcast into Turkey from Europe.

Diasporic communities can also be a source of funding. Many violent non-state actors have turned to fundraising and taxation of activated transnational networks, tapping the resources of the community (Byman et al., 2001; Kaldor, 2013). Sometimes this assistance is voluntary while other times the support is coerced. Sometimes motivated by the discrimination taking place in their homelands, diasporic communities send remittances from abroad which can be converted to fund the purchase of weapons from various forms of asset transfer (Sheffer, 2006: 124). Direct assistance for arms came from Irish Americans to the IRA, Armenians to Nagorno-Karabakh and Canadian Tamils to Tamil Tigers in Sri Lanka.

Diasporic communities can also assist with cross-border networks that can be used to engage in illicit activities. Many violent non-state actors are integrated into illegal trading hubs and profit from the sale of counterfeit products and drugs. The People's Workers Party benefits from cross-border trade in counterfeit cigarettes and drugs. Kinship ties among Kurds across the region help assist with this trade. The global network of the LTTE was also involved in all kinds of business ventures across the globe. These included real estate, shipping, retail and grocery stores, gas stations and restaurants (Jayasekara, 2007). The group was also involved in film

(Continued)

(Continued)

production, TV, radio and newspapers. The World Tamil Coordinating Committee was later found to be an LTTE front organization for many illegal businesses.

One example of the role of the diasporic community is the case of Kosovar Albanians. During the 1990s, almost one-third of all Kosovars had worked or lived abroad. With almost 400,000 living in western Europe, the Democratic League of Kosovo (LDK) had thick transnational social networks with western Europe. This party used diasporic communities to help fund the creation of parallel political structures or a de facto state (see Chapter 6). Almost all of the funds were used to promote a parallel education system (Adamson, 2005).

The PKK also took advantage of the Kurdish diaspora. Throughout the mid-1980s and early 1990s, the group was able to operate legally in most of Europe. It promoted cultural, social and political organizations that could exist in parallel with its underground structure (Adamson, 2005). The PKK organized cultural festivals, youth camps and immigrant support groups in Europe. The group was particularly active and adept at raising money in Germany, where political demonstrations organized by the group would capture huge crowds of 50,000 people. These demonstrations were then filmed and circulated throughout the diasporic community (Chapin, 1996).

The LTTE have also been able to build a transnational movement through support from the Tamil diasporic community, which has been the backbone of the campaign (Thiranagama, 2014). However it was not until the riots of July 1983 that the LTTE was able to raise money outside of Sri Lanka for its insurgency. After the riots, tens of thousands of Tamils left for Tamil Nadu in India or Western countries and were welcomed as political refugees. Over 450,000 Tamils took refuge in over 50 countries (Gunaratna, 1998).

As a result of the wide presence of the diaspora, the LTTE was able to build offices and cells in 54 countries (Chalk, 2008). By the 1990s, the Tamil Tigers had highly effective transnational funding organizations. The average funding coming from the diaspora totalled $2 million a month by 1995, with $1.5 million coming from the UK, Canada and Australia alone (Byman et al., 2001). Eventually the group was earning $100 million a year, with $60 million of it coming from overseas (Kumaraswamy and Copland, 2013: 181). A World Bank estimate is more generous, claiming that Tamil diasporic organizations were raising about $450 million per year during the 1990s (Demmers, 2007: 10). The money was acquired through donations from Tamil migrant communities, Tamil NGOs and Tamil-run businesses across the globe. The vast network disseminated propaganda, engaged in fundraising and helped the group obtain weapons.

Other times extortion is used to persuade the diasporic community to contribute to violent causes. The PKK has threatened the diasporic community of Kurds living abroad to contribute to their cause (Shelley, 2014: 138). Millions of dollars have been extorted from Kurdish legitimate businesses in Europe. At times it taxed individual salaries and business profits, upwards of 20%. In the UK, in 1993 alone, the PKK extorted £2.5 million from Kurdish immigrants and business-men (Roth and Sever, 2007: 910). The Tamil Tigers were even more successful. Tamil businesses in Toronto were forced to provide $1 million a month to the Tamil Tigers (Shelley, 2014: 138).

Hezbollah exploits Middle East ex-pats around the world, especially in Latin America. About 10% of Hezbollah's funding, or $10 million a year, used to come from Paraguay in the tri-border area. Hezbollah controls money-laundering channels in West Africa. Often those involved in supporting violent groups are otherwise law-abiding citizens who have no blemishes on their record, and are often long-time residents.

Transnational ethnic linkages may also influence whether or not grievances escalate into con-flict. Members of the transnational component of an ethnic group may be more confrontational since they don't face state repression (Gleditsch, 2007: 298). Alienated diasporic groups can provide funding, ideas and techniques. They can help develop and disseminate propaganda, assist with training and provide on-the-ground intelligence. Some are specialists in making false documents. When the diasporic community is close by, they can be easily recruited (Salehyan, 2007). The diasporic community may have a larger pool of resources to draw upon for mobilizing conflict. They can also provide resources that the group in the home country could not access.

The role of diasporic communities illustrates that a conflict far away can affect communities all over the world. It is therefore important to take a regional approach when it comes to tackling violent non-state actors. And though the answer may appear to be stemming the flow of immigration, it is preferable (as this is not feasible or beneficial) to seek out solutions that protect the diasporic community from exploitation and alienation (for more on this, see Chapter 12).

CONCLUSION

Global factors are important to explaining the strength and effectiveness of violent non-state actors. Global factors are also relevant to consider in terms of what motivates violent groups to form. The end of bipolarity and the creation of a global world has, on the one hand, compressed the world, but has also led to the proliferation of violent non-state actors and enhanced their power vis-à-vis the state. Globalization has levelled the playing field of the state versus non-states, something that has had both positive and negative consequences for security.

Summary Points

- The end of the Cold War fostered significant changes in the strength of non-state actors.
- In particular, one alarming trend with globalization is the privatization of security and the weakening of the state.
- Global factors are important mostly for explaining how violent groups are able to flourish.
- Globalization has created ungoverned spaces that violent non-state actors can profit from.
- Violent groups take advantage of diasporic communities and rely on their support, which has been facilitated by improvements in technology.

Key Questions

1   In what ways did the end of the Cold War lead to the rise of violent non-state actors?
2   How has globalization motivated actors to commit acts of violence?
3   How has globalization facilitated the success of violent non-state actors?
4   How has globalization affected the types of violence being committed?
5   In what ways have diasporic communities been able to profit from globalization in order to further the violent groups that they may support?
6   Theory: How do realists, liberals and constructivists characterize globalization? Do they see the effects as largely positive or negative? What aspects of globalization can be harnessed in a positive way to prevent the rise of violent non-state groups?

FURTHER READING

Aas, K.F. (2013) *Globalization and Crime* (SAGE). Overview of the downside of globalization, including an examination of urban crime and human trafficking, as well as an analysis of the controversies over the war on terror and migration.

Appelbaum, R.P. and Robinson, W.I. (2005) *Critical Globalization Studies* (Psychology Press). Critical essays on globalization, in particular the effects of globalization on social justice. In doing so, it develops new perspectives on globalization.

Aydinli, E. and Rosenau, J.N. (2005) *Globalization, Security, and the Nation State: Paradigms in Transition* (SUNY Press). Examines the effects of globalization on security and states.

Kahler, M. and Walter, B.F. (eds) (2006) *Territoriality and Conflict in an Era of Globalization* (Cambridge University Press). Explains how globalization has changed the way conflict takes place.

Kirshner, J. (2013) *Globalization and National Security* (Routledge). A reader on how globalization affects security in the US, Europe, Russia, the Middle East, China and Japan; also helps explain how global migration may affect security.

Schneider, G., Barbieri, K. and Gleditsch, N.P. (2003) *Globalization and Armed Conflict* (Rowman and Littlefield). Explores the relationship between globalization and conflict, such as whether or not economic integration fosters or tempers disputes.

STATE-LEVEL EXPLANATIONS

While global factors help explain what facilitates the formation and endurance of violent groups, state-level factors provide a more direct explanation for why these groups might emerge in the first place. This chapter first looks at motivational factors that help to explain the emergence of violent non-state actors at the state level, such as socio-economic factors, repressive policies and an absence of services. The second half of the chapter will explore theories that explain the opportunities for violent groups to emerge, such as institutional weakness and incapacity. State-level factors have largely come to play when explaining the development of all different types of violent non-state actors.

MOTIVATIONAL FACTORS

What factors encourage violent non-state actors to form? The next section examines the role of factors that motivate their formation.

SOCIO-ECONOMIC CONDITIONS

For insurgencies and rebels, there is a strong correlation with poverty. In particular, conflict tends to occur in poor, resource-dependent countries. Paul Collier and Anke Hoeffler (2004) see it as reflecting lower opportunity costs of fighting in low-income economies. There are several reasons this may be the case. Impoverished countries are unable to provide public goods to their citizens, and may be too poor to repress rebellions. Many of the initial demonstrations in Syria were fuelled by the poor economy and high levels of unemployment in areas outside the main urban centres that had been neglected by the regime (Hinnebusch and Ehteshami, 2002: 107). The removal of subsidies and agricultural inputs also led to the abandonment of the agricultural sector. Housing costs soared, and poor neighbourhoods around the cities burgeoned with the influx of out-of-work farmers and Iraqi refugees. Thus, chronic underdevelopment coupled with economic and social exclusion can be exacerbated by short-term shocks. The loss of social services can be a source of grievance from below, just as it fuels top-down violence (Keen, 2012). This helps to explain the mass explosion of armed groups in Syria.

Though it is not entirely clear if unemployment directly feeds the formation of violent insurgencies and rebel groups, some case studies demonstrate that it may be a source of grievance. Unemployment may also provide potential rebels with free time to join violent organizations. Some scholars have noted that where alternative opportunities are few, due to poor employment, the incidence and duration of wars are likely to be greater (Patrick, 2006). For example, in the case of Sierra Leone, chronic unemployment led many youth to join rebel organizations (Keen, 2012). In the case of Nepal, instability and conflict were driven by frustrations with the government's handling of the economy and high levels of unemployment. While the labour force increased by 300,000 a year, underemployment levels were as high as 47% (Goodhand, 2001: 28). Left-wing Filipino insurgencies formed after decades of economic neglect by the government (Cragin et al., 2007). In line with this argument, youth bulges are also a source of violence. An abundant supply of youths with low opportunity costs, due to unemployment, provides greater opportunities for conflict (Urdal, 2006).

The predominant narrative on the economic status of terrorists is that they are poor, unemployed and living in squalor, with nothing to lose. Policymakers have argued that the conditions in developing countries are breeding grounds for terrorists and that poverty is a root cause to breed resentment. Deprivation and alienation radicalize people to join extremist groups. Several authors have claimed that most terrorist volunteers who are selected for missions come from the poorest parts of societies (Berman, 2011; Stern, 2000). However, many other micro-level studies of terrorist groups have demonstrated that there has been no direct connection between education, poverty and the propensity to participate in terrorism (Atran, 2003a; Berrebi, 2003; Krueger and Malečková, 2003). Instead, it is more likely that perpetrators come from educated and middle-class backgrounds (De Mesquita, 2005). Thus some argue that poverty and lack of education are *not* the root causes of terrorism, particularly suicide terrorism (Krueger and Malečková, 2003). (For more on these micro-level studies, see Chapter 5.)

When looking at the target country, there is research which contradicts the argument that poverty and terrorism are unrelated (O'Neill, 2002). Scholars have found that economic development in a given country and its trading partners decreases the likelihood of terrorism in that country (Li and Schaub, 2004). Other studies have also found that levels of foreign direct investment correlate with reduced transnational terrorism over time (Robison, Crenshaw and Jenkins, 2006). Lia and Skjolberg (2004) test the contention that terrorism happens least in the world's poorest countries (for example, sub-Saharan Africa), but found that Africa has the highest number of terrorism-related injuries. Scholars have also noted the importance of large-scale poverty in explaining the rise of the Boko Haram (an insurgency that has killed over 6,000 civilians in terrorist attacks in 2014 alone) in Nigeria

(Tonwe and Eke, 2013). Yet demonstrating how controversial this literature is, Walter Laqueur claimed that 'in the 49 countries currently designated by the United Nations as the least developed hardly any terrorist activity occurs' (Laqueur, 2003: 11).

Other scholars have claimed that terrorist groups may be most likely to form in countries with many people in the middle – people who are not so poor that they have to focus only on survival but are not so rich that they are satisfied (Callaway and Harrelson-Stephens, 2006). It may be unemployment coupled with higher levels of education that breeds this type of resentment and anger (Angrist, 1995). Survey research in Northern Ireland demonstrates that Protestants with higher incomes and higher levels of education are more moderate and less supportive of terrorism (Davis and Cragin, 2009).

The bigger issue may not be the economy of a country as such, but how *unequal* it is, and whether one group feels deprived; this is known as 'relative deprivation'. Political violence may be due to the gap between what people want and what they get – the difference between expectations and gratifications (Davies, 1962: 5; Gurr, 1993, 2015). More recent studies have demonstrated that higher levels of income inequality lead to more terrorism and insurgency (Krieger and Meierrieks, 2011). Inequality can compound the sense of grievance by those who feel they are living in an unjust society (Donnelly, 2004). In particular, it is the perception of inequality that is most important in helping understand how terrorist groups may form (Young, 2003). In Northern Ireland, factors that drove the formation of the IRA were years of economic deprivation and educational under-performance (O'Leary, 2007).

For organized crime, but more specifically gangs, inequality is a major problem. Teresa Caldeira claims that 'now the most visible forms of violence stem not from ideological conflicts over the nature of the political system but from delinquency and crime' (qtd by Rodgers, 2004: 3–4). The new type of violence is due to social and economic exclusion, and it is enabled by the weakness of the state (Aguirre, 2006). The research is fairly conclusive that crime is related to inequality and relative deprivation. Countries with higher levels of inequality have much higher levels of violent crime (Bursik and Grasmick, 1993; Chester, 1976; Hagedorn, 2007; Webber, 2007).

Inequalities are also a major factor behind the emergence of privatized security services to deal with rising crime and violence. The rich also deal with crime by creating a 'fortified network for urban elites, privatization of security and construction of high speed roads and roundabouts which exclude the poor' (Rodgers, 2004: 13). The rich retreat to gated communities, separating themselves further from their fellow citizens.

Case Study Boko Haram

Since Nigeria returned to democracy in 1999, the country has seen a rise in violent non-state actors (Forest, 2012). No group has gained more attention than Boko Haram. The group was responsible for more attacks on civilians in 2014 than even the IS. Boko Haram is an extremist Islamic group based in the north-east of Nigeria that claims to shun Western education. Since its emergence in 2003, it has developed into a full-blown insurgency, threatening stability in Nigeria and the region, and recently pledging allegiance to the IS. Much of the explanation for Boko Haram's appeal has been Nigeria's chronic poverty, growing inequalities, increasing unemployment and deteriorating social services (Aghedo and Osumah, 2012).

(Continued)

(Continued)

Though rich in resources, Nigeria is very poor. In addition to having 80% living under $2 a day, a 2010 survey revealed that 92.5% of the population perceive that they live in poverty (Rogers, 2012). Though Nigeria has enjoyed some economic growth this past decade, the nature of the growth has exacerbated patterns of regional inequality and social cleavages between the Muslim majority in the north and the Christian majority in the south. The north has faced persistent educational disadvantages, recurrent droughts, agricultural neglect, de-industrialization and an absence of the public sector. Poverty levels in the north are 40% higher than those in the south and unemployment is three times as high. Additionally, only 20% in the north are literate compared to 80% in the south (Rogers, 2012).

Thus it is not surprising that the worst political violence in Nigeria originates from the most socio-economically deprived parts of the country, the north-east. In Borno State, where Boko Haram originates, 'only 2% of children under 25 months have been vaccinated; 83% of young people are illiterate; 48.5% of children do not go to school' (Rogers, 2012: 3).

Given this backdrop, Boko Haram initially emerged to protest against corruption and poor governance, which the group believed could be solved through the implementation of strict adherence to Sharia law. Led by Mohammed Yusuf, the group was critical of the leadership in northern Nigeria. The group offered impoverished Nigerians one meal a day and provided small loans for commercial activities. The group shifted to more violent extremism after its leader was killed in 2009. It mutated into an aggressive and violent organization under the leadership of Abubakar Shekau, targeting churches, schools and bars, and engaging in kidnapping and suicide bombing, something that had been foreign to Nigeria (Agbiboa, 2013).

Boko Haram's membership mostly comprises political thugs, drug addicts, uneducated dropouts and unemployed people. Though the group has attracted some intellectuals and some members of the economic and political elite, the bulk of its membership is very poor. Most members come from the Kanuri tribe, which is 4% of the population who are concentrated in the north-eastern states of Nigeria (Agbiboa, 2013: 146).

A 2014 study revealed that 80% of Nigerian Muslims do not support Boko Haram and view it unfavourably (Onuoha, 2014). But Boko Haram is not the only problem for Nigeria's troubled north. Membership in youth gangs has also flourished in the region. Rapid urban migration is also unravelling communal support mechanisms. Though some may blame Islamic extremism for Nigeria's violence, the persistent inequalities are something that the country has to address.

REPRESSIVE POLICIES

Many studies of why politically violent groups emerge have centred on the role of repression and perceived repression (for more on the role of repression as a counter-strategy, see Chapter 12). Repression can provoke groups to form and use violence (Schmid, 2011; Victoroff, 2005). State repression has been cited as a necessary condition for terrorism and insurgencies (Callaway and Harrelson-Stephens, 2006). This is especially the case for nationalist separatist or ethnic sectarian groups, both insurgencies and terrorists. Continued violent repression of a specific group can cause the group to evolve into a violent actor. When they can gain access to arms they may be able to wage a full-blown insurgency.[1] In a study of Italian terrorists,

---

[1] This is where opportunities may be important; there are many repressed minorities around the world that don't form insurgencies or terror groups, but this may be a matter of lack of opportunity (Silke, 2003: 33).

it was argued that perceived state brutality, such as death of activists in prisons, was a major reason for the formation of violent groups (della Porta, 1992: 158). Excessive use of force can turn moderates into extremists (Crenshaw, 2015). State repression creates martyrs and myths that fuel recruitment to violent groups.

Actors often claim that it is the government's treatment of their group that motivates the formation of the groups, such as trying to erase their identity and undermine their dignity. Attempts to force Muslim communities to assimilate in the Philippines were a major factor in the emergence of violent groups in the Philippines. Kurdish groups also have claimed that efforts by the Turkish government to eliminate their language and culture bred resentment. Many of these groups also cite infringements on their personal freedoms and security as another motivating factor (Post et al., 2003).

In the case of the IRA, to deal with the added unrest, British troops were deployed in Northern Ireland in 1969, which was originally welcomed by nationalist communities as a stabilizer against sectarian attacks (Kearney, 2013). Eventually, heavy-handedness would cause ethnic tensions to intensify. The turning point for the organization came in January 1972, when British troops killed 14 unarmed civilians protesting in Derry in an event known as Bloody Sunday. This led to massive recruitment for the IRA and legitimized their struggle. It also generated Irish nationalist sympathy and extensive financial support from Irish and Irish Americans (Fierke, 2009: 498). Bloody Sunday was a culmination of a series of events that led to a loss in trust of the British government (Fierke, 2009). Much of the IRA's support was the result of British counter-terror policies such as checkpoints, house-to-house searches, large-scale raids and bombings of roads at the Irish border (Mobley, 2012: 25–6). In particular, the house searches conducted were considered to be humiliating, alienating many who were not committed to the cause (Dixon, 2009).

The national origin of international terrorists is also highest from countries that have high levels of political repression compared to the targets they select (Krueger and Laitin, 2008). When groups are repressed and dissidents are discouraged from being incorporated into the political process, groups will turn to violence. Though democracies may be more likely to be a target, repressive states may be more likely to be a breeding ground (Von Hippel, 2002: 35).

For parties that have become terrorist groups or insurgencies, the constant use of repression against political parties associated with the same cause is a motivation to use violence. In the case of Turkey, the state has repressed all Kurdish parties. The following Kurdish parties have been outlawed and closed down: the Social Democratic People's Party (SHP) in 1993; the Democracy Party in 1994; the Democratic People's Party (DEHAP) in 2003; and the People's Democracy Party in 2003. Members have also been arrested or imprisoned, important politicians have been banned and, in the case of the Democracy Party (DEP), 48 of its officials murdered.

Box 4.1　Political Institutions and Violent Non-state Actors

There is an abundant literature on the role of political institutions and their impact on the emergence of politically violent non-state actors. We focus briefly on the most notable contributions, looking at the role of government design, electoral systems and strength of parties, legislatures and party systems.

(Continued)

(Continued)

First, scholars have noted that federal systems may be better at preventing insurgencies (Brancati, 2006). Groups are given more control over their own lives and this may dissipate conflict concerning who controls the central government. Federalism can be seen as a useful tool to manage the potential for ethnic insurgencies in particular.

Second, scholars have argued that proportional representation is both better for decreasing the chances of an insurgency developing (Saideman et al., 2002) and terrorist groups (Li, 2005; Reilly and Reynolds, 1999).[2] In proportional systems, minority groups are more likely to have some form of representation in the legislature. Their members are more satisfied that their voices are being heard, preventing the chances for violence. For example, the UK's majoritarian system may have been an issue in helping Catholics in Northern Ireland feel disenfranchised. Insufficient political representation has been cited as an important factor in the Northern Ireland conflict (O'Leary, 2007).

Third, effective parties and legislatures are also important in preventing insurgencies (Rothchild and Groth, 1995: 74). They help mediate and resolve conflicts between groups (Randall and Svåsand, 2002). Tanzania provides another example of the role of parties in alleviating potential insurgencies. Tanzania has more than 140 different ethnic groups, yet unlike other diverse countries in Africa that have devolved into conflict, power-sharing mechanisms within the ruling Chama Cha Mapinduzi (CCM) party have been used to accommodate demands. In particular, religious diversity between Tanzania's powerful Christian and Muslim communities led to an alteration in power between Christian and Muslim leaders. Without the structure of the party to implement this informal power-sharing mechanism, tensions between the primary religious communities could have erupted into conflict (Hydén, 1999).

As for terrorism, what is important is the strength of the party system. Countries with weak party systems will have too many weak parties represented in the legislatures and governing coalitions. This is problematic because weak party systems are often unable to moderate and integrate the different political forces into legal political behaviour. Instead, extremist, anti-system political forces in government are empowered, such as has been the case in Israel, India and Colombia (Piazza, 2006).

LACK OF SERVICE PROVISION

In general, scholars have noted that providing public goods is an important way for the state to achieve legitimacy. The inability of states to provide services disrupts the social contract between citizens and the state and may lead to a crisis of the state's legitimacy. As the regime is perceived to be increasingly illegitimate, the likelihood of groups forming that are willing to use violence increases (Weinberg and Pedahzur, 2004). This may be true of all violent groups with the exception of terrorist groups (see the case study on Failed States and Violent Non-state Actors later in this chapter). States that lack legitimacy may 'provide the space and oxygen' for these groups to thrive and step in to fill the void (O'Neill, 2002: 20). Violent non-state actors, such as Hezbollah and Hamas, have supplied clean water, sewage treatment and utilities. The Sandinistas built health clinics. Russian mafia groups have organized sports teams. Drug cartels have provided money for schools and established community centres.

---

[2]Proportional systems usually mean that a percentage of the vote roughly translates into a percentage of seats in the legislature.

For many politically violent groups, integral to their strategy of attracting support is to provide social welfare services where the state is unable or unwilling to do so. Charitable services are used as a tool to shape the local population's views, possibly towards a more violent agenda. These groups undermine the state by competing against it. Although the Shining Path lost support due to its use of extreme violence on its own support group, it did provide a host of services throughout the rural highlands, including support for educational development and economic production. The Tupamaros of Uruguay also gained high levels of popularity initially in the late 1960s when they provided food and blankets to impoverished areas and funnelled money to hospitals and primary schools. They also stole $200,000 from a casino and used some of the money to set up a fund for casino employees (Grynkewich, 2008).

Though few studies have evaluated the relationship between administrative institutions and insurgencies, it is theoretically possible that such a relationship exists. When the state stops providing social services, this may be a potential source of tension. A recent study demonstrated that the provision of public goods makes the onset of an insurgency less likely (Getmansky, 2013). When the Algerian government stopped providing social services during the late 1980s, violent groups emerged to fill the void (Grynkewich, 2008). For many poor states, stability is very tenuously maintained by the distribution of resources through patronage networks. When the state is no longer able to distribute this patronage due to either corruption or an economic crisis, violent groups can form to get control over whatever resources the state may have to offer (Clunan and Trinkunas, 2010: 63).

There is also evidence that the inability of governments to extract revenue is associated with a greater risk of conflict (Collier and Hoeffler, 2006: 11). Governments have a higher incidence of conflict when they cannot defend themselves from insurgencies and rebel groups, a situation that is far more likely when governments are incapable of extracting revenue (Collier and Hoeffler, 2006). Without sufficient income to invest in defence, governments are vulnerable to predation by rebel groups and conflict erupts. Because administrative institutions play a critical role in revenue extraction, it is possible, then, that higher-quality administrative institutions lessen incidences of internal conflict. Further research is necessary, however, to evaluate this prediction.

Some studies have also indicated that when the state delivers goods based on ethnic loyalties, it may make minority groups feel excluded and lead to challenges to the state (Crawford and Lipschutz, 1998).[3] Individuals who feel excluded from clientelistic networks may be more likely to form violent groups. In the Ivory Coast, unity of the different ethnic groups and nationalities had been expertly maintained under President Felix Houphouët-Boigny (1960–93) as the administrative institutions never favoured one ethnic group over the other. When he left power, the practice of discriminating against Burkinabé immigrants from Burkina Faso led to rising tensions and eventually to the formation of rebel groups in 2002. The practice of ethnic favouritism is a sign of low levels of state legitimacy.

Some studies have shown that organized crime is linked to corruption in the administrative institutions (Buscaglia, 2008) (for more on this, see Chapter 12). There is also evidence that states failing to provide administrative services help legitimize crime groups. Crime groups have risen in the Brazilian favelas due to state neglect. The state

---

[3]Many groups have internationalized their demands and received support from international actors.

is negligent in providing the citizens with their basic needs such as safe housing, water, security and education. As there is no reason to be loyal to the state, citizens seek the support of violent gangs who offer protection in violent environments.

OPPORTUNITIES

As the previous section illustrated, a regime that is perceived as illegitimate, unjust and repressive will serve as a breeding ground for violent groups. But there also needs to be the opportunity for these groups to form. The next section focuses on whether violent non-state actors are more likely to flourish in countries that are democratic, suffer from security gaps, or both.

REGIME TYPE

The literature on regime type of violent non-state actors has mostly focused on whether or not democracies facilitate terrorism. As far as insurgencies are concerned, as stated in the section on political institutions, regime type does not necessarily have an impact, because exclusionary policies can happen in democracies as well, which makes it more important to examine the nature of the political institutions.

In terms of the terrorism literature, there is a plethora of studies that have examined the relationship between democracies and terrorism. There are several questions that this literature explores. Are democracies more likely to be the target of terrorist groups? Are democracies more likely to host terrorist groups? And, finally, are terrorists more likely to emerge from democratic countries?[4]

Much of the literature has generalized that democracies are more likely to be targets of terrorism and are more likely to host terrorist groups than strong and capable authoritarian regimes because they have lower opportunity costs for terrorists (Eubank and Weinberg, 2001). Democracies may be more likely to be targeted because the laws that protect civil rights and political liberties also protect terrorist groups. There is more freedom of movement and association in a democracy. Individuals living within democratic societies are able to communicate and disseminate their ideologies more easily. There is greater access to government buildings. Democracies may have a more difficult time in apprehending and convicting would-be terrorists due to restrictions on whether or not the state can violate individual rights (Crenshaw, 1983, 2015; Gurr, 2000). There are more procedural limits on government counter-terrorism tactics, and for this reason, they may experience more transnational terrorist tactics. The recent moves by democratic governments to enhance their abilities to engage in counter-terror tactics would call this into question, however. Moreover, some scholars caution that it may just be states with at least an intermediate level of political freedom that are more prone to terrorism (Abadie, 2004).

The evidence, however, seems to support the argument that authoritarian regimes allow for few opportunities for terrorist incidents to take place. One study claimed that an authoritarian regime that is not politically oppressive has an 80%

---

[4] We assume democracies are countries with free and fair elections and extensive civil liberties.

chance of not having a single terrorist incident in a given year (Lisanti, 2010: 12). Another study confirmed this finding, claiming that countries that have authoritarian rule also had the lowest risk of terrorism (Abadie, 2004). Aidan Hehir (2007) supports this claim by arguing that some of the more authoritarian states in the world have few if any recorded terrorist incidents, citing examples such as Belarus, Cuba, North Korea, Zimbabwe, Zambia and Equatorial Guinea, whereas another study claims that democracies have had approximately four times as many incidents per capita as non-democratic regimes (Blomberg and Hess, 2005). A recent study argues that what matters is the *type* of authoritarian regime. Single-party regimes, which have a wider range of coercion and co-optation methods are less likely than personalist or military regimes to experience terrorism (Wilson and Piazza, 2013).

Media freedom also plays an important role in the likelihood of terrorism (Altheide, 2007). Modern terrorists are aware of the new opportunities to exert a psychological impact on a mass audience. Some terrorist attacks seem to have a theatre-like quality to them (Weimann, 2005). In democracies where the media is freer to operate, the relationship between violent groups – terrorists in particular – is symbiotic. According to some scholars, without the media's coverage, the act of terror is wasted (Hoffman, 2008). Democracies with a free media help terrorists reach a wider audience. The media functions as a tool to help diminish the power asymmetry between a terrorist group and its target.[5]

One of the reasons terrorism and democracy may go hand-in-hand is the very specific objectives of terrorism in the first place. The strategy of terrorism is about signalling to the public the vulnerabilities of the target regime. A democracy is more likely to heed to the public outcry of a terrorist act than an authoritarian regime. Suicide bombings, in particular, target mainly democracies because they can lead to a policy shift (Pape, 2005).[6] The 2004 Madrid bombings by a group possibly linked to al-Qaeda illustrate this case. In non-democracies that are not occupied by foreign forces, terrorizing civilians provides no direct or even indirect influence over the government.

Further research has also supported the claim that the main targets of terrorist groups are most likely to be powerful democracies. Robert Pape's work from 1980 to 2001 argued that most terrorist attacks aim to 'compel modern democracies to withdraw military forces from territory that the terrorists consider to be their homeland' (Pape, 2005, 7). India has been subject to continual terrorist attacks regarding the territorial dispute in the Kashmir, which could have an impact on the democratic populace (Hehir, 2007). It is the role of public opinion in democracies that make democracies vulnerable to terrorist groups and their demands. Authoritarian regimes are usually not swayed by public opinion and have the option of not succumbing to terrorist demands.

The terrorism and democracy literature is full of interesting studies on the dynamics of the relationship. However, the mechanism that is important to understand may not be regime type, but whether or not the terrorist group believes the

---

[5]However, it is important to note that the media in democracies may help to bias the number of reported incidents, because attacks may not be as likely to be reported in authoritarian regimes (Li, 2005).

[6]This is also supported by Wade and Reiter (2007) but is it also correlated with the number of religiously distinct minority groups within the country.

population of the target state has some influence on the state. Therefore, electoral democracies or competitive authoritarian regimes are likely targets. In addition, it's also important to look at whether or not the act of terrorism is being signalled to an external actor that is democratic, such as the United States in the case of the surge in terror attacks in Iraq. The other important point to mention (although not within the scope of this book to address in full) is that it is authoritarian regimes that are most likely to *sponsor* terrorist groups (Carter, 2012; DeRouen and Newman, 2014). Democracies face harsher constraints for sponsoring terrorist groups compared to other violent non-state actors because of the controversial nature of the terrorist label (Lynn-Jones, 1998).

Regarding economically motivated groups, there is also no clear connection between the proliferation of organized crime and gangs and regime type. However, some recent studies have argued that democratization facilitates organized crime. A study of 59 democracies revealed that organized crime was highest in countries that were moderately democratic or undergoing a democratic transition since there were more opportunities for organized crime during the institutional transition (Karstedt, 2012; Sung, 2004). As for PSCs, no country has made more use of these actors than the United States, but the literature is still nascent on this topic and further research is necessary.

SECURITY GAPS

One of the most commonly cited reasons for why violent non-state actors are able to emerge is weak security institutions or security gaps. Because there are so many more armed actors, security becomes privatized (Rodgers, 1999: 4). For many individuals living in poor slums, it is violent non-state groups that provide protection. Most citizens of favelas in Rio de Janeiro and Sao Paolo claim that they feel that the local drug lords do a better job than the police of ensuring their protection (Davis, 2010). The only interaction that the residents of favelas have with the state is with the police, who are perceived as corrupt, violent, untrustworthy and dangerous. This perception of corruption is fuelled by the notion that the police collaborate with those involved in the drug trade when it suits them (Koonings and Kruijt, 2004: 9). Citizens in Mexico also turn to private police for protection. These violent groups then gain more freedom of action, popular support and legitimacy. The other problem is that when security is provided by non-state actors such as drug lords or gangs, most of the time they are inferior to what the state could provide if it wished to do so (Rodgers, 1999: 5).

Security gaps can exist anywhere, even in strong democracies and wealthy countries. Terrorist groups and criminals have set up a hub in Ciudad del Este, the tri-border area in South America of Brazil, Argentina and Paraguay (Gray and LaTour, 2010: 158). All three states have reasonably strong institutions, but security gaps are possible. These ungoverned spaces are havens for violent non-state actors.

In some cases the security gap occurs along ethnic lines. This is more likely to be the case when militaries recruit along exclusive ethnic lines. When security institutions recruit along ethnic, sectarian or regional lines, the apparatus may be more reluctant to protect a particular ethnic group or region and the absence of security for minority groups can lead to the formation of an insurgency (Burton, 1987). Minority groups that feel unprotected by the national security forces may create guerrilla units to fill this void in security, such as has been the case in Lebanon and

Colombia. In the Ivory Coast under the Laurent Gbagbo government (2000–11), minority ethnic rebel groups believed that Gbagbo was filling the police and military units with those of his own ethnic group. The rebels in the northern and western regions claimed that they instigated a conflict in order to protect members of their own ethnic groups (Kirwin, 2006: 48–9; Posen, 1993).

Because states with failed security institutions have no control over their borders, they are often filled with weapons which can be used by violent groups (Takeyh and Gvosdev, 2002: 101). The arms acquired in various training camps by al-Qaeda in Afghanistan far exceeded anything any terrorist group had achieved in the past (Gunaratna, 2002: 27). Security gaps also provide violent groups with greater opportunities to establish businesses to fund their attacks and activities. The law enforcement laws are too lax, providing a perfect environment for illegal business activities and smuggling, especially drug trafficking (Takeyh and Gvosdev, 2002: 99).

States that have collapsing security institutions will also be rife with PSCs. In the case of Africa, which has weak security structures and a legacy of civil conflict, PSCs are pervasive (Singer, 2011: 9). PSCs have been contracted to work all over Africa, including Sierra Leone, the Democratic Republic of the Congo, Liberia, Ivory Coast, Somalia, Burundi and Angola to provide military training and military support in cases where there is no security. But PSCs are also active in states with stronger security institutions that have important commodities that need to be guarded, such as in Saudi Arabia, Kuwait, Indonesia, Kazakhstan and Australia (Singer, 2011). Thus, we cannot draw the conclusion that state failure is always connected to the proliferation of violent non-state actors. The following case study discusses this point further.

Case Study   Failed States and Violent Non-state Actors

Many policymakers and academics alike have argued that failed states pose a major threat to security. A failed state is a country in which the institutions of the state are not functioning. The state is either unwilling or unable to provide services such as security, representation, welfare or the rule of law. The Rand organization claims that failed states 'breed terrorism, generate all manner of security problems, such as civil conflict and humanitarian crises, arms and drug smuggling, piracy, and refugee flows' (Rabasa, 2014: 1).

While it is true that insurgencies and especially warlords and rebels usually emerge in failed states, since they emerge when there is a security vacuum, the connection between terrorism and organized crime/gangs and state failure is flawed in both theory and empirical evidence. There is no causal relationship and there is also little evidence of a connection (Hehir, 2007: 308, Newman, 2007: 483).[7] Terrorist groups and criminal syndicates have dominated even the richest countries in the world. The following section explains why there is no conclusive connection between failed states and terrorist groups or organized crime/gangs.

(Continued)

---

[7]As for international terrorists, it may be unlikely that the perpetrator comes from a failed state. They would have a more difficult time passing through border controls. Terrorist groups tend to recruit individuals who can fit into developed societies and who bear passports 'that do not arouse suspicion' (Simons and Tucker, 2007: 388).

(Continued)

The concept of terrorist sanctuaries first gained popularity during the Cold War era. During this period, terrorism and insurgency were seen as being largely synonymous; thus a number of countries experiencing civil war – such as Vietnam, Guatemala and the Philippines – were described as 'terrorist havens' (Jackson, 2008). The terrorist sanctuary denoted any area where non-state actors were able to undertake activities that supported their terrorist operations (Gray and LaTour, 2010).

Much of the confusion over the concept of terrorist sanctuaries comes with the conflation of insurgencies, rebel groups and terrorists. Terrorists do not need a lot of room to operate since they do not hold territory. For international terrorist groups, many developed states are attractive to terrorist cells because of their welfare systems, communications and trade networks (Hehir, 2007). For example, the UK has been very attractive to international terrorist groups. Al-Qaeda may be present in over 70 countries including strong states such as Switzerland, Belgium and Ireland (Hehir, 2007: 321). The attacks of home-grown terrorists in Madrid and London also demonstrate that stable, rich, democratic states can provide terrorist havens.

Insurgencies and marauding rebel groups, however, are more likely to emerge when the state is weak or failing. Insurgencies capitalize on state weakness or neglect to seize territory. Rebel groups and warlords take advantage of the security void to capture resources to take over small plots of territory. Marauding rebel groups and warlords emerge out of the chaos. Warlords provide 'security' as a commodity. Insurgencies can appear in states that are overall stronger, but they have most often appeared in states with regions of the country that are completely abandoned by the security forces. While insurgencies and marauding rebel groups may be more likely to form in failed states, the same cannot be said for terrorist groups and organized criminal groups (Fearon and Laitin, 2003). Both need a certain amount of infrastructure to survive.

Terrorist groups are often involved in high-level planning. The deteriorating infrastructure that typifies failed states does not make them an attractive locale for terrorists to set up a base. The physical terrain and the political and economic environment may also make failed states undesirable (Menkhaus, 2006). Though failed states may be free from security, they are also free from the public goods and necessary infrastructure that states provide (Hehir, 2007). Sageman (2004) writes that electronic connectivity is important. States must have strong Internet services and other telecommunications infrastructure in order to maintain the networking to connect with different cells. The technological constraints of failed states have made European states seem like more suitable bases of operations for cells of al-Qaeda (Hehir, 2007). If failed states were so attractive on their own, states like the DRC, Chad, Haiti and Liberia would be hotbeds for terrorist groups. Newman argues that there are many states with weak or failed capacity, poor service delivery and poverty whose territory has not become a terrorist haven.

The lack of roads also hampers the effectiveness of the terrorist group. Though there is no state in the southern Philippines, which is where the Moro Islamic Liberation Front (MILF) is located, these same lack of roads also make it difficult for this group to leave. Al-Qaeda also tried to infiltrate the weakest states in the Horn of Africa, but was unable to do so because they found the lack of infrastructure and terrain to be too difficult. There were not enough flights and the roads were too bad and too remote. Though al-Qaeda had to contend with a much more hostile government, the increase in infrastructure, air connections, communication and integration of the economy made Kenya a more attractive option to set up a base (Hehir, 2007).

Scholars in the past have claimed that organized crime flourishes in weak states by exploiting holes in state capacity such as the rule of law, taxation, law enforcement, border controls and contract enforcement (Rotberg, 2003: 5–6). In theory, criminals would prefer to operate in environments where they can go about their business unbothered. Because failed states may lack control over their territory, they can serve as production centres for illicit items. Because they don't have control over their borders, they can serve as distribution networks for these goods. Because institutions are weak and unaccountable, opportunities are created for corruption at all levels. In states where crime has become more entrenched, the state and the people may be less disposed to use whatever capacity they have to fight it.

State weakness is a necessary condition but not a sufficient one in explaining crime. Although weak states may seem most attractive, the sole quality of being weak is a not a sufficient explanation for the emergence of organized crime. There needs to be something that criminals can profit from (Patrick, 2006: 38). These groups are likely to become involved in the drug trade as a consequence of their geographical location and proximity to drug cultivation. Thus, the presence of drug cultivation or other illegal resources presents a lucrative opportunity for armed groups such as organized criminals. Oil and gems are also important to organized crime. These commodities are smuggled in easily into central Asia from Afghanistan. From 1997 until 1998, Kyrgyzstan claimed that over 155 tons of oil was smuggled into the country (Thomas and Kiser, 2002: 28).[8]

Moreover, it is more difficult to yield high returns to tap into the global market without the presence of modern financial services, telecommunications and a transportation infrastructure. Because maximizing profits is the sole motivation for criminal groups, criminals may accept higher risks of operating in states with higher levels of capacity for greater rewards (Patrick, 2006: 39).

Criminals are adept at exploiting weak states in conflict such as Colombia. Where political authority has collapsed in some areas, criminal groups have taken de facto control and have intimidated the state. But the Colombian state functions well enough to afford these groups some luxuries that they could not exploit elsewhere. Moreover, and most importantly, there exists an important commodity, namely coca production, that can be easily used to generate huge profits.

Trafficking of drugs may be due to state weakness in managing borders, but other types of crime may not be linked with state weakness. Money laundering, for example, occurs in small offshore financial centres of wealthier nations primarily because weak states lack the banking systems (Patrick, 2006: 39). Financial fraud, cybercrime and intellectual property theft are not correlated with state weakness. Money laundering is so widespread that it accounts for 2%–5% of the world's GDP, according to former International Monetary Fund director Michel Camdessus (Patrick, 2006: 38).

Gangs can also thrive in relatively strong states. Powerful gangs have emerged in the United States, the United Kingdom and Russia. Like organized crime, gangs need something to profit from and can survive in strong states that may have ungoverned or failed communities (Bunker, 2014: 49). There are many states that overall function well but may have urban areas that are pockets of instability. In these cases, the state may be complicit, unwilling or unable to do much to change the status quo.

Drawing from this, Richard Jackson claims that 'It is actually states with limited institutional capacity that face the greatest challenges in dealing with terrorist campaigns and organized crime' (Jackson, 2006: 11). Terrorists are more likely to find weak but functioning states, such as Pakistan or Kenya, agreeable bases of operations. This means that states which have uneven levels of institutional decay and strength may enable terrorist groups to operate freely. The same can be said for organized crime. Criminals need some aspects of the state to be functioning so that there is something to profit from.

---

[8]The IS controlled more than 60% of Syria's oil production capacity and less than 10% of Iraq's oil production capacity, representing a profit of as much as $4 million (Brisard and Martinez, 2014).

Box 4.2   State Support for Violent Groups

As the case study on failed states and violent groups revealed, state failure is not always related to the formation of violent groups. There are many cases of strong states covertly supporting violent groups either by providing them sanctuary or significant funding, such as Syria with the PKK, Iran with Hezbollah, the US with the Contras, and South Africa with the National Union for the Total Independence of Angola (UNITA), to name a few. When violent groups are dependent on outside support from states, the state is better able to impose its will and control over the violent non-state group (Asal et al., 2012).[9]

In the case of Afghanistan and its hosting of al-Qaeda, although the Taliban was an international pariah, there is no evidence that Afghanistan's security institutions were weak. It had an authoritarian grip on power and exercised almost complete control over its territory. Evidence of this strength is how rapidly it was able to eradicate 97% the production of opium in 2000–1. Thus, it was not state weakness that attracted bin Laden to Afghanistan but state *support*. Bin Laden also initially received support when he stayed in Sudan. He did not set up a base in the anarchic, lawless south, but in the controlled city of Khartoum (1991–96), where he enjoyed the protection of the National Islamic Front (NIF) and the Sudanese state. When his presence was no longer tolerated, he left. In this commonly cited case, it was not institutional weakness that caused the link between al-Qaeda and Sudan and Afghanistan but state support.

There are also cases where organized crime benefits from state support. In extreme cases, the state perpetuates crime and is filled with politicians who have been bought off by organized crime or actual criminals who were 'elected'. The police, customs, courts, politicians and other agencies responsible for fighting corruption actually support organized crime (Karklins, 2005: 28). When this happens, it is known as 'state capture'.

This problem has been especially acute in central Asia. Drug enforcement agencies in the region were infiltrated by known drug traffickers and criminals. In Tajikistan, low-paid government officials in law enforcement are bribed to look the other way as smugglers take a shipment through. More importantly, high-level government officials have also been known to be involved in the trafficking of drugs, implying not simply passive corruption in the form of bribe-taking, but the actual direct involvement of officials (in other words, state complicity) in the drug trade. Many government officials have been accused of being narco-barons. In May 2000, Tajikistan's ambassador to Kazakhstan was caught with 63 kilograms of heroin in his car (Cornell, 2005a: 581). Warlords from the civil war have been absorbed into the government, and have close ties with trafficking. After the war ended, the United Tajik Opposition (UTO), one of the groups involved in the civil war, took a 30% share in the government, though they continued to engage in drug trafficking (Markowitz, 2012).

Despite an extremely powerful state, organized crime in the Soviet Union thrived, providing evidence of the role of the Soviet state in supporting it. Links between the state and organized crime were also left undisturbed in the post-Soviet transition. Organized crime in Russia has always had tremendous bargaining power due to alliances with state officials and outright state complicity (Kupatadze, 2012: 182).

---

[9]There are also other cases of states killing their own people. Although beyond the scope of this book, there are many cases of authoritarian regimes purposely killing their own citizens, known as 'democide'. For example, in Iran under the Shah, over 6,000 people were killed by the secret police and the military in 1963. In the 1982 Hama massacre in Syria, over 20,000 people were killed by the state.

Before Georgian President Mikheil Saakashvili (2004–13) came to power and enacted a series of effective reforms to curb corruption, Georgia was consistently one of the lowest-ranked countries on the corruption perceptions index. A World Bank study of Georgia found that the prices of 'high-rent' public positions were 'well known' among public officials and the general public, suggesting that corruption is deeply institutionalized (World Bank, 2012). Organized crime had deeply penetrated the state and evidence later emerged of high-level government collusion with organized crime. Many of President Eduard Shevardnadze's (1995–2003) cabinet were credibly alleged to be directly involved in organized crime (Kukhianidze, 2009). (For more on how Georgia reformed itself, see Chapter 12.)

In the case of Mexico, counter-narcotics units have often been co-opted by drug cartels. Some heads of state at the highest levels have been implicated with collusion with the drug industry (Cornell, 2005a). Non-state actors in Thailand, Laos and Vietnam have also captured parts of the state to help facilitate the cultivation of the opium and heroin trade (Dupont, 1999). In some countries in Africa, government officials have linked up with or directly run smuggling rings. In Liberia and Sierra Leone, both governments were easily penetrated by criminal elements involved in the smuggling of diamonds (Reno, 1999, 2000).

CONCLUSION

State-level factors are very important in understanding the root causes of violent non-state actors. There is a rich literature of theories to help us understand why violent groups form and what motivates them to action. In particular, socio-economic and political factors were examined in depth. State-level factors can also help explain how opportunities may vary across regimes, with authoritarian regimes less likely to be a target of terrorism, but more likely to sponsor terrorist groups. State-level factors are also important in explaining the opportunities that have led to the rise of insurgencies, with failed states much more likely to face insurgencies, but not necessarily terrorist groups or organized crime. Thus an examination of state-level factors is critical to grasping why and how violent non-state actors form and thrive.

Summary Points

- Poverty and inequality are important in explaining the rise of insurgencies, rebel groups and gangs.
- Countries with democratic and authoritarian features may be the most likely to face terrorism.
- States that provide administrative and judicial services are less likely to face any kind of violent group.
- State failure leads to the rise of rebel groups and insurgencies but does not necessarily lead to terrorism and organized crime.
- Many states willingly provide a safe haven for terrorist groups.

Key Questions

1 In what ways do socio-economic conditions help explain crime? Are these conditions also important in explaining political violence?
2 What types of political institutional arrangements are important for diminishing the chances of political violence?
3 Why are democracies more likely to be targeted by terrorist groups?
4 Why are failed states likely to facilitate rebels and insurgencies but not terrorism?
5 What is 'state capture'? How does state capture facilitate the drug trade?
6 Theory: How important are domestic-level factors in explaining security according to realists, liberals and constructivists? What is the logic of their arguments?

FURTHER READING

Byman, D. (2005) *Deadly Connections: States that Sponsor Terrorism* (Cambridge University Press). Provides an explanation of states that sponsor terrorism.

Fearon, J.D. and Laitin, D.D. (2003) 'Ethnicity, insurgency, and civil war', *American Political Science Review* 97 (1): 75–90. Essential article on what factors lead to insurgency, examining the effects of ethnicity.

Howard, T. (2016) *Failed States and the Origins of Violence: A Comparative Analysis of State Failure as a Root Cause of Terrorism and Political Violence* (Routledge). Up-to-date analysis of how weak and failing states have helped lead to the emergence of different violent groups. The book does not distinguish between terrorists and insurgencies, but offers detailed case studies of the emergence of violent groups in southeast Asia, Latin America, the Middle East and Africa.

Rotberg, R.I. (ed.) (2004) *State Failure and State Weakness in a Time of Terror* (Brookings Institution Press). Covers everything about state failure and the challenges facing countries in the developing world and how this has led to the rise of violent non-state actors.

Weinberg, L. (2013) 'Democracy and terrorism'. In L. Richardson (ed.) (2013) *The Roots of Terrorism*. (Routledge). New edition that examines the relationship between democratic government and political terrorism. It adds a new section on how the Arab Spring has increased the frequency of terrorism in the region.

5

INDIVIDUAL- AND SOCIETAL-LEVEL EXPLANATIONS

Key Terms

- Al-Aqsa Martyrs Brigade
- Black widows
- Group processes
- Narcissistic aggression
- Terrorist personality

OVERVIEW OF INDIVIDUAL-LEVEL THEORIES

Individual and societal theories attempt to explain why individuals join violent groups or engage in acts of violence. Most of the research has focused on terrorist groups, but the chapter will also examine the factors that motivate actors to join economically motivated groups such as organized crime and criminal gangs. The chapter will not devote attention to insurgents, however, for several reasons. First, there has been little individual-level work done on insurgents, and second, the literature tends to conflate insurgents with terrorists. Any study that examines insurgency will be noted. In addition, as very few individual-level studies have been done that have examined warlords, marauding rebels, PSCs and parties with militant wings, these groups will not be examined. The chapter focuses on how individual- and societal-level analyses can add to our understanding of why individuals join violent groups.[1]

---

[1]There are several important points to mention about individual-level factors. Social psychologists and sociologists focus on group-level factors and criticize psychological approaches that focus on personality traits as committing an attribution error by failing to consider significant situational factors in society. They argue in favour of looking at the group-level variables such as the dynamics between social networks and what types of social interactions take place. It is also important to emphasize that the pathologies and individual characteristics of members of violent groups may be very different from the leaders of these groups, particularly in the area of politically motivated violent non-state actors. It is also critical to clarify that the number of people who join economically motivated groups is much larger than those who join insurgencies. And only a very small number of people join terrorist organizations (Kruglanski and Fishman, 2006).

We will turn to psychological approaches and societal/social psychological approaches in understanding why individuals join violent groups. Before exploring the psychological and societal approaches, we will look at some individual-level demographic factors such as origin, age, education level, employment and economic status.[2] In a departure from the last two chapters we do not divide the chapter into motivational and opportunity factors. The section on psychological factors constitutes a motivation while social psychological approaches demonstrate both motivational factors and opportunities.

DEMOGRAPHIC FACTORS

URBAN VS. RURAL

Studies have demonstrated that the origin of a violent non-state actor is dependent upon the type of actor and its political orientation. In general, most gang members and criminals originate from urban areas where there is some mode of profit (Manwaring, 2005). There has been a large focus on gangs in urban settings because urban areas have a much greater level of gang activity (Conly, 1993). Gangs are prevalent in decaying inner cities and low-income urban areas.

Insurgents originate from the area that they are fighting to hold on to, which is often a rural area, but urbanites have been recruited as well. Knowing the area of operation is one of the most important aspects of guerrilla warfare (Arjona and Kalyvas, 2009). Terrorists can be best divided by looking at their ideological orientation. Left-wing terrorists tend to come from urban areas, whereas right-wing terrorists tend to come from rural backgrounds. Urban areas are favoured by left-wing terrorists because they serve as an easier base of operation. Right-wing terrorists might favour being geographically isolated in compounds in rural areas (Miller, 2006).

AGE

The most common demographic of violent non-state actors is that most violent actors are young. Once individuals get to a certain age, they may be less likely to take the risks involved in being a part of a violent group. They may also not live very long. Youth is also a period of experimentation and identity formation (Smetana et al., 2006; Steinberg and Morris, 2001). Youth are more likely to be influenced by peer pressure, especially as parental bonds become less prominent.

The chance of engaging in crime rises in the early teen years and reaches a peak between the ages of 15 and 17. This prevalence then decreases over the rest of a person's life (Gottfredson and Hirschi 1990: 124–44). Gang members are usually

---

[2]Most individuals of violent organizations have nothing notable about their appearance, except possibly that they are usually healthy and in sufficient shape to perform the tasks at hand.

Marital Status: Gang members are usually unmarried, but because organized criminals are older, many may be married. Most insurgents and terrorists of the 1970s and 1980s have been single due to the needs for flexibility and dedication (Hudson and Majeska, 1999). However, a study of 400 al-Qaeda members found that 75% were married and the majority had children (Sageman, 2004).

much younger than members of organized crime (Smith et al., 2013). A 2008 study of US gang members showed that slightly over 40% were under the age of 18. Another study demonstrated that gang members in the US and the UK entered gangs between the ages of 12 and 18 (Rizzo, 2003; Spergel, 1995). In El Salvador, the average age that individuals join maras (gangs) is 15 (Bruneau et al., 2011). In contrast, a UK study showed that the average age of organized criminals was 32 (Francis et al., 2013). A Dutch study found no organized criminal members to be under the age of 18. In fact, 75% were 30 years and older (Smith et al., 2011: 481).

On the ideological dimension, most left-wing insurgent groups tend to be younger than right-wing groups, though the average age for being arrested is about the same according to a 2006 study: 35 was the average age of arrest for left-wing groups, compared to 39 for right-wing groups (Miller, 2006). Research has shown that terrorist groups usually disband when their members grow old, as many are tired of waging a struggle (Reinares, 2004: 473). Terrorist group members, in particular, have difficulty maintaining the intensity needed to be a part of a terrorist group. Organized criminal groups are best able to make the generational transition as it is not difficult to maintain the motivation to generate profits (Cronin, 2009). In a 1983 study, a sample of 350 urban terrorists from 18 different organizations showed that the average age was between 22 and 25 (Russell and Miller, cited by Krueger and Malečková, 2003). Not surprisingly, 70% of ETA members were recruited between the ages of 18 and 23. Hezbollah fighters tended to be in the late teens and early 20s (Gill et al., 2014)

Leaders of organized criminal groups, insurgencies and terrorist groups are generally much older than their members; gang leaders, however, are generally only slightly older than their members (Hudson and Majeska, 1999). Leaders of groups such as the Shining Path, the PKK, the FARC, the Baader-Meinhof Gang and the major drug cartels have typically been older because experience, know-how and amassing strong personal networks is paramount to running an organization effectively.

EDUCATION

There have been many studies that have looked at education levels of violent individuals. For economically motivated actors, the results are mixed. Gang members typically suffer from very low levels of education. Education of organized criminals varies because some members come into the organization due to their noted skill set.

There have been many studies that have examined the relationship between education levels and terrorists. Terrorists generally have higher levels of education and few are illiterate, but distinctions can be made based on political orientation. A study demonstrated that more than half of left-wing terrorists have college degrees while only 10% of right-wing terrorists do (Miller, 2006). While right-wing terrorists tend to be less educated (Smith and Morgan, 1994), studies in both the US and Germany demonstrated that education was unrelated to violence against foreigners (Krueger and Malečková, 2003).

Studies of religious groups have found that education levels of members have been high. A study from 1966–76 of 350 terrorists from various countries found that two-thirds had some university training (Berrebi, 2003: 55). Many members of the Jewish Underground who were active in the late 1970s and early 1980s were well educated (Berrebi, 2003). A study of 129 Hezbollah members killed in paramilitary action in the late 1980s and early 1990s lived above the poverty line and had a secondary school education or higher (Krueger and Malečková, 2003). At least 60% of 400 al-Qaeda members studied had a college education, most in technical fields. Over 75% were professionals from scientific disciplines. Of the central staff members of the movement, 88% had finished college and 20% had doctorates (Sageman, 2004). Another study that examined the education backgrounds of 75 terrorists involved in attacks against Westerners found that a majority had a college education, mostly in engineering, and only nine attended madrassas, and these nine were involved in only one attack, the Bali bombing (Bergen and Pandey, 2005). Terrorism in particular may attract highly educated individuals who have not been as successful as they feel they should be.

———————— Case Study   Female Terrorists ————————

Women are generally not involved in organized crime, gangs, rebel groups, insurgencies and terrorist groups (Forst et al., 2011). There are no female warlords. However, there are increasingly more women involved in terrorism and insurgency, with terrorism being the most common (Library of Congress, 1999). About 20% of terrorists are female (Huckerby, 2015).[3]

Women join violent political groups for four reasons. One reason is that a partner, relative or friend is involved in the group. Women who were recruited into ETA, a Basque group, did so because of personal bonds with men who already belonged. An emotional relationship was critical in deciding to join a terrorist group for those that might otherwise have reservations about violence (Reinares, 2004). Suicide bombing for women in Chechnya has been a family affair. More than a quarter acted with other family members in carrying out their attacks (Speckhard and Akhmedova, 2006).

A less plausible, though oft-cited reason, is feminism. Some female terrorists have come from societies where women have been culturally repressed or are stuck with very traditional gender roles, such as in Chechnya, various parts of the Middle East and even parts of Southern Europe (Hudson and Majeska, 1999). Violent groups may try to lure women into joining based on some sort of message of equality, but these women are mostly being exploited, and messages of equality are contradictory. Left-wing terrorist groups are predominantly male, but do include more women in leadership positions and rank and file compared to other violent groups (Miller, 2006). But for most groups, women are rarely in leadership positions or taking part in the decision-making process. Palestinian women are not allowed to be a part of the ranks in most violent groups. Women are not even paid equally for the same effort. A Hamas spokesman claimed that terrorist organizations provide a stipend of approximately $400 per month to the families of male suicide bombers but only $200 per month to the families of female bombers (O'Rourke, 2009: 102). Additionally, there are many instances where women have been raped or sexually abused by fellow members of the violent groups they are a part of.

Other arguments claim that women become involved after they have experienced some sort of trauma, such as the death of a family member or shame, such as a recent divorce, infertility or rape. Shame may have been the case for Wafa Idris, the first Palestinian female suicide bomber, who was infertile and divorced (Pedahzur, 2005: 138–9). Palestinian women have been motivated by a desire to recover family honour (Bloom, 2005). 'Black widows' from Chechnya were motivated by the death of a loved one, often a spouse (Bloom, 2005: 145). All of Chechen women interviewed for a study had suffered from deep trauma (Speckhard and Akhmedova, 2006). Almost all of these women did not have children.

---

[3]The study did not clarify whether or not terrorist was being conflated with insurgent.

Some scholars have argued that women join terrorist groups because they are pawns (Bloom, 2005). They join solely because they are forced into doing so. There have been accounts that the PKK forced women to become suicide bombers, killing those on the spot who refused (Ergil, 2000). Other scholars have countered that the Chechen women were not coerced but were self-recruited in order to seek revenge (Speckhard and Akhmedova, 2006).

Women have been used more and more in terrorist groups in general, since they are instrumental to the organizations. Female suicide attacks gain eight times as much press coverage as male attacks (Bloom, 2012: 23). Women also have higher kill rates and can get closer to the target compared to men (Bloom, 2012: 22). They are less likely to be detected and can hide bombs and weapons more effectively under their clothes. For example, female suicide bombers can hide explosives around their midsection, giving the impression that they are pregnant (Bloom, 2012: 22, 68). In the case of Chechen terrorist groups, women carried out some of the most risky operations (Speckhard and Akhmedova, 2006). Female terrorists have been characterized as strong, dedicated, and composed and cool under pressure. They are less likely to talk to law enforcers and will not spill information to receive a reduced prison sentence. When women do get involved they are more emotionally involved and have a deeper commitment than men (Hunsicker, 2006). There are also more female recruits, because these organizations may need more participants. In the case of the LTTE, women have taken part in actual fighting and have been given training, due to a shortage of numbers during the 1980s. Women in the LTTE had their own army division by 1985 and proved themselves to be strong fighters.

Though still not common, there are also more female suicide bombers than before. The first female suicide bomber was a 17-year-old Lebanese girl named Sana'a Mehaydali who blew herself up near an Israeli convoy in Lebanon, killing five Israeli soldiers on behalf of the Syrian Socialist National Party (SSNP/PPS). Women took part in half of the 12 suicide attacks conducted by the SSNP. The second group to use women was the LTTE, where about 25% of the suicide attacks were perpetrated by women. The third group to women for suicide attacks was the PKK, which used women 75% of the time. From 1985–2005, there have been 220 female suicide bombers, or about 15% of the total (Bloom, 2005).

More than half the time, females attack on behalf of a secular organization. According to Pape (2005), the rate of females attacking on behalf of secular organizations was 57%, with some studies claiming that this is as high as 85% (O'Rourke, 2009). The Al-Aqsa Martyrs Brigade eventually set up a special unit to train female suicide bombers and named it after Wafa Idris. It has used women in suicide attacks about 15% of the time. Hamas also claims that it has received letters from Palestinian women asking to participate more directly in the conflict and become martyrs (O'Rourke, 2009)

Al-Qaeda has claimed to set up a female squad of suicide bombers, but in general, conservative militant Islamic organizations have avoided using women. Hezbollah has never used women in suicide missions. In contrast, Chechen Wahhabist groups have women in suicide missions more often than men, about 66% of the time. These women were also all exposed to and involved in the violent Wahhabist jihadist ideology and wanted to become martyrs in order to be reunited with their deceased family member in paradise (Speckhard and Akhmedova, 2006).

Most female suicide bombers are in their 20s, but the age range of female suicide attackers is older than men. Most are not married. Only 15.4% of the Chechen female suicide bombers were married at the time. None of the PKK suicide attackers were married (O'Rourke, 2009). Many female suicide attackers are not poor and are fairly well educated, but this depends on the country they originate from. Some have few career options. Mia Bloom writes that Kurdish and Sri Lankan female suicide bombers are often 'unsophisticated and poorly educated and simply follow their leaders blindly' (Bloom, 2005: 165).

SOCIO-ECONOMIC STATUS

Socio-economic status matters more for criminal groups than political ones. Richer individuals are less likely to participate in organized crime and more specifically gangs because they have more to lose (Becker, 1981). Individuals with less education are more likely to join gangs if they have low wages and few economic opportunities (Becker, 1981). Gang members almost always come from low-income backgrounds and have a low socio-economic status (Spergel, 1995). In spite of this, there are many youths in low-income areas that may even have similar personality traits to other gang members but never choose to join (Pennell et al., 2001). Organized crime is motivated by opportunity costs. Individuals choose to engage in organized crime if the rewards exceed the probability of detection (Becker, 1981; see also Box 5.1).

As Chapter 4 noted, most terrorists have not come from the poorest deciles of society. Left-wing terrorists in the 1960s and 1970s were not poor. And although right-wing extremists are usually much less educated than left-wing ones, there is no evidence that economic status motivates right-wing extremism. A study of 1,247 Israeli university students demonstrated that right-wing sentiments were not related to any socio-economic variables (Canetti and Pedahzur, 2002). Other studies of terrorist organizations have shown that the members come from mostly middle-class families (Hudson and Majeska, 1999; Russell and Miller, 1977). Relatively poor individuals may be more distracted by survival, trying to provide for their families, and may not have the time or energy to devote to violence. Violent groups that are more selective, like terrorist groups, screen potential members for quality, selecting those from the middle class. Thus, the extremists are not the have-nots – rather, they are those who simply want more (Krueger and Malečková, 2003).

Scholars studying the motivation of politically violent non-state actors have focused on the role of relative deprivation (Gurr, 1993, 2015). While economically violent non-state actors may be more focused on 'egotistical' deprivation – individuals feel deprived because of their position within a group – politically violent non-state actors may be more motivated by fraternal deprivation – where their group is positioned compared to other groups (King and Taylor, 2011: 610). Terrorists and insurgents (see Chapter 4) are more likely to live in societies where their groups have experienced economic hardship, inequality and dim economic prospects, such as Chechnya and Palestine (Ehrlich and Liu, 2002; Fields et al., 2002). These individuals believe that the groups they are a part of are disadvantaged, discriminated against and oppressed. In some cases, these feelings of fraternal deprivation translate into collective action. This may be especially true in cases where minority groups feel as though the path to their goal has been blocked (Gurr, 1993, 2015).

UNEMPLOYMENT

Unemployment can be both a motivation and an opportunity to join a violent group. Gang members are recruited at such a young age that joining a gang may constitute their first 'job'. Many potential gang members live in difficult living conditions and lack employment opportunities (Vowell and May, 2000). However, organized criminals typically are involved in some other occupation beforehand that provided them with a skill set that is needed for the organized criminal group.

As for politically motivated groups, there is no clear consensus. For example, the height of Palestinian terrorism took place when employment levels in the Palestinian community were rising. However, historically, scholars have claimed that Marxist groups have recruited unemployed students with little direction (Merkl, 1986). As for religious groups, there is some variation. While al-Qaeda has mostly recruited professionals (with only 25% that could be considered unskilled with few job prospects), in the case of Yemen it has recruited those who are unemployed and directionless (Sageman, 2004). Many of the IS's recruits come from Tunisia, more specifically the poorest suburbs of Tunis. This reflects the disillusionment that Tunisians may feel after they put so much effort into the revolution and face unemployment and continued marginalization in their society.

Left-wing groups are more likely to be composed of professionals, however, such as physicians, attorneys, professors and social workers (Miller, 2006). Right-wing groups attract more blue-collar workers; however, the prevalence of right-wing extremist groups is not related to the employment rate (Krueger and Malečková, 2003). Areas of the US with a high prevalence of groups the like the Ku Klux Klan were not affected by unemployment. The literature suggests that in contrast to studies of politically motivated groups, gang membership can be decreased by reducing unemployment and improving access to education.

Box 5.1   Rational Choice Theories

Rational choice approaches attempt to explain human behaviour by assuming that individuals are rational, calculating actors who weigh the costs and benefits of their decisions and are capable of acting strategically. The rational choice approach has been used extensively in explaining criminal activity. Rational choice theories assume that criminals offend because it is the most effective means to derive income and wealth. The choice of methods for carrying out the crime and the decision-making involved are instrumental behaviour to serve the criminal's objectives (Piquero, 2012: 41). Organized crime in particular is argued to be highly planned, directed and committed by determined offenders with strong economic motivations. Rational choice approaches focus on the fact that organized crime is purposeful and that it is a business. The rational choice perspective, however, has less to say about why individuals choose to become involved in organized crime and more to say about how crimes are carried out by organized criminals (Piquero, 2012: 41).

Crime is a function of rewards and punishment, something individuals calculate (Cornish and Clarke, 2014). Those involved in organized crime have a higher expectation of material returns from criminal activities compared to conventional means. For gangs, teens in low-income areas may make deliberate decisions to join gangs if they believe that they have few legitimate alternative means of earning income (Sánchez-Jankowski, 2003). Other studies argue that economic incentives and opportunity costs have an important influence on joining a gang and terminating a criminal career (Pezzin, 1995: 134).

In contrast to explanations for violent criminal behaviour, explanations for political violence have historically not used rational choice approaches. Past studies of politically violent groups argued that political violence is driven by those with fiery personalities, or those who were 'crazy' and emotionally disturbed (Hacker, 1976). Walter Laqueur (1977: 125) stated that terrorists were fanatics and fanaticism frequently makes for cruelty and sadism. Earlier, Brian Crozier (1960) claimed that it takes a rebel to rebel and that one's condition in life being intolerable was

(Continued)

(Continued)

not a sufficient explanation. Individual factors such as temperaments matter. Crozier argued that 'Human frontal lobe cortical planning based on rational calculation of costs and benefits is forever subject to limbic tyranny. Passion often trumps rationality. Thus, in the past, theories of politically violent groups characterized insurgents as zealots and terrorists as mentally deranged. These past perspectives have largely been discredited.

Given the shortcomings of theories that assume violent actors are deranged extremists, rational choice approaches have been used to explain the logic of political violence. The most notable proponent of rational choice for politically violent actors – and terrorism more specifically – is Robert Pape. Pape's (2005) work has focused on the logic of suicide bombing. As he sees it, suicide bombing is a rational tactic to inflict terror and fear. It is violent, dramatic and inexpensive. Thus, resorting to terrorism is not due to defective personality traits but is a strategically rational act, one that works more often than it fails.

It is true that many people die and are injured in suicide attacks. On average, suicide operations worldwide kill about four times as many individuals as other kinds of terrorist attacks. In Israel, the average is even higher: suicide attacks inflict six times the number of deaths and roughly 26 times more casualties than other acts of terrorism (Hoffman and McCormick, 2004: 270). Suicide attacks are also very dramatic – a usually young victim has chosen to die on behalf of their cause (Hoffman and McCormick, 2004: 250). They attract more media attention. They are also economical. The improvised explosive devices worn or carried by a suicide bomber, for example, can cost less than $150 to produce.

Suicide attacks are also not particularly damaging to the manpower of the perpetrating organization. Though the attackers die in these attacks, never are important members used as a sacrifice. Suicide bombers used in networks of Palestinian terrorists are usually not central figures in the organization. They are usually peripheral members, whose sacrifice will not constitute a major blow (Pedahzur & Perliger, 2006).

However, the rational choice approach does not explain why individuals decide to join these groups, but why this type of violence is used as a strategy. Martha Crenshaw (1987) has tried to use a rational choice approach to explain why individuals use violence to further political goals. As she sees it, individuals may take risks to engage in violence, but feel as though these risks are worth it since they believe they are supporting a necessary cause or that their own lives may be in danger if they don't take action.

Critics also argue that violent political actors don't always behave rationally. In the Palestinian case, Fatah always acted strategically, while Abu Nidal has been very extreme (Abrahms, 2004). Some organizations are strategic and others less so. The rational choice explanation is that insurgencies and terrorist groups are mostly focused on maintaining their own existence. This drive for survival may lead to actions that seem inimical to the organization's long-term political objectives (Langdon et al., 2004). Violent political groups may make decisions that ensure organizational survival and social connections rather than achieving political goals (Abrahms, 2008; Harmon, 2001). Moreover, the leaders of these organizations may engage in behaviour that is aimed at sustaining their important position in the group rather than achieving other ideological goals of the organization (Oots, 2006).

PSYCHO-ANALYTICAL APPROACHES

Psycho-analytical approaches assume that individuals who commit acts of violence such as terrorism have personality defects and a damaged sense of self. Psycho-analytical approaches look at the role of relationships and unconscious forces. Scholars such as Jerrold Post (1990), John Crayton (1983) and Richard Pearlstein (1991) have argued that terrorists suffer from 'narcissistic aggression'. Terrorism thus serves as a way of stabilizing and restoring an individual's self-esteem and sense of self (Post, 1990). Furthermore, a humiliating experience might produce an adult narcissistic injury that may re-awaken an infantile one (Gill and Young, 2011). The result may be an egotistical drive to attain some sort of glory under the guise of altruism. The rage in this instance may be projected onto the terrorist's victim as a way of rectifying the intolerable feelings that the terrorist has about him- or herself (see also Akhtar, 1999).[4] In a study of German terrorists from the Baader-Meinhof Gang, it was demonstrated that this group was composed of children without fathers (Becker, 1981). Their fathers were former Nazis, which caused them to hate their parents and lash out against the greater society. The government was blamed for not being able to resolve these personal problems. But other authors have cautioned against the generalizability of these studies on West German terrorists since they may have suffered from unique pathologies (Wagenlehner, 1978). In general, the conclusions about narcissistic injury and rage are not empirical. Furthermore, it is unclear whether terrorists are more likely to exhibit narcissistic traits compared to the general public.

Other studies have noted that many terrorist leaders and members have survived traumatic experiences. Using case studies, Gallimore (2004) argues that terrorists emerge after a painful and dysfunctional childhood where the individual forms a personality and identity disorder. Interviews with five Palestinian suicide bombers revealed that they all reported having a traumatic experience with the Israeli military, such as a friend being killed or beaten (Soibelman, 2004). Timothy McVeigh, the right-wing terrorist who attacked the Oklahoma City government building, suffered trauma during his military service in the first Gulf War and was humiliated as a child by constant bullying (Gallimore, 2004). A study of Baader-Meinhof Gang leader Ulrike Meinhof claimed that she had low self-esteem and an obsession with belonging as a result of traumatic events. Other studies of female Italian terrorists also revealed psychic injuries and low self-esteem due to tyrannical fathers and weak mothers (de Cataldo Neuberger and Valentini, 1996). Another notable study of female Chechen suicide terrorists that used personal interviews found that all of those sampled suffered trauma (Speckhard and Akhmedova, 2006). Their personal trauma caused them to seek out an ideological inspiration to find meaning in their lives.

In spite of these interesting anecdotal cases, many scholars have written that there is no 'terrorist personality' (Atran, 2003b; Fabick, 2004). Many studies of the Italian Red Army brigades, the Basque ETA and various Palestinian groups did not find a unique psychological make-up. In fact, scholars have argued that the most notable thing about terrorists is how normal they are. A study of 172 people linked to al-Qaeda found that few suffered from narcissism or childhood or personal trauma (Sageman, 2004). A study of prisoners in Northern Ireland found no evidence that any of them were mentally ill; they generally came from stable backgrounds (Horgan, 2014: 56).

Critics have argued that terrorism cannot be fully tested using psychological theories. One of the issues of diagnosing terrorists is that due to a lack of primary data based on interviews, psychological diagnoses have to be done at a distance,

---

[4]Other scholars have examined the role of humiliation in motivating acts of terrorism. Humiliation can also drive terrorist violence to take revenge against the perpetrator (Juergensmeyer, 2005).

which many scholars have argued against doing (Silke, 2003). Studies have mostly been conducted based on speculation from small number of cases. The findings have been criticized for being unreliable. However, these criticisms have led to a premature abandonment of psychological assessment of terrorists. More recent studies have demonstrated a need to reconsider psychological factors. For example, a data set of 119 lone-actor terrorists demonstrated that lone-actor terrorists are more likely to be mentally ill compared to group terrorists. (For more on lone-actor terrorism, see Box 2.1.)

As stated before, few studies have examined individual-level psychological factors that may explain which individuals are at risk of joining gangs. Some risk factors identified are the following: experiencing trauma, displaying antisocial tendencies and low parental supervision. This literature suggests that there is no one risk factor that can predict exactly who will join a gang, since these same factors can predict other outcomes, but youth who do join a gang usually possess certain risk factors (Decker et al., 2013). For example, many gang members may be motivated to join due to feelings of humiliation and anger (Agnew, 2006). Psychological studies have argued that gang members suffer from low self-esteem and a tendency towards aggression (Donnellan, et al., 2005). Those with weak bonds are more likely to look up to youth in gangs who appear to be more confident. Gang membership is based on the need to meet emotional and developmental needs (Decker and Curry, 2000).

SOCIAL PSYCHOLOGICAL APPROACHES

Social psychological approaches to understanding terrorism have received the most scholarly support. This approach focuses on group processes. Group psychology is argued to be more important than individual traits of terrorists. In this school of thought, the avenue by which individuals join violent groups is what is most important to understand (Hoffman 2006; Merari 1998; Post et al., 2009; Sageman, 2004).

One of the most commonly cited characteristics of those that have been recruited to join politically motivated groups is alienation. Loneliness and feelings of being excluded motivate individuals to join a tight-knit group that can serve as a surrogate family. Terrorist groups provide these individuals with a sense of belonging (Doosje et al., 2016). Terrorist groups in particular are incredibly tight compared to other groups, due to the need for secrecy and the bonds that form in high-risk groups. Psychologists argue that it is alienation that causes a cognitive opening to accept the need to take extreme measures (Wiktorowicz, 2004).

Studies show that members of the Ku Klux Klan want and need to belong to a group (Gallimore, 2004: 155). Excluding separatist and nationalist organizations, terrorist organizations appeal to those who feel socially alienated. Data on the demographics of terrorist organization members demonstrate that most are composed of unmarried young men or widowed women who may be lonely (Abrahms, 2008: 96). Terrorist groups offer strong collective identities for alienated individuals (Crenshaw and Pimlott, 2015).

Terrorist groups may also target discriminated immigrants. Data from 1993 to 2003 show that 86% of 212 suspected and convicted terrorists were Muslim immigrants (Leiken, 2005). This illustrates the importance of alienation and social dislocation from their native homeland as a factor motivating individuals to join violent groups. A study of 172 al-Qaeda members showed that 80% were unassimilated first- or second-generation immigrants in non-Muslim countries, usually in Europe. Muslim migrants to Europe often feel disconnected and unwelcome. Feeling economically discriminated against and politically disenfranchised, they seek out other Muslims for guidance and companionship (Dalgaard-Nielsen, 2010). This offers support for the argument that most individuals participate in terrorist groups for social solidarity (Abrahms, 2008: 97). Networks then form that become increasingly radicalized, with small group meetings being most important for radicalization (Sageman, 2004: 158; Wiktorowicz, 2006). Through these networks, individuals become more aware of political events and injustices taking place. Individuals incite one another to become more radicalized. Violent agendas are legitimized in these small groups. Peer pressure is much higher in small group settings; the pressure pushes the individual to conform. However, bonding also takes place in small groups, which provides the individual with a sense of belonging.

Even if individuals are not totally alienated from society, friendship and kinship ties seem to be a deciding factor in joining violent groups. In this way, joining a violent group was dependent on opportunities. In many studies of the Basque ETA, the IRA, the Red Brigades, the Baader-Meinhof Gang and Turkish terror organizations, the desire to join an armed struggle was not as much a result of a political or ideological agenda as it was to cultivate social ties with other members of these groups (Reinares, 2001; Weinberg and Eubank, 1987). A survey of over 1,000 individuals of a Turkish terrorist group claimed that they were ten times more likely to join an organization due to friends already being members than due to the group's ideology (Abrahms, 2008: 97). The same could be said of al-Qaeda, Aum Shinrikyo, Fatah, Hamas and Hezbollah as well as Chechen terrorist groups. A study of al-Qaeda showed that 75% of terrorists were found to have pre-existing familial bonds to members already involved in terrorist organizations, or joined as a group with friends or relatives (Sageman, 2004). A study of Middle Eastern groups, both secular and religious, found that peer pressure was important. As one terrorist claimed, 'Everyone was joining' (Post et al., 2003, 173). These individuals joined terrorist groups to improve their relationships with other members of violent groups and to feel less alienated from society (Sageman, 2004: 158; Wiktorowicz, 2006). The social bonds were more important than the commitment to the ideology (Abrahms, 2008: 98).[5]

But this presents a puzzling picture. On the one hand, people are most likely to join politically motivated violent groups if they are alienated and lonely. On the other hand, individuals are also much more likely to join a group through pre-existing social networks. How do we make sense of this? A likely scenario is that an individual living either in a host community or in a disputed homeland may feel isolated and seek out social ties. They may want to solidify these social ties more intensely and join groups that help alleviate these feelings of alienation, dislocation and lack of direction. It is also likely that some individuals join groups less out of loneliness and more out of peer pressure.

It is important to distinguish between groups that are sanctioned by their societies and those that are not. Scholars like Post (1987) already distinguished between 'anarchic-ideologues' and 'ethnic/nationalist separatist' groups. For the former, these individuals are a part of groups that are not supported by the wider society. For the

---

[5]Shaw talks about the importance of narcissistic injuries and escalatory events coupled with personal connections to other group members (Shaw, 1986: 365). Other scholars of network theories also acknowledge that a personal crisis is important to create the cognitive opening (Wiktorowicz, 2004: 16).

latter, societal peer pressure may influence the decision to join. Thus, for individuals joining an ethnic/nationalist separatist group like Basque ETA, the IRA or the various Palestinian groups, there would be strong social support within their group. They are more likely to be integrated in their communities and can move in and out of their communities with ease. These individuals may be less likely to join a group due to alienation and more likely to join due to peer pressure. For individuals of anarchic-ideologue groups, they may lack ties to society because their objectives and means of achieving them are not widely popular. They are also often prohibited from socializing with outsiders. This is because establishing mutual trust and a complete commitment by members is paramount. Conformity is imposed upon them, as is total secrecy. This social isolation contributes to a lack of empathy for outsiders.

Criminologists claim that individuals are more likely to commit crimes when they are less integrated into society (LaFree and Freilich, 2012). Yet, for those involved in organized crime, it is important to have built up suitable social ties and social contacts. Though criminals are outside the law, they do not interact in a social vacuum (von Lampe, 2016: 19).

Social contacts provide opportunities for involvement in criminal networks. Because building strong social ties is important and building up such relationships takes time and energy, scholars reason that those involved in organized crime are not loners who are mentally ill (Kleemans and Van de Bunt, 1999; Peterson et al., 2014). Social ties and opportunity structures are more important reasons that certain individuals progress to certain types of organized crime. Recruitment is usually based on who you know. In the past it was thought that outsiders are recruited for their ability to carry out dirty jobs and climb the ranks due to their abilities. Scholars now argue that social ties and how knowledge is transferred matter more.

Being involved in organized crime is much more likely if an individual is born into a family in which parents or older siblings are already involved (Thornberry et al., 2003). One reason that organized crime is likely to be a family affair is that family members are more likely to cooperate, which means that there is less violence needed to keep family members under control. This diminishes the risk of being betrayed (Gambetta, 2000). In the case of gangs, family is also important (Eitle et al., 2004). Some studies have noted that in poor neighbourhoods, belonging to a gang is a family tradition. Some parents may even encourage their children to join if they had been members themselves (Sánchez-Jankowski, 2003).

Potential gang members are also motivated in large part by a need to belong. Studies of gangs also emphasize the social component of joining a gang. Many potential gang members feel excluded from society (Decker et al., 2013). They join to find people that they can befriend and fit in with and to find companionship. They feel a strong connection to other gang members. Antisocial and impulsive behaviour in a gang is praised rather than criticized (Egan and Beadman, 2011). They depend on the moral support of their comrades. They join to gain a sense of moral fellowship with other individuals whom they already know and value (Binder et al., 2001). Gang members seek an identity and solidarity. They may also feel extensive peer pressure to join (Esbensen and Weerman, 2005). It is the psychology of adolescence that explains and encourages gang membership (Alleyne and Wood, 2010).

CONCLUSION

This chapter acknowledges that the role of individual factors is very controversial. Scholars have criticized the methods used in these studies and have cautioned against making generalizations about individuals who are members of violent groups. There may be a host of reasons why individuals join violent groups, such as genuine grievances, peer pressure, survival and coercion (Humphreys and Weinstein, 2008). Individual-level factors have been downplayed in favour of social factors. However, many political psychologists assert that ignoring the explanatory power of individual-level factors is premature, cautioning that more research needs to be done (Victoroff, 2005). Additionally, examining past work that has looked at individual-level factors helps enhance our overall understanding of what may be important in driving the motivation to join a violent group and what is not.

Summary Points

- Gang members often come from poor backgrounds, but this is not necessarily the case for organized criminals or terrorists.
- There are very few women involved in violent groups, with terrorist groups attracting the most women.
- Most of the terrorist literature has critiqued psychological approaches to predicting which types of individuals are most likely to commit acts of terrorism.
- Ethnic and separatist groups often attract more support from the wider community for their efforts; individuals who join these groups are often not alienated from society.
- Criminals and terrorists often join violent groups through linkages with friends and family.

Key Questions

1 What are the demographic factors that matter most for explaining criminal compared to political activity?
2 Why do women join terrorist groups?
3 Is there a terrorist personality? What are the strengths and weaknesses of psycho-analytical approaches?
4 What psychological factors are important in understanding why individuals join gangs? Are these factors more important than demographic ones?
5 What is the importance of networks in understanding criminal violence and political violence?
6 Theory: What role have psychological approaches played in explaining security? Why have other theories been so critical of these approaches?

FURTHER READING

Alleyne, E. and Wood, J.L. (2012) 'Gang membership: the psychological evidence'. In F-A. Esbensen and C.H. Maxson (eds) *Youth Gangs in International Perspective* (Springer). Overview of what drives individuals to join gangs and what psychological factors may explain this.

Bongar, B., Brown, L.M., Beutler, L.E., Breckenridge, J.N. and Zimbardo, P.G. (eds) (2006) *Psychology of Terrorism* (Oxford University Press). Extensive reader on how individuals are affected by terrorism and the effects of the media; also offers essays that explore the psychology behind why individuals may turn to terrorism.

Horgan, J. (2014) *The Psychology of Terrorism* (2nd ed.) (Routledge). Looks at the individual approaches that explain why and how individuals become terrorists, why they engage in violence and why they may disengage.

Kruglanski, A.W., Gelfand, M.J., Bélanger, J.J., Sheveland, A., Hetiarachchi, M. and Gunaratna, R. (2014) 'The psychology of radicalization and de-radicalization: how significance quest impacts violent extremism'. *Political Psychology*, 35 (S1), 69–93. How individuals become radicalized, focusing on the need to attain personal significance.

Post, J.M. (2007) *The Mind of the Terrorist: The Psychology of Terrorism from the IRA to al-Qaeda* (Palgrave Macmillan). Fascinating book on the psychology of different terrorist group members in the past and present, with each chapter offering a historical background and political context to each group's emergence; presents a compilation of the psychoses of different individual members of these violent groups, though these diagnoses are conducted from afar.

PART III

TYPES OF VIOLENT NON-STATE ACTORS

In Part III, we introduce different types of violent non-state actors. They are as follows: de facto states and insurgencies (Chapter 6), terror organizations and terror networks (Chapter 7), marauding rebels and warlords (Chapter 8), organized criminals and gangs (Chapter 9) and PSCs and paramilitaries (Chapter 10). Table III.1 presents an overview of the various actors and key characteristics associated with each.

Table III.1   Types of Violent Non-state Actors and their Key Characteristics

Group	Motivation	Strategy and tactics	Key group threatened/ victim	Organizational structure	Scope and power	Legitimacy and popularity
De facto state	Political: set up a state	Provide state services and armed defence; hold territory	State	Tightly organized; hierarchical	Very powerful; territorial control	High legitimacy
Political organizations with militant wings	Political: influence policy	Provide party platform and armed defence	State	Tightly organized; hierarchical	Somewhat powerful	High legitimacy; public support
Insurgency	Political: varies	Mostly armed conflict; hold territory	State and society	Somewhat tightly organized; somewhat hierarchical	Somewhat powerful; some territorial control	Some legitimacy
Terror organization	Political: varies	Engage the media; psychological warfare; kill civilians	Society	Tightly organized; somewhat hierarchical	Not powerful	Little legitimacy

(Continued)

Table III.1 (Continued)

Group	Motivation	Strategy and tactics	Key group threatened/ victim	Organizational structure	Scope and power	Legitimacy and popularity
Terror network	Political: amorphous	Engage the media; psychological warfare; kill civilians	Society	Cellular/loose; somewhat hierarchical	Not powerful	Little legitimacy
Marauding rebels	Economic/ opportunistic	Loot and pillage; kill civilians	Society (state may have already collapsed)	Loose	Not powerful; temporary control of some towns or villages	Little legitimacy
Warlord	Economic/ opportunistic	Loot and pillage; predation	Society (state may have already collapsed)	Somewhat organized around charismatic warlord	Somewhat powerful; some control over territory	Little legitimacy
Organized crime	Economic/ opportunistic	Corruption, crime and violence	State, society, individuals	Tightly organized; formerly hierarchical, now flatter hierarchy	Very powerful; some territorial sphere of influence; may control transactions and flows of goods	Little legitimacy
Gang	Economic/ opportunistic	Petty crime and violence	Individuals and society	Somewhat loose; somewhat hierarchical	Not powerful but becoming more dangerous	Little legitimacy
PSC	Economic/ opportunistic	Gun-for-hire; earn profit and maintain stability	State, other violent non-state actors	Tightly organized; hierarchical	Somewhat powerful but does not control territory	Little legitimacy
Paramilitary	Economic/ political	Armed conflict; possibly hold territory	State, other violent non-state actors, individuals	Tightly organized	Somewhat powerful; sometimes controls territory	Little legitimacy

6

INSURGENCIES

This chapter explains what is meant by insurgencies. It demonstrates that the primary raison d'être of these groups is to achieve some political goal (such as more autonomy or improved socio-economic conditions) by challenging the host state through armed struggle or challenging other paramilitary groups. The most important goal of the chapter is to demonstrate what the difference is between an insurgency and a terrorist group, two concepts that have often been conflated. Insurgencies can commit acts of terrorism, but they are not the same as terrorist groups. This chapter explains why this is the case.

DEFINITION

An insurgency is a substate group that wants to bring about political change, obtain power and political control, and seek some transformation of governance (Kiras, 2007). Thus they want to undermine a constituted authority through an armed struggle. They often have greater military capacity vis-à-vis the state, compared to other violent non-state actors; they also have a standing army to help them accomplish their goals. Because insurgencies are engaged in battle, they have a more visible structure and are usually not clandestine organizations, like a terrorist sleeper cell. One of the key distinguishing features of an insurgency is that they exercise some territorial control, which they use as their base. Being able to control territory constrains their strategy, and is indicative of other capabilities. Because they can control territory, they also often need to build governance structures in the areas that they control (de la Calle and Sánchez-Cuenca, 2012). Thus they are not just trying to fight more effectively than the state, they are also trying to administer more effectively as well. Today's insurgencies also have more advanced recruitment methods and greater access to weapons (Beckett, 2005). They can operate in urban terrain and are more involved in organized crime.

POLITICAL IDEOLOGY AND OBJECTIVES

Insurgencies emerge over a range of issues involving territory, history, ideology and leadership (Rid and Hecker, 2009). However, insurgencies often have very concrete political goals, usually separatist or ideological. They want to spread their ideology and often may hold popular assemblies and local meetings (Palma, 2015: 490). Here we focus on four different types of insurgencies: liberation, separatist, reform/revolutionary and religious/traditional.

'Liberation' insurgencies seek independence from colonial rule. These were common after World War II when many states, particularly in Africa, were seeking independence from foreign control, such as in the insurgencies that developed in Algeria, Mozambique and Angola. In the case of Algeria, the National Liberation Front (FLN) was the umbrella organization that advocated armed efforts to gain independence from France, which had ruled Algeria since 1834. In 1954, the FLN formed an armed wing known as the ELN. As with many liberation insurgencies, after independence was achieved, the armed wing was converted into the regular armed forces.

'Separatist' insurgencies want to represent an ethnic group and form an independent state. They renounce the political community and aim to create a new independent political community. The drive for secession is sometimes mostly ethnic, but could be also religious, racial or a combination of these (Harris, 2010). In some cases, they may be willing to accept greater autonomy. Separatist insurgencies can take place in strong states that happen to have substate identities that are particularly intense such as the Tamil Tigers in Sri Lanka and the Chechens in Russia.

'Reform' or 'revolutionary' insurgencies seek radical reform of the national government, such as the National Resistance Army in Uganda or the Ethiopian People's Revolutionary Democratic Front in Ethiopia. This category of reform insurgency is similar to the category of an 'egalitarian' insurgency, which is focused on creating a new system based on an equal distribution of income that can help radically transform society (O'Neill, 2001). Most revolutionary and reform insurgencies aim to make society more egalitarian and to advocate on behalf of the poor, such as the FARC and Shining Path of Peru. Many leftist insurgencies became obsolete after the Cold War ended because these groups were no longer receiving state support from the Eastern bloc nations and the USSR. The end of the Cold War also led to less ideological commitment to socialist/communist ideals (Robison et al., 2006). In some cases, the reform insurgencies were able to become part of the government, such as was the case in Nepal, with its Maoist insurgency.

'Religious' insurgencies are focused on transforming the state into one that promotes certain religious ideals. Islamic fundamentalism is often noted for being the inspiration for insurgencies around the world, such as against the Soviets in Afghanistan, against the Philippine government and in Sudan and Iraq. Some scholars have argued that religious insurgencies are most likely to take place in states that are heterogeneous, and where Islam may be forced to confront Western values (Metz, 1994). Others have argued that religious insurgencies can also be anarchic because they aim to eliminate institutionalized political arrangements that they deem to be illegitimate (O'Neill, 2001). Some of the religious insurgencies appeared to have this aim, refusing to engage in the conventional political system or to respect the idea of the state, simply because it is viewed as a Western import. These religious insurgencies discourage participation in the current political system and focus on advocating values that are rooted in their religion. Some elements of the Iraqi insurgency appear to be rejecting government as a whole (Berman, 2011). Other Iraqi insurgency groups aimed initially to expel the US from Iraq, but also provide Sunni tribes with greater representation and power. Examples of insurgencies are presented in Table 6.1.

Table 6.1 Examples of Insurgencies that Commit Acts of Terrorism and Examples of Terrorist Groups

Insurgencies that commit acts of terrorism (hold territory)	Terrorist groups (do not hold territory)
Boko Haram (Nigeria)	ETA
IS (Syria and Iraq)	Baader-Meinhof Gang
FARC (Colombia)	Weather Underground
Al-Shabaab (Somalia)	Armed Forces of National Liberation (FALN)
Taliban (Afghanistan)	Red Brigades
PKK (Turkey)	Aum Shinrikyo
LTTE (Sri Lanka)	Abu Nidal Organization
Naxalites (India)	Abu Sayyaf
Haqqani Network (Afghanistan)	Jemaah Islamiyah
Moro Islamic Liberation Front (MILF) (Philippines)	Japanese Red Army
Shining Path (Peru)	Egyptian Islamic Jihad

Case Study   The Zapatistas

Few insurgent movements are able to maintain a commitment to their ideals without having to eventually compromise these ideals by resorting to acts of violence, theft and crime that are worse than the misdeeds of their opponents. The Zapatistas are one of the few insurgent groups that have not fallen prey to the lure of more lucrative options of funding.

The Zapatista National Liberation Army (EZLN) is an insurgent group committed to calling the world's attention to the growing gaps between rich and poor, highlighting the plight of the poor people of Chiapas in particular. The group called for greater democratization in Mexico and land reform which had been mandated by the 1917 Constitution but ignored by the ruling Institutional Revolutionary Party (PRI) for over six decades. The group did not demand independence but aimed for greater autonomy, with natural resource extraction in Chiapas benefiting the people of Chiapas directly.

The group's origins stretched back over a decade before the armed insurgency took place, initially attracting peasants. Focusing on an egalitarian agenda, young women were also encouraged to join. The Zapatistas went public on 1 January 1994 – when the North American Free

(Continued)

(Continued)

Trade Agreement came into effect. They claimed that they needed to opt for an armed struggle because peaceful protests had yielded few results. An estimated 3,000 armed insurgents seized key towns in Chiapas, freed prisoners in one of the jails and set fire to several police buildings and military barracks. The next day the Mexican army was able to counter-attack and intense fighting broke out, with the Zapatistas suffering heavy casualties and being forced to retreat into the jungle. Massive protests in both Mexico and abroad, however, forced a halt to the offensive, and a ceasefire on 12 January 1994 ended the armed clashes. The Zapatistas retained some land for over a year, but by February 1995 the Mexican government had broken the ceasefire and overran the territory under Zapatista control.

The Zapatistas enjoyed tremendous popular support through their media and propaganda campaign. The Internet provided the means for rapid dissemination (Cleaver, 1998). Though much of civil society did not want to engage in an uprising against the Mexican government, it was also not apathetic enough to do nothing, and the general mood of civil society was supportive of negotiations (Esteva, 1999). This support did not come just from local sources but also from around the globe. Grass-roots activists from over 40 countries and five continents attended both intercontinental meetings that the group later held (Cleaver, 1998). Much of the support was generated by the uncompromising ideals of the organization. While other violent non-state actors have resorted to targeting citizens or getting involved in organized crime, the Zapatistas are one of the few who have avoided these traps, sticking to their ideals.

The goals of the Zapatistas extended beyond greater autonomy for the poor people of Chiapas and the rights of indigenous groups. It is a movement that targeted those who have been excluded and oppressed and negatively affected by neo-liberalism (Olesen, 2004: 261). At the same time, the movement did not reject liberal democracy but focused on improving the quality of democracy both at the national and international level. Thus part of the group's wider critique took aim at the International Monetary Fund, the World Trade Organization and the World Bank.

STRATEGY AND TACTICS

Insurgencies engage in long and tense campaigns of irregular warfare (one exception was the insurgency in Cuba led by Fidel Castro which was a very quick victory). Tactical offensives, with local numerical superiority, are carried out to further stretch enemy resources. Insurgencies use guerrilla hit-and-run attacks on supply lines and small and isolated units. They usually have time on their side, as they may have a stronger commitment than the state to wage a long war of attrition. Insurgent groups have lasted several decades in countries such as Guatemala, Eritrea, Western Sahara and Laos. They focus on using their strengths in mobilizing and organizing against the weaknesses of the more powerful state.

Insurgencies can engage in campaigns against an opponent where they have better knowledge of the terrain and are able to control territory better. Afghan guerrillas had better knowledge of the mountains than the Soviets. Chechen fighters had better knowledge of the urban jungle, buildings, etc. than the Russians (Schaefer, 2010). Iraqi insurgents had better knowledge of Fallujah. States often abandon the countryside to defend more valuable resources of the state in urban areas and military bases. Insurgencies can get control over some space, especially if the government is not strong enough to control the entire country.

Because the goal of insurgencies is to gain the loyalty of a large support group, this impacts their choice of tactics. Insurgencies of the past mostly focused on targeting the state in an armed struggle. Insurgencies of the past had engaged in selective violence, usually targeting the state and the military. Though civilians may be victims of insurgencies, they are not the prime target. Insurgencies of today have been more likely to use terror tactics or at least have made alliances or links with noted terror organizations. In spite of their more frequent use of terror, they are equipped to be able to fight against a military. The IS is an example of an insurgency/de facto state that uses and encourages the use of terror (for more on the IS, see Chapter 7).

In comparison to terrorist groups, insurgencies typically were bound by conventions that entailed moral distinctions between belligerents and neutrals, combatants and non-combatants. Some targets were deemed inappropriate and illegitimate. Terrorists, on the other hand, refuse to accept the conventional and moral limits that defined actions by insurgencies. In the past, the use of terrorist tactics have been discouraged by insurgencies (Wickham-Crowley, 1990). Civilians were not usually targeted by insurgencies because it undermines the legitimacy of the group. But today, acts of terrorism can also occur in the context of an armed conflict where basic human rights are repeatedly violated. Some insurgency campaigns are particularly dirty, targeting civilians such as was the case with UNITA. Today, many insurgency campaigns are no longer bound by conventions and have created terror cells that engage in brutal behaviour on behalf of the insurgency.

One of the more powerful insurgencies that used terrorism as part of an armed struggle strategy is the LTTE (for more on the Tamil Tigers, see the case study in this chapter). In addition to fighting the Sri Lankan government by conventional means, the LTTE targeted civilians and targets with high symbolic value.[1] The group has killed high-profile political figures in both Sri Lanka and India, including Indian prime minister candidate Rajiv Gandhi in 1991, Sri Lankan President Ranasinghe Premadasa in 1993 (the only group able to assassinate a sitting president), and former Sri Lankan Prime Minister and presidential hopeful Gamini Dissanayake in 1994. Former president Mrs Chandrika Bandaranaike Kumaratunga was also wounded in a botched suicide attack in December 1999, permanently losing her eye. It has also killed moderate Tamil politicians. Of 37 prominent politicians assassinated by LTTE cadres, 24 were Tamils.

In 1987, the LTTE began an unrelenting suicide campaign, often targeting civilians. From 1984 to 2004 the LTTE killed 3,045 civilians and injured 3,704. The bloodiest year of the terrorism campaign was the year the campaign started, 1987, when 547 civilians were killed. In total, the group has been responsible for 1,660 acts of terror (START database; Kumaraswamy and Copland, 2013).

STRUCTURE AND RECRUITMENT

STRUCTURE

Insurgencies of the past were very hierarchical and organized around the Maoist notion of the need to have a core leadership with a degree of hierarchy. Given the military function of insurgencies, they often have to operate with some hierarchy. Hierarchy is also needed to ensure that forces remain intact. However, the more an

---

[1] The LTTE used a suicide truck bomb on the newly inaugurated World Trade Centre in Colombo in October 1997, killing 18 people and injuring over 100.

organization is decentralized, the more it is able to survive and regroup after an attack on the organization (Brafman and Beckstrom, 2006). The other issue is that groups that are too hierarchical may have charismatic leadership that is resistant to bureaucratization, which is important for administering territory (Asal et al., 2012).

The Shining Path is an example of an organization that had a mixture of both network and hierarchy. The group was founded by Abimael Guzmán and aimed to overthrow the Peruvian government and implement a communist system. Before it dismantled, the group had a national directorate, a central committee and several regional commands. It was Guzmán, however, who made the final call on all decisions on the group's strategy, objectives and aims. The rank-and-file members were organized into cells that had little contact with the hierarchy and were able to make many day-to-day decisions on their own. The network allowed the group to operate over a vast geographic area (Dishman, 2005).

The PKK has had a hierarchical leadership with Abdullah Öcalan at the top and a chairmanship council, a central committee and a central disciplinary board below him, in descending order. Öcalan has been considered ruthless and willing to suppress any internal leadership challenges. From 1983 to 1985, Öcalan ordered the murder of 11 high-level former or current PKK members (Marcus, 2009). Öcalan also wanted to ensure that no other autonomous Kurdish organization emerged that could challenge his claim to represent the Kurds. The PKK has been successful at creating a central system in which all Kurdish organizations are chained hierarchically. Öcalan has been able to maintain youth, women's and students' organizations under his organizational command. Media sources are also under his influence. Unofficial members known as commissars always accompany Kurdish politicians. Kurdish political elites are investigated thoroughly by PKK leadership. In 1999, Öcalan was captured and he has remained behind bars. However, his imprisonment did not signal the end of his grip on the PKK. He has had regular contact with lawyers who are able to deliver his orders to his followers, such as whether to engage or refrain from violence (Roth and Sever, 2007).[2]

The LTTE was tightly organized and led (until 2009) by its highly charismatic leader, Velupillai Prabhakaran. Prabhakaran was known for his brutality and uncompromising attitude. He allowed little dissent to his power and ideas. In fact, any dissent within the organization over strategy and direction led to murder within the group, with many Tamil leaders killed as a result (Whittaker, 2013).

Increasingly, modern insurgencies have become more and more operationally decentralized. The FARC in Colombia was more hierarchically controlled, while the Taliban in Afghanistan was more networked (Sanin and Giustozzi, 2010). Insurgencies in Iraq are also much more networked and diffuse. They are looser and more ambiguous (Hoffman and McCormick, 2004). There is a constellation of cells that are gravitating towards one another, carrying out armed attacks, trading weapons, partaking in joint training and exchanging intelligence. These alliances are constantly shifting, however (Williams, 2009: 13).

Insurgencies have an army that may be well organized into fighting units, with a command and rank structure. Insurgencies have developed training routines and may even wear uniforms (Palma, 2015). They are also specialized in executing operations. FARC developed an impressive military structure that was

[2]From prison Öcalan directed followers to refrain from violence in 2002, but in 2004 he ordered his followers to restart the conflict, and violence resumed.

designed to confront the national military head-on if needed. The organization deliberately paralleled that of the Colombian army. FARC's primary tactical unit consisted of 150–200 armed combatants. In 2000, FARC had control over 70 different fronts that were organized into seven regional blocs, but by 2008 it had lost over 20 fronts and half of its fighters.

Some individuals may be focused on military operations while other individuals are responsible for recruitment or the dissemination of propaganda. Insurgencies often have internal rules of conduct of violent actions, to help maintain the legitimacy of the group (Kiras, 2007). They may have guidebooks that detail their choice of targets and what their relationship should be with the population. These guides may also provide information on how prisoners should be treated and how recruitment should take place.

Insurgencies may also have military manuals that outline their military tactics, operations and strategy. FARC operated with a complex manual. The Naxalites, a communist insurgency in India, had a 332-page army and air-defence manual. The Taliban's manual was over 150 pages (Bangerter, 2012). These military manuals also make clear how the command structure works, how decisions are made and who has the power to make decisions. This is especially helpful if insurgencies have just experienced a merger between several groups.

Though Chechen groups have historically operated very independently, they have always retained some obligation of mutual defence during times of war. Clans could be quickly linked and connected into larger clan confederations that could cooperate to defend themselves. The Chechen insurgency initially resembled a commander and cadre organization, which was more similar to the Russian army. It then transformed into horizontal networks after the first war instead of using a unified guerrilla army. In general, Chechen networks do not have a clear hierarchy and have quicker operational flexibility. There is faster exchange of information between nodes because information does not have to travel up the command structure. There may be a central gang dominated by a powerful leader, but the organization is more networked with many different groups radiating from the centre. The lack of a clear command after the assassination of Chechen leader Jokhar Dadaev in April 1996 led to an increased assault on Russian military outposts, as attacks were no longer waiting to be coordinated from the top.

RECRUITMENT

Insurgencies try to establish moral superiority with the local population. They have to carry out a campaign of political indoctrination to attract new recruits. Insurgency troops tend to come from the lower classes and are often composed of young males. They also target an alienated population who have been disenfranchised. Although often forced to join, they may be lured in with money and resources. Child soldiers have often been used as well. Also common is to recruit students and peasants. Ethnic-based and religious-based insurgencies focus on their constituency, often targeting religious establishments in the case of the latter. Insurgencies also recruit from the prison populations. The Shining Path targeted mostly young vulnerable students who would eventually become teachers returning to their villages to carry on the movement's message. The group also recruited among the highland indigenous communities.

In the case of the LTTE, rank-and-file members are mostly recruited from the lower middle classes and all LTTE cadres come from the lower castes. The most militant members have been drawn from the higher castes and tend to be university-educated, English-speaking professionals (Hudson and Majeska, 1999). Tamil Tigers have recruited child soldiers, relying on a 'baby brigade' of boys and girls aged 10–16. In 1998, a Sri Lankan military report claimed that 60% of all Tamil fighters were 18 years or younger. The LTTE was accused of having up to 5,794 child soldiers in its ranks since 2001. About one-third of its membership is women, and women have participated in about one-third of the group's suicide attacks (Schweitzer and Schweitzer, 2002: 84)

The LTTE kept the numbers of the group small and maintained a high standard of training. LTTE members were prohibited from smoking cigarettes and consuming alcohol in any form. They were required to avoid their family members and avoid communication with them. Initially LTTE members were prohibited from having love affairs or sexual relationships as they could deter their prime motive, but this policy changed after Prabhakaran married Mathivathani Erambu in October 1984.

The major challenge in the recruitment of insurgents is maintaining a large number of capable fighters and a steady flow of motivated recruits. This is all the more difficult given that insurgents are perpetually engaging in acts of violence that impose risk (Gates, 2002). Large death tolls not only diminish the number of active members but may also discourage more individuals from joining the organization. Moreover, the most valuable recruits are usually the hardest to retain (Frisch, 2012).

FUNDING AND SUPPORT

FUNDING

Insurgencies of the past relied on state support to fund their operations. Many left-leaning countries were accused of supporting insurgencies. However, state support has waned in recent years. This loss of state support has led to three consequences. First, insurgencies have started to rely on more economic tactics in warfare, such as terrorism, instead of targeting the state through an armed struggle, which is much more costly. Second, insurgencies have had to forge links with criminal gangs and other violent non-state actors. Third, insurgencies have had to find other sources of funding to finance themselves.

Decline in state sponsorship has led to more involvement in the drug trade, smuggling, extortion and kidnapping. Insurgencies that are heavily involved in different forms of illegal businesses are referred to as commercial insurgencies (Metz, 1994; Palma, 2015). Chapter 2 detailed the crime-terror nexus and the emergence of hybrid groups. These insurgencies began with political motivations but became lured by profits to focus most of their activities on illegal activities that were highly lucrative. The LTTE were highly involved in organized crime such as credit card fraud and drug trafficking, but they also received support from the diaspora, particularly in Canada. Some of these donations were legitimate while others were obtained by means of coercion and extortion. Boko Haram receives most of its funding from bank robberies, extortion, ransoms and kidnappings. They have also received some funding from the al-Qaeda global network. Al-Shabaab has also engaged in theft, stealing equipment from various organizations and looting UN compounds and private media stations (Kelley, 2014).

Many insurgencies, such as the Shining Path, are also involved in the drug trade. Involvement in the drug trade helped the group to improve its military capabilities. It moved into the coca-cultivating Upper Huallaga valley in 1984 and established itself as a middleman. It charged landing fees for any aircraft that was transporting drugs to Colombia to be processed and trafficked (Kay, 1999: 102). Though the Shining Path has had a reputation for sticking to a highly dogmatic ideology, it became more flexible and moderate in its relations with the local population producing coca. The PKK is said to control about 30% of the laboratories that refine heroin in and around Turkey, with the rest being controlled by the Turkish mafia (Steinberg, 2008). The PKK and IRA have also been linked with the smuggling of contraband cigarettes (Shelley and Melzer, 2008).

Of the nine major drug-producing countries, only Bolivia and Thailand have not experienced armed conflict. Most insurgents exacerbate the drug trade since they have a serious need to finance their conflict efforts. Only the Zapatistas have avoided getting involved in the drug trade. They have received significant funding from donations and believe that their involvement in the drug trade would jeopardize such donations (Dishman, 2001: 47).

Laos has an insurgency comprising the Hmong minority that inhabit the country's opium-producing hills, which has enabled the group to wage a low-intensity insurgency with the communist government since 1975. All of the major non-state actors in Afghanistan have also been heavily involved in the drug trade, such as Gulbuddin Hekmatyar's Hezbe-Islami and factions of the Northern Alliance (Goodhand, 2000).

SOURCES OF SUPPORT

An insurgency is often supported by a popular movement, fuelled by deep-seated grievances such as relative deprivation (terrorist groups may also have deep-seated grievances). They aim to win over the population and undermine authority. No insurgency can be successful without the support of the population; its centre of gravity is the population's support. Because of this, insurgencies will try to achieve a different level of embeddedness with overall society, which makes them different from totally marginalized organizations. The insurgency has to show that it can be stronger than the state or other insurgencies.

Insurgencies gain support by provoking the state and demonstrating strength. With the former, known as the 'provocation effect', an insurgency uses violence against the state to force the state to overreact, which will only serve to reinforce the insurgent's cause. Over-retaliation and oppressive measures will push more people to support the insurgency. With the 'demonstration effect', an insurgency attempts to appear stronger than it is. Insurgencies need to demonstrate to the public that the state is ineffective and that the insurgency will likely win, making it important to join the winning side (McCormick and Giordano, 2007).

Insurgencies need sizeable support for their cause, which moderated their behaviour in the past. Che Guevara rejected using terrorism as a tactic due to fears that it would alienate the population (Hashim, 2013: 8). Today's insurgencies seem to care little about whether or not they should resort to terrorism. Since terrorism as a tactic has become more commonly used, most insurgencies target civilians at some point.

Insurgencies of the past often received significant support from foreign governments and possibly other violent non-state actors (Schneckener, 2006, 2007). Venezuela has supported FARC. Libya has supported the MILF and the Moro National

Liberation Front (MNLF). Countries such as Eritrea, Iran, Syria, Saudi Arabia and Djibouti have been accused of offering support for al-Shabaab through weapons and funding. Kashmiri insurgents have long been supported by Pakistan (for more on this, see Chapter 4).

Ethnic political organizations often have a wide range of external support (Byman et al., 2001). Though direct support declined after World War II, alternative forms of support such as from diasporic groups, advocacy groups and even refugees have played an important role in providing financial and human support to ethnic insurgencies (Byman, 1998). This non-state support is based on a common ethnic identity and shared political and ideological objectives.

POWER AND IMPACT ON THE STATE AND SOCIETY

Insurgencies involve adversaries that are not symmetrical in equipment or training. Insurgents avoid direct confrontations with their opponents but they are capable of seizing territory. Because of this, they most often emerge in very weak states where the state does not have a monopoly over the legitimate use of force for the entire territory. Insurgencies often begin in rural areas or mountainous areas that are beyond the government's control. They have to demonstrate that they are powerful enough to protect those whom they are advocating on behalf of. They also have to protect their core group members from destruction or capture.

Insurgencies usually operate within a defined territory. As mentioned before, we distinguish insurgencies from terrorist groups in that insurgencies control territory or occupy a common territory. The control of territory indicates that the space is being patrolled, managed and administered by that group (Mobley, 2012: 14). The control of territory is instrumental to the definition of what constitutes an insurgency. Though insurgencies sometimes have transnational objectives, they are mostly territorially bound.

Controlling territory is also different than a safe haven, which is used to describe a space where a terrorist group might find refuge from its adversaries. This is more the result of state sponsorship or due to the remoteness of the territory than due to the group's capacity and popularity to take territory by force. ETA was never strong enough to control Spain's territory (Sánchez-Cuenca and de la Calle, 2009: 34). They had to flee to a safe haven in France. Though the region that they were trying to separate from was occupied by Basques, only 1% of Basques offered ETA full support (Sánchez-Cuenca, 2007, 305). In contrast, at the height of its power, the Shining Path controlled large areas of Peru. The Tamil Tigers controlled large parts of northern and eastern Sri Lanka (de la Calle and Sánchez-Cuenca, 2012: 582). In contrast, in southern Thailand, none of the many violent groups are insurgencies. They do not control or administer territory.

The issue of whether or not the IRA was an insurgency or a terrorist group is highly contested. The IRA did have paramilitaries, and at one point it was on the verge of becoming an insurgency. In the early 1970s, the IRA had de facto control over some neighbourhoods in Belfast and Derry (Sánchez-Cuenca and de la Calle, 2009: 35). In the rural area of South Armagh, the IRA presence was so strong that the British army had to travel by helicopter to avoid sniper fire (Kennedy-Pipe and McInnes, 1997). Nevertheless, paramilitaries in Northern Ireland never controlled territory. Scholars have claimed that it was the 'motorman' operation of the British in July 1972 that prevented this from happening (Smith and Neumann, 2005).

Once insurgencies have seized some territory, they exercise de facto control and may start to provide some administrative services. They have replaced the authority and sovereignty of the state and can now create a parallel state. They seek to demonstrate that the government is illegitimate while establishing themselves as a preferable alternative to the state. They need to provide an alternative form of governance. Insurgencies therefore have to be able to provide some services that reflect their values and concerns. Insurgents may therefore engage in state-building by providing security, collecting taxes and setting up administrative structures in cases where the government is absent (Kalyvas, 2006). Bernard Fall suggests that when a country is 'being subverted it is being out-administered, not out fought' (qtd by/Fall, 2015: 55)

Seizing territory implies control over the population and high levels of interaction with the citizens. Many living under their territory may be forced to join the ranks (Kalyvas and Kocher, 2007). Insurgencies also use the territory that they seize to train these new recruits in remote, safe bases. The seizure of territory allows the group to further expand in capacity, attain greater military resources and employ more effective hit-and-run tactics against the state. Controlling territory has many advantages, but it also makes the group a fixed target that its opponent can more easily attack. It also creates greater demands on the group to provide services and win over the population (Mobley, 2012: 15).

Box 6.1   De Facto States

A de facto state is a geographic entity, usually consisting of a particular ethnic group, which wishes to secede from the parent state that it is a part of and be recognized as a de jure state by the international community (Pegg, 1998: 26). De facto states are in control of the territory that they lay claim to. For example, the de facto state of Nagorno-Karabakh in Azerbaijan exercises considerable control, and has a clear armed forces structure, police force, border troops and customs posts (Lynch, 2002: 838). In some cases, de facto states may have an organized political leadership, some administrative capacity to provide services and popular support. De facto states often go unrecognized by the international community for fear that this would harm the relationship with the sovereign state and that it could set a precedent that would lead to more cases of secession around the world. Because de facto states are not recognized, they are considered violent non-state actors.

For most de facto states, the parent state offers little motivation to remain. They do not offer enough services or are too repressive of the residents of the de facto state. The authorities of de facto states often believe that the economies of the parent state are either just as bad as theirs or worse (Lynch, 2002: 843).

Though the parent state is unappealing, de facto states usually have very low functioning institutions, low levels of democracy and corrupt economies. Power is usually personalized and corruption and patron-clientelism tend to be high. Repression is more likely to be used rather than accommodation and compromise (Lynch, 2002: 836). De facto states cannot legally trade with the outside world, which encourages illegal business activity. They have little transparency and have high levels of crime. Revenues tend to go into private pockets (Kolstø, 2006).

De facto states do offer some administrative services. However, most de facto states are too weak to provide much. The de facto state of Abkhazia is able to maintain a legislature,

(Continued)

(Continued)

executive and judiciary but is unable to provide many services to the population (Sanchez, 2006). Transnistria has aimed to offer an attractive alternative to Moldova. It declared itself independent from its parent state Moldova in 1992, and fighting broke out between the Transnistrian Republican Guard and Cossack units. The Russians provided military support, but after four months of fighting there had been no solid resolution and Transnistria remains a de facto state. Though not yet internationally recognized, Transnistria has worked to improve its educational system. It has no programme for state health insurance but does provide free medicine and covers the cost of urgent operations. It relies heavily on Russian support for the development of textbooks and higher education and for medical infrastructure (Blakkisrud and Kolstø, 2011: 192).

De facto states must have strong militaries to defend the territory they have gained. The military in Nagorno-Karabakh may have as many as 20,000 troops (with possibly as many as 30,000 in reserve); there are 2,000 in South Ossetia and 5,000 in Abkhazia. This is not large compared to the host state but it is considerable. This leaves fewer resources available for welfare, education, healthcare and building infrastructure. The role of the military for survival is predominant, leading to the militarization of society (Kolstø, 2006: 732).

Some de facto states have difficulty providing security since they are constantly facing the threat from the parent state. In Abkhazia, the state has not been able to provide law and order and security is guaranteed by Russia, NGOs and other international organizations (Lynch, 2002: 836). In some cases, security has to be outsourced – as Russia, for example, has provided security for Abkhazia and South Ossetia. Security institutions in Abkhazia, South Ossetia and Transnistria are often headed by Russians or officials who are 'de facto delegated by state institutions of the Russian Federation' (Popescu, 2006: 11). Chechnya had a de facto state that was on the brink of anarchy between the first and second Chechen wars. There were no state institutions, schools were closed and there were no thriving businesses – with the exception of smuggling, stealing and kidnapping (Tishkov, 2004).

De facto states pose great challenges for peace and stability. De facto states weaken the sovereignty, capability and security of the parent state as resources are diverted from providing services to competing against the de facto state. They often perpetuate frozen or active conflicts with the sovereign state. These conflicts tend to be intractable with settlements nearly impossible (Lynch, 2002: 838).

Insurgencies can also seriously threaten security. One of the most dangerous insurgencies was the LTTE in Sri Lanka. In its terrorist campaign, the group aimed to cause tremendous damage to strategic targets with high financial and symbolic value such as commercial buildings, naval vessels and aircraft. In October 1997, the LTTE used a truck bomb to damage the newly inaugurated World Trade Centre in Colombo, killing 18 people and injuring over 100. Four days later, a flotilla of 20 small boats attacked two Sri Lankan navy gunboats off the coast of Sri Lanka by ramming an explosive-laden boat into one of the navy gunboats, sinking it and killing nine navy sailors. Its July 2001 attack on the Colombo airport is the most destructive terrorist act in aviation history, destroying or damaging 26 aircraft. This constituted half of the national airline's commercial planes and 25% of the air force fleet (Aryasinha, 2001: 30).

The PKK launched its insurgency against the Turkish government in 1984 which caused major damage and a high death toll. The insurgency began by attacking military posts, but many civilians were later targeted. Those who worked for state hospitals and schools were targeted as well. From 1984–87, 217 teachers were killed or kidnapped by the PKK (Phillips, 2008). In total, the conflict killed over 40,000 people, destroyed thousands of villages and displaced millions.

Case Study   Tamil Tigers (LTTE)

The LTTE is an insurgency that has been fighting for independence from Sri Lanka for decades. At its height it was one of the most dangerous and powerful insurgencies in the world. The LTTE has used both a rural guerrilla campaign and an urban suicide attack campaign. The urban suicide attack campaign was carried out by the terror wings that worked as part of the LTTE, known as the Black Tigers and the Black Tigresses, which were formed by the LTTE in 1987. To distance itself from this type of violence, the LTTE has not officially claimed attacks against non-military targets (Hoffman and McCormick, 2004: 262). In spite of its numerous acts of terrorism, the LTTE is an insurgency because of its ability and aim to control and administer territory.

Tensions between Tamils (who constitute about 12% of the population) and Sinhalese (about 74% of the population) had been ongoing for years. These tensions came to a head after the 1956 election of the Sri Lanka Freedom Party which implemented a 'Sinhala Only' policy. In response to this discrimination, many Tamil groups formed to advocate on the group's behalf. The Tamil United Liberation Front (TULF) was founded in this context (Nadarajah and Sriskandarajah, 2005). Frustrated with the TULF's lack of action, a youth guerrilla movement formed that comprised 35 competing groups, eventually whittled down to a handful of groups. One of these groups was the LTTE, which had been founded on 5 May 1976. The LTTE were quickly able to marginalize the other competing groups. It ordered civilians to boycott the local government elections of 1983 in which the TULF took part, leading to 10% voter turnout. Thereafter, Tamil political parties were largely unable to represent Tamil people as insurgent groups took over their position.

The turning point for the LTTE in terms of attracting recruits came in July 1983 (known as Black July) after an upsurge in violence took place against Tamils, seeing thousands murdered by Sinhalese mobs in response to an LTTE ambush that killed 13 Sri Lankan soldiers. Over seven days 8,000 homes and 5,000 shops were destroyed and another 150,000 people were made homeless. Recruits flooded the organization hoping to join the movement.

The LTTE was estimated to have 8,000–10,000 armed combatants with a core of trained guerrillas in the order of 3,000–6,000. The LTTE had a well-developed militia. It has a naval capacity with 12 vessels, one of the few insurgencies with this capability. It is also the first insurgency to acquire air power and use light aircraft in some of its attacks.

As a result of this extraordinary power, the LTTE was able to set up a de facto state. It has exercised control over 70% of the Tamil areas of the north and east, though not the five main population centres which have been under government control. The LTTE has built up a civil administration, a police force, a justice system and a humanitarian assistance agency. It also has a health and education board, a bank, a radio station and a television station. To help pay for the administration, the LTTE has a taxation system for the territory under its control and the government-controlled areas. It also developed a customs regime at the borders of the front lines.

On 16 May 2009, the LTTE was finally defeated by the Sri Lankan government. The death of their charismatic leader, Velupillai Prabhakaran, three days later seemed to signal the end of the group, with most fighters surrendering to the Sri Lankan government. An estimated 90,000 people were killed in the conflict.

Box 6.2   Self-Defence Militias

Militias are self-defence units that are outside the formal security sector and central government. They do not support the formal state. They are irregular armed forces usually operating within failing or weak states. They are usually composed of volunteers who are trying to defend their localities. These are groups such as the Kurdish Peshmerga that may form to protect de facto states. Militias are particularly prevalent where particular ethnic factions or religious groups feel that they do not receive adequate protection from the state (Williams, 2009). They are the militaries that form to provide some sort of defence. Thus they often represent specific ethnic, religious, tribal, clan or other communal groups and have high levels of legitimacy in the areas they protect; loyalty levels are high. Because they are defensive units, they do not always receive formal training but in some cases, if they have experience in battle, they are skilled if unconventional fighters. Self-defence units were formed by the Tutsis and Hutus to stop the massacres taking place in Rwanda in 1994. Self-defence units were also set up by the African National Congress Party (ANC) in South Africa to defend themselves from the Inkatha militias. Another example is the Mahdi army, which is the armed wing of the Sadrist movement in Iraq.

CONCLUSION

Insurgencies are armed organizations that are strong enough to contest the state in some form of unconventional warfare. They usually aim to take hold of territory and are strong enough to do so. Although the popularity and legitimacy of insurgencies varies, they usually have to take into account how their strategy of violence affects their popularity and the population they control. Terrorism may be part of their grand strategy, but their ultimate aim of ruling or gaining more autonomy means that engaging in warfare and offering services are more critical components for achieving their aims.

Summary Points

- Insurgencies have often been mistaken for terrorist groups.
- Insurgencies are much more powerful than terrorist groups, but they are also more constrained.
- Insurgencies often use terrorism as a tactic, but their primary strategy is to engage in armed struggle and to win over the hearts and minds of a constituency.
- Insurgencies have had to change how they fund themselves due to losses in state sponsorship.
- Insurgencies that want to secede from their host state and have control over a defined territory become de facto states.

Key Questions

1   What are the primary strategies of insurgencies?
2   Why are insurgencies likely to receive so much support?
3   In what ways have insurgencies changed from the past?
4   In what ways do insurgencies pose a threat to states?
5   Why is the LTTE considered to be an insurgency? Do you agree with this? Why or why not?
6   Theory: What are the different ways in which realists, liberals and constructivists would assess the power of insurgencies?

FURTHER READING

Beckett, I.F.W. (2001) *Modern Insurgencies and Counter-insurgencies: Guerrillas and their Opponents since 1750* (Psychology Press). Overview of the history of insurgencies and the efforts to counter them; provides information on the roots of insurgency and guerrilla warfare.

Data on Armed Conflict: www.prio.org/Data/Armed-Conflict

Horowitz, D.L. (1985) *Ethnic Groups in Conflict* (University of California Press). Overview of historical ethnic insurgencies, explaining why these groups form and militarize and strategies for dealing with these groups.

Salehyan, I. (2009) *Rebels without Borders* (Cornell University Press). Explores the effects of insurgencies that are transnational, and how these conflict spillovers affect stability.

Salehyan, I. (2010) *Transnational Insurgencies and the Escalation of Regional Conflict: Lessons for Iraq and Afghanistan* (Strategic Studies Institute). More information on insurgencies with more detailed analyses of Afghanistan and Iraq.

Taras, R. and Ganguly, R. (2015) *Understanding Ethnic Conflict* (Routledge). Thorough overview of different types of insurgencies with a particular focus on ethnic insurgencies.

7

TERRORIST ORGANIZATIONS AND TERROR NETWORKS

Key Terms

- Affiliates
- Aum Shinrikyo
- Black Tigers and Tigresses
- Osama bin Laden
- Religious terrorism
- Terrorist networks

This chapter provides an overview of terrorist groups of the past and compares them to how they operate today. As the chapter will detail, tightly knit terror groups of the past are being overshadowed by terror networks that take advantage of advances in technology. We offer an in-depth look at al-Qaeda, the best-known terror network of the 21st century and compare it with the IS, a former terrorist group turned insurgency/de facto state.

DEFINITION

There is no widely accepted definition of what a terrorist group is. Labelling a group a terrorist group is a way of delegitimizing an opponent who may have legitimate grievances, which is why the term is so controversial. In spite of this, it is possible to identify several common characteristics of terrorist groups. We highlight four criteria that are important for distinguishing terrorist groups from other violent non-state actors: (1) Like insurgencies, terrorist groups seek political change through the use of violence; they are largely politically motivated. (2) In contrast to insurgencies, terrorist groups are weak actors militarily and often politically as well. They do not have the power or possibly the aim to hold territory. They often have to base themselves in other countries, hiding out in sleeper cells in order to operate. They have to remain clandestine and more underground (McCormick, 2003: 486). They are comparatively much weaker vis-à-vis the state. They target civilians because they do not have enough support and strength to use other methods. (3) Terrorist groups' main power derives from their ability to attract a large audience by engaging in shocking and unconventional violence (Lisanti, 2010). Their impact is more psychological than physical. (4) Though other groups may use terror as a tactic, for terrorist groups the use of indiscriminate violence against civilian targets is not only central to their strategy but is also their defining characteristic (Williams, 2012).

Based on these criteria, today there are fewer terrorist groups than there were in the past. Many terrorist groups have changed and have become more networked and multifunctional. They are often linked up with insurgencies and vice versa. Confusingly, there are more and more insurgencies that create terror wings, such as was the case with the LTTE and the Black Tigers and Tigress units. Because of this, the distinction between terrorist groups and other violent non-state actors has become increasingly blurred. It is also important to note that terrorists can gain strength and transition into full-blown insurgencies once they control territory, which is what happened in the case of AQI. This is common when an ethno-nationalist group represents a popular movement and becomes stronger. They also may be able to escalate into an insurgency, possibly due to support from an outside actor. It is also possible that as an insurgency loses strength and cannot hold territory, it goes underground and resorts to a terror strategy.

POLITICAL IDEOLOGY AND OBJECTIVES

Terrorist groups of the past often had very specific objectives and staged extraordinary attacks in order to exact concessions from the state or rich individuals and groups. New forms of terrorism have focused more on challenging the value systems of the liberal international system. They are less specific, more amorphous; they represent conflicts between value systems.

The goals of past terrorist groups were mostly ideologically (left- or right-wing) motivated or nationalistic. Previously, terrorism often challenged the pre-existing territorial boundaries and political hegemony of states. Many of these groups were ethno-nationalistic groups, and were often inspired by socialist ideals. Comparatively speaking, ethnic and sectarian groups usually have a concrete goal with many different potential compromise options. While many are fighting for complete independence, middle ground may be reached by attaining more autonomy. These groups are seeking to free themselves from oppression and assert their own political, social and economic rights, as well as their cultural identity. They may be turning to terrorism as a last resort after years of repression. However, left-wing groups that originated in Western countries were less specific in their aims. They were also concerned with rejecting the past and the existing order, but there was little ground for negotiation and compromise. Due to loss of state support, there has been a decline in groups motivated by socialism.

Religious terrorism has become more dominant in recent decades, and the role of religion has also changed. Religious terrorism has become more transnational in nature (Mickolus and Simmons, 2002). In the past, religious terrorism was often conflated with ethnic terrorism. The ultimate goal of religious groups was actually based on a secular identity, such as the role of Catholicism in the conflict in Northern Ireland. Religious terrorism is still being driven by complex national, cultural and historical contexts, but the national objective is unclear. New religious terrorism is more deadly because there is no need to adhere to international norms, or to compromise and show empathy. Much of the new religious terrorism also appears to be interested in violence for the sake of violence in reaction to a general loathing for the existing world order. From 1968 to 2005, the casualty rate (wounded and killed) for religious attacks, excluding al-Qaeda, was 38.1 compared to 9.82 for leftist groups, 2.41 for right-wing groups and 9.06 for nationalist separatist groups (Piazza, 2009). In addition to being violent, the political agenda is purposely inflexible and difficult to accommodate.

Terrorists tend to see the world in a polarized way, which makes it difficult to moderate their views to accommodate the masses (Alex, 2004: 214). The goal is not to persuade based on convincing others that the policies the group hopes to achieve are preferable, but to make it clear that refusing to submit to the demands of the group will have dire consequences (Goodwin, 2006: 2038). Terrorist groups have extreme ideologies and uncompromising demands (Hoffman, 2006). The uncompromising ideals of a terrorist group were clearly illustrated by Red Army Faction founder Ulrike Meinhof: 'Protest is when I say I don't like this. Resistance is when I put an end to what I don't like. Protest is when I say I refuse to go along with this anymore. Resistance is when I make sure everybody else stops going along too' (qtd by Davis et al., 2013: 171). The world is seen in a polarized way: us versus them. At the same time, the ideologies of terrorist groups can be confusing and incoherent.

STRATEGY AND TACTICS

Terrorist groups have always targeted civilians, but today maximum damage is used to attract more media attention for their ideology and grievances. Causing greater damage also appears to be attractive to potential recruits (Enders and Sandler, 2000). Each act of terror attempts to outdo the preceding one to try to find new ways to attract attention. Terrorist groups are no longer trying to exact a specific concession but are engaged in a war of attrition. More lethal technologies have facilitated this as has the erosion of taboos. Terrorist groups lack restraint, particularly since many of the perpetrators are amateurs who are loosely connected to a base. Some scholars have claimed that religiously motivated terrorists are more likely to conduct mass casualty attacks because unlike politically motivated terrorists, they are not constrained by the fear that excessive violence will offend, because they only care about their support group. Terrorist groups also escalate the levels of violence in efforts to outdo other political organizations, such as has been the case with Palestine Liberation Organization and the Popular Front for the Liberation of Palestine (PFLP). It is not just a means of attracting the attention of the state, but also a strategy to crowd out rivals.

Terrorist groups of the past did not aim to inflict such high casualties as they do today (Hoffman, 2006). For example, IRA violence was mostly aimed at the state rather than Protestant civilians. About 42.6% of those who died were civilians, though the death toll per terrorist attack was only 1.3 (O'Leary, 2005: 235).[1] Thus the goal was not to inflict huge numbers of casualties, which could have backfired, causing the group to lose all of its support or resulted in a crackdown that might have forced it to shut down completely, or at least complicate its functioning.

---

[1] The IRA's weapon of choice was car bombs (O'Leary, 2005: 234).

Terrorist groups today are much bloodier, not killing in the tens but in the hundreds. Terrorist groups of the past believed that recruitment and support levels would wane if they caused too much damage.

The disregard for death tolls has led to a rise in suicide bombing, the deadliest terrorist tactic. Because it is so cheap and effective, suicide bombing is commonly used by terror groups. There were 382 suicide attacks in 2013, 592 in 2014 and 452 in 2015. Suicide terrorism is characterized by the willingness of individuals to die in the course of destroying or attempting to annihilate enemy targets to further certain political or social objectives (Schweitzer and Schweitzer, 2002). Individuals purposely cause their own death by blowing themselves up along with a chosen target (Schweitzer and Schweitzer, 2002: 78). It is a tactic of the weak, designed to put the group on a more equal footing with the state, as dramatically and inexpensively as possible. It also is used to disrupt a peace process when the actor has not been included.

Hamas began to use suicide terrorism as a tactic on 6 April 1994 in efforts to derail the Oslo peace process taking place between the Palestine Liberation Organization (PLO) and Israel. After Hamas felt that it was losing support from many of its rivals, including secular nationalist Palestinian groups and religious groups such as Palestinian Islamic Jihad (PIJ), it established its military wing, the al-Qassam wing, in an effort to make a name for itself as a serious contender to represent the Palestinian cause.

Box 7.1   Suicide Terrorism

Suicide terrorism aims to capture the headlines, convince potential members that it has what it takes to win, and extend its base of active support. For this reason, suicide attacks are a form of strategic signalling. Suicide terrorism signals to a group's supporters that they are willing to challenge the state. Suicide attacks may also encourage the state to retaliate in ways that push the public to support the terrorist group, helping the group to mobilize.

Suicide attacks can be a source of unity between the terrorist group and its political constituents. The death of martyrs is presented as a collective loss, not only for the organization with which they were affiliated, but the community from which they volunteered. Opinion polls in 2002 reported that more than 70% of the Palestinian population living in Lebanon support suicide attacks against Israel (Winkates, 2006).

Most media attention has focused on the massive suicide campaigns from Palestinian groups, assuming that Palestinian suicide terrorism was largely religiously motivated. Not only is Palestinian suicide terrorism not always religiously influenced, but the concept of martyrdom is not just a religious construct. In fact, one of the most ruthless and bloody suicide campaigns carried out in history was perpetrated by the ethno-nationalist LTTE through their Black Tigers and Tigresses, which were formed in 1987. The LTTE pioneered new methods of how to use suicide bombings effectively and used them on a scale that had never been seen before, even managing to kill Indian Prime Minister Rajiv Gandhi. They also have the notorious claim to fame of inventing the suicide vest and belt.

Studies are not in agreement about the role of religion in driving suicide terrorism. Some scholars have noted that only about 60% of the suicide attacks carried out between 1993 and 2003 were conducted by religious organizations (Hoffman and McCormick, 2004).

(Continued)

(Continued)

Others claim that the number is as low as 40% (Pape, 2005). The secular LTTE was one of the groups that used suicide attacks the most (137 attacks), the Algerian armed Islamic group Laskar-e-Taiba not as much. This trend seems to be changing in that the target countries of suicide attacks are mostly countries with Islamic majorities: Iraq, Syria, Nigeria, Pakistan and Afghanistan. Iraq has been the most dangerous country for suicide attacks by some distance. Over 1,000 suicide bombings took place between 2003 and 2010 with 12,000 civilians killed during this time period (Burnham, 2011). In Afghanistan, the use of suicide terrorism is a more recent phenomenon. It was never part of the struggle against the Soviets in the 1980s. It was only used as a tactic after 2004 based on its success in Iraq.

There have been 36 countries and territories over the last 30 years that have experienced suicide terrorism. Though al-Qaeda does not utilize suicide bombing as often as it could, when it does use this tactic, it creates mass casualties. In fact, the most deadly attacks have been committed by al-Qaeda, followed by Hezbollah and Jemaah Islamiyah.

Though attacking civilians has been considered morally reprehensible, targeting them is increasingly used. Scholars explain this by pointing out that terrorism is a form of asymmetrical warfare available to a weak actor to attempt to level the playing field. They also may feel helpless. Using a terrorist tactic is a way to symbolically express power over forces that were viewed as oppressive (Alex, 2004: 212). The terrorist is trying to demonstrate the state's impotence and vulnerability. As noted in the statement of the Provisional Irish Republican Army (PIRA) to the Thatcher government after the Brighton bombing, 'Today we were unlucky, but remember we only have to be lucky once. You have to be lucky always' (BBC, 1984).

Militarily speaking, terrorist groups are relatively weak actors. Terrorist groups are not strong enough to compete against or target the state directly. Of course there are strong insurgencies that have resorted to terrorism, but this is usually because winning a conflict by purely conventional methods was not possible. Terrorism is a relatively cheap and easy method to kill in large numbers. Terrorists also want to exploit their enemies' heavy-handed response to an illegitimate act of violence.

The specific tactics of terrorists have changed over the years. In the 1970s, more than 100 plane hijackings took place. These types of acts were spectacular and planes were used in order to create hostage crises. Attacks on embassies have also been used as a tactic to hold hostages. Kidnapping high-profile victims was also popular, the most memorable being the 1979 kidnapping and murder of Italian Prime Minister Aldo Moro by the Red Brigades. In Colombia, M-19 seized the Supreme Court in November 1985, with the government refusing to yield to demands, resulting in the death of over 100 people including 11 court justices. Kidnappings were initially used to gain political concessions, but they became increasingly used as a way to fund violent groups. Hundreds of millions of dollars have been earned through kidnappings. There have been hundreds of kidnappings, though some groups have claimed that they no longer use kidnapping as a tactic. Bank robberies were used more initially, though not as often as other tactics. A notable bank robbery was the PLO and Christian Phalange attack on the major banks in Beirut that led to as much as $100 million being stolen – the biggest bank robbery of all time (Adams, 1986).

Typical tactics today include kidnapping, hostage-taking, sabotage, murder, suicide attacks, vehicle bombs and improvised explosive devices, as well as potentially the use of material for weapons of mass destruction (e.g. 'dirty bombs'). Potential targets range from military sites, police stations and official government buildings to companies, airports, restaurants, shopping malls and means of public transport. Terrorist groups have used a host of different weapons, including grenades, hand guns, rifles and different small types of bombs.

STRUCTURE AND RECRUITMENT

The structural changes to terror organizations constitute one of the biggest differences between old and new groups. Past terrorist groups were organized more hierarchically with charismatic leaders at the helm. Policies, tactics and ideas were generated directly from the leader. Though the leader would rely on subordinates to take on different responsibilities, the leaders were in charge of maintaining discipline and managing the activities of the organization. Leaders of terrorist organizations relied on creating intense loyalties among group members to prevent defection and dissent within the organization (Crenshaw, 2010). The command and control structure was clear.

Most nationalist and left-wing groups were more tightly organized. Left-wing and nationalist terror groups were often sponsored by another state, which necessitated a tight control from the state patron to the group's leader. A hierarchical model was important for giving assurance to state patrons of operational goals, since rogue actions by cells could undermine the state patron's objectives. However, with time more successful groups could not survive if they were too hierarchically organized. Many groups changed their structure in response to counter-terror measures (Gunaratna and Oreg, 2010: 1046).

Terrorist networks today no longer have a single leader or command cadre to manage the organization. Decision-making is decentralized, as are the operations. Modern terror networks are composed of different, largely autonomous cells. Independent behaviour is allowed among the cells, as is local initiative and autonomy. Cells are mostly self-organized and self-enrolling. The leaders of the cells usually have the most experience. The leader of each cell ensures that tasks are successfully carried out. All external contact is handled by the cell leader. Cell leaders are also responsible for maintaining ideological fervour (Dear, 2013; Fellman and Wright, 2014).

There may be multiple leaders within the network. The leaders of the hub of the network have challenging tasks. They have to ensure that the cells adhere to the same ideology and general goals, aims and beliefs. They also have to ensure that the nodes are regularly communicating. Hub leaders are dynamic individuals with extensive social networks (Sageman, 2004). They attract recruits and help guide and train them. They also help link up with different cells and help cells communicate with each other. The cells may receive needed material support and some ideological support.

Networked groups have less institutional presence – they may disappear at any time and can attach and detach. There is no affiliation with a specific territory. There is more flexibility in ideology, allowing the group to align with different regional conflicts or allies, though there is adherence to a grand vision. The use of networks elongates the lifespan of the terrorist group as it can survive the decapitation of the leader and other disruptions (Comas et al., 2015; Sageman, 2004).

The biggest problem for decentralized groups is informational asymmetry, but this has been largely overcome with the help of technological advances (Johnston, 2008). Today's groups have been able to exploit improvements in technology and communication. Communication technologies have enabled new terrorists to maintain links between cells more easily. Satellite and mobile phones and the Internet are used to exchange information and give orders. Communication and planning is less intense than in hierarchical structures, making it harder for law enforcement to dismantle these groups. Communication also moves very freely (Matusitz, 2013; Nacos, 2016).

In the most extreme forms, there are very loose linkages and little supervision and control over the nodes. There are few if any formal commitments (Mishal and Rosenthal, 2005). Amateurs may want to join networks, and may receive no training or logistical support, learning from publications on the Internet. These groups are especially difficult to identify and counteract since they have no infrastructure; thus there is little to target (Nacos, 2016).

For example, those responsible for the Madrid bombings in 2004 were not directly linked with al-Qaeda, though they were inspired by it. The group responsible was known as the Moroccan Islamic Combat Group, which consisted of a local group of immigrants that were inspired by al-Qaeda's focus on the worldwide battle between Islam and the 'new world order'. However, this group was not actively embedded in the network, and any damage to the cell – all members died or were arrested – had no impact on al-Qaeda.

RECRUITMENT

In the past, recruitment for many terror organizations was top-down. Groups would target particular individuals who might be vulnerable or sympathetic to their cause. Terror groups were based on an extreme ideology. Because of this, they appealed to few, and membership was small. Membership was exclusive and recruits were thoroughly vetted. For many left-wing groups, the use of pretentious language meant that many recruits were the children from affluent homes. They were mostly recruited from extremist political groups at universities. For many revolutionary terrorist groups, being part of a secret society was an integral part of the appeal.

Nationalist movements focused on recruiting co-national or co-religion persons. In contrast to ideological groups, the recruits were often not from wealthy families, but individuals who felt disenfranchised. The IRA recruits were mostly young males of Catholic origin, coming from working class, lower middle class or small farmers. Few recruits were prosperous professionals and most recruits came from families that had supported the IRA in the past (O'Leary, 2005: 230).

Aum Shinrikyo focused on recruiting those who were both skilled and alienated. The group recruited those who could be useful for the organization's drive to attain weapons of mass destruction but also those who were alienated from the current system, such as dropouts and lonely or needy individuals. Once one became a member of Aum Shinrikyo, it was very hard to leave. The cult used many bizarre methods to ensure no one escaped, such as drugs, sleep deprivation, electric shocks and poor diet. Once members joined, they were forced to cede their identities completely, which helped reinforce group norms and prevented anyone from challenging the authority of the leader (Cameron, 1999: 284).

Today recruitment is largely bottom-up. Local cells are formed around friendship and kinship ties, promoted by local religious leaders and further radicalized by propaganda on the Internet. In the case of Islamic terrorism, recruiters hold informal gatherings in private homes, mosques, cultural centres, religious summer camps and schools. Potential candidates have one-on-one conversations where their motivations and qualifications were assessed. Recruits are often very young. For example, the Jemaah Islamiyah in Indonesia has a network of over 50 Islamic boarding schools that are sympathetic to its goals, which it recruits from.

Al-Qaeda has effectively used the Internet to promote local home-grown jihadi operations. Al-Qaeda has recruited by disseminating textual propaganda and videos, providing training on how to hack computer networks, and publishing online magazines like the *Voice of Jihad* (Sawt al-Jihad) (Rudner, 2013: 968). Al-Qaeda assigns handlers to oversee recruits and enforce discipline to prevent penetration by authorities. Al-Qaeda prefers to recruit those who can pass through surveillance and border controls easily. Ideally, recruits know how to blend in with their host communities and carry multiple passports and documents, as well as professional credentials.

FUNDING AND SUPPORT

FUNDING

Terror groups usually rely on clandestine support for their organizations, but more and more they have been involved in organized crime. Terror groups today are more criminalized and less dependent on state sponsors; trafficking drugs is their number one source of funding (Richmond, 2003: 291). In addition to the drug trade, they are engaged in siphoning off raw materials and smuggling weapons. To deal with these earnings, they have legitimate businesses that they use to launder the money they earn from illicit activities. Terrorist groups also skim money from NGOs and charities. Finally, they earn large sums of money through membership dues and overseas donations. Much of the IRA's £10 million came from theft and racketeering, but as much as 12.7% of all revenues came from overseas donations (O'Leary, 2005: 230).

Al-Qaeda has transnational fundraising abilities through the use of informal networks. In the early 1990s, bin Laden founded a network of business enterprises in Sudan from small farms and fishing operations to multinational investment and construction companies (Mannes, 2003: 34). When these transfers were disrupted in the US and Europe, al-Qaeda was able to rely on under-regulated financial systems in the Arab world (Basile, 2004). Al-Qaeda is able to receive money through a number of untraceable means, such as front corporations, secret bank accounts, and legitimate charities. Some al-Qaeda cells are also involved in drug trafficking in Afghanistan and the illegal diamond trade in Africa.

Even religious groups have resorted to criminal activities to fund their operations. The Armed Islamic Group of Algeria (al-Jama'ah al-Islamiyah al-Musallaha; GIA) has always survived by smuggling. Al-Qaeda in the Islamic Maghreb (AQIM), has acquired many of the smuggling networks once controlled by the weakened GIA.[2] AQIM also makes money by taxing drug traffickers (Shelley, 2014: 237). It is not

---

[2]AQIM was previously known as the Salafist Group for Preaching and Combat.

entirely clear whether AQIM has taken on a direct role in drug trafficking, but it has worked with traffickers and offered them protection (Pham, 2011). There are also other al-Qaeda cells that are involved in drug trafficking in Afghanistan and the illegal diamond trade in Africa. Some terrorist groups actually produce the drugs themselves. Aum Shinrikyo, which was responsible for sarin gas attacks in Tokyo in 1995, was the most significant producer and distributor of methamphetamines in Japan.

The costs of maintaining a terror cell are much lower than maintaining an insurgency. Insurgencies must have access to weapons and military training in order to hold territory. Simply maintaining a small cell may not be financially difficult. A suicide bombing planned by one cell would not need a steady flow of income because the group would cease after the attack. Hamas and Hezbollah have claimed that an act of terror costs from $500 to $3,500. The USS Cole bombing in 2000 cost al-Qaeda less than $5,000 (Hutchinson and O'Malley, 2007). The Madrid train bombings, which killed 191 people and caused over 2,000 injuries, cost approximately $10,000 (Sandler and Enders, 2004). Sporadic crime requires few specialized skills and little division of labour. Moreover, cells that are home-grown avoid the costs of circumventing international and national law enforcement.

SUPPORT

Terrorist groups of the past were more like tiny gangs of bandits than serious political movements. Terrorist groups usually lack popular support for their struggle, which is why they resort to non-conventional tactics.

Terrorist organizations usually receive more public support when they avoid a strategy of targeting too many civilians. For terrorist groups whose supporters are just as 'radical' as the terrorists themselves, the organization is less constrained in terms of killing civilians in indiscriminate ways, such as in the case of Palestinian groups. Civilians account for 70% of victims in Palestinian terrorist attacks, as opposed to around 40% for the Basque ETA and the IRA. As for public opinion, in Palestine, 90% of respondents in the West Bank and the Gaza Strip approve of armed attacks against soldiers and settlers in the occupied territories, and more than 50% support the killing of civilians inside Israel (Sánchez-Cuenca and De la Calle, 2009: 303). When nationalist groups have a collective sense of legitimate grievance, the citizens can be as 'radical' as the activists. Groups that act on behalf of these groups will be less constrained in how many civilians are killed and how indiscriminate the attacks are.

There are many foreign governments that have chosen to support terrorist groups, though in contrast to most insurgencies, this takes place more clandestinely. Libya has made supporting terrorist groups a centrepiece of its foreign policy. It has supported the IRA and ETA along with the PFLP. Syria supported the Japanese Red Army. States can offer numerous sources of support. Iraq has offered a sanctuary in the past to anti-Iranian and anti-Turkish groups (Byman, 2005: 3). Libya's support of the IRA enabled huge arms shipments that helped the organization sustain a prolonged fight against the UK. When states work with terrorist groups, some become more deadly and potent while others are restrained. At times too much state support can cause the group to lose contact with its constituency. States may decide to host terrorist groups, provide them with weapons, training and funding.

POWER AND IMPACT ON THE STATE AND SOCIETY

The primary impact of terrorist groups on the state and society is psychological. They aim to inflict fear and terror. They want to affect people's freedoms. They are the weakest of all of the violent non-state actors, but they attract the most media attention. The economic costs of terrorism are much lower than other forms of violence, with the losses from criminal violence incurring 32 times greater losses. In spite of this, the economic costs of terrorism continue to increase, having risen by 61% in 2014, reaching a total of $52.9 billion, a ten-fold increase since 2000 (Global Terrorism Database, 2015).

Though there have been increasing economic costs, terrorist groups lack the power to engage in armed conflict or challenge the state head-on and must engage in subversive tactics. In comparison, insurgencies possess military power to challenge the target directly. Unlike insurgencies, terrorist groups do not control any territory. They also do not have the ability to administer and rule (de la Calle and Sánchez-Cuenca, 2012). Terror groups were usually not territorial and the individuals never wore uniforms like an army. Terror groups usually do not have recognized war zones; operations can be carried out anywhere. They may be able to establish a safe haven, but this is distinct from controlling territory. In the former, the terrorist group is given some free rein to exist because the state is either looking the other way or deliberately providing a home base. The safe haven is due to state willingness or state carelessness – not because the terrorist group has overpowered the host state. Though some terrorist groups may have territorial ambitions to create their own state, they lack the capabilities to do so (Schneckener, 2006).

Once terrorist groups begin controlling and administering territory, they can be classified as insurgencies. Groups that have control over territory operate differently than groups that have no control over territory (Schneckener, 2006). Control of autonomous territory allows the group to establish an extensive military infrastructure, training bases, offices and more. It also means that they can bring volunteers from around the world to train there. On the other hand, controlling territory makes it more vulnerable to attacks from the state (Schneckener, 2006). It is also much more expensive.

The actual death toll caused by terrorist groups is much lower than all of the other violent groups. They are simply not powerful enough to inflict much damage. Even so, terrorist groups have become more deadly. In 2014 there was an 80% increase in terrorist activity, with the death toll rising from 18,111 in 2013 to 32,685 in 2014. The total number of people who have died from a terrorist attack has increased nine-fold since 2000 (Global Terrorism Index, n.d.).

As the following section illustrates, one of the most deadly groups is al-Qaeda. From 1998 to 2008, al-Qaeda and its affiliates launched 84 terrorist attacks, with 16 mass assaults that resulted in 4,299 deaths and 6,300 injuries in Australia, central Asia, China, Europe, the Middle East, North Africa, North America, Russia, and South and Southeast Asia. Between 5 January 2002 and 25 August 2013, there were 307 incidents of terrorism perpetrated by al-Qaeda or its affiliates (Global Terrorism Database, 2015).[3]

---

[3]This does not include the work of its associates such as Abu Hafs al-Masri Brigades, the group responsible for the 2004 attacks on the public transport system in Madrid that killed 191 people.

AL-QAEDA, TERRORIST UMBRELLA ORGANIZATION

Al-Qaeda is a global network that provides training, financing and technical expertise for Islamic terrorists all over the world. Al-Qaeda has funded insurgencies and terror cells and is involved in organized crime. Al-Qaeda is not just nationally based; it has a global presence. It is impossible to fully understand the structure and capacity of al-Qaeda because it is constantly changing. It is best described as a global terror network.

IDEOLOGY AND OBJECTIVES

Unlike many terrorist organizations, al-Qaeda's ideology has often been called amorphous, though its origins are extremist, influenced by Qutubbism and Salifism. Its ideology has gained the support of different forms of Sunni Islam. In spite of its purported Islamic origins, al-Qaeda has been critiqued for mostly killing and targeting Muslims. In fact, despite Islamic terror groups' claims to support Muslims, it is the Muslim countries that suffer the most attacks and Muslim citizens who suffer the most, constituting over 80% of the casualties, though the number could be much higher (Global Research, 2016).

ORIGINS

Al-Qaeda was established initially to serve as an auxiliary organization that helped assist volunteers coming to Afghanistan to fight against the Soviets. It provided the infrastructure to assist with tracking soldiers and sending in troops and aid (Mishal and Rosenthal, 2005: 282). Through its leader Saudi-born Osama bin Laden, it started to forge alliances with militant groups all over Egypt, Pakistan, Algeria and Tunisia. It engaged in many different types of operations such as deploying fighters to Chechnya and Tajikistan. It also established satellite offices in many different countries. It operated 'horizontally' with about 24 different constituent terror organizations.

Originally, al-Qaeda focused on internal jihad or overthrowing authoritarian regimes in the Middle East. In the late 1990s, it shifted its strategy to external jihad in an attempt to draw in the United States. Several attacks on US targets would ensue with the 1998 bombings of the US embassies in Kenya and Tanzania, which killed 225 and injured 5,000 (most of whom were local), followed by the 2000 attack on the USS Cole in Yemen, which killed 17 marines. None of these attacks helped to attract the mass following that the organization was hoping for.

By late 1996, after being forced to leave Sudan, bin Laden was able to create, with the help of the Taliban in Afghanistan, a headquarters to train fighters. Over 70,000 recruits travelled to Afghanistan when the Taliban was in power to take part in military training camps run by al-Qaeda. While based there, al-Qaeda developed several parallel structures that functioned like militias. Brigade 055 was a guerrilla army with an elite force of about 2,000 men who were trained to fight alongside the Taliban. Because it had a massive base to work with, it could use the territory to recruit, train and house fighters, developing the capacity of an insurgency.

STRUCTURE AND ORGANIZATION

At this point, the base of al-Qaeda's organization was mostly hierarchical. Each unit was subordinated into a pyramid structure into the organization's leadership. Bin Laden was at the top, with a consultative or command council below, directing four key committees (military, finance, Islamic study and media), whose members were hand-picked by senior leadership (Gunaratna and Oreg, 2010: 1054). By mid-2001, the group merged with Egyptian Islamic Jihad, which was led by Ayman al-Zawahiri (al-Qaeda's current leader and former deputy leader). An additional five people were added to the core membership, including Mohammed Atef, who served as the military chief. The core members helped set general policies and approve large-scale attacks, constantly consulting the leader (Gunaratna and Oreg, 2010: 1056). The military committee was especially important in the planning of 9/11. The military committee conducted surveillance, gathered intelligence and helped with military training, but it was bin Laden who also played a hands-on role in planning the attacks. He hand-picked operatives and ultimately rejected recommendations to abort the attacks (Dishman, 2005).

Meanwhile, al-Qaeda remained well networked with other like-minded groups, providing training and expertise. It acted like a large charity organization for terrorist projects that were affiliated with it. Al-Qaeda worked to establish a connection with indigenous Islamic terrorist groups. It also penetrated Islamic NGOs so that the organization was enmeshed with Muslim communities worldwide. In some cases, al-Qaeda was very hands-off – just giving some guidance but encouraging the group to raise its own funds.

UMBRELLA ORGANIZATION

Al-Qaeda was forced to decentralize after the war on terror began in 2001. It lost 70% of its leadership and lost its safe haven in Afghanistan. In the words of a high-ranking British intelligence official, 'Al-Qaeda has split like a piece of mercury into different groups in different countries' (Rudner, 2013: 957). The international financial crackdown also affected its finances. Communication between the centralized command and its operatives was disrupted, which has meant that the central staff plays a less direct role in planning attacks. Al-Qaeda is now a system of systems (Rudner, 2013: 957). Operational commanders and cell leaders exert more influence, though cells should be less able to carry out spectacular attacks (Dishman, 2005). Cell leaders are often veterans from Afghanistan who had received advanced training on how to establish and lead terror cells of 2–15 members. They were encouraged to show initiative in their operations. A promising operation might receive some funding and support and technical assistance.

Today there is no agreement on the exact structure of al-Qaeda. Some scholars claim that al-Qaeda no longer exists as an organizational entity – that it is more of an ideology without an organization (Sageman, 2004). Though there were many cells fuelled by its ideology, it lacks a central authority. Cohesion was mostly achieved through members' personal relationships and exchanges. The main threat to al-Qaeda was bottom-up, not top-down. Local cells and networks were carrying out their attacks with little coordination from the top, though the top still provided a general agenda to help maintain some appearance of unity. Al-Qaeda is now decentralized and de-territorialized.

Others, however, claim that al-Qaeda has regrouped in the tribal areas of Pakistan, Iraq and Syria. It was argued that every major terrorist attack against the US, the UK and most European countries emanated from al-Qaeda or from allies acting on its behalf. Once the war in Iraq started, al-Qaeda had another centralized base to work with, offering logistical support for the Sunni insurgency in Iraq. Most fighters that were entering and exiting Iraq went through al-Qaeda; many were Syrian jihadis (Hoffman, 2013: 637).

The reality may be, however, that al-Qaeda has both top-down and bottom-up planning capabilities. There have been many plots that were generated by independent, home-grown groups in Europe. These local cells of home-grown terrorists have formed loose associations with al-Qaeda and have orchestrated attacks from the bottom up.

In addition to being associated with and inspiring many groups around the globe, al-Qaeda comprises affiliates or local branches such as AQIM and al-Qaeda in the Arabian Peninsula (AQAP). Although they have a relationship with al-Qaeda, they have their own infrastructure, base of operations and chains of command. A group can partner with al-Qaeda and not abandon its own agenda. The affiliates are usually required to seek approval before conducting attacks outside their assigned regions, and when attacks are conducted outside their region, the group must adhere to parameters designated by al-Qaeda. Franchises must also seek approval before assisting other groups with external operations.

Al-Qaeda had grandiose vision, pulling off the most deadly terrorist attack in history, but today it is comparatively much weaker, with al-Qaeda central consisting of fewer than 200 people (Mueller and Stewart, 2016). Today we focus more attention on the groups that have spun off from al-Qaeda than al-Qaeda itself.

THE EMERGENCE OF AL-QAEDA IN IRAQ (AQI) AND THE ISLAMIC STATE

One of the most powerful affiliates to emerge that has now taken a life of its own is AQI, which has since mutated into the IS. Because the IS holds territory and even administers over territory, it is not a terrorist group but an insurgency/de facto state (Cronin, 2015). AQI was originally founded in 1999 under the leadership of Jordanian Abu Musab al Zarqawi whose aim was to topple the Jordanian monarchy, build an Islamic state and purge the world of Muslims who were not staunch believers. Initially called Jama'at al-Tawhid wal-Jihad, the group changed its name to al-Qaeda in Iraq (AQI) in 2004 when it began to participate in the Iraqi insurgency. Zarqawi at this time pledged allegiance to bin Laden in return for assistance with funding and forging contacts. Zarqawi had multiple contacts in senior leadership positions in Afghanistan. Zarqawi convinced the Salafist Group for Preaching and Combat (GSPC) to merge with central al-Qaeda. The group that emerged has been one of the most brutal and effective insurgent groups, controlling the resources and flows of foreign fighters into Iraq.

From the beginning, the alliance between Zarqawi and bin Laden was fraught with tensions. Zarqawi had little respect for bin Laden because he believed that legitimacy was derived from the battlefield, not ruling from behind the scenes.

In turn, al-Qaeda was concerned with Zarqawi's excesses, over-the-top violence such as beheadings, and campaigns against both Shiites and Sunnis. For example, when AQI bombed three hotels in Amman, Jordan, in 2005, it was strongly rebuked by al-Qaeda. Zawahiri warned Zarqawi that his group's actions would alienate moderate Sunnis.

In June 2006 Zarqawi was killed and the group changed its name in October to the Islamic State of Iraq (ISI). By 2013 it changed its name again to the Islamic State of Iraq and the Levant (ISIL), and in June 2014 it officially declared a caliphate in Iraq and Syria and changed its name to the Islamic State (IS). From August 2011, the IS was led by Abu Bakr al'Baghdadi. His brash actions deepened the rift between the IS and al-Qaeda. The official split of the two organizations came in February 2014.

Though the IS originated from al-Qaeda, the two groups are distinct in many ways. The first major difference is the leadership. Al-Qaeda's leadership has come from the upper middle classes and is much better educated than the IS's. Members from al-Qaeda have come from all over the world, but have been mostly recruited from 'Afghan Arabs', or men from Arab countries who went to Afghanistan to fight against the Soviet Union. Some of al-Qaeda's top leaders are Egyptian. In contrast, the IS is primarily comprised of ex-Saddam Hussein militants, Syrians as well as some other Salafist jihadists. The core comes from Saddam Hussein's Republican Guard and intelligence units. The IS has three deputy leaders, who are ethnic Turkmen, but the leadership is dominated by Iraqis.

Al-Qaeda still remains more clandestine than the IS; it is more of an umbrella organization to help support other terrorist cells (Farrell, 2010). Al-Qaeda does not have a clear base of operation, though it is probably somewhere in Pakistan. Al-Qaeda has been mostly effective in supporting affiliates in Iraq, Yemen and Nigeria. The IS's base today is clearly Mosul (where it may have some genuine support due to high levels of dissatisfaction with the Iraqi government), in Iraq, though it also has a base in Raqqa in Syria. Once the IS took over Mosul in June 2014, the organization became a state and was no longer a shadowy terrorist group.

The IS also differs from al-Qaeda because it has a semi-conventional military, with units divided into brigades, regiments and platoons (Warren, 2015). It has access to heavy weaponry, confiscated from the US military after winning battles in Iraq. As such, the IS has had more military victories. The head of security and intelligence for the Kurdistan Regional Government (KRG) in northern Iraq, Masrour Barzani, claimed that it is their knowledge of conventional war that makes them so powerful. He added, 'They know how to plan, how to attack, how to defend....Otherwise they'd be no more than a terrorist organizations' (Muir, BBC, 2016). Though the strength of the IS's military has been disputed more recently (see Chapter 12), it has been more powerful than the Iraqi military. When the IS does engage in acts of terrorism, they are more brazen and not as thoughtfully planned. The IS is more willing to take credit for any act of brutality against the West regardless of what the backlash might be, whereas al-Qaeda appears to be more concerned with not alienating Muslims.

As the name denotes, the IS has set up a state that is highly structured. There are councils that work on finance, military matters, security and intelligence, foreign fighters' assistance, media and legal matters. Unlike al-Qaeda, it aims to establish a caliphate and a single transnational Islamic state based on Sharia law. A Shura council is set up to ensure that all decisions comply with the group's interpretation of Sharia (Stern and Berger, 2015).

After capturing territory, the IS was able to generate massive revenues through the sale of oil (see Chapter 2). This in turn, has enabled the group to provide some meagre administrative services such as welfare, healthcare, food kitchens, road maintainance, electricity and water (Napoleoni, 2014). It also keeps annual reports and tracking statistics of the cities that it has taken over. But much of its emphasis is on security and maintaining intelligence on all of its residents. Checkpoints were erected and individuals are constantly checked against databases. Moral police cruised around IS captured territory trying to find individuals violating rules of conduct, such as playing music, having satellite TV, and not covering up, etc. (Muir, BBC, 2016). In contrast, al-Qaeda has not tried to control much territory on its own. Most of its funding allegedly comes from private donations and ransoms, which it uses to offer logistical support to terror cells and affiliates.

Because the IS has a bureaucracy, it has had to develop a payroll system with clearly defined salaries. Though the pay scale is egalitarian, fighters are not necessarily paid competitive wages compared to what the average illiterate Iraqi male would earn. Oddly, pay was lower for riskier jobs, illustrating the importance of martyrdom for the organization in its recruitment. Members seem to be driven by the need to have value in their lives more than monetary compensation (Shapiro and Jung, 2014).

Although few thought any group could be more deadly than al-Qaeda, the IS has proven to be more brutal and violent. Between 2002 and 2015, the IS, its affiliates and its precursor organization, AQI, were responsible for the death of 33,000 people by terrorist attacks. In that period, it was responsible for 26% of all terrorist attack deaths and for 24% of all kidnapping victims (Global Terrorism Database, 2015). In total, some 70 terrorist attacks have been committed by or on behalf of the IS in 20 countries, with over 1,200 victims. The group has stepped up suicide bombings due to recent pressures on its front lines. Since the height of its power in 2014, the IS has lost as much as 20% of the territory it held in Syria and 40% of the territory it held in Iraq. According to the US, air strikes have killed about 20,000–25,000 IS combatants (BBC, 2016).

The IS has had no qualms about using child soldiers. According to its propaganda, in 2014 it used 89 boys, some as young as eight. Researchers also found that in 2015, 39% of boy child soldiers were killed in suicide car bombings and 33% were killed in combat (Longman, 2016). As the following chapter will explain, many terrorist groups and insurgencies are now comporting themselves like warlords.

CONCLUSION

Terrorist groups have become more networked and more resilient. Many terrorist groups no longer resemble small tightly knit organizations filled with zealots. Instead, many terrorist groups today consist of a loose conglomeration of cells, which are engaged in organized crime. Terrorist groups today and the networks they are a part of are more lethal and violent than past terrorist groups; there are fewer classical terrorist groups engaged in low-casualty, urban guerrilla warfare campaigns. Though they are increasingly linked with various different types of groups, they are actually the weakest of all violent non-state actors; in spite of the media attention and fear they generate, terrorist groups are the least deadly.

Summary Points

- Terrorism and insurgencies have often been conflated, but terrorist groups are not as powerful and they do not last as long.
- Terrorist groups of the past are structurally different than terror networks today.
- Terrorist groups have a massive psychological impact but a minimal impact to our overall security.
- Suicide terrorism has been both secular and religiously motivated.
- Al-Qaeda was an insurgency, but today it is a terror umbrella organization.
- Most suicide terrorism was secular.

Key Questions

1 What are the key factors that differentiate a terrorist group from an insurgency?
2 How have terrorist groups changed over time?
3 Why are terrorist groups so much more resilient than in the past?
4 Do terrorist groups have a major impact on the state and society? What are the ways in which this is the case?
5 In what ways does al-Qaeda constitute an umbrella organization more than a traditional terrorist group? Why is the IS not a terrorist organization?
6 Theory: Is terrorism a rational strategy for violent groups? According to realists, should states respond to terrorism? Do terror groups threaten security according to realists?

FURTHER READING

Enders, W. and Sandler, T. (2011) *The Political Economy of Terrorism* (Cambridge University Press). Provides both a qualitative and quantitative investigation of terrorism, examining its economic effects and economic reasons that may drive terrorism.

Hoffman, B. (2006) *Inside Terrorism* (Columbia University Press). An essential book, focusing on what drives terrorism, the interaction between terrorist groups and the media, and the tactics, targets and technologies used by terrorist groups.

Martin, G. (2015) *Understanding Terrorism: Challenges, Perspectives, and Issues* (SAGE). A useful starting point for understanding terrorism.

Pape, R. (2005) *Dying to Win: the Strategic Logic of Suicide Terrorism* (Random House). Presents a rational choice approach for understanding why there has been an increase in suicide terrorism, showcasing its utility as a tactic.

Rapoport, D.C. (ed.) (2013) *Inside Terrorist Organizations* (Routledge). Edited volume on the structure of terrorist organizations and their motivations to use violence.

Sageman, M. (2004) *Understanding Terror Networks* (University of Pennsylvania Press). Excellent overview of the new types of terror organizations, how they are structured, function and recruit.

8

WARLORDS AND MARAUDERS

Key Terms

- Charles Taylor
- Child soldiers
- Kalashnikov culture
- National Patriotic Front of Liberia (NPFL)
- Neo-warlord
- Resource wars
- Revolutionary United Front (RUF)
- Sobels
- Warlord militia

In a departure from the previous chapters which have focused on organizations with largely political goals, this and subsequent chapters focus on organizations with primarily economic goals. Chapter 8 introduces the concept of warlords and rebel marauders, which have become notable for their role in delegitimizing and weakening the state in countries like Afghanistan, Tajikistan, Somalia, Liberia and Sierra Leone. Though these groups aim to control territory and people, their motivations are primarily economic rather than political.

DEFINITION

Warlords are leaders of armed groups that control local territory. They are motivated by greed – they aim to acquire territory, money and resources through the use and threat of violence, while keeping a weak central authority at bay (Duffield, 1998: 81). Warlords emerge in collapsing and collapsed states and where the security institutions, in particular, are weak or non-existent. Scholars have argued that when the state's power is fragmented, localized power may emerge (Freeman, 2015; Hills, 1997: 35). Sometimes they originate in the military, with a faction leader defecting and setting up an alternative power base (Freeman, 2015).

After the security institutions have fallen apart, warlords aim to maximize their profits from state disorder. In contrast to organized criminal groups, warlords have an interest in sustaining state collapse. While organized criminal groups need some semblance of stability and regulations in order to have an environment where high profit margins are likely, warlords prefer total chaos. The criminal, in contrast, depends on the stability of the state for his commercial gains.

Warlords also emerge in post-conflict zones, where power, law and civil order have disappeared (Freeman, 2015; Hills, 1997: 35). Max Weber noted that warlords are permanent figures in a chronic state of conflict. The warlord often has some form of professional or paramilitary experience, but he is much more selfish than heroic. The warlord can take advantage of war or post-war economies by exploiting local resources and the local population through looting or levying taxes.

Warlords appear to provide security, but they also manufacture insecurity to justify their existence. Warlords and their militias need insecurity in order to flourish. Those living in war zones fear constant attacks from armed looters. As physical security decreases and society breaks down, individuals need local protection in order to survive. This makes them more dependent on local warlords (Hills, 1997). Thus physical force provides limited stability instead of moral or legitimate authority.

Warlords are distinct from insurgents – insurgents draw support from the population, whereas warlords prey on the population and recruit from the local community (Mackinlay, 2000: 56). The warlord does not depend on any popular support; the only service they provide, if any, is security. Waging military campaigns may be necessary to maintain some legitimacy, but overall they are not committed to a higher cause. They often target the population rather than protect it from harm.

Insurgents and warlords do have in common the possession of an armed fighting force.[1] Though warlords' militias are not well trained or disciplined, warlord militias constitute a fighting force with access to arms. An organized criminal group usually does not have an armed militia, though they may have access to guns for hire. Even the most simple and barbaric warlord still institutes some form of training and indoctrination for the fighters. New fighters in the Lord Resistance Army in Uganda were given a spiritual education and indoctrinated into the organization with formal processes such as spreading shea butter on them.

Warlords seek control over resources and thus some control over territory where resources exist. They want political power over a territory in order to exploit resources. In Sierra Leone, warlords were involved in the diamond trade, while in Burma and Afghanistan, warlords were involved in the opium economies. Warlords make revenues from exploiting resources and in setting up a quasi-taxation regime, extracting capital from business activities of their subjects. They target minerals, drug producers, drug traffickers and other smugglers. Commercial insurgencies are possible in countries that have something to loot such as drugs, mineral deposits, timber or rubber. Warlords in Tajikistan have taken control over key resources; an example is the warlord Ibodullo Boimatov, who once controlled the country's only aluminium smelter. Makhmud Khudayberdiev also ruled over the agricultural area of Kurgan-Tubbe as an independent city state.

Warlords are not entrepreneurial. Their economic objectives drive them to avoid acquiring any kind of fixed economic asset. They rarely invest in the territory

---

[1]When warlords offer some sort of pseudo-political agenda, they control rebel groups. When they have no pretence of a political agenda, their fighting force is just referred to as a warlord militia.

under their control because it entails great risk to their power. They are governed by their access to resources which generates hard currency, which they use to purchase arms. A warlord's power is often dependent on his ability to govern the war economy (Le Billon, 2001).

MARAUDING REBELS

Marauding rebels are groups of ad hoc fighting units, usually controlled by warlords, factional demagogues and political entrepreneurs. They are demobilized or scattered fighters who often engage in looting, pillaging and terrorizing defenceless civilians. They have been described by scholars as violent thugs who use their access to weapons to loot (Azam, 2006). They plunder property and threaten security and do not aim to offer anything to citizens. They have very little loyalty to the state; they are loyal only to the leader who directs them, yet they are not just a self-defence militia to protect the warlord. They see themselves as being part of a political-military organization, though their main activity is looting. In Iraq, the Fadhila party, the Islamic Supreme Council of Iraq (SIIC) Badr organization and the Mahdi army are mostly fighting for the control of oil both for legal exports and smuggling. The Fadhila party used to control the Iraq oil ministry until 2006 but is challenged by other militias. These groups behave like criminal gangs, though armed clashes have taken place (Williams, 2009).

Scholars have noted that it is the prevalence of resources that helps explain why rebel groups form instead of insurgencies. The latter consists of an organization that typically depends on the local population for support. Therefore, it will employ a 'stationary bandit' approach, and attract high-commitment recruits who believe in the organization's ideology and will employ violence selectively. Rebel groups have access to natural resources, making them more likely to attract low-commitment recruits who are primarily interested in profit and who have little regard for the lives or livelihoods of civilians, or in establishing a stable system of long-term tax collection (Weinstein, 2005).

Like warlords, marauding rebels also emerge during and after conflicts have taken place or after the security institutions of a state have completely disintegrated. They benefit from chaotic situations and where the government has lost control over specific areas. The M-23 Movement, for instance, has taken control over Goma in the Democratic Republic of the Congo because government forces all but disappeared and UN soldiers were unable to offer much resistance. The movement forced Congolese to abandon their homes to escape the brutal attacks (Vinci, 2007). Marauding rebels also emerge after a more organized and recognized force has broken up. They may consist of a particular ethnic group or clan, but are often composed of young men, even teenagers and children. Though there are some skilled unconventional fighters, most are not well trained.

These forces are irregular and the individuals involved may engage in dual activities. Some may have actual day jobs, possibly even working for the regular military. In the case of Sierra Leone, some individuals were soldiers by day and rebels by night. There were 30–50 groups of 50–80 fighters each that were referred to as 'sobels'. Sobels consisted of members of underfunded armies who would engage in criminal activities such as looting, robbery and protection. In Somalia, access to weapons for young unemployed fighters granted many of them new-found power. Their main purpose became setting up roadblocks and looting. As a result, these fighters were referred to as 'Moorjans' (looters) (Marchal, 2007).

POLITICAL IDEOLOGY AND OBJECTIVES

Warlords do not have political motivations, though they sometimes may pretend to. Their main motivation is self-enrichment, not state-building or any sort of collective interest. Jean-Germain Gros writes that they have the 'emotional immaturity of teenage fighters' (Gros, 1996: 459). Other scholars concur that warlords are one-dimensional and mostly engage in indiscriminate violence against the population under their control (Lezhnev, 2006). They are devoid of any ideology and, unlike leaders of insurgencies, they do not have to constantly reinforce some sort of ideology.

Because the warlord controls some territory, they sometimes provide some governance structures, but they do not have anything that even comes close to resembling a bureaucracy. The warlord organization has no distinction between the political and military organizations. The militia intervenes in all aspects of political life and the civilian/military balance is dysfunctional (Rich, 1999: 6).

Warlords usually do not provide any sort of public good or service, and if they do, the recipients are carefully chosen. The most they usually offer as a public good are distributions of cash, gifts and arms to their supporters. Any goods that the warlord provides only cement their clientelistic networks (Giustozzi, 2004). In the rare cases in which a warlord has provided some public goods, the net benefits are still low. One example is Mutiullah Khan, a warlord who operated in the Oruzgan Province of Afghanistan. He built 70 mosques on his territory and provided scholarships to local students to study in Kabul (Filkins, 2010). However, the highway in his territory was unsafe to pass, making trade on the highway limited. Moreover, very little economic growth was allowed to take place outside of businesses that he controlled. In general, warlords do not care if the territory they control deteriorates.

In contrast, the insurgent has no interest in the decline of the area that they are operating. Insurgencies are also not always overthrowing a collapsing state. The motivation of the insurgent is political, not commercial. The insurgency also actually wants to govern. The warlord wants to maintain a low-intensity conflict, while the insurgent wants to attain power to provide a political good. Insurgents may seek to replace an existing government, gain more autonomy or secede from a state. For example, the Chechens wanted to secede from Russia. Though they committed terrible atrocities against the Russians (and vice versa), some of the Chechen violent non-state actors had a legitimate political agenda.

In spite of their lack of ideological agenda, most warlords operate under the pretence of having a political agenda. In fact, many warlords pretend to helm some sort of political organization, such as Charles Taylor in Liberia, Joseph Kony in Uganda and Foday Sankoh in Sierra Leone. They only aim to control territory and defy the state. The militia that works under their command may not operate under the assumption that they are fighting on behalf of a political movement, however.

In spite of this lack of political interest, nearly all warlords in Somalia, the Democratic Republic of Congo, the Republic of Congo and Liberia held high office at one point prior to emerging as warlords. In Somalia, Mohammed Aidid was the defence minister for Somali president Siad Barre (1979–91). Through his position he was able to acquire arms clandestinely prior to the civil war. Charles Taylor was able to do the same when he ran the state procurement agency under President Samuel Doe (1980–90). Though many warlords do not pretend to have any political aims, some warlords seize opportunities to take high positions of power.

Marauding rebel groups also attempt to disguise their profit-oriented motivations behind a political discourse (Osorio, 2013: 17). This is what distinguishes a marauding rebel group from a warlord militia. Marauding rebel groups often claim to have a political objective and they may have been originally motivated by some sort of political grievance such as discrimination. A warlord militia is just the army that a warlord uses for protection and does not pretend to have any political objective. In contrast, a marauding rebel group may have a loose mantra that binds them; they may legitimately detest the regime. The Revolutionary United Front (RUF) in Sierra Leone claimed to believe in putting arms and power in the hands of the people. RUF soldiers maintained that they wanted to build a fairer society, where education was more widely available, though they offered no explanation as to how this would be achieved.

The initial grievance provides political justification for their illegal profits, however (Kaldor, 2013: 113). But the warring factions in Africa are more aptly described as racketeering enterprises rather than political groups. Many scholars have noted that rebels within these fighting groups have a nihilistic outlook on life and have become focused on a life of plunder and violence. They do not consistently adhere to some ideological principle. In the Liberian war, no one knew exactly who the armed combatants were. Though they had uniforms, they do little to politicize the villages or leave any impression beyond terror. They made no effort to put their message across to the outside world.

In some cases, marauding rebel groups have a shared ethnic group or history, but often they are mixed groups with weak ideological connections. Taylor attracted groups that had been oppressed, such as the Mano and Gio ethnic groups under Samuel Doe. He encouraged them to attack rival groups such as the Krahn and Mandigo (Reno, 1997: 498). But ethnicity was a tool to mobilize groups of people and camouflage other ambitions. The National Patriotic Front of Liberia (NPFL) had few if any ideological benefits.

Once these groups take power, they do little to provide any sort of administration. They offer no compelling ideological plan and are devoid of ideas of how to govern. The main interest is to replace the old patronage network with their own network. While the insurgent is focused on taking over the state and administering, the warlord does not have such objectives. Remedying local injustices is secondary to reaping the benefits of the chaos. They join groups that permit them to access loot. The RUF's main interest was in mining diamonds in the territory they held. Marauding rebel groups have an interest in maintaining the conflict to maintain their position of power and access to resources (Makarenko, 2004: 140).

STRUCTURE AND RECRUITMENT

STRUCTURE

Warlord rule is based on personal networks that are informal. The militias that they control are organized around their frightening behaviour and appearance or due to high levels of personal charisma (Marten, 2012: 47). Their legitimacy is rooted in this charisma and patronage ties. The warlord can use this charisma to motivate militias to hate their opponents. Much of the warlord's popularity is based on his own charisma rather than his military abilities or venerable characteristics. In Somalia, warlord Mohammed Aidid ran his fiefdom with hired guns that were partially paid in drugs. Some groups in Liberia were led by drunks such as Prince Yormi Johnson. Warlords usually do not reward those loyal to them; they prefer to rely on force.

Warlords operate at the top, exercising hierarchical forms of leadership. They have some trusted subordinates but generally do not rely on any formal structure. The rank structures within warlord armies are ambiguous (Thomas et al., 2005: 125). For this reason, warlord systems do not survive the death or decline in power of the warlord. The entire system is based on one person, which leaves favoured individuals in the lurch. The warlord's power relies on force, charisma and patronage.

Marauding rebel groups may have started off with some hierarchy, but fragmentation usually takes place in which local army commanders act as local warlords, such as in the case of Tajikistan. Most positions were ad hoc with the exception of the key appointments. There may also be an abundance of generals and field officers who do not have a real command status.

Marauding rebel groups do not have the attitude or structure of a professional army, as an insurgency might. Smaller subunits would form, disperse, form new configurations and command structures. Factions were made to seem larger than they were due to the flow of transient local fighters who fought part-time. They display a relatively low level of organizational cohesion and move from one place to another. They tend to have low levels of discipline and a breakdown of any sort of military hierarchy. Much of the lack of discipline is due to the fact that often rebels and marauders are not given a cash salary. They are given food but are forced to fend for themselves by looting.

In the case of the 15,000 combatants involved in the conflict in Somalia in 1991, fewer than 1,500 were organized in any sort of classic military formation. The groups had no clear lines of authority or structure (Pérouse de Montclos, 2003: 42). In contrast, Afghan fighters during the war against the Soviets were organized and relatively cohesive. They demonstrated discipline and tenacity. Afterwards, warlords emerged and groups disintegrated without much discipline, plundering the population they had once fought to defend. The warlord militia member avoids battle, picks on unarmed civilians and focuses on making money (Keen, 2000: 26).

RECRUITMENT

Recruitment for warlord militias and rebel groups is lax, with low entry requirements. Some marauders used to be part of the previous regime, possibly working as border guards, presidential guards or internal security forces. A former faction leader of the military can create his own militia, tapping into the frustration of other poorly paid, poorly educated soldiers (Freeman, 2015). Many of those recruited lack basic skills, but covet access to food and services (Kaldor, 2013: 113). Recruits are often very young and unaware of what political goals the group may have originally had. Once they gain access to loot, this further fuels their motivation.

In the case of marauding rebel groups in Sierra Leone and Liberia, the units were mostly young, with low levels of education, experience and motivation. Many were displaced youth while some others were deserters from the armed forces. Ethnic background is sometimes a common bond of fighting groups, but it is not always

the case that the warlord and his militia are co-ethnics. Charles Taylor was an edu-
cated and urban Americo-Liberian whereas most of his initial army were from the
Gio and Mano people who were reacting against the brutality of the Doe regime.
By 1994, Taylor was recruiting from larger demographic zones.

Taylor's NPFL could call on 12,000 soldiers of different levels of ability. They
were an array of troops who had been trained in the US, and those with no education or experience. Many were only semi-literate villagers who were frustrated by
their lack of opportunities and access to food. Most did not even receive a cash
salary. Their food and essential survival needs had to be looted from local sources.
The RUF in Sierra Leone recruited disaffected youth and those that had been
arrested by Taylor in Liberia. More recruits to the RUF came from abductions
conducted at refugee camps.

A study that examined recruits in the RUF found that only 10% of those
recruited claimed to have any sort of ideological motivation for joining. Nearly half
of all recruits claimed that they joined out of fear, and as many as 88% claimed that
they were abducted and forced to join (Humphreys and Weinstein, 2008: 436).
Most of those who joined had very low levels of education and could barely eke
out a living in logging and mining camps (Peters and Richards, 1998). For the M-23
Movement in the Democratic Republic of Congo, most of the recruitment was
forced. The group forcibly recruited army soldiers, medical officers, police and civilians into its ranks. Those that join willingly reason that it is safer to be part of a
rebel organization than to become a victim of one (Keen, 1998).

The recruitment of child soldiers has also been commonplace among marauding
rebel groups. In at least 20 countries, children are direct participants in war (Antonio
Ocampo, 2005). Child soldiers have been used in countries such as the Central
African Republic, Chad, Somalia, Uganda, Myanmar (Burma), Sudan, Iraq, Colombia,
Serbia and Sri Lanka. Child soldiers are cheap and only have to be paid in food and
basic essentials, yet they can be deadly once equipped with heavy weaponry.

When Charles Taylor invaded Sierra Leone in December 1989, 30% of the soldiers were under the age of 17, with about 6,000 child soldiers in total. Taylor even
created a Boys Own Unit with some as young as eight. Many of those in the Boys
Unit were recruited from the streets of Freetown in Sierra Leone, who, prior to
recruitment, had been involved in petty theft for survival. Children were handed
semi-automatic weapons such as AK-47s, giving them the opportunity to engage in
theft and violence on a larger scale (Denov, 2010; Small Arms, 2008).

In total, there were 11,000 child soldiers recruited for the Sierra Leone Civil war,
mostly for the RUF. They were most often used to attack villages and to guard
diamond mines and weapons stockpiles. Recruited children were often forced to
murder their parents (Zack-Williams, 2001). To make the children more maniacal
and fearless, they would rub cocaine into open cuts. It has been common for other
groups to also force children to use cocaine, crack, methamphetamines and 'brown-
brown' – cocaine mixed with gun powder (Betancourt et al., 2008).

STRATEGY AND TACTICS

There are no clear tactics or strategy for warlord militias and rebel groups.
Marauding rebels are often fuelled by alcohol or drugs. The strategy is marauding
terror. Warlord violence is usually also very savage. The military objective is unclear

and lacks a political purpose. The military units have no discipline in the actions that they commit. Units are mostly unreliable and the violence is very unpredictable, with random shootings. The Liberian war was characterized by sudden attacks by armoured gangs who emerged from the bush to destroy villages, ambush roads and murder, rape and steal.

For both groups, violence against civilians takes place indiscriminately. They spend no time trying to develop an underground movement, since their main aim is to rob the local people (Mackinlay, 1998). Compliance is ensured through threats of violence. They rely on the use of fear of barbaric force. As a result, the warlord and rebel groups are very careless of the civilian population. Unlike in the case of insurgents, in the case of marauding groups, widespread indiscriminate violence against civilians takes place as well as looting of civilians by warlord militias and rebel groups (Azam, 2006).

Because marauding rebel groups have no political agenda, they do not have a politically sensitive path to navigate or need to adhere to an ideology. They do not need to persuade a constituency since threats of violence are enough to ensure compliance. They prey on civilians rather than attempt to represent them. This contrasts with insurgencies, which have a connection to society. This connection with society for the insurgency prevents too much looting and barbaric acts of violence against their own constituency. Marauding rebel groups, however, may ambush citizens, and locations known to be populated by civilians are targeted (Hoffman, 2004: 212). The tactics used in the war in Tajikistan were mostly terror rather than engaging in combat. Hostage-taking, kidnapping, murder and looting were common during the war. Much of the violence was fuelled by retaliation against previous acts of violence.

The violence can also be especially brutal (Gberie, 2005; Hills, 1997: 42). There are usually no moral restrictions for the warlord or the rebel army. They avoid the conventional moral burdens of power. They can use the justification of self-preservation to excuse extreme measures. For example, in the wars in Liberia and Sierra Leone, rebels acted with recklessness, indiscriminately shooting with automatic weapons. Amputations and rape of women were common, a practice that started in Freetown, Sierra Leone, in 1999 (Gberie, 2005: 182). Warlords such as Sam Bockerie introduced chopping off limbs of men, women and children, as well as other forms of mutilation and rape.

Much of the brutality can also be explained by the levels of education of the fighters. Those that had some military training and professional experience may discourage looting and savagery against civilians. Less educated ones indulge their reputations for brutality. They adopt crazy nicknames, piratical dress and use human remains as warning symbols at roadblocks (Mackinlay, 1998). Drugs and alcohol fuelled the barbaric behaviour of recruits. Not surprisingly, an estimated 25%–30% of those who emerged from the war had a serious drug problem (Mueller, 2013: 19).

In contrast to the warlord and marauding rebel group, insurgencies are constantly engaged in wars against a much stronger opponent. Warlords and marauding rebel groups rarely engage in conflict with government forces or other warlords in open battle (Thomas et al., 2005: 125). They would rarely confront an opposing armed faction of equal strength. Weapons are fired, but high-intensity fighting is not the norm (Mackinlay, 1998). Battles are fought that consist of shots being fired for 15 minutes, followed by fleeing. The warlord often withdraws when an opponent comes within fighting distance. The warlord usually focuses on seizing lands that are outside the control of the government and that have potential value for its raw materials. Thus, the main battlegrounds are unmanned trade and aid routes, ports and diamond mines.

FUNDING AND SUPPORT

FUNDING

Like other economically motivated violent non-state actors, warlords and rebel groups fund themselves. However, unlike organized crime, the funding is not generated by sophisticated organized criminal operations but through different forms of looting and predation. Warlords in African states have gotten rich from looting and taxing territory under their control.

For individual rebel group members, looting is not necessarily a lucrative job but is necessary for survival. In some cases, militaries that have not been paid begin to engage in criminal behaviour such as looting, as was the case in Joseph Mobutu's Zaire. The disintegrating military's access to weapons facilitates this behaviour. In other cases, the warlord may encourage looting (Allen, 1999). The M-23 Movement has engaged in constant looting of homes, offices and cars.

In the case of the NPFL under Charles Taylor, looting was the main source of income for individual soldiers. Looting houses that had been captured was seen as a generous reward (Alao et al., 1999: 46). One of the more egregious cases of looting took place in Somalia under the direction of warlord Mohammed Aidid. Aidid's officials told UNICEF that there were 25,000 starving Bardera people instead of the actual 6,000. A few days later, the figure was inflated to 56,000 people needing food. The food aid was then siphoned off by Aidid's group (Duyvesteyn, 2000).

Warlords manipulate scarcity and access to goods to extend their authority. Mutiullah Khan of Afghanistan provided protection to US military convoys and owned a rock-crushing company that sold gravel to the US military, employing over 15,000 people with these businesses, but the area that he controlled suffered from high levels of insecurity.

Warlords can control some simple criminal networks but often favour business enterprises such as protection. Warlords want protection to be seen as a scarce and valuable commodity. Warlords also like to offer protection from economic competition and force their rivals out of business. They limit the range of commercial activities in their areas.

When the government is weak or non-existent, warlords can tax goods in transit and create checkpoints to extract cash from passing trade (Hills, 1997: 41). Because of this, warlords are often associated with illegal border activity. They smuggle weapons, narcotics and people across borders, and avoid customs duties. They can also just rob or extort from the local population, such as was the case in Somalia. When foreign aid or relief comes in, warlords can intercept this and directly pocket it.

In spite of the lack of a complex organization, if a warlord or rebel group gets control over an area of the state where there are valuable natural resources or a key asset, they can become very wealthy. For this reason, many conflicts involving warlords and rebels are often referred to as 'resource wars'. Warlords are often able to sell local resources on the international market and develop export trade with foreign firms, which brings in hard currency that can be used to buy weapons or to enrich themselves. Thus warlords can sustain themselves by selling primary commodities under the table.

Charles Taylor of Liberia offers a good example. Taylor had no elaborate infrastructure, just raw materials that he sold for hard currency on the international market.

Taylor's 'businesses' were run by loyal partners, mostly relatives. For example, Taylor's brother, Gbatu, organized the plunder of the abandoned German-owned Bong Iron Ore Company. Taylor supported himself through his involvement in illicit trade of diamonds, other minerals and agricultural products and timber (Reno, 1995: 28). Through the vast networks he created with foreign investors and regional commercial networks, he was able to net himself an income of over $400 million per year (Reno, 1995: 10). A British mining company paid Taylor as much as $10 million a month just to keep a railroad site to a port operational (Reno, 1993: 181). This provided him with access to foreign exchange which he could use to buy weapons.

SUPPORT

Warlords and marauding rebel groups sometimes receive international support. Warlords may offer their territory as a safe haven for access to resources to other states, groups or businesses. Alliances can be made with PSCs, organized criminal groups and terrorist groups (Mair, 2005: 50). But these alliances are always temporary. Collaborations are also subject to fluctuations in response to threats and opportunities.

Foreign states may opportunistically offer support for warlords. Border states can use warlords to challenge the domestic sovereignty of weak neighbours (Marten, 2012: 12). Local warlords were supported by states bordering Afghanistan, such as Iran, Uzbekistan, Tajikistan and Pakistan. Warlords also may receive support from bureaucrats and state leaders who link up with local strongmen out of necessity, but for the most part, the warlord is completely independent from the state. The state needs the warlord's compliance more than the warlord needs the state.

In general, warlords lack deep political relationships or allies. Allies are usually bought and have a similar interest in destabilization (Mackinlay, 1998). When warlords do make alliances, they still manage to maintain their independence. In the conflict in Somalia, warlords tried to strengthen their power position by mobilizing alliances with other clan groups in order to fight against a common enemy, but these alliances were mostly short-lived.

Warlords do not require an underground movement to generate power. Popular support is not necessary for the warlord. They just need to muster enough followers to bear arms alongside them and gain access to local resources. In contrast, insurgents are more dependent on society and rely on some popular support, which they use as their base to combat the government.

POWER AND IMPACT ON THE STATE AND SOCIETY

As a previous section illustrated, warlords and their militias and marauding rebel groups often emerge in countries where the state has already disintegrated or is experiencing a conflict. The chances of stability in post-conflict zones lessen when warlords emerge. The main problem is that warlords have an interest in maintaining state collapse and insecurity. They care little about saving the infrastructure of the state since they will never control it. Warlords use the resources they have for parochial interests and defy centralized authority.

These groups also present a significant obstacle to the reconstruction of society. Warlords and marauding rebel groups have fostered the emergence of a 'Kalashnikov culture', where political disputes are settled through the use of arms. This culture has been especially notable in the Pakistan and Afghanistan border areas, where some people own more than one automatic weapon.

Compared to the states where they operate, warlords are very powerful. They may have access to powerful weapons. Marauding rebel groups are also often equipped with weaponry that is potent, such as Piranha armoured personnel carriers, rocket launchers (M-116s), mortars and major aircraft.

Box 8.1   Small Arms

Small arms are weapons that are intended for use by an individual. They include pistols, rifles, sub-machine guns, assault rifles and light machine guns. For warlords and rebel groups, small arms are widely accessible. They are widely produced, cheap, easily transportable and widespread and are difficult to trace and monitor.

There are over half a billion small arms (640 million) and light weapons, enough for one in every 11 people, and causing 11 deaths per day (Hazen, 2008). More than eight million small arms circulate in West Africa. Some eight million new guns are being manufactured every year by at least 1,249 companies in 92 countries. In Uganda, an AK-47 can be produced for the same cost as a chicken. Inside Mozambique and Angola, an AK-47 complete with a couple of clips of ammunition can be bought for less than $15.00, or for a bag of maize (Small Arms Survey, 2008). They are also easy to use. They can be used by children and informal militias. They require no form of training. Because small arms are so easy to use, wars can be more likely to involve children as recruits.

Small arms are also easily transportable. They are light and easy to hide. They have been moved in South Asia using mules and camels. Small arms are difficult to trace because, although much of the trade in small arms is legitimate and accounted for, most of the weapons are assembled with components sourced from many countries (Small Arms Survey, 2013). They are also easy to ship or smuggle into areas of conflict. They can be easily hidden in legitimate cargo or warehouses. They are hard to monitor and easily stolen, with more than one million firearms being stolen or lost worldwide.

War-torn countries and countries with poor border security are flooded with surplus weapons. Weapons are easily stolen and can end up in the hands of violent non-state actors. During the Somali conflict, most of the heavy weapons in Somalia were inoperable. However, 30,000 people were killed by light weapons in 1991 and 1992. Some 500,000 weapons that were abandoned by the Somali army fell into the hands of General Mohamed Farah Aidid and Ali Mahdi. Weapons also flooded into Somalia after the collapse of the Mengistu regime in Ethiopia in 1991. The US also donated 5,000 M-16 rifles and 5,000 handguns to the Somali police, an unnecessary move to a country already flooded with weapons. Soon after, brand-new M-16s were sighted in the hands of criminals (Ezrow and Frantz, 2013: 74).

The proliferation of small arms has had a long-lasting effect on human security. In countries considered to be at peace, the level of violence due to small arms is considered to be as high as in war zones. In 90% of conflicts since 1990, small arms have been the primary weapons used in fighting, and have contributed to the increased proportion of civilian deaths in those conflicts (Bourne, 2007). The proliferation of small arms has also made it easier for rebel groups and warlords to continue to threaten stability and defy a collapsing state (Boutwell and Klare, 1998).

The areas that are under the control of warlords and marauding rebel groups are rarely safe for citizens. There may be some security for those loyal or able to pay off the warlord, but for everyone else the area becomes more risky and dangerous. In the case of Somalia, the warlord-controlled areas were supposed to be safer, to protect businessmen and their goods. Warlord militias were supposed to ensure the safe passage of goods from numerous checkpoints and roadblocks, but robbery and looting still prevailed. In the case of Tajikistan, some areas are still under warlord control. Though the civil war ended decades ago, some territories are no-go zones unless you have a prior arrangement to enter the territory. Though warlords are usually not powerful to take over an entire state, their militias are strong enough to seize a large piece of territory.

In rare cases, warlords and marauding rebel groups are able to take control over not only large territories in the countries they originate from, but also from neighbouring weak countries as well. In the case of Liberia, with the help of his 50-man NPFL, Taylor was able to control parts of Liberia but also parts of Sierra Leone and frontier zones of Guinea and the Ivory Coast, referred to as 'Taylorland'. His soldiers were perfectly at east in the Ivory Coast. With the complicity of the Ivoirian army, they did as they saw fit (Reno, 1997: 498–500). Taylorland had its own currency, banking system, TV and radio station, international airfield and deep-water port.

Box 8.2　War Economies

The war economy is defined as 'the production, mobilization and allocation of economic resources to sustain a conflict' (Goodhand, 2004: 157). It is based on the economic interactions that directly sustain combat. Violence emerges as a good that is marketable and the means of force becomes more and more privatized and decentralized. The few actors involved benefit from the status quo and have a vested interest in the continuation of the conflict and instability.

Some of the activities of the war economy include control over natural resources, which is important for funding the purchase of weapons (or the sale of resource exploitation rights to foreign companies). Controlling resources and other assets to fund the war effort is a violent process that involves pillaging, predation and extortion against citizens (Goodhand, 2004).

Another activity in war economies is providing security checkpoints. In most cases this comes in the form of bribes at security checkpoints and roadblocks (Goodhand, 2004).

The effects of the war economy overall are very negative, not just because the citizens are forced to live in an environment of heightened insecurity and violence, but also because all legal forms of entrepreneurship are discouraged, which leads to a mass exodus of the entrepreneurial and upper and middle classes. Neighbouring economies are also often affected by the instability and violence.

States with warlord-controlled areas are negatively affected by their operations. They cause economic inefficiency and stunt economic growth. They disrupt free trade, and make any sort of commerce and investment unpredictable and risky. They make economic transactions more inefficient, expensive and insecure. This leads to capital flight and low levels of other forms of investment. People must focus on short-term profits while they can. The future can change rapidly with warlords, which makes it difficult to make long-term deals. To illustrate the instability caused by warlords in Tajikistan, in November 1992, in the town of Kolkhozobod, the centre of cotton production changed hands six times due to infighting amongst warlord militias.

Warlords and marauding rebel groups generate revenues in a parasitic manner. They extort, tax and create the need for protection (Thomas et al., 2005). They tap into the resources of the state and its people and siphon off what they want. In Somalia, where warlord rule was the norm, very little investment took place. Business contracts could only be enforced through informal protection pacts, and business owners had to rely on warlord militia. Small business owners could not afford the costs of security which priced them out of the market.

Warlords not only cause irreparable damage to security, the economy and the state, but also to future prospects for democracy. Warlords have no democratic mandate and usually have no interest in democracy. They also do not adhere to international and human rights laws (Robinson, 2001). It was the frustration and disgust with warlords in Afghanistan that led to the emergence of the Taliban in the mid- to late-1990s.

Warlords also negatively affect peace processes. On the one hand, they do not have the power to make peace. On the other hand, they routinely disrupt and destroy peace. They have no interest in a settlement because it would diminish their power (Hansen, 2006). A post-conflict situation is very complicated when warlords have gained power. They may agree to be incorporated into the state, but they thrive on an insecure environment and may serve a dual role of using their new position in the state to serve their own financial interests while also continuing to ensure that the country remains insecure to justify their provision of protection. Civil war in Tajikistan (1992–97) led to the development of warlord militias and bands of vigilantes and other illegally armed formations. Once they became involved, these groups had an interest in protracting the conflict. There were several attempts at a ceasefire early in the conflict that were undermined by warlords. Warlords violated the truce due to their desire to maintain control over lucrative enterprises such as cotton plantations and oil refineries. Marauding rebel groups are usually fairly easy to disband once the warlords who led them have been dealt with. They are often made up of members who are too young and inexperienced to challenge a peace process once it has been initiated.

—————— Case Study   Warlords in Afghanistan ——————

Warlords in Afghanistan have constantly threatened state sovereignty. The state has rarely exercised a monopoly over the legitimate use of force, giving ample room for non-state actors to take control over small territory and provide 'protection'. The power of warlords has been so great that they have even been incorporated *into* the state. The Hamid Karzai (2001–14) government placed warlords in key positions of the government regardless of their expertise or experience. According to a delegate, at one point in the Loya Jirga, '85% of the elected were with the warlords or were warlords' (Kolhatkar, 2003).

Warlordism in Afghanistan became more notable after initial uprisings took place against the Soviet-backed state government in the late 1970s (and against the actual

Soviet invasion in 1979). This instability led to the rise of independent commanders. After the war began, refugee camps spawned new insurgent groups. In regions where the insurgents successfully fought off the state and Soviet forces, their commanders planted opium poppies as a source of independent income and took control over transportation checkpoints to collect unofficial taxes from travellers. Many warlords emerged more powerful than ever after the conflict with the Soviet Union ended.

Warlords have undermined the capacity and legitimacy of the state in Afghanistan because they have usurped revenues that could be collected by the government. For example, all of the revenues from the transit trade in the region of Herat (one of the richest regions in the country) have gone directly to warlord Ismail Khan, who emerged after being a prominent military commander in the war against the Soviets. Ismael Khan is sometimes referred to as a 'neo-warlord' – one who provides some form of public good over the territory under his control. Earning millions in revenues due to his control over international trade that passed through his region, he was able to provide tight security and even some economic opportunities. The Afghan government tried to incorporate him into the state, and he has served as the Minister of Water and Energy since 2005, though he has favoured Herat at the expense of other regions.

Attempts to incorporate other warlords into the army have mostly backfired. Warlords have paid lip service to the Afghan government but have been able to exercise power more or less autonomously.

CONCLUSION

Warlords and marauding rebels are comparatively more powerful than the state, but that is only because they emerge in states that are either completely collapsed or in the process of failing. They have no interest in state-building or ending low-intensity conflicts. They are also difficult to negotiate with. Because they are often emerging in post-conflict zones, the prospects for peace are that much more difficult when powerful warlords are involved. Nevertheless, their lack of political objectives means that they are more easily bought off. But buying off these groups is only a temporary fix. The long-term solutions to preventing the strengthening and emergence of these types of groups necessitate increasing the capacity of the states they emerge in.

Summary Points

- Warlords and rebels emerge in states that are failing or have collapsed; they emerge in post-conflict zones.
- Warlords and rebels offer few political benefits and mostly prey on their populations.
- Warlords and rebels undermine state legitimacy but have no ability to administer.
- Warlords and rebels create tremendous security and instability though they claim to offer protection.
- Warlords and rebels have an interest in prolonging a low-intensity conflict to take advantage of the war economy.

Key Questions

1   In what ways do warlords and rebels differ from organized criminal groups?
2   In what ways do warlords and rebels differ from insurgencies?
3   What are the conditions where these groups are most likely to emerge?
4   Why are warlords and rebels so detrimental to stability?
5   In what ways do the proliferation of small arms and the abundance of resources facilitate these groups?
6   Theory: How do rational choice approaches explain conflict?

FURTHER READING

Ballentine, K. (ed.) (2003) *The Political Economy of Armed Conflict: Beyond Greed and Grievance* (Lynne Rienner Publishers). An in-depth explanation of the economic factors that drive conflicts. It offers case studies on the role of resources that have driven many of the conflicts in Africa.

Berdal, M.R. and Malone, D. (2000) *Greed and Grievance: Economic Agendas in Civil Wars* (Lynne Rienner Publishers) Similar to the Ballentine book, provides an overview of the literature on economic motives that drive wars.

Burgis, T. (2016) *The Looting Machine: Warlords, Oligarchs, Corporations, Smugglers, and the Theft of Africa's Wealth* (PublicAffairs) Offers an in depth overview of the looting that has taken place on the continent.

Reno, W. (1999) *Warlord Politics and African States* (Lynne Rienner Publishers). Excellent book on warlords in Africa and how they maintain themselves in power.

Smillie, I. (2013) 'Blood diamonds and non-state actors', *Vanderbilt Journal of Transnational Law*, 46: 1003–1024. Excellent overview of how diamonds funded warlords and what has been done to regulate the industry.

Thomas, T.S., Kiser, S.D. and Casebeer, W.D. (2005) *Warlords Rising: Confronting Violent Non-state Actors* (Lexington Books). Examines warlords mostly in the region of greater Central Asia.

9

ORGANIZED CRIME AND GANGS

Organized criminal groups and gangs are the most ubiquitous of all of the violent non-state actors and exert the biggest threat to security. Most criminal organizations operate across borders and have links and presence in a number of countries. Today organized crime networks are more fluid and interested in striking new alliances with other networks. This chapter discusses the role of gangs and organized criminal groups in destabilizing the state and society.

DEFINITION

Organized criminal groups are structured groups of three or more people that exist for a period of time and aim to regularly commit more serious crimes in order to obtain material benefit. Though the group may be constantly evolving to evade detection, the basic structure remains the same. In contrast, sporadic crime is more isolated and ephemeral. Sporadic criminals have low skills and knowledge and cannot manage a complex and risk-laden environment. Organized crime involves enduring networks of actors engaged in making money illegally.

Most organized criminal groups are involved in multiple illegal businesses to achieve their earnings, though they aim to gain a monopoly (Abadinsky, 2012). The crimes include smuggling, robbery, fraud, blackmail, piracy, contract killing, money laundering, and trafficking of drugs, weapons and humans, along with other illegal or counterfeit goods. Though they often use bribery, organized criminal groups are violent non-state actors because they are willing to use illegal violence to achieve their objectives.

Organized criminal groups are frequently based on family ties and ethnic networks. For example, the major organized criminal groups are the Italian, Chechen and Russian mafias, the Japanese Yakuza, the Chinese Triads and the Colombian and Mexican cartels (Rotman, 2000). When organized crime is based on a code of conduct where local fraternities have been created, it is often referred to as a 'mafia'. The Mafia is better known for certain types of criminal activities, such as protection, arbitration and contract enforcement. They may also be involved in loan-sharking, gambling, drug trafficking and fraud.

GANGS

Gangs are a group of three or more persons that have a common identifying sign, symbol or name, and who individually or collectively engage in criminal activity which creates an atmosphere of fear and intimidation (Barker, 2010). Gangs have existed for centuries, but they received more attention during the 1980s. Many gangs do not have a clear hierarchy; they vary in terms of their level of organization. Gangs and organized crime differ mostly in terms of progression and sophistication. In comparison to organized criminal groups, gangs may not hold regular meetings or have clear written rules about the organization and their businesses. Gangs are not as well organized, complex or capable. Gangs have a very young membership compared to organized criminal groups. In fact, it is the youth of gang members that is one of the key defining characteristics, compared to organized criminals (Esbensen et al., 2001). Additionally, the members of gangs are comparatively less educated and less skilled (Klein and Maxson, 2010). Gangs also offer different enticements from organized crime groups, providing much less in terms of economic rewards and financial gain. They may appeal to those who have few economic opportunities and feel disenfranchised. Gang members often come from difficult family backgrounds, and are often alienated from school. Gangs provide a social setting that their family and economic status cannot provide (Vigil, 2010: 168). Though gangs are not as well organized as organized criminal groups, they do provide group members with a strong sense of solidarity and a distinct identity (Esbensen et al., 2001).

GANG EVOLUTION

Scholars have noted that there has been an evolution of gangs over time, though most gangs still remain fairly unsophisticated (Bunker and Sullivan, 2013). First-generation gangs don't engage in high levels of violence and have a loose leadership. Violence never extends outside the boundaries of their turf. They focus their attention on maintaining gang loyalty and protecting their turf, which is often just a few blocks in a neighbourhood. Any criminal activity is opportunistic rather than well planned because they have limited scope and sophistication. Gang soldiers made very little per hour in the 1990s (Forst et al., 2011: 105). First-generation gangs were not involved in any sort of trafficking. Gang homicides were likely to be turf-related rather than drug-related. For example, gangs were only minor players in crack sales in California. They did not get involved with the major cartels, but some were recruited to become hitmen. They were primarily used as lookout enforcers (Sullivan and Bunker, 2002: 41).

Second-generation gangs are engaged in businesses, such as drugs, though this usually entailed whatever the drug cartels did not already control. The appearance of cocaine and crack in Central America changed things. The lucrative nature of the cocaine and crack trade forced gangs to better organize themselves to take advantage of new profits (Cruz, 2010: 390). For example, gangs in Guatemala are able to obtain cocaine in powder form, which they reprocess into pebble-sized tabs and sell (Dudley, 2011: 898). They protect markets and use violence to control any competition. They have a broader area that they operate out of. Their operations may involve multiple countries. Their leadership is more centralized and their operations are more sophisticated. These gangs were better funded and organized. The more responsible and reliable members of these gangs would be recruited to work as foot soldiers or bodyguards (Sullivan and Bunker, 2002: 41).

Third-generation gangs have their own power and are interested in controlling their economic apparatuses. They have transnational links and are much better networked. About 28% of gang members interviewed in El Salvador in 2006 claimed that they kept contacts with gang members in other countries (Franco, 2007). These gangs can engage in mercenary activity and work as cartel enforcers (Sullivan and Bunker, 2002: 36). 'Enforcer' gangs are specialists in violence that are hired by larger organizations such as drug cartels to provide security and ensure protection of the group. They engage in contract killings, assassinations, kidnappings and threats of violence. Gangs are often a labour force for crime groups. Enforcer gangs change in composition and membership constantly. Many are killed, disabled or arrested. There is a constant need for new recruits, but enforcer gangs are becoming more widespread.

Today many gang members from the Central American Mara Salvatrucha and the 18th Street Gang are working as mercenaries for Mexican drug cartels. Some Maras have even gained control of illegal immigrant and drug trafficking through Mexico and to the US. They can also provide prison protection for important Mexican cartel members if they are incarcerated. Guatemalan gangs have begun to work as spotters and enforcers for larger criminal groups, but they have not reached this mercenary phase yet. They are assassins for hire, but not in any systematic way (Dudley, 2010).

Third-generation gangs may have some political and social objectives. They may even extract taxes and provide limited services. They are not just interested in protecting markets but in acquiring power. Because of their capabilities, they strain government capacity more than other gangs. They may even establish small businesses and use violence to compete unfairly with legitimate businesses. They have much more sophisticated and powerful weapons and more prone to violence (Sullivan and Bunker, 2002: 41).

The case of Nicaraguan gangs illustrates how gangs can transform from first-generation gangs to much more sophisticated entities. Nicaraguan gangs (*pandillas*) initially had mainly operated traditionally in close groups. They consisted of individuals who wanted to create a sense of cohesion, solidarity and respect. They were not involved in violence and had only limited participation in criminal activities, with the exception of minor robberies. They were primarily aiming to gain resources to buy drugs and alcohol. Unfortunately, they have now become more involved in drug trafficking, distributing drugs locally and providing arms for drug-trafficking groups (Rodgers, 2006).

——————————— Case Study   Evolution of Los Zetas ———————————

Los Zetas was one of the most powerful and violent enforcer gangs to emerge in Mexico, with its operations extending into Central America. Though it no longer wields much power today after a series of successful counter-narcotics efforts, it set a new bar for how violent an organization could be.

Los Zetas originally worked as the enforcer gang for the Gulf cartel and later for the Beltran Leyva organization. They engaged in cross-border killing sprees on behalf of the Gulf cartel in 2004–5 in the Laredo–Nuevo Laredo along the US border. The group eventually transformed into its own independent drug cartel, almost becoming an insurgency, holding territory, but having no political agenda. Instead, the group used the territory it controlled to monopolize criminal activities. The group was originally organized along military lines, but eventually flattened its structure. It is also run surprisingly like a business with quarterly meetings, business records and a voting procedure for key assassinations.

The origin of Los Zetas is similar to the foundation of many paramilitary groups; it drew from a pool of already trained professionals. Los Zetas was primarily composed of former members of the Mexican special forces known as GAFE (Airmobile Special Forces Group). To fight the big drug cartels, the Mexican Army and Air Force Development Plan designated the fight to be a military task. The state then created drug-fighting units and provided them with advanced specialized training. Though they were well trained, they were poorly paid, and none of the individuals were thoroughly vetted. These groups were easily recruited by the drug cartels that had either been purged due to corruption or were attracted to better pay. In 2000–3, nearly 50,000 soldiers had deserted, though it could have been has high as 150,000 (Turbiville, 2010).

One noted defector from GAFE was Arturo Guzmán Decena. He left GAFE in the late 1990s and brought with him over 30 fellow GAFE members. Originally recruited by the Gulf cartel, he was asked to help recruit the most vicious hit squad for the cartel. Guzmán revealed that the best place to recruit was the army (Grillo, 2012). Along with other military and police recruits and civilian thugs, he formed Los Zetas, a reference to Guzmán's code name in 1997. Some cells spun off and served as enforcer gangs or other cartels, while others worked as drug-trafficking factions in their own right.

The former GAFE men had acquired training in desert, mountain and jungle operations. They were trained in using weapons (such as firearms and explosives), intelligence gathering and surveillance, intimidation and coercion. They had extensive knowledge of tactics, techniques and procedures of the police and the military. They had means of communication, including mobile phones, satellite phones and other radios and computers.

They had knowledge in deception and information management. They were equipped with transportation resources such as SUVs and had training in offensive and defensive driving. They knew effective recruitment methods. They were also well disciplined, enabling the group to execute complex plans (Turbiville, 2010: 132). They were easier to train and had tactical advantages during battles.

Los Zetas not only demonstrated expertise in complex assaults, but also possessed massive firepower. Los Zetas was the first drug cartel to employ military arsenal, moving from AK-47s to shoulder-fired missiles, armour-piercing ammunition and heavy machine guns. Like insurgencies, they also have used fragmentation grenades and improvised explosive devices.

While some of these weapons were stolen from the Mexican military, most were simply bought legally in the US and just smuggled into Mexico (Kan, 2012: 46).

The knowledge, expertise and brazenness of Los Zetas led to an escalation of violence in Mexico since 2007. The violence is reminiscent of the type of violence taking place in a brutal civil war. Los Zetas were also willing to take on the military in direct firefights, but eventually key arrests caused a major setback for the cartel. As of December 2015, it has begun to identify itself as 'Cartel del Norte', or Cartel of the North, and is considered to be much weaker than it once was.

POLITICAL IDEOLOGY AND OBJECTIVES

Organized criminal groups do not have an ideology or political agenda that drives them. They may serve on behalf of politicians or political groups, but they are not usually politically motivated, except supporting politicians or actors that can help their businesses become more lucrative. Many gang members in El Salvador may have been the sons of leftist guerrillas, but they have little knowledge or passion for socialism. They are mostly interested in profits and becoming embedded in a social network. In contrast to terrorists who believe that they are altruistic and serving a good cause in order to achieve support from a wider constituency, criminals are interested only in their own 'personal aggrandizement and material satiation' (Hoffman, 1998: 43).

Some cartel leaders have had political aspirations and have run for public office. Drug lords like Carlos Lehder of the Medellin cartel actually wanted to achieve political power. He organized a political party named the Latin Nationalist Movement and ran for the Colombian Senate. Pablo Escobar of Colombia was elected as an alternative deputy to the Congress in 1982. Drug lords also spent huge sums of money financing campaigns, such as the Ernesto Samper presidential campaign, which was assisted by major contributions from the Cali cartel in the mid-1990s. Tajik organized criminals are current members of the parliament (Engvall, 2006). Tajikistan's former deputy defence minister was imprisoned after using a military helicopter to smuggle drugs. The country's trade representative was caught with 24 kilograms of heroin. The secretary of Tajikistan's Security Council admitted that many of the representatives of Tajik state agencies are involved in drug cartels (Engvall, 2006). Kazakhstan's ambassador was twice caught transporting drugs.

Organized criminal groups and gangs usually do not care about influencing public opinion, but there have been plenty of examples of organized criminal groups wanting to gain some legitimate support from the population. Once an organization is powerful enough to control some territory, they can provide public goods. Because the drug trade is so lucrative, successful traffickers are able to make investments in infrastructure to maintain roads and build landing strips and tunnels (Shelley, 2014: 220).

Organized criminal groups from time to time have had a populist agenda that includes providing some social services. Drug lords such as Escobar and Juan Matta Ballesteros of Honduras started to provide public goods to the local population to generate goodwill. Escobar provided a local welfare system in his home town and built a housing development in a slum, where he gave away 1,000 houses to low-income residents. Roberto Suarez, the drug kingpin from Bolivia, used some of his immense wealth to underwrite most of the education costs for an entire district. He also regularly provided technical or college education abroad for young people in the area he was from. Some scholars have claimed that many organized criminal groups are highly nationalistic. The Latin American crime groups have claimed that they are hiring thousands of poor individuals and challenging Northern imperialism. But rational choice theorists would counter that criminal groups can operate with greater ease if they have the support of the population (Albertson and Fox, 2011).

STRUCTURE AND RECRUITMENT

STRUCTURE

Criminal organizations are often organized with some degree of hierarchy. With a standard hierarchy, there is a single leader, strong internal discipline and strict rules for regulation with a strong social and ethnic identity. Organized crime is complex enough to have a clear division of labour. Members are specialized in certain types of crimes. They may use chemists, pilots, drivers, accountants, lawyers and architects, in addition to assassins.

Today there are only some organizations that are highly organized and bureaucratic where the decision-making is centrally concentrated and subordinates executive activities. These groups are anomalies in the global underworld, since it takes years to develop such complex structures. Thus, it is only groups that have been around for hundreds of years that may have these structures (Cheloukhine and Haberfeld, 2011). This is representative of the Italian, Chinese, Colombian and some eastern European crime groups. In comparison, Russian mafia groups are more decentralized.

More and more criminal organizations are networked (Pearson and Hobbs, 2003). Network organization refers to horizontal organizations with few hierarchical levels and a high degree of flexibility. The network structure is more adaptable, more resilient and harder to target, making them more resilient to law enforcement and intervention (Morselli, 2009). In hierarchical groups, communication from top to bottom can be intercepted. Furthermore, death or incarceration of top personnel can leave the group with big gaps and any sort of infiltration at the upper levels jeopardizes the group.

Structurally, Chinese Triads (organized crime) have a clear division of labour, with the upper levels functioning as resolvers of disputes. They follow a Confucian code of conduct, respecting elders, but those on the low end of the ladder have much more lateral movement. Members do not need permission from a head of a Triad to engage in a criminal act, even if this may mean partnering with someone outside the group. Profits will go to the gang, not to the entire organization. Thus the hierarchy is not as strict as the Italian Mafia.

Yakuza groups are very centralized and bonded by elaborate hierarchies, composed of groups in pyramid structures. Members once initiated must subvert all other allegiances in favour of the Yakuza. These hierarchical relationships are cemented by the creation of father/son or brother relationships that are not actually based on bloodlines.

In Mexico, the Gulf cartel was also hierarchical, which made it easier for the Mexican government to target it, compared to El Chapo's Sinaloa cartel which was more networked. In Colombian drug cartels today, flexible networks are the norm (Kenney, 2007). With the fall of the big cartels, smaller cartels with flatter hierarchies are more adaptable and efficient (Mair, 2005).

Due to successful 'decapitation' strategies (eliminating the leadership), Mexican cartels have been forced to decentralize. As a result, Mexican drug trafficking leaders are pushed further away from their traditional centre, being forced to maintain distance from their members to avoid law enforcement (Dishman, 2001). The issue with the new cellular structure is that they can begin to act independently without regard for the organization. Organized criminal groups may also want to retain some hierarchy in order to train, monitor, reward and punish members. They want to prevent defection and too much fragmentation, to preserve the organization. Sometimes these networked groups have a loose structure, but there is still a core group of a limited number of individuals that is tightly organized with strong internal discipline.

A regional hierarchy has a single leadership structure and line of command from the centre, but with a degree of autonomy at the regional level, such as Hells Angels, with chapters in different countries. Some groups may also have a clustered hierarchy, where there are a number of criminal groups that have a governing arrangement but the cluster has a stronger identity than the constituent groups.

There is no clear consensus in the literature on the exact structure of gangs (Windle and Briggs, 2015). Early research claimed that gangs of the past were only loosely organized, subject to constant changes in structure, composition and purpose (Decker and Van Winkle, 1996; Hagedorn, 1998; Klein and Maxson, 2010). Studies argued that gangs did not have the organization or the discipline to engage in effective drug trafficking (Decker and Van Winkle, 1996; Forst et al., 2011; Reiner, 1992). However, other authors countered that gangs cannot be characterized as loose social networks (Ruble and Turner, 2000). Gangs can be hierarchical with clear leadership, which are organized and governed by a set of rules and roles (Sánchez-Jankowski, 1991, 2003; Venkatesh and Levitt, 2000). But these perfectly well-organized gangs may be the exception rather than the norm. Gangs with some hierarchy at the top, but with looser social networks may be the most common structure (Curry, 2015; Decker and Curry, 2000). Though more sophisticated gangs (third-generation gangs) have emerged that have been able to make inroads in the drug trade, many gangs still have very loose coordination when it comes to drug sales (Decker et al., 1998; Dell, 2015).

RECRUITMENT

Organized crime has a limited or 'exclusive' membership. In contrast to politically motivated violent non-state actors, organized crime is not trying to actively recruit as many people as possible. The Yakuza mainly recruit from juvenile delinquents, though sometimes there are university graduates within the ranks. Some are also boxers and martial artists. Training lasts six months to a year. Once initiated, gang members pay monthly fees, in the hope that their membership will bring lucrative opportunities.

Members of organized crime share high levels of risks. They may not be as cohesive as political groups, which should make them vulnerable to state infiltration. Criminal groups get around this problem by creating a unique sub-culture and clear identity, such as having elaborate induction rituals (Gambetta, 1996). For the Yakuza, members must subvert all other allegiances after they have been initiated. Ceremonies are ornate traditions which go on for hours. Members are subject to a code of discipline that is backed by punishments, such as amputating the smallest finger (yubitsume) (Kaplan and Dubro, 2012).[1] Members of organized

---

[1]In 1993, 45% of Yakuza members had undergone this form of punishment. However, now this practice is being phased out to fit in with society more, with the exception of more serious offences. Common punishments today include shaving off one's hair, monetary fines and temporary imprisonment and expulsion (Bosmia et al., 2014: 1–2).

criminal groups emphasize their membership and closeness through the use of specific colours, clothing, language, tattoos and initiation rites (Finckenauer, 2012: 8). The Chinese triads also have very intricate and fixed rituals for initiation that can last several days; symbols and ceremony are important. Triads may make use of secret signs, code names and tattoos. Taking an oath is also important. As generating high levels of trust is critical, one of the worst offences is ratting out another member (Bolz, 1995). The triads also use rituals, oaths, secret ceremonies and incentives to secure personal loyalty, and individual membership provides credibility and influence. For Latin American crime groups, a narco-culture has developed that distinguishes each group from the other (Kalyvas, 2015).

Another way of ensuring high levels of loyalty is to recruit based on ethnicity. The Aryan Brotherhood and Black Guerrilla Family depend on racial and criminal considerations (Finckenauer, 2005). Groups that do not share a close ethnic connection may have some other form of pre-existing ties to prevent betrayals. Rarely do individuals join criminal groups as complete outsiders, though more recently former members of elite security forces and militaries have been recruited to serve as mercenaries in enforcer gangs. This has been the case of Los Zetas in Mexico, recruiting from the Mexican government's special forces and (see the case study on Los Zetas in this chapter), even recruiting former members of the elite special forces (Kaibiles) in Guatemala (Manwaring, 2011: 862). As Chapter 5 explained, individuals usually join organized crime groups by establishing criminal relations with persons who are already involved in criminal acts. The Colombian drug organizations recruited individuals who had experience in other areas of crime. Prisons are also important places for criminal networking. Detainees have the proper credentials and track record in crime (Albanese and Reichel, 2013). The case of Russian organized crime illustrates this.

In contrast to Colombian, Italian, Mexican, and Chechen organized crime groups, Russian organized crime is not based on ethnic or family structures. In the former Soviet Union the connections were based on the need for mutual participation in criminal activities, not ethnic or familial bonds. These are known as associational networks. With associational networks shared participation in prison or youth crimes leads to bonding, communication, mutual support and the creation of a code of conduct (von Lampe, 2016). Organized criminal groups in the Soviet Union formed in prison, where a professional criminal class developed, some of which started during the era of the gulag in 1924. Criminals in prison together adopted clear values and rules which helped bond them tightly together, living according to the 'thieves in law' codes. This helped the Russian criminal groups maintain the bonds and trust necessary to carry out organized crime (Abadinsky, 2012).

In contrast, members of Chechen crime groups are very socially cohesive and bound by kinship. The Chechen mafia does not adhere to the 'thieves in law' codes of their Russian counterparts. Instead they have a tribal structure (Galeotti, 2002). These bonds are so strong that it has been near impossible for Russian agents to infiltrate their groups. There have rarely if ever been turf wars between Chechen crime groups and insurgencies. Chechen crime groups have rarely cooperated with other crime groups, though they have been located across the globe. There were many instances of cooperation between Chechen separatists and Chechen criminal rings, especially in the counterfeit and illegal arms trade (Bovenkerk et al., 2003). They have also cooperated with each other in diverting oil to boost earnings. But Chechen groups lack the flexibility of Russian crime gangs due to their emphasis on tribal loyalty (Williams, 2014).

For gangs, recruitment takes place at a very young age. In Central American gangs, the average age of initiation is 14.5 years. Often gangs are able to lure potential members by offering very little. Mexican cartels offer street gang members money, mobile phones and guns (Grillo, 2012: 166). In contrast to organized criminal organizations, most gangs don't have a huge vetting process. In the case of the El Salvadoran gangs, Mara Salvatrucha and the 18th Street Gang, the gang member needed to endure a 13-second or 18-second beating, respectively, by five or six members of a clique. More recently, both gangs have been ordering recruits to execute a violent mission as part of their initiation (Boeri, 2014; Starita, 2007).

The 18th Street Gang in El Salvador changed their recruitment strategy in response to the government after it passed a series of draconian policies known as Mano Dura. To avoid detection from the government, the gang suspended recruiting youth with criminal records. The Mara Salvatrucha Gang responded to the policies by being more aggressive in their recruitment, swelling the membership to about 30,000 members, compared to the 18th Street Gang that has about 18,000.

A study of gangs in the UK revealed that recruitment takes place through peer influence, with vulnerable individuals targeted, particularly those who have been excluded from mainstream school (Windle and Briggs, 2015: 1176). Another study in the UK found that having a prior relationship with an existing gang member is important, because being a gang member requires high levels of trust. Those who do not have a pre-existing relationship are 'beaten in' as a way of earning trust (Densley and Stevens, 2014).

STRATEGY AND TACTICS

Organized criminals use violence in order to achieve their financial objectives. In contrast to terrorist groups specifically, organized criminal groups usually do not want a lot of media attention if that is going to undermine their ability to make money. Because of this, their use of violence is often selective so as to not attract too much attention. These groups usually prefer to remain under the radar and want to conceal all of their profits.

In spite of this, the level of violence associated with organized crime groups has intensified, with the violence escalating into war-like levels.[2] The rate of homicides along the northern and southern borders of Mexico is considered epidemic, even worse than Iraq. In Guatemala and El Salvador, death tolls are higher than during the civil wars (Kalyvas, 2015: 13). In Guatemala, gang members are responsible for 10%–13% of the homicides committed each year. The rest of the homicides are committed mainly by a number of organized groups such as narco-traffickers and rough groups related to the state security apparatus (Richani, 2010: 447).

The traditional norms governing violence have completely eroded. Killings take place in broad daylight, victims are displayed publicly and the violence is more gruesome (such as beheadings and mutilations). Machine guns, grenades and barrels of acid are now used. Women and children are also the victims of violence. Doctors treating the wounded have also been killed as have prominent journalists, teachers and bureaucrats. Drug lords today prefer to have impunity

---

[2]Firearms, grenades and explosives are often used where many innocent bystanders are now being killed.

to operate and will opt for wide-scale levels of violence to attain this. Violent tactics are designed to shock and instil fear. Cartels are more willing to take the state head-on. Police radios are hacked so that police can hear death threats delivered to them. These campaigns have taken their toll on police morale. They have to go against both the cartels and their corrupt colleagues. Many police have quit due to low morale (Sullivan and Elkus, 2008).

The Chechen-organized criminal groups are especially noted for their use of violence as a means to shape attitudes as part of a long-term strategy. Chechen gangs have eclipsed the violence exercised by Russian gangs, operating outside of the norms regulating behaviour among criminal groups. This distinguished the Chechens from other criminal groups. The excessive violence was a warning to anyone who attempted to take them on. Even the Sicilian Cosa Nostra has been alarmed by the Chechens: one Italian criminal reportedly noted that 'where we would first threaten someone, the Russians would kill him. The Chechens would kill his whole family, too' (Galeotti, 2002: 3).

In general, organized crime is at its most violent when there are periods of uncertainty. Though the major drug cartels have been dismantled in Colombia, the smaller cartels or cartelitos are incredibly violent. Russian-organized crime was at its most violent when groups were vying over spheres of influence. Violence was generated by personal vendettas being settled. Russian-organized crime was particularly violent during the 1990s, when it was characterized by hundreds of contract killings. After agreements were reached on spheres of control and influence, the violence decreased.

Box 9.1　Mexico's War on Drugs

The most recent drug wars in Mexico have caused in excess of 120,000 deaths. About 10,000 homicides a year can be attributed to Mexican organized crime from between 2006 and 2011(Molzahn, et al., 2012: 11). What explains the increased violence? In addition to the use of former military personnel to serve as enforcer gangs, violence is at its height among criminal groups when there is more fragmentation and uncertainty. Splintering of criminal groups has led to more violence to overwhelm new challengers (Carpenter, 2010). The violence has been over the top as groups try to outdo one another. Murders are accompanied by a message to try to intimidate civilians and rival groups. The violence by Los Zetas has led to copycats. Many old drug lords have been put in prison and replaced by a new breed that is more callous and reckless. Groups are also trying to minimize civilian defection by engaging in more violence.

The fragmentation of the cartels has been linked to more infighting and violence because commanders have lost control over the rank and file, giving them free rein to engage in gratuitous violence. In 2006 there were six major drug cartels in Mexico, but by 2010 there were twice as many with over 60 local criminal groups (Calderón et al., 2015). New armed groups are springing up as old cartels have been forced to splinter and evolve. The explosion of new cartels has led to a loss of equilibrium that helped to maintain some levels of stability. These newer cartels are more ruthless, more skilled in military tactics, better at psychological warfare and eager to expand into all different types of crime.

The Mexican government's decision to take on the drug cartels head-on, using its military, has also led to an increase in violence. The state response has not been discriminative, which has also caused the violence to escalate (Grillo, 2012: 128). The major cartels (Tijuana, Sinaloa,

Juarez and Gulf) primarily fought amongst themselves, but now they wage a war on the security forces as well. In the case of Colombia and Italy, the state was able to effectively take on the major cartels and the Mafia. This has not happened yet in Mexico (Williams, 2008: 16). This may be due to the fact that Mexico has less capacity and is also facing a much more formidable threat. Excessive violence is also used to show how incapable the state is (Kalyvas, 2015: 14). An example of the intimidation strategy: during one week in May 2008, five police chiefs were assassinated.

The fall of the ruling PRI in 2000 also led to an increase in violence. There was a complete breakdown of government protection deals that police and judicial agents had provided to criminal organizations. This period of uncertainty led to an escalation of violence. There was more mistrust and competition (Carpenter, 2010: 410). This forced the cartels to adopt new, more aggressive, strategies to defend their own turf. It also offered them opportunities to try to conquer new territories (Trejo and Ley, 2013).

FUNDING AND SUPPORT

FUNDING

Organized criminal groups are involved in many different types of enterprises that help them to earn billions. The richest organized criminal group is Solntsevskaya Bratva, which makes most of its money from the drug trade and human trafficking, earning revenues of $8.5 billion. It is very involved in the heroin trade originating in Afghanistan and sold in Russia. In total, the Mafia in Italy generates revenues of $33 billion, with the top earners being the Camorra and 'Ndrangheta mafias, earning $4.9 and $4.5 billion, respectively. The Sinaloa cartel makes 60% of the $6.5 billion made by the Mexican cartels, or about $3 billion a year (Matthews, 2014).

Drug trafficking in particular is extremely lucrative, and is the largest source of profits for organized criminals. It contributes to $200–$250 billion a year to organized crime, but possibly as much as $500 billion – more than the global trade in oil. Drug trafficking accounts for 2% of the global economy and 7% of international trade (Palma, 2015: 478). Thailand's annual $85 billion made from drug trafficking is double the country's exports.

Another major source of funding is the protection racket. In El Salvador, 76% of extortions were committed by youth gangs. Nearly $4 million was demanded in 2011 and $2 million was collected in a suburban neighbourhood in Guatemala. Guatemalan maras extort money from local businesses, nearly $4 million a year (Gurney, 2014). Being in a gang has become a lucrative occupation. In countries where the per capita income is no more than $4,000 a year, a single gang member in El Salvador earns more than that in one month, while Honduran and Guatemalan gang members collect slightly less (Cruz and Durán-Martinez, 2016).[3]

---

[3]A single Salvadoran gang member weekly collects around US $1,250, whereas a Guatemalan gang member collects $975, and a Honduran gang member makes $935. Per capita income levels are $4,023 in El Salvador, $3,886 in Guatemala and $2,365 in Honduras.

EXTERNAL SUPPORT

Drug cartels and organized criminal groups don't need to secure financial aid, but they do need a compliant state that is willing to look the other way. It is often the organized criminal groups that do the paying up, not the other way around. There are exceptions to this, however, if the organized criminal group has a specific good that can be offered to a government.

There has long been speculation that major drug cartels and mafia groups enjoy some political support, but this was especially true for the Latin American drug cartels during the Cold War. The Central Intelligence Agency (CIA) in the US was complicit in making deals with key drug lords in exchange for support to purchase weapons that could be funnelled to paramilitary groups, notably the Contras in Nicaragua in their fight against the left-wing guerrilla movement, the Sandinistas.

Many key drug lords were on the CIA payroll, such as Matta Ballesteros of Honduras. Like many drug lords, Matta Ballesteros was a specialist in transportation and owned a fleet of planes and airstrips. His aviation company, SETCO (Services Ejecutivos Turistas Commander), received its first contract to ship arms from the US to the Nicaraguan Contras in 1983. Matta Ballesteros's company took in about $186,000, but more importantly, the US would look the other way as he smuggled in massive amounts of narcotics into the US through Mexico. In total, the US government paid over $806,000 to known drug traffickers for 'humanitarian assistance' to the Contras (Cockburn and Clair, 1998: 303).

POWER AND IMPACT ON THE STATE AND SOCIETY

Criminal organizations can have tremendous power and of all the violent non-state actors, they pose the biggest threat to security. Organized criminal groups are capable of planning sophisticated crimes and may be in possession of high-tech equipment such as military weapons. They are powerful enough that their reputation alone should be enough to generate obedience.

Organized crime does not seek to destroy the state. It is most interested in controlling or subverting the legal structures to be able to maintain their operations unbothered. It aims to undermine the state rather than destroy it completely. It wants to act with complete freedom of movement in order to achieve its financial objectives (Manwaring, 2011: 863). Nevertheless, crime groups' long-term financial interests require the preservation of state structures (Shelley, 2014: 1). A case in point is that organized crime tends to be higher in urbanized and industrialized areas that require the state's existence.

In extreme cases, organized criminal groups begin to fill the void of the government. They may assume parallel government functions. They can control the entry of businesses into the market. They can impose taxes, tariffs and protection fees. They exert their influence often through violence and coercion, which directly challenges the state's monopoly over the legitimate use of force. They also may provide public goods. This can include repairing schools and hospitals. By providing these goods, they may be able to gain the support and assistance of people in neutralizing efforts by law enforcement. In some states, because of the ineptitude and corruption of the government, groups that would normally oppose organized crime will instead support it because it may provide some stability.

For the most part, organized crime is parasitical. It aims to take from the state. To do so, organized crime co-opts and threatens. Co-optation is more common among economically violent non-state actors. Organized crime can offer huge bribes to the state that the other groups cannot. Though Mexican cartels are competing against the state violently, they are also co-opting it. For the Russian mafia, bribing politicians is a major business expense. This allows them to exert greater influence. In these cases, organized criminal groups are not just forming parallel governments which coexist with an existing one, but have captured the state (for more on this, see Chapter 4).

In the case of Colombia, the cartels directly weakened the quality of the judicial institutions. Judges were routinely threatened by the drug traffickers and offered bribes to not make rulings that would punish the drug cartels. Many principled judges were forced to go into exile. In November 1985, the guerrilla group M-19 was commissioned by the Medellin cartel to assault the Palace of Justice in Colombia while the judges were ruling on the extradition of prominent drug traffickers to the US. Over 100 people were killed in the attack, including nine Supreme Court justices. After an extradition agreement with the US was finally put in place in Colombia in 1987, the Medellin cartel responded by assassinating judges, journalists and five presidential candidates.

Brazilian criminal groups have also had a significant impact on public security. On 12 May 2006, Sao Paulo was paralyzed by warfare between police and members of the PCC, a gang with origins in the prison system (for more on the PCC, see Chapter 2). On a weekend when 10,000 prisoners were given a day pass to visit families outside of prison, the PCC was able to take advantage of the lax security conditions. In response to a plan to transfer PCC members to a top-security penitentiary, a wave of attacks took place against police stations and other symbols of state power. Public security members were hunted down at their posts and in their homes, even in front of family members. Most of the city was shut down, bus services were cut off and businesses were closed. Almost 300 assaults took place and 215 hostages were taken in 80 prison riots. Some 82 public transport buses were burned; as many as 140 people were killed on the first day, with another 53 wounded (Sullivan, 2006).

Case Study   Maras in El Salvador

Maras are a vast network of groups associated with the two major street gangs now dwelling in Central America, Mara Salvatrucha (MS-13) and the 18th Street Gang. They are transnational groups and have organized protection rackets. They emerged from the conflicts in El Salvador, Nicaragua and Guatemala. During the conflicts, millions of people fled to the United States in the 1970s and 1980s. These immigrants found themselves unable to find work, as most were uneducated and unskilled. For many of the young men, they were discriminated against and treated poorly. Many drifted into gangs and started to develop their own gangs as a means of self-preservation.

The 18th Street Gang was formed by El Salvadoran immigrants who had originally joined Mexican gangs, who had not been accepted into existing Hispanic gangs. It was the first Hispanic gang to accept members from all races and to recruit members from other states. Mara Salvatrucha was made up of El Salvadoran immigrants who were later joined by people

(Continued)

(Continued)

from other parts of Central America. From 1993 until 2003 the US enacted a policy where any immigrant who had any brush with the law was sent back to Central America, without giving their governments much warning. In total, 150,000 people were deported, and 43,000 had a criminal record. Many deportees were members of the major gangs. This helped gangs become a transnational problem and facilitated their growth. The maras overwhelmed the local governments, police and legal systems (Ribando, 2007).

These two gangs soon spread with ease in the marginal barrios of San Salvador to the two most violent areas of the city, the Sonsonate and Santa Ana departments. Active gang members claim that they were able to organize and recruit without detection, capitalizing on the limitations of the state and the poor conditions in the marginal areas (Richani, 2010: 437).

Though many gang members were deported, most of the deportees had never been members of the main maras. The deportees were young, vulnerable males that were accustomed to completely different cultures. Some barely spoke Spanish and had weak ties to their original home country. They arrived often without their family, and needing to find a sense of family quickly joined the gangs. Contacts were facilitated by the heavy presence of tattoos, particularly on the face, the dress code and the means of communication (Cruz, 2010: 388).

Initially, it was impossible to identify any sort of formal leadership within a gang. The members would deny that any internal or external structure existed. They were all members of one grand mara that comprised a federation of clikas. The structure of cohesion of gangs changed due to the Mano Dura plans that took place in several Central American countries from 2001 to 2006. The law made it illegal to be a gang member. Crackdowns were harsh. Anyone who had an ostentatious tattoo could be apprehended. The prison population swelled as the number of gang members inside the prisons went from 4,000 to 8,000, making up one-third of the prison population (Dudley, 2011: 897).

While in prisons, gangs have organized themselves better and have created more structured organizations. Gangs were separated in detention centres according to gang affiliation, with authorities reasoning that this would lessen the violence within the prisons. Gang members from the same gang federation but from different clikas came together from different places and established contact with each other. These conditions allowed gangs to set up their networks inside jails and crate national structures that could also expand outside of jails. Gangs were able to rethink their operations that took place outside of prison. They started meeting in private areas as opposed to public locations. They moved in vehicles instead of walking on the streets. They linked up with drug cartels while in prison and started to impose a protection tax to extort local businesses in zones that they controlled. As a result, some gangs have become more sophisticated and powerful.

CONCLUSION

Organized criminal groups and gangs are ubiquitous actors and pose the biggest threat to security. They take advantage of what the state has to offer, while also thriving off state weakness. They don't usually emerge in the weakest states in the world, but those with ungoverned spaces and failed communities. Unfortunately, the violence over time has increased from these groups. No longer held back by norms that prevented collateral damage, they use violence to send a message. Though they have little if any political motivation, they are increasingly connected to other powerful actors. Understanding how these groups emerge and thrive is thus critical to mitigating their impact.

Summary Points

- Organized criminal groups are capable and complex organizations.
- Gangs have evolved and become much more violent and powerful, but they are not as sophisticated as organized criminal groups.
- While gang members are incredibly young and seek out gangs due to a need for camaraderie, organized criminals are often older and more skilled.
- Of all the violent non-state actors, it is organized crime that has the biggest impact on the state.
- Both gangs and organized crime can emerge in strong states that have failed communities or areas of institutional weakness.

Key Questions

1 What are key differences between a gang and an organized criminal group?
2 In what ways are organized criminal groups involved in political activity? Why do they choose to do this?
3 Why have organized criminal groups and gangs become more violent?
4 What are the three generations of gangs? How have gangs evolved over time?
5 What are the major impacts of organized criminal groups and gangs on the state?
6 Theory: How do rational choice theories explain criminal behaviour?

FURTHER READING

Abadinsky, H. (2012) *Organized Crime* (Cengage). Textbook on organized crime, providing comprehensive analysis of its origins and structure.

Albanese, J.S. (2010) *Organized Crime in Our Times* (Routledge). Overview of all of the developments in organized crime, its history and the theories to understand organized crime. It also offers an explanation of the key organized crime figures, their transnational links and how criminal justice can respond to it.

Franzese, R.J., Covey, H.C. and Menard, S. (2016) *Youth Gangs* (Charles C. Thomas). Recent update on youth gangs, including an overview of the literature on why youth gangs form; chapters are devoted to different types of gangs, such as ethnic and female gangs.

Knox, G.W. (1994) *An Introduction to Gangs* (Wyndham Hall Press). Textbook covering everything on gangs, including the societal conditions in which they emerge, their organization, group characteristics and how they differ from organized crime.

United Nations Office on Drugs and Crime. www.unodc.org/unodc/en/data-and-analysis Statistics and data on organized crime and drug trafficking.

10

PRIVATE SECURITY COMPANIES AND PARAMILITARY UNITS

Key Terms

- Blackwater
- Contras
- DynCorp
- Plausible deniability
- United Self-Defence Forces (AUC)

This chapter provides an introduction to private security companies (PSCs), paramilitary units and death squads. The former are hired by states to achieve stability. They are mostly motivated by profits but they are more political than they first appear. The latter two are contracted covertly by states to do their dirty work. Both usually fight at the behest of a government, but their motivations are largely economic. These actors merit attention in order to better understand how they negatively or positively contribute to security. The chapter will offer examples of US PSCs and the now defunct South African group, Executive Outcomes.

DEFINITION

PSCs are non-state actors that are recruited by governments to fight in combat units. PSCs can provide training, consulting and planning, maintenance and technical assistance, operational and logistical support, intelligence services and post-conflict reconstruction. PSCs promise to respond to crises with armed personnel to re-establish stability. Private *military* companies are engaged in actual direct combat, whereas PSCs imply that the group could provide a range of services. Private military companies provide offensive services and are designed to have a military impact. PSCs offer defensive services and are designed to protect individuals and property. PSCs have mostly originated in rich countries with large security industries such as the US and the UK, but have also been prevalent in countries like South Africa.

Unless noted otherwise, throughout this chapter we will refer to private military and security companies both as PSCs.

In the last three decades, there has been an explosion of PSCs. In the 1991 Gulf War there was one contractor for every 50 active duty personnel. By 1999 in Kosovo, this number was one in ten. In Iraq, there may be equal number of contractors to US military personnel (Chesterman, 2016: 5). This explosion of PSCs has led to concerns that there is a privatization of violence taking place, which may bring with it negative consequences for overall stability (Chesterman and Fisher, 2009).

Box 10.1   Mercenaries

'Mercenaries' is a term that differs from PSCs only slightly. The main difference is that mercenaries are banned under international law, while private security and military companies are supposedly acting on a legalized and licensed basis. A mercenary is a soldier who is not a national of one of the groups in conflict, who is willing to sell his military skills to the highest bidder. Mercenaries are paid in excess of paid combatants of similar ranks and functions in a state military. In practice, it is not clear whether or not mercenaries only fight for monetary gain. Some have fought against communists during the Cold War and some for religious reasons in the Balkans and Afghanistan. Like PSCs, mercenaries are not just restricted to combat. They may also engage in training, organizing, equipping and gathering intelligence for their home government. They are often used to maintain stability.

In spite of this, mercenaries are associated with escalating conflicts and taking part in overthrowing governments or propping up dictatorships. Mercenaries may be less likely to adhere to international laws and human rights. But critics claim that the articles (Article 47) of the Geneva Convention which condemn mercenaries do not adequately address the role of PSCs by sovereign states, which are also engaged in combat roles (Chesterman, 2016).[1] Thus the division between what constitutes a mercenary and what constitutes a PSC is hazy.

PARAMILITARY FORCES

Paramilitary forces are organizations that are outside of the formal security sector and central government command that use violence to target groups that are aiming to change the status quo. Though they formally lie outside of the state, they are often viewed as an extension of the state. They usually receive support from factions of the state and may make alliances with multiple power holders in the system, such as the economic elite (Grajales, 2011). Though they remain outside the law, they often enjoy some of the resources, access and status that is exclusive to the state. Paramilitary forces sometimes identify themselves as self-defence groups while their critics call them death squads. As a later section will illustrate, a death squad is a specific type of paramilitary unit.

Paramilitaries are often used to counter reform efforts. They are interested in defending the political and economic status quo. They emerge in settings where

---

[1]This refers to the Geneva Conventions of 12 August 1949 and 8 June 1977.

there is an oligarchy, which has a monopoly over the country's resources and wealth. They also emerge in states where there may be a significant degree of wealth for parts of the population. In contrast to warlords and marauders, they don't just emerge in failed states. They emerge with the complicity of the state (Mazzei, 2009). In contrast to organized criminals, they are not using violence to directly capitalize on wealth. In contrast to PSCs, they are not used in an official sense to create stability in exchange for payment. However, they are provoked and stimulated by financial factors. They want to defend the interests of the wealthy, which in turn may directly affect their own wealth. Security groups thrive from the financial support that they may gain from the state.

DEATH SQUADS

A death squad is an armed group that conducts extrajudicial killings and other violent acts against clearly defined groups of people that present a challenge to the legitimacy of the state and the elites. Death squads are usually clandestine and irregular organizations, but they often have the support of domestic or foreign governments. They emerge in states that are unable to maintain a monopoly over the legitimate use of force. They are subcontracted by the state to allow legitimate state authorities to avoid any association with the atrocities committed by death squads. They operate in areas where the government does not want to go.

The term 'death squad' denotes that military, paramilitary and irregular units are involved. They operate somewhere in between the state security apparatus and the criminal underworld of killers and torturers (Breuil and Rozema, 2009: 415). They are a result of policing being more and more frequently subcontracted out to the highest bidder (Huggins, 2000: 204). Death squads can be found all over the world, and in the last 40 years were responsible for millions of deaths. They did not disappear with the end of the Cold War. They are not uniquely a developing world problem as there have been historical cases of death squads in the US, Europe and Asia as well.

Box 10.2   Tonton Macoutes

The Tonton Macoutes was a paramilitary death squad in Haiti set up by François Duvalier in 1959. Unlike most death squads, the group was officially part of the Duvalier regime, though it was never part of the regular armed forces (at its height, the group never had more than 10,000 members). The group wore a uniform of straw hats, denim shirts and sunglasses. Though they looked as though they were heading to a picnic, they were armed with machetes. Their official name was the Volunteers for National Security (Volontaires de la Sécurité Nationale; VSN), but their nickname was derived from the Creole term for a mythological bogeyman.

The group was set up to provide information for the Duvalier regime and detect any subversion. Like other death squads, they were used to strike terror into anyone that advocated a progressive agenda. Anyone who opposed Duvalier was killed, and opponents would often disappear at night. Their methods were particularly violent. Showing no mercy towards civilians, they would often stone people and set them on fire. Dead bodies were showcased in order to terrorize the public. Even the smallest infraction could lead to a violent reprisal by the group. Because they were poorly paid, they often resorted to stealing and exacting private contributions by force (Ferguson, 1987). In total, the group slaughtered more than 600,000 Haitians (Fuller, 1991).

Unfortunately, death squads are still commonplace in Haiti today. The most feared group is the Front for the Advancement and Progress of Haiti (FRAPH). It attempts to mask itself as a political party, but it was responsible for terrible atrocities in targeting and killing supporters of democratically elected president Jean-Bertrand Aristide (who was deposed in a coup in 1991) and controlling the public during the de facto military rule period until 1994. The group was led by Louis Jodel Chamblain, who had been a sergeant in the Haitian Armed Forces until 1990 (Wucker, 2004). The US government originally supported the group until 1995, when the abuses became internationally known. Many members went into hiding and its leader, Chamblain, was convicted of taking part in the assassination of a noted pro-democracy businessman in absentia.

POLITICAL IDEOLOGY AND OBJECTIVES

PSCs and mercenaries are supposedly motivated by profits and have no political goals. PSCs are intended to be in the business of providing security and stability. They are not supposed to represent the interests of one particular country or ideological viewpoint, and in theory will make their services available to countries that are suffering from conflict, instability or both. They may be used on both sides of a conflict. They also lend their services to NGOs and international agencies such as the United Nations and corporations.

But the apolitical nature of PSCs must be called into question. Many PSCs are made up of ex-military and government personnel. Former government officials and military officers enter the private sector and are able to exert their political influence through their connections and insider knowledge (Mathieu and Dearden, 2007). They may also have links with powerful elites in multinational corporations, such as has been the case of the American PSC Blackwater. Blackwater's vice-chair, Cofer Black, worked for the US State Department as the coordinator for counter-terrorism. He also directed the CIA's Counter-terror Centre (Isenberg, 2009). Joseph Schmitz, the chief operations officer for Blackwater's parent company, was also the Pentagon's inspector general. Employees from Titan, another American PSC, have been former senior air force officials and a Pentagon official. Thus, there is a revolving door between government and military personnel and PSCs, which poses a challenge to the notion that these organizations are entirely apolitical (Mathieu and Dearden, 2007).

The process of how contracts are awarded has been criticized for being driven by financial and political interests coinciding between the PSCs, the multinationals and the governments that solicit their services. Many of the contracts were not awarded based on full and open competition. Oversight is also complicated by the extent of subcontracting that takes place (Holmqvist, 2005).

Because PSCs are in the business of being involved in conflicts, they also have clear political preferences for who holds power. To illustrate the political nature of PSCs, in 2001, the ten leading US private military firms spent more than US $32 million on lobbying, and donated more than $12 million to political campaigns.

DynCorp, yet another American PSC, donated more than $500,000 between 1999 and 2002, with 72% of the donations going to the Republican Party. Titan spent $2.16 million from 1998 to 2004 on lobbying, which seems like money well spent: 96% of its $1.8 billion in earnings in 2003 came from contracts it had with the US government (Mathieu and Dearden, 2007). They have also tended to provide security and combat for an incumbent regime and have had a proclivity for offering support to more conservative regimes.

Because PSCs are in theory apolitical, they can be used to avoid political pitfalls. When it may be politically costly to deploy actual government troops, governments who want to intervene are able to use PSCs with fewer political costs. Sending private contractors working for profit, of their own choice, does not require the same level of political mobilization as sending national troops, serving their country. In Iraq, PSCs provided extra support to address the Iraqi insurgency without the political and bureaucratic lead time required for mobilizing military forces (Elsea et al., 2008).

Paramilitary organizations tend to have the same political views as military hardliners (Mazzei, 2009: 30). They use violence to protect the established order, and are never attempting to overthrow it. They enable the state to perpetrate violence against state enemies while still maintaining a clean international appearance. Death squads are also usually right-wing and counter-revolutionary in that they oppose any group that aims to challenge the status quo. They are more likely to emerge in societies where there is an alliance between the military and the economic elite.

For both groups, their political objectives are largely motivated by financial exigencies to enforce the status quo and maintain the economic powers of the elites. They don't defend the interests of society as a whole, but aim to defend the interests of the established order. Paramilitary organizations are often set up to protect property rights against landless peasants and to prevent any sort of agrarian counter-reform (Grajales, 2011). Though they have strong financial factors that influence their activity, unlike PSCs, recruits join out of some grass-roots activism and not just for a salary.

In Nicaragua, the Contras (Frente Democratico Nacional; 1981–88) were one of the most notable right-wing paramilitary groups. They were made up of recruits from the former national guard of the Somoza dictatorship. Various factions from the Somoza regime started a series of rebellions to overthrow the Sandinista government, cooperating only very loosely (Miranda and Ratliff, 1992). Their official role was to undermine the military support structure in Nicaragua from the Cuban government (Roberts, 1990: 78).

Some death squad members may also be motivated by a sense of social responsibility to maintain order which they feel the formal government is unable to do. They may believe that society needs to be socially cleansed of 'non-desirables' such as abandoned street children, prostitutes, drug addicts and petty criminals. Interviews with Brazilian policemen involved in death squads reveal the apparent motives for the violence. They view it as a more effective way of fighting crime. The operatives see themselves as purposed because the state is incapable and corrupt. The death squads in El Salvador's civil war viewed themselves similarly. They are doing what the army needed to do but could not because their hands were tied.

Box 10.3   Vigilantism

Vigilantism is a form of self-policing by a non-state actor. Vigilantes break the law in order to achieve their goals of protection, justice, order and revenge. Though there is usually no cooperation between vigilante groups and the state, often the state is completely ambivalent. Vigilantes may garner some support in the community (especially when there are low levels of trust in the police), but they deny the role of the state in providing social order, and create a parallel order that is unregulated (Haas et al., 2014). In Russia, vigilante justice has been used by organized crime and religious groups who target prostitutes and drug addicts (Tyler, 2000). In Nigeria, where crime has skyrocketed, vigilante groups such as the Bakassi Boys have emerged, taking the law into their own hands with tacit approval of the government. But while some governments may decide to look the other way, vigilantism can prolong conflicts and increase tensions between sectarian groups.

In Northern Ireland, vigilantism was a fixture of the conflict. Vigilantism was written about in the IRA training manuals, articulating that it would be part of their overall strategy (Morrison, 2015). From 1970–2000, around 115 people were killed due to vigilante attacks, with another 4,000 hospitalized (Silke and Taylor, 2000). Vigilantes in Northern Ireland used a wide range of tactics, starting with warnings and followed by curfews, fines and acts of public humiliation. In more serious cases, paramilitaries resorted to beatings, shootings, expulsions from Northern Ireland and, finally, assassination. Over 1,300 were victims to punishment beatings and over 2,000 have been victim to punishment shootings (Silke, 1998). Though beatings may inflict more bodily harm, victims of humiliation claim that the damage is more traumatic (Nicholas et al., 1993). In particular, tarring and feathering is an extreme form of public humiliation, with women being the prime targets. Victims are doused with hot asphalt and then covered with feathers, usually tied to lampposts with signs attached indicating their alleged crimes. The victim's hair is chopped off to add to the humiliation. Removing the tar at the hospital is also incredibly painful (Silke, 1998).

Unfortunately, vigilantism in Northern Ireland has not ceased, as a host of new groups have emerged, targeting the communities that they supposedly represent (Horgan and Morrison, 2011: 651). Vigilantes claim that the victims are all getting what they deserve, but the actions of vigilantes undermines the rule of law, weakens the credibility of the state and in some cases may exacerbate tensions in a conflict (Tankebe, 2009).

Many groups have members that are motivated by the financial gain that being part of a death squad offers. In the case of the Davao Death Squad (DDS), which targets criminals in the Philippines, members are paid ten times as much as they would earn normally. Some of the members of the death squads began to offer their services as guns for hire.

STRUCTURE AND RECRUITMENT

STRUCTURE

PSCs are structured like a military with a clear chain of command, though they can deploy more quickly. They can also field the exact kind of forces that are needed and have access to military equipment. PSCs are usually composed of former soldiers who have received training and may have had experience working together. They may be more cohesive than ad hoc multinational forces, but they may not wear uniforms.

Paramilitaries are organized, trained similarly to a professional military, but they are not included as part of the state's formal armed forces. However, in contrast to insurgents, they do not aim to rebel against or overthrow the state. They use violence to move within the system, not to oppose it (Barkey, 1994: 195). They are unofficial security forces that serve a military or quasi-military function. They are structured to resemble a command or military organization and they vary in size. Unlike death squads, they are not secret organizations, but they do not always wear uniforms. They may display a symbol such as a flag or insignia on their arm band. They may dress similarly to showcase their identity and sport distinctive clothing or signs. For example, paramilitary forces in Kosovo wore black and camouflage uniforms, red bandanas, black masks and red scarves. They also had shaved heads and wore a red insignia on their uniform (Krieger, 2001: 57). Paramilitary units in Northern Ireland often did not wear uniforms, but many received military training (Helsinki Watch Organization, 1991: 116).

As death squads are very clandestine, it is hard to know their exact structure. Death squads are a form of paramilitarism usually linked to the state's security apparatus or some rogue element of it. Because many of the members of these organizations come from the military, there is evidence that they are highly structured organizations, usually structured along military lines though they are legally autonomous from the state. Unlike vigilantism, they are not spontaneous. Their operations are well planned, financed and executed. They differ from lone assassinations that may be the work of a single individual. For example, the DDS started off with only ten members, but was composed of 500 members by 2009 (Breuil and Rozema, 2009).

Death squads have a more permanent organization and are set up to conduct ongoing operations on a fairly large scale. There may be a tiered system with a leader, higher-ranking individuals and personnel consisting of hitmen, drivers and lookouts. They may also be divided into small cells. The chain of command may start from high levels of the security forces. The head may have direct contacts with other security forces, and pays off and recruits foot soldiers, though the foot soldiers may not know who the leader of the organization is.

In the case of the El Salvadoran death squads, all activity was directed by the National Republican Alliance (ARENA) party in association with the security force members. ARENA party leader Roberto D'Aubuisson sometimes gave directives directly while at other times, underlings of the party took their own initiative. ARENA was essentially an umbrella organization for a diverse group of death squads, all controlled by the same paymaster. The prevalence of so many death squads gave the appearance of mass participation and multiple sources of responsibility (Arnson, 2000).

Death squads were well equipped with weapons, often because members already were in possession of them. To avoid being noticed, death squad members usually do not wear uniforms, though sometimes they may wear masks. In the case of the Davao death squad in the Philippines, members did not wear uniforms, only jackets, even during hot weather, and buttoned shirts, to hide firearms and knives, and baseball caps. They did not wear masks. They rode around on motorcycles, but to conceal themselves did not have licence plates.

RECRUITMENT

Most of the staff members of PSCs are recruited from ex-military personnel, police, civil affairs officers and special operations forces. PSCs can recruit personnel with particular skills, such as with language or area expertise. These companies recruit from databases of mostly retired military and police personnel, making it easier to hire people with particular experience. PSCs can recruit quality personnel by offering them two to four times what they could earn in their own country's forces and fielding them for (potentially) short periods of time (about six months at a time).

Recruitment is not always that thorough, however. Many PSCs do not thoroughly vet their personnel. Some companies have had slack procedures for recruitment. US and British firms often use employees from other countries, which complicates the procedures for prosecution in the case of misconduct. Individuals who have been drawn in to work in the private security sector of Iraq have not had great human rights records. Blackwater confirmed that in Iraqi contracts, commandos were recruited from former forces that were loyal to Chilean dictator Augusto Pinochet (Holmqvist, 2005).

Paramilitary units are usually recruited from elite well-trained sections of a country's military and police force. Many are soldiers that have been made redundant, or even whole units of redundant or breakaway soldiers, which sometimes include common criminals. Paramilitary fighters were recruited in Colombia by luring discharged active duty military officers with generous salaries, cars, and even land (Human Rights Watch, 2015). The AUC of Colombia had a huge membership, as high as 80,000. The recruitment of death squad members also usually comes from the secret police forces, special counter-insurgency units, government soldiers and regular police members. They may be able to recruit mercenaries or expelled police officers. They may also consist of police or members of the military who need more income. Police officers could be working at a desk by day and covertly operating as a member of a death squad at night, as has been the case in Brazil.

When the attorney general investigated the Colombian death squad Muerte a Secuestradores, which had been linked to the drug cartels, they found that 59 members accused of belonging to it were on active military service (Pearce, 1990: 177). An investigation carried out in 1991 showed that 27% (8,000 police officers) of the Rio de Janeiro police force had been invited, at one time or another, to join these groups. Another report in the 1990s claimed that half of the city's death squad members are off-duty or ex-policemen (Brookes, 1991). Reports claimed that in Brazil a death squad member could earn about $500 for killing an adult 'undesirable' and $40 to $50 for killing a street kid (Brookes, 1991). Low police salaries help to lure policemen to join the death squads.

Many of the recruits to the DDS were members of the security apparatus, most notably the police, but the death squad also recruited young men and boys who may have been petty criminals, had no job and no place to live. Many had been involved in a bit of drug pushing before joining the death squad. Individuals whose friends or relatives were members of the DDS claimed that they joined for the easy money. The payment for each operation is about $100 to $1,000 and can be as high as $2,000 (Human Rights Watch, 2009: 58).

STRATEGY AND TACTICS

What PSCs are allowed to do is not entirely clear. They do not always have well established mandates for what their tasks are supposed to be. They are not part of a long-term strategy as they are usually hired to provide a quick surge of armed personnel to increase security. Though they do not aim to combat troops, their actions are sometimes indistinguishable from military forces. Some PSC employees have detained people, erected checkpoints without authorization and confiscated identity cards.

PSCs are supposed to have defensive tasks, but they sometimes get trigger-happy. The most notable example of this was the Nisour Square Massacre in Iraq which took place on 16 September 2007, involving the Blackwater security company. Employees of Blackwater opened fire on unarmed pedestrians and motorists in Baghdad's bustling Nisour Square. The massacre left 17 civilians dead and two dozen wounded. Blackwater mercenaries have also been accused of allegedly shooting at a taxi in Baghdad during 2005, killing the passenger and injuring the driver (Risen and Mazzetti, 2009; Scahill, 2011).

Paramilitaries are mostly offensive, not defensive in nature. The tactics used by PSCs compared to paramilitary organizations helps to illustrate one of their differences. PSCs are supposed to respect human rights, target combatants only and must adhere to the rule of law. Whether or not they are awarded a contract again may depend somewhat on how they handled the operation. A paramilitary organization's success is not dependent on being considered legitimate domestically or to the international community. Paramilitary groups are used on behalf of the political establishment to handle the dirty business of targeted kidnappings and killings, massacres, ethnic cleansing and forcible resettlements. In contrast to insurgencies, their success is also not dependent on casting a wide net of support from the local population. They do not need to appeal to the masses. Though, like insurgents, they sometimes engage in co-optation, destabilization and intimidation, they mostly engage in physical elimination of targeted groups.

In Colombia, the AUC was involved in many atrocities and organized crime such as drug trafficking, oil theft, extortion and kidnapping. The biggest victims of the AUC were ordinary Colombians. Many indigenous communities were displaced. They even taxed local citizens and regulated how they could dress (Grajales, 2011).

In Guatemala, the Fuerzas Armadas Rebeldes was founded by disgruntled Guatemalan army officers in 1963. They practised a scorched earth campaign, razing 626 Mayan villages. Though most of the violence took place between 1980 and 1982, selective assassinations continued up into the 1990s (Sanford, 2003). The Guatemalan paramilitaries kidnapped, tortured to death and buried peasants in hidden graves. In Nicaragua, the Contras terrorized Nicaraguan villages, bombed health clinics, schools, irrigation projects, power plants, oil pipelines, ports and bridges.

In the Colombian conflict, paramilitaries were responsible for 80% of the killings (Sanford, 2003: 76). Most of the victims were unarmed civilians, often people who worked for NGOs, churches, unions and community activists. Even as late as 2002, paramilitaries killed far more civilians than did guerrilla combatants, but were barely a target of the government.

A death squad's most common activity is murder, but they also engage in torture, rape, arson, bombing or forced disappearances. The killings are often conducted in ways meant to ensure the secrecy of the killers' identities. They are not usually targeting combatants or irregular forces. They mostly target civilians. Death squads aim to eliminate the leaders of 'subversive' movements and terrorize or kill their sympathizers (Gurr, 1988). In the case of Argentina, death squads used by the military regime (1977–1983) would kidnap the children of captured 'subversives' and torture them in front of their parents, and vice versa.

The victims are a wide array of individuals. Some death squads target those that they view as undesirable. Others target anyone who is seen as a challenge to the status quo. Trade union members are especially targeted, and have been a common target in Colombia. Colombia accounted for more than half of all unionists killed globally from January 1990 to March 1991. Community leaders are also a common target. Between 1991 and 1993, in the area of Rio de Janeiro alone, extermination squads executed 31 community leaders. In the case of El Salvador, anyone suspected of communism was killed by death squads. Before the 1982 elections in El Salvador, hundreds of unarmed peasants, including women, children, and elderly people, were massacred as they attempted to flee to Honduras (Mason and Krane, 1989: 190). Death squads have no qualms about exterminating adults, adolescents and small children alike.

FUNDING AND SUPPORT

FUNDING

PSCs were formed to gain profits. They provide security in return for a lucrative contract or access to an entrepreneurial venture. The combined revenues for all PSCs across the world have skyrocketed. British PSCs earned £1.8 billion in 2004 alone, up from £320 million in 2003 (Richards, 2006: 2). The global market for private security will reach $244 billion by 2016 (Griffin, 2013). Though proponents of these companies claim that they help cut costs of providing security, costs savings have been elusive in the case of Iraq.

In addition to the revenues that PSCs gain from lucrative contracts, they also earn money by gaining a foothold in the industries of the countries that they are offering protection for. In particular, offering protection to the extractive industry infrastructure is a key element of PSC operations. PSCs have sought out political elites of weak or failing states that were also rich in oil or mineral extraction. For weak countries, PSCs can offer protection in return for future commercial opportunities. In return for drilling or mining concessions, political leaders could afford their services to protect the country's important resources while also marginalizing threats from political opponents. Thus they finance their services through the exploitation of resources in areas they have neutralized, often to the detriment of the local population (Cilliers and Mason, 1999).

Paramilitaries and death squads may receive some government backing, but much of their income comes from wealthy supporters. Paramilitary groups are also largely self-funded. They have become involved in black market activity, illegally selling weapons, drugs or other valuable commodities such as oil and diamonds. Some have even become involved in kidnapping for profit. Once paramilitaries become established in rural areas, they start to ask for protection taxes or side payments. Some farmers who are forced to pay for protection may wind up hiring their own paramilitary forces to protect them at a lower cost (Sanchez, 2006).

In the Colombian case, the AUC was very involved in criminal activities. It grew, refined and domestically moved its own cocaine, even trafficking its drugs to international markets.

SUPPORT

PSCs have various sources of support. They have support from the states that hire them to maintain security, from multinational corporations that solicit their business, and from NGOs, humanitarian agencies and international organizations. The United Nations, for example, has made use of private security firms to provide local intelligence, logistics, transport and communications services for their mission in East Timor. PSCs are legal, and states contract them to maintain stability.

Paramilitary organizations do not operate within the state structure, but they do operate with state support and frequently work closely with the state. They are often funded, equipped and trained by state authorities. Though the state may never officially acknowledge the links with paramilitary organizations, they do little to eliminate them. Thus, unlike PSCs, these organizations are not private. They are semi-private. It is elements within the state itself that play a role in their creation and direction, though the state usually refuses to recognize any links to the group. Paramilitaries in Colombia emerged in the 1960s after legislation was passed that permitted the formation of local self-defence groups. Thus, paramilitaries like the AUC had the assistance of the Colombian government to fight left-wing insurgencies. They also had the support of the drug cartels who often used their services to provide protection from left-wing guerrilla groups.

Paramilitary organizations are also likely to receive support from foreign governments who share their goals. US President Ronald Reagan decided to offer his support to the Contras, providing millions in funding in the 1980s. The US government has also offered its support for various paramilitary organizations in Haiti in its attempt to oust democratically elected president Jean-Bertrand Aristide in 1991 (Whitney, 1996).

Death squads almost always operate with the overt support, complicity or acquiescence of the government. The violence is sanctioned by the regime either explicitly or implicitly by not trying to curtail the acts. Nevertheless, it is difficult to prove the government's role in supporting or dictating the activities of death squads. Providing proof usually comes at a great cost to local human rights organizations and monitors, who are themselves often among the prime targets of the death squads. There are some cases where the links are clearly established, such as was the case in El Salvador with the ARENA party under D'Aubuisson. Though they usually have government support, there are death squads that have been formed and supervised by drug lords or warlords.

Officials within the US-supported unity government in Iraq had unofficial ties to the death squads that began operating in Baghdad around 2006. As the murder rate escalated in the capital city to dozens per day, evidence of the connections between the perpetrators and their organizations and officials within the government were uncovered. Members of the Iraqi police force were found to overlap with the individuals making up paramilitary groups, who were carrying out gruesome attacks and leaving a trail of corpses (Kaufmann, 2007).

POWER AND IMPACT ON THE STATE AND SOCIETY

Though some PSCs may provide stability, there are several negative spillovers of having private armed groups that can challenge the state's monopoly over the legitimate use of force. They affect the quality of democracy, commit human rights abuses, engage in the proliferation of weapons in conflict zones and are ineffective in long-term conflict resolution.

PSCs have a direct impact on democracy in the countries that use them. One of the most notable reasons for this is that legislative branches are often not involved in making contracts with these groups, giving the executive more power and diminishing the effects of democratic restraint. Privatization of security erodes the established tools for accountability and makes it easier to take action. When the US wanted to support the rebel Sudanese People's Liberation Movement, they awarded a contract to DynCorp as a way to avoid Congressional oversight, according to a US government official (El Tom, 2009).

States may also be more likely to use force if they face fewer political costs for doing so. States have a greater capacity to become involved in politically sensitive conflicts without facing the repercussions of risking their own troops. Using them also allows governments to circumvent legal obstacles. In 1991, a UN arms embargo prohibited the sale of weapons to, or training of, any warring party in the former Yugoslavia. The US government was able to circumvent this embargo by having one of its PSCs forge a contract with Croatia to provide training, allowing the US to evade responsibility for the human rights abuses that took place. By using PSCs, the state can distance itself from events and create 'plausible deniability' (Elms and Phillips, 2009).

Moreover, because legislative branches are often not involved in the decision process, they have little information available. This reduces transparency and makes it easier for actors who are commercially interested to impact policy. It also reduces the information available to the public and obscures governmental responsibility if there are breaches of international laws and standards. In addition, there tends to be much less media coverage of contractors compared to troops. PSCs themselves provide little information, which would normally be available by state security forces (Avant and Sigelman, 2010).

PSCs are also above the law when they commit human rights abuses. Many may be liable for their actions under international law, but bringing a case against them is very difficult (Carney, 2005). This is especially true in states where the rule of law is weak and ineffective. Determining the human rights abuses taking place in conflict situations is especially difficult. The US government in particular has faced accusations of creating rules-free zones by groups such as Amnesty International. PSCs can stipulate in their contracts that they are immune from prosecution in the weak states where they operate. This is the case for all non-Iraqi military personnel under Coalition Provisional Authority CPA Order 17 for acts performed within the terms of their contracts, giving unprecedented power to foreign nationals.

Regulating PSCs is difficult. There are no real checks on their activity beyond not renewing contracts. Contracts often allow a wide range of unspecified duties to be carried out, with few standards, safeguards or monitoring mechanisms, and sometimes spanning more than one country. Oversight is further complicated by the extent of subcontracting between PSCs and the fact that many PSC staff members are actually freelance consultants. Where oversight is impossible, self-regulation is ignored. A further complicating matter of accountability is the fact that many PSC employees do not wear uniforms, making it harder to identify when they have been involved in abuse (Avant, 2005a).

PSCs also do not contribute to conflict resolution and long-term security for all. They have an interest in ongoing conflicts. They can only end conflicts with force, not peaceful methods of resolution. These victories are only temporary and do not always lead to a lasting peace (Mathieu and Dearden, 2007). They have also been accused of channelling weapons into conflict zones. PSCs also create a false image of security, making it harder to properly assess security needs. It also further weakens the establishment of legitimate security institutions by crowding them out. The proliferation of PSCs has produced an unequal distribution of security in many weak states. Those who can afford their own security are advantaged over those who cannot, since law and order in their countries is not upheld.

The demand for all of these services undoubtedly reflects the increasing blurring of the boundaries between internal and external security. Private security guards outnumber the police in South Africa. At the height of the Iraq conflict, there were over 100,000 PSCs in Iraq (Lane, 2010).

Case Study   Executive Outcomes

Executive Outcomes is one of the best-known PSCs, though it is now defunct. Unlike many PSCs, it generated a largely positive image for its work stabilizing the wars in Angola and Sierra Leone. The organization was founded in South Africa by a former lieutenant-colonel of the South African defence force, Eeben Barlow, in 1989. Executive Outcomes did not have a standing army or a major stockpile of weapons. It did, however, have very well trained soldiers who served as a stabilizing force in Africa (Howe, 1998).

Executive Outcomes was first contracted by the Popular Movement for the Liberation of Angola (MPLA) government to defeat Joan Savimbi's UNITA force. Ironically, many employees of Executive Outcomes had previously fought to defeat the MPLA. Due to their superior training, Executive Outcomes was able to quickly help recapture the diamond areas by mid-1994 and the oil installations. The cost of the contract was relatively low for the Angolan government. The Angolan government spent over $500 million on its military but only $41 million to contract Executive Outcomes (Howe, 1998).

In May 1995, the Sierra Leone government contracted Executive Outcomes to help combat the RUF. The war had been going on for four years, with the Sierra Leonean government unable to fight off the RUF. Executive Outcome soldiers arrived by May 1995 and trained 150 government soldiers in a few weeks. They were able to quickly push the poorly organized RUF troops out of the capital and protected the diamond districts (Singer, 2011). They also were able to help open the roads to Freetown to ensure that food and fuel transport reached the capital. As was the case in Angola, Executive Outcome's activities were cited as critical to facilitating a ceasefire (Howe, 1998).

Executive Outcomes has remained very loyal to its employers, not switching sides or threatening the government. It also was selective about its clients and refused to work for non-sovereign states (Chesterman and Lehnardt, 2007). It has also not avoided combat when it was necessary. In spite of this positive reputation, critics claim that the company became very involved in gaining access to long-term concessions in the resource industries. For example, some resource extraction corporations may have financed the costs of Executive Outcomes when the Sierra Leone government could not pay the organization.

Paramilitaries can be highly fragmented, and once created they are often difficult to control. They can evade government control and develop their own agenda (Dasgupta, 2009). Paramilitaries usurp or delegate part of the state's monopoly over the legitimate use of violence. Many paramilitary organizations emerged in Central America during the Cold War with the encouragement of the US to help deal with communist subversion. The paramilitaries were more violent than the insurgencies that were assigned to fight and paid no attention to the notion of human rights.

Death squads also affect the legitimacy of the state and encourage a culture of impunity, though they sometimes operate with the public's consent, as has been the case with the upper and middle classes in Brazil. They operate with immunity from any sort of prosecution. They can threaten witnesses and intimidate judges. They are also not brought to trial due to inefficiencies in the judiciary. For other countries, such as in Central America, the death squads' pursuit of impoverished citizens has deeply affected the public's trust of the state.

Like paramilitaries, death squads enable the state to claim 'plausible deniability' (Sluka, 2000: 227). The state never takes responsibilities for the atrocities committed. Some of these atrocities are quite significant. In El Salvador, in 1983 alone, there were 1,259 documented killings by death squads. The Contras were responsible for killing as many as 8,000 civilians, and assassinating as many as 910 state officials (Brody, 1985).

The use of both paramilitaries and death squads also causes violence levels to escalate. They may cause the targeted group to increase its own attacks. In the case of Spain, Grupos Antiterroristas de Liberación (Anti-terrorist Liberation Groups; GAL) were death squads established illegally by officials of the Spanish government to fight ETA, the Basque terrorist group (see Chapter 7). GAL members carried out paramilitary actions in both Spain and France. Some thought that they may be mercenaries hired by the public, but it eventually emerged that the Spanish government had created them, though the prime minister at the time, Felipe Gonzales (1982–96), was never found guilty.[2]

In the end, GAL was responsible for the deaths of 27 people (Woodworth, 2001). Nine of the 27 were not even ETA members. ETA responded to GAL's activities by increasing its own activities. ETA attacks went beyond targeting the security institutions and Franco-era politicians. Young Spanish politicians and journalists were targeted, leading to a much heavier death toll (Barros et al., 2006).

CONCLUSION

PSCs and paramilitary groups are two sides of the same coin. PSCs appear to be apolitical, economically motivated actors, while the opposite is true of paramilitary organizations. However, a closer look reveals that both actors work on behalf of states to provide stability, and are largely focused on maintaining status-quo policies as well as profits. They are examples of how states can appear to be disengaged

---

[2]The interior minister, Jose Barrionuevo, and the secretary of state for security, Rafael Vera, and the civil governor of Vizcaya, Julian Sancrisobal, were convicted in 1998 for the kidnapping of Segundo Marey and sentenced to ten years in prison.

from politics, while avoiding culpability and responsibilities for their actions. The privatization of security – even when it is legal and sanctioned by states – is an alarming trend that poses unique challenges for ensuring transparency in how security should be achieved.

Summary Points

- Since the war on terror began, there has been an explosion of PSCs, usually American and British companies.
- The use of PSCs makes it easier for countries to deploy forces and avoid responsibility.
- Paramilitary groups and PSCs are both economically motivated; both also usually seek to maintain the status quo .
- Many paramilitary groups have committed more human rights abuses than guerrilla groups.
- Death squads are often working covertly at the behest of a government or a wealthy group.

Key Questions

1. Why do countries choose to rely on PSCs?
2. In what ways do PSCs pose a threat to democracy?
3. How do the tactics and strategies of paramilitary groups differ from PSCs?
4. Why are PSCs and paramilitary groups most likely to be used to defend conservative interests?
5. Can PSCs and paramilitary groups contribute positively to stability? Why or why not?
6. Theory: Realists are concerned with measuring power. How do PSCs and paramilitaries impact how state power is measured?

FURTHER READING

Avant, D. (2005) 'Private security companies', *New Political Economy*, 10 (1): 121–31. Explains what private security companies are and gives an overview of the array of services that they provide; analyses the pros and cons of private security forces in Iraq.

Avant, D. and Sigelman, L. (2010) 'Private security and democracy: lessons from the US in Iraq', *Security Studies*, 19(2): 230–65. Critiques private security forces in Iraq and how they have undermined democracy.

Chesterman, S. (2016) 'Dogs of war or jackals of terror? Foreign fighters and mercenaries in international law'. http://papers.ssrn.com/sol3/papers.cfm?abstract_id=2814889 (27 July 2016). Provides an overview of the evolution of mercenariness and the efforts to regulate it.

Holmqvist, C. (2005) *Private Security Companies* (Stockholm International Peace Research Institute). Extensive explanation of how private security forces emerged, how diverse they are, how much more they have been used since the war on terror began and the lack of options available to regulate them.

Mazzei, J. (2009) *Death Squads or Self-Defense Forces? How Paramilitary Groups Emerge and Challenge Democracy in Latin America* (University of North Carolina Press). Presents how paramilitaries in Latin America have challenged human rights in democracy; explains why they have emerged in the region and provides definitions of paramilitaries and death squads.

Singer, P.W. (2011) *Corporate Warriors: the Rise of the Privatized Military Industry.* (Cornell University Press). Thorough investigation of the explosion of private security companies, how they operate and what impact they may have.

PART IV
DEALING WITH VIOLENT NON-STATE ACTORS

11

MODERATION AND POLITICIZATION

Key Terms

- African National Congress Party (ANC)
- Mozumbique Liberation Front (FRELIMO)
- Structuralist approach
- Hezbollah
- Hamas
- Sandinistas National Liberation Front (FSNL)
- Sinn Fein
- Strategic approaches

POLITICAL ORGANIZATIONS WITH MILITANT WINGS

As Gerald Seymour pointed out in his 1975 book, *Harry's Game*, 'one man's terrorist is another man's freedom fighter' (62). The line that distinguishes violent non-state actors taking part in atrocities against civilians and legitimate actors pushing to rectify legitimate grievances is often blurry. Violent non-state actors use violence to achieve their objectives, but what happens when they are also willing to do so through conventional methods? In order to best understand how to deal with groups that have chosen to play by the rules, it's necessary to take a critical look at political organizations with armed wings. This chapter examines the political wing of violent groups, focusing on political parties that turn to violence, followed by the reverse. We also look at groups where the violent and political wings emerge simultaneously or emerge as part of the same movement. In doing so, we define and conceptualize political parties that are attached to and/or associated with violent groups, and investigate the reasons these types of violent non-state actors emerge in the first place. The chapter explores the questions of whether violent groups can eventually transform into purely political actors, and how to prevent purely political actors from turning to violence. If they do, should states allow parties to contest elections if they are associated with a violent wing or group?

DEFINITION

What are political parties with violent wings?

Some violent political groups have both a political and militant wing, but it is not always the case that the political wing of the group constitutes an actual political party. There are several important criteria to note. The political wing should have a well-developed political platform and ideology and highly organized political units. It may be capable of drafting coherent public policy. It can stimulate associational activities and provide information (Lipset, 2000). These groups often have high levels of legitimacy and political support. The political party tries to represent a constituency (Sartori, 2005). The political wing may try to build up its membership by providing services to the community such as education, healthcare, education and other acts of charity. The political wing is committed to contesting elections and engaging in conventional politics, working with the state and not working to subvert it. The political wing could publicly deny that they are attached to the militant wing, but they share similar goals. It is possible that the political wing is merely part of the same movement, but it is difficult to know whether a relationship exists when it is clandestine.

Political parties with violent wings are engaged in two different types of activities. The political wing is engaged in above-ground activities and plays by the rules of the game. Conversely, the militant wing operates covertly and engages in acts of violence to help achieve its political outcome (Siqueira, 2005). In some cases, the violent wing constitutes a militia and is engaged in combat or is ready to engage in combat or self-defence. In other cases, the violent wing may use a terror strategy targeting civilians. The militant wing either emerged before, after or simultaneously with the political wing. The militant wing could be considered a terrorist group or an insurgency (for more on these groups, see Chapters 6 and 7). In general, studies have shown that violent groups with links to parties are more successful and persistent than those that lack these relationships (Crenshaw, 2010).

POLITICAL OBJECTIVES AND IDEOLOGY

Political parties with militant wings have a very clearly articulated political agenda and objective. The goals are concrete and clearly stated in a charter, and the ideology is relatively coherent. Most of the goals should be achievable through conventional politics. The group's agenda could be based on a specific ideology, fighting for an ethnic group or implementing a religious doctrine. The ideology may have to be moderated to appeal to a wider cross-section of the public, but this may not take place until after the group has had the chance to contest elections. There have been many right-wing and ultra-nationalist groups that develop militias in order to intimidate their opponents.[1] A subsequent section will also show that many political parties with armed wings have been based on left-wing agendas, emerging in the context of right-wing repression and colonization.

---

[1] In one of the more peculiar cases, in Hungary a paramilitary wing formed to provide security to support a nationalist movement. The Hungarian Guard Movement was the paramilitary wing of the nationalist Jobbik party in Hungary. Its members had to take an oath of loyalty to Hungary after its founding in August 2007, but it was dissolved by the Budapest tribunal by July 2009. Its members were never armed.

STRATEGIES AND TACTICS

The strategy of armed groups connected to or associated with a political party that is contesting elections is distinct from the strategy of an insurgency or terrorist group. Political parties with militant wings are walking a dangerous tightrope. They want to maintain popular legitimacy but they also feel it is necessary to retain or be associated with an armed wing. Therefore, any violence that the military wing embarks on is very calculated and controlled. They do not want to be too deadly. We will illustrate this with the complicated case of the terrorist group ETA in Spain and the various parties that might be considered to be associated with it.[2] Though ETA is not officially associated with a political party, the popularity of these parties was affected by how violent ETA was.

In the case of ETA, there is no official linkage between the organization and other political parties. However, ETA is unofficially attached to many of the political parties that push for Basque rights. One such party is Euskal Herritarok. Euskal Herritarok (formerly called Herri Batasuna, or Popular Unity) began as a faction that split off from the Basque Nationalist Party (Partido Nacionalista Vasco, or PNV). Euskal Herritarok has had the same goals as ETA and has never produced a statement claiming that it rejected violence (Bourne, 2015). Euskal Herritarok was banned in 2003, but before that it was strong enough to win several seats in national parliamentary elections were held. When a truce took place between ETA and the Spanish government, it received its highest vote share in history with 17.7%. This vote share dipped to less than 10% after the truce was called off. When ETA killings took place in 2001, Euskal Herritarok was by far the biggest loser in the 2001 elections.[3]

Sinn Fein, the party associated with the IRA in Northern Ireland, has seen its popularity soar since the IRA stopped using violence. Before a truce took place in 1994, Sinn Fein had less than 10% of the vote. After the truce, it received 16.1% of the vote. After the Good Friday Agreement in 2001, it garnered 21.7% of the vote, which then rose to 24.3% in 2005. As of 2016, it has about 25% of the seats in Northern Ireland's assembly.

Parties that are associated with militant wings have to win over those who sympathize with the group but may not condone violence. This group is often quite large, which necessitates that any violence be planned with strict attention to the outcome. When the support group of the violent party is more moderate, there is a trade-off between how much offensive action they want to take and how much popular support they want.

Parties with militant wings want to avoid civilian targets and provide reasons for citizens to support them. This is a strategy to increase a group's legitimacy. For

---

[2]ETA is not a political party with a militant wing. It is a terrorist group that has recently chosen to stop using violence. It has killed over 820 people since 1968, 240 of whom have been civilians. It has also injured hundreds more and kidnapped several dozen people. In 1980 alone, it killed 92 people. The last year that ETA killed more than 20 people was 2000; since 2002, the yearly number has been less than ten. Though laws prohibit ETA from running in Spanish elections, the group's dwindling popularity means that even if the group had the chance to compete, it would not reap huge electoral rewards (Muro, 2013).

[3]In February 2011, the Sortu Party – described as the new Euskal Herritarok – was launched, rejecting all politically motivated violence. By the end of March, the Supreme Court had banned Sortu as well, claiming that it was linked to ETA (Türkeş-Kılıç, 2015).

example, Hezbollah has struck at military and diplomatic targets 40% of the time. Hezbollah's strategy has entailed keeping civilian death tolls to a minimum while offering many services to the public. The Hezbollah strategy has largely succeeded in increasing the group's legitimacy in Lebanon, though not in the West. Islamic charity is a central part of Hamas's strategy.[4] Hamas aims to infiltrate society by providing social welfare (Grynkewich, 2008).

ORGANIZATION AND RECRUITMENT

Parties with militant wings have sophisticated levels of organization and recruitment. The political wings should be able to recruit more members than even insurgencies. Compared to terrorist groups, which are more selective of their members, parties are aiming for mass levels of recruitment. The apparatus itself should be better organized, institutionalized and bureaucratic. It may have a wider reach of branch offices. It may have a clearer compartmentalization of roles and duties within the organization. These parties are also relatively cohesive due to some levels of hierarchy within the organization.

In the case of Hezbollah, the level of organization is impressive. The political wing has evolved into the larger, more significant and more influential part of the organization. The organization has a hierarchical leadership system with an information office, social service divisions, branch offices, active participation in the parliament and executive cabinet, and alliances with other parties. An observer of Hezbollah points out that 'this hierarchical division of labour (which permits certain degrees of flexibility) enables the party to move comfortably between the military and the political apparatus, depending on the circumstances' (Wiegand, 2009: 678). Thus it has formal and direct links between the different segments of the organization. There is a high authority decision-making council comprising seven special committees: ideological, financial, military, political, judicial, informational and social affairs, with committee members elected every two years.

There is no official membership in Hezbollah. Its leaders rely on clerics to influence people towards the organization and it does not attempt to recruit official members. The deputy secretary general of Hezbollah explained the reason for the mixed structure: 'We concluded at the end (of organizational discussions) that we needed a structural organization which was in some respects rigid enough to be able to prevent infiltration by the enemy and at the same time flexible enough to embrace the maximum sector of people without having to go through a long bureaucratic process of red tape' (Jaber, 1997: 8).

Hamas does have a membership and a clear recruitment strategy of using its social services to link up with potential members. It has a diverse range of members with some being more moderate and some being more militant. It is also more secular than it appears to be, with little religious training of its leadership. Though Hamas has a governing council and a politburo, it is mostly non-transparent (Bhasin and Hallward, 2013).

---

[4]The violence conducted by Hamas has been an anomaly in that its popularity does not seem to be affected by the level of violence. Though it conducted 206 terrorist attacks causing 67 deaths and 210 injuries in 2004, by 2006 it was popular enough to win 76 of 132 seats in the Palestinian parliament (Grynkewich, 2008).

FUNDING AND SUPPORT

Parties with militant wings have ample support and funding. They are considered to be legitimate by a section of the population. Because parties with militant wings rely on conventional methods of action, they have to appeal to a wider constituency than an insurgency or terrorist group not connected to a political wing that contests elections. According to Roger Petersen (2001), citizens offer different levels of support for politically violent groups. As he sees it, the following levels can be identified: (1) those who disagree with the armed struggle and the killing of innocent victims, but vaguely sympathize with the organization's goals; (2) those who vote for the party associated with the terrorist/militant organization or participate in the social movements that develop around the organization; and (3) those who actively help the organization in various ways (by providing information, housing, money, etc.) or engage in lesser acts of violence. Groups that are involved in contesting elections may try to win over those who vaguely sympathize. The key for these parties is often their ability to appeal to this group.

They also receive support and funding from other states, who either support their agenda or want to provide support to this group as a way of balancing against another state who might be threatened by the violent non-state actor. For example, Hezbollah is a threat to Israel, which is why it receives most of its support from Iran (for more on this, see Box 1.1 on Omni-balancing in Chapter 1). Hezbollah has survived with the help of other external benefactors, such as Syria before its civil war began in 2012. The Mozambique Liberation Front (FRELIMO) (see Box 11.1) party in Mozambique during its struggle for independence received support from China, the USSR, the Scandinavian countries and some western NGOs. Because parties are contesting elections, they may be able to receive more overt support, rather than just clandestine support from other states.

Political parties with militant wings are often well networked as well. The party may receive more financial support from citizens who want to help further their chance of winning elections. These parties have received millions in support from a vast network of donors. Hezbollah and the IRA are also deeply involved in organized crime. Hezbollah receives $50–$100 million from the tri-border region in South America. Cells operating there raise money through counterfeiting, money laundering and extortion (Shelley, 2014).

POWER AND IMPACT ON THE STATE AND SOCIETY

Parties with militant wings often engage in competitive state-building. This means that they provide services that the state should be providing to its constituency. Hezbollah's effective organization has offered a host of different social services since 1983, filling the void that the Lebanese government is unable to fulfil, particularly in southern Lebanon. It has provided health services, water distribution, electricity, garbage removal, education, welfare services and cultural centres. In 1988, it began collecting garbage which had been building up for years, replacing the government function. It is the most efficient political organization in the country and provides better social services than the Lebanese had previously received from the state. After an Israeli bombardment of Lebanon in 1997, Hezbollah rebuilt 5,000 homes in 82 villages.

The Gaza Strip where Hamas operates experiences extreme poverty. As such, Hamas is the most influential social welfare organization in the Gaza Strip. It has done an effective job of providing social services compared to the highly corrupt Fatah. Its political wing has provided services of all kinds, in the areas of education, healthcare and welfare. In fact, about 80%–90% of its funds go towards funding these services (Altier et al., 2016: 85).

Unlike political parties that are not attached to violent wings, parties with militant wings threaten security and undermine the legitimacy of the state. The violent wings have often caused serious damage to life and property. Hamas has been especially violent. Since Hamas's inception, the organization has carried out over 476 terrorist attacks, killing over 1,000 people (Global Terrorism Database, 2015). Brigadier General Ya'acov Amidor conceded that Hamas is a serious challenge to Israeli security. 'You can trim its branches,' he suggested, but it was going to be difficult to 'pull out its roots' (Hoffman and McCormick, 2004: 268). Hezbollah has also inflicted damage. It carried out over 179 terrorist attacks, killing more than 800 and injuring over 1,500.

THEORIES OF PARTIES AND VIOLENCE

Political parties remain committed to playing by the conventional rules of the game when they are able to achieve their objectives by doing so. Parties are constrained by the rules that allow them to participate and how much support they receive. In some cases the group enjoys high levels of support but is limited by repressive rules. High levels of insecurity may also force parties to form a militia to protect themselves. In other cases, they are limited by mass passivity to their cause, and splinter.

POLITICAL PARTIES THAT TURN TO VIOLENCE

As Chapter 4 illustrated, there are many grievances held by groups stemming from gross inequalities and repression. Given how difficult it is to overcome these inequalities and repressive conditions, achieving any sort of positive outcome is difficult. Thus turning to violence and forming a militant wing may be a response to the repressive conditions that parties face. This may be especially true for countries that are suffering from a crisis of national integration where groups/minorities are not feeling represented (Weinberg et al., 2008). If we make the assumption that parties are responding to conditions, this is known as a 'strategic' model (Abrahms, 2008: 78).

Drawing from rational choice theory, strategic approaches assume that parties are rational actors and weigh the expected costs versus the expected benefits of their actions. Thus when groups have consistently chosen non-violent measures that produce no net positive payoffs, they may search for another option. In other instances some event may have taken place where it no longer appears rational to continue to pursue non-violent methods to achieve their objectives. According to this model, violence is chosen as a last resort and when better political options arise, violent groups will turn their backs on violent measures. Thus for groups such as the FLN in Algeria, bombing French civilians proved to be the most effective tactic compared with non-violent methods. Motivated individuals weigh their political options and resort to terrorism only after determining that alternative political avenues are blocked. Resorting to terrorism may be a sign that the previous strategy was no longer working.

The use of violence may be due to the frustration with the gap between the party's goals and the feasibility of accomplishing these goals, due to low levels of support (Weinberg, 1991; Weinberg et al., 2008). In Italy, the Prima Linea-related Democratic Proletarians won less than 2% of the vote in the crucial 1976 national elections (Horgan, 2011: 124). But to counter the strategic approach, one reason parties may turn to violence is that these types of parties often have grandiose and impossible objectives to achieve, such as forming a new state (Weinberg et al., 2008).

In general, the response of the state can have a large impact on whether or not parties turn to violence. When the state uses violence, this helps the party see the prevailing order as illegitimate, which can lead to violence. There are many cases where repressive conditions gave parties few options but to create a militant wing. The act of repression confirms the party's commitment to its mission (Weinberg, 1991; Weinberg et al., 2008).

Many parties form militant wings in order to achieve independence after years of being colonized. For many of these groups, the European powers left without a major struggle, but in cases where conflict erupted, the nationalist/independence parties were forced to resort to violence, usually rural guerrilla warfare. In fact, the formation of many political parties in much of the developing world was driven by the need to achieve national liberation (Weinberg et al., 2008: 13).

In South Africa, the ANC had endured years of repression under the apartheid regime, but a severe injustice took place that served as a catalyst for the group to turn to violence and create an armed wing known as Umkhonto we Sizwe (MK). This wing was co-founded by ANC leader Nelson Mandela after the Sharpeville Massacre in March 1960 in which 69 black South Africans were killed by the police during a peaceful protest. The ANC came to the conclusion that it could no longer meet its aims through non-violent protests. It warned the South African government that acts of terror would ensue if the government did not move forward with constitutional reform to increase the political rights of black South Africans. These warnings were ignored and as a result, the MK launched its first terror attacks against government sites on 16 December 1961. The South African and US governments classified the ANC as a terror organization and banned it.

Box 11.1 FRELIMO

The Mozambique Liberation Front (FRELIMO) is a party that was associated with a massive guerrilla movement in Mozambique fighting for independence from Portugal. In June 1962, three regionally based nationalist organizations (the Mozambican African National Union, the National Democratic Union of Mozambique and the National African Union of Independent Mozambique) merged into one broad-based guerrilla movement under the leadership of Eduardo Mondlane, with its headquarters in Dar es Salaam, Tanzania. After the Mueda massacre where innocent civilians were killed by Portuguese security, the FRELIMO was convinced that a peaceful struggle was not feasible. It launched a war for independence in September 1964, though

(Continued)

(Continued)

it maintained a party that advocated mostly socialist ideals. As the political campaign became more comprehensive and effective, the military campaign also made significant gains. It controlled about one-third of Mozambique by 1969, though it was unable to seize control over any urban areas. By June 1975, it finally gained independence using a guerrilla force of only 7,000 against a Portuguese force of over 60,000 soldiers.

In many countries in Latin America, large gaps between rich and poor and repressive conditions offered few alternatives for left-wing groups but to create a violent wing (Weinberg et al., 2003). It was customary for groups in Latin American with political ambition that opposed the repressive ruling government to create armed groups to engage in acts of violence as a defence mechanism, such as was the case in El Salvador, Uruguay and Guatemala, to name a few (O'Brien, 1996).

Political parties also may feel compelled to develop militias in order to protect themselves. This may be especially necessary in the context of a conflict. Thus, external or domestic conflict may explain why political parties link up with violent organizations (Weinberg et al., 2008: 16). In Georgia, at the onset of its conflict after it had achieved independence, each political party except the Greens had their own militia. During the Lebanese civil war, many political parties developed armed wings, not just Hezbollah. The Zgharta Liberation Army was the armed wing of the Lebanese Marada Movement. The militia was originally formed by President Suleiman Frangieh in 1967 as the Marada Brigade, and was commanded by his son, Tony Frangieh. It mostly fought in Tripoli and Zgharta but it also had a presence in Beirut, fighting against Palestinian and Lebanese Muslim militias. The Croatian Party of Rights also had a militant arm known as the Croatian Defence Forces from 1991 to 1992. The Croatian Defence Forces were used to fight in its war for independence. After a ceasefire was declared, the Croatia Defence Forces were absorbed by the Croatian army.

POLITICAL PARTIES THAT SPAWN OR SPLINTER INTO MILITANT ORGANIZATIONS

There have also been many cases of political parties splintering off due to growing dissatisfaction with the direction of the party's leadership. In these cases supporters of an established party spawn a splinter faction that then forms an independent violent group. This took place in Italy in the 1950s when the New Order was created after a split with the neo-fascist Italian Social Movement. The militant group splinters off to ensure its own autonomy due to perceptions that the strategies of the political parent organization are ineffective. This is how ETA emerged. In Spain, the PNV had formed in 1895 to represent the interests of the Basque community. By 1959, after years of frustration with the lack of action from the PNV, students, many of whom had been forced into exile, formed secret cells committed to taking on the Spanish government directly in 1959.

This is particularly true for extremist parties that find that they are encountering too much passivity (Ross, 1993: 323). The Italian Red Brigade, for example, emerged in 1970 and was mostly formed by the more radical members of the Communist Youth League who were disenchanted with the Italian Communist Party's lack of activism. As a result of the split, the activities and presence of the independent Red Brigade seemed not only to have harmed the Italian Communist Party's political prospects, but their actions may have also helped sustain the Christian Democrats' hold on power for a considerable period of time (Laqueur, 1996). According to Weinberg (Weinberg, 1991; Weinberg et al., 2008), this scenario is quite common.

VIOLENT GROUPS THAT TURN TO POLITICS

With the onset of greater levels of democratization around the world, there are increasingly more cases of violent groups that decide to form a political party. In these cases the party that forms may even deny that it is linked to the violent group in order to maintain its own legitimacy. This was the case in Ireland with the PIRA and its sponsorship of its political wing, Sinn Fein. Sinn Fein denies allegations that it is connected to the PIRA, but the Irish government has alleged that senior members of Sinn Fein have held posts on the IRA council. Scholars have also argued that the two groups are connected, claiming that Sinn Fein plays a role in maintaining a propaganda war, providing the political voice of the movement while the IRA has waged an armed campaign (O'Brien, 1999: 128). A 2015 assessment revealed that the PIRA still exists, but in a reduced form, and that the IRA members claim that its army council oversees the activities of both the PIRA and Sinn Fein.

In other instances, the violent group undergoes a strategic shift and decides that violent operations are no longer working; it rebuilds itself as a political party and then participates in democratic elections. The Irgun organization in the Palestinian mandate used acts of terrorism against British rule but then transformed into a political party, the Herut Party, after Israel gained independence, with its leader, Menachem Begin, eventually becoming prime minister of Israel (Shapiro, 1991). In other instances, the parent organization was a political party, which then turned into a violent organization and then transformed back to a political party in order to take part in conventional politics.

What causes these shifts? There are several arguments, based on the idea that internal group structures matter. One is that a change takes place within the group that leads to changes in decision-making. A change in the group's leadership can make a big difference. The case of Hezbollah illustrates this, with secretary general Hassan Nasrallah taking over in 1992 after the death of Abbas al-Musawi, who was a more extreme leader. Changes in Sinn Fein's tactics took place when Gerry Adams became a key figure in the late 1970s. The leadership believed that it was only a change in tactics that could help realize long-term goals (Whiting, 2016).

Some groups also change in structure, moving from more hierarchical to more democratic structures. Internal debates can take place that are more pluralistic, which may help groups evolve to reflect changing external environments. Change in internal group structure may also help transform what the boundaries are for justifiable action, or what the margins are that a group can credibly change its political goals. In this scenario it is also possible that more members enter the group who are more inclined to support non-violent measures to achieving their aims. The balance of power between the political and military wings is constantly fluctuating, which may lead to changes in strategy (Weinberg et al., 2008).

In other cases, members may splinter in terms of strategies. A strategic shift may take place – the violent organization may persist but one faction jumps to pursue their political goals through conventional means. Maintaining the ideals that are passionate enough to support the use of violence is difficult. In cases where the group is not destroyed, they may experience burnout or commitments to using violence may wane. Some members may become bored while others may no longer hold such extreme beliefs. Generational shifts may have taken place.

A 'structuralist' approach argues that the strategy that a group chooses is affected by the institutions that they must operate under. In some states, groups (including political parties) are constrained by various institutional barriers that explain why some political parties use violent tactics instead of using mainstream political practices (Ross, 1993). Institutional barriers create grievances for individuals who belong to marginalized political organizations; these grievances cause them to ally with or create militant wings that engage in terrorist activities (Crenshaw, 1981: 384). The first barrier is regime type. Though much of the literature has claimed that democracies are more prone to being targets of terrorism, democracies may also allow for more conventional participation for other potentially violent political groups.

The same can be said for electoral systems. More proportional systems that are more inclusive may allow for more participation of political groups. John Huber and G. Bingham Powell (1994) argue that majoritarian systems may not be representative of the interests of minority groups. In contrast, proportional systems may produce more representative cabinets and legislatures. Marta Reynal-Querol (2002) argued that proportional systems are less likely to produce discontented groups, reducing the likelihood of civil war. Quan Li (2005) also claimed that majoritarian systems are more likely to experience acts of political violence than proportional systems. Electoral systems that prevent citizens from feeling represented will have more dissatisfied citizens (Danzell, 2010).

Many scholars have emphasized the importance of political inclusion and accommodating institutions to elicit moderation (Dayton and Kriesberg, 2009; Schwedler 2011). A large body of literature also supports using power-sharing strategies to push radicals towards moderation (Garry 2014; McEvoy, 2014; McEvoy and O'Leary, 2013). Critics claim, however, that this only helps radical groups take part in conventional politics without forcing them to change their position and possibly reinforcing divisions further (Horowitz, 2014).

MOVEMENTS THAT HAVE BOTH VIOLENT AND NON-VIOLENT GROUPS

There are also many cases of violent groups and non-violent groups that have the same views and are part of the same movements, but with one group preferring to use conventional means to achieve their objectives and another group choosing the violent option. In this case, the party and the political movement may be in competition with one another. In Sri Lanka, Tamil nationalism led to the creation of two groups. The LTTE were committed to using violence to achieving their objective of Tamil independence. The TULF, on the other hand, was a political party consisting of older, more conservative Tamils who believed that independence could be achieved without resorting to violence. At times, these groups were more at odds with each other than they were allies (Horowitz, 1989).

In other cases, these two organizations may be accused of being more intricately connected. With the case of ETA, various political parties have formed, such as the Batasuna Party, the Communist Party of the Basque Lands and the Sortu Party, which have been accused of being linked to the terrorist group. Though party leaders claim they are separate entities, they are part of the same general movement advocating Basque autonomy. This pattern possibly took place with the case of the new left movement in Italy during the 1970s, Lotta Continua. Some supporters promoted the political party, the Democratic Proletarians, which contested elections, while others turned to violence with the Prima Linea (Horgan, 2011).

Burma (Myanmar) provides another example of a two-pronged strategy which included the non-violent political dissent of Aung San Suu Kyi's National League for Democracy (asking for international support) and the violent ethnic guerrilla factions on the country's borders in the 1990s (providing protection) taking part in the same movement.

The coordination of the political and militant wings has led to success before. In Cyprus, the National Organization of Cypriot Fighters (EOKA) coordinated the efforts of its militant group with that of the community's political leader, Michael Mouskios, who later became the country's first president (Hoffman, 2006).

Case Study Violent Groups That Form Political Parties

Hezbollah is a case of a militant group that became more involved in politics, eventually forming a political party capable of winning elections and providing services. Hezbollah has a dual status but it has moved away from its radical policies of kidnapping and destruction of the Lebanese political system. The organization also has lifted some of its secrecy that shrouded its motivations and decision-making processes.

Hezbollah emerged soon after the 1982 Israeli invasion of Lebanon with backing from Iran and Syria, and quickly became popular among Lebanon's Shiites. Hezbollah gained notoriety in the West for its use of violence against Israel, and its deadly attacks on international and communal targets. The April 1983 bombing of the US embassy in Beirut and the October 1983 suicide bombing of the US and French contingents of the multinational force stationed in Lebanon, in which 241 American marines were killed, placed Hezbollah on the list of foreign terrorist organizations by Western nations. Hezbollah was also suspected of the hijacking of TWA flight 847 in June 1985. Hezbollah still has a unit that engages in acts of terrorism and a unit that engages in guerrilla warfare. Hezbollah has also offered active support for the Syrian government in the Syrian conflict since 2012.

Nevertheless, in spite of years of violence, the group transitioned its political wing into a genuine political party by 1985, when it produced a manifesto in an open letter. In this manifesto, Hezbollah called for creating an Islamic state based on the model of *velayat efaquih* that was popular in Iran during its revolution. Hezbollah directly appealed to Shiites who were underrepresented in the Lebanese political system and excluded economically.

The most significant change was the decision to participate in mainstream Lebanese politics by taking part in elections in 1992 with Ayatollah Khamenei giving his blessing. The concept of jihad was reframed in order to take part and the militant arm of Hezbollah was downsized. The militant wing was also de-linked from the civil wing in order to give the civil wing the internal space to participate in mainstream politics (Wiegand, 2009).

(Continued)

(Continued)

Another important event was the election of Hassan Nasrallah as the new secretary general of Hezbollah. More moderate than his predecessor, Nasrallah ushered in a new era of moderation and pragmatism for the organization. Subhi al-Tufayli was the more radical previous leader; he would later be expelled from the group. In contrast, the views and statements of Nasrallah were often reasonable. He claimed, 'We don't want to have control over Lebanon, or to have governance over Lebanon or to impose our ideas over the people of Lebanon, because we believe Lebanon to be a special and diverse country that needs collaboration of everyone' (qtd by Worrall et al., 2015: 107). Thus the party has had to accept that Lebanon is a multi-religious state.

Once the organization entered politics, it was deliberately vague regarding its goals of restructuring the Lebanese government. In order to win seats, it immediately embarked on a campaign to gain positive publicity and sponsored community outreach programmes, accomplishing this feat in less than 50 days since it announced that it would run in elections. This political strategy worked, as it won 12 of 128 seats in its first election in 1992. It was able to successfully frame itself as a legitimate organization committed to both civic representation and resistance against aggression.

The Lebanese electoral system, though heavily criticized for encouraging deeply entrenched sectarian identities, has encouraged some interreligious coordination. Hezbollah has been pragmatic in its decision to form coalitions with political groups of all different ideologies and backgrounds, including both Sunnis and Christians and its former rival, Amal. It has also participated in parliamentary elections in 1996, 2000 and 2005 and in municipal elections in 1998 and 2004. It has run on joint electoral tickets with the Lebanese forces, Syrian Ba'thists, communists, the Syrian National Socialists and the Christian Free Patriotic Movement. With the latter party, Hezbollah signed a memorandum of understanding in 2006. During the 2013 electoral reform debate, Hezbollah backed the Orthodox Gathering proposal that was put up by the orthodox Christian communities.

Hezbollah has also engaged in some restraint in terms of its use of violence. It used rockets and anti-aircraft missiles 24 times and killed 43 Israeli civilians from 2000 to 2006 in clashes over the Shebaa Farms, but has not fired rockets since the ceasefire. It has also given a nod of legitimacy to the Lebanese forces in 1997. In May 2008, Hezbollah shifted its strategy from non-violent protests and parliamentary votes to using political violence again. This led to the death of 65 people.

Though Hezbollah has remained pragmatic, it is unlikely that it will ever disarm anytime soon. Hezbollah's main objectives have been based in Islam and jihad against Israel (Wiegand, 2009: 672). In order to achieve these objectives Hezbollah has offered support to Palestinian groups engaged in terrorist attacks, by providing training in the Bekaa Valley. Hezbollah also still remains committed to liberating the disputed Shebaa Farms territory, which has been claimed by the Lebanese government, though the United Nations recognizes it as part of Israel (Wiegand, 2009: 673). Though Hezbollah remains committed to taking part in elections, it also undermines the state's legitimacy in Lebanon and is a symptom of how weak the Lebanese state is.

Case Study   Political Parties That Form Militant Wings

Hamas was founded sometime in 1988 soon after the First Intifada broke out, as an offshoot of the Egyptian Muslim Brotherhood that was formed in 1928 (Berman, 2003). In its Gaza branch, it had been non-confrontational towards Israel. It had refrained from resistance and was hostile to the PLO. The Hamas Charter affirmed that its main purpose was to liberate Palestine from Israeli occupation and establish an Islamic State in the West Bank and the Gaza Strip. It has moderated its view that it may accept a ten-year truce with Israel if the state was willing to withdraw to the 1967 borders and allow Palestinian refugees from 1948 as well as their descendants to return to what is now Israel.

Hamas's militant wing formed later in 1992, known as the Izz ad-Din al-Qassam brigades, has an estimated 10,000 operatives of different degrees of professionalism and experience that support the brigades. Its military capacity has increased from rifles to Qassam rockets and the use of suicide bombings against civilians. The brigades operate independently of Hamas and at times possibly against the aims of Hamas, but internal discipline is strong enough to contain them. Hamas officials seem to differ in terms of how they see the militant wing. A senior Hamas official said: 'The Izz al-Din al-Qassam Brigade is a separate armed military wing, which has its own leaders who do not take their orders from [Hamas] and do not tell us of their plans in advance' (qtd by Kass and O'Neill, 1997: 267). An opposing view claims that Hamas is directly responsible for coordinating acts of violence. The founder, Sheikh Ahmad Yassin, stated in 1998: 'We cannot separate the wing from the body. If we do so, the body will not be able to fly. Hamas is one body' (qtd by Phillips, 2011: 75).

Hamas has remained committed to maintaining its political wing, running candidates for elections, offering ceasefires and negotiating the exchange of political prisoners. It first decided to take part in elections running as the Reform and Change Party in 2006, seizing on the opening caused by the weakness of Fatah, weak electoral rules, the death of Yasser Arafat, Hamas's growing popularity and the rise of more moderate leadership within Hamas itself. The party has offered governance and welfare services to Palestinians. Maintaining the political wing has remained important to gaining support for its cause and also for ensuring funding from external donors.

Prior to the 2006 elections, there were no regular elections held and no local elections. There were few incentives to work within the political party framework. It is unknown whether it decided to participate in elections to undermine Fatah or because it was truly committed to democratic processes. For the moment there are no signs that Hamas will disarm. The organization views its militant wing as a necessary component to achieving its goals of liberating Palestine. One of its senior leaders has said, 'If we can fulfil our goals without violence, we will do so. Violence is a means, not a goal. Hamas's decision to adopt self-restraint does not contradict our aims' (qtd by Hoffman and McCormick, 2004: 268). However, as the previous section mentioned, Hamas has been incredibly violent and has yet to back down on its use of violence.

POLITICIZATION OF VIOLENT GROUPS

Would states be better off allowing violent groups with political parties to run in elections? How do these parties respond when they take part in democratic procedures and institutions? Pessimists argue that such groups' own revolutionary nature drives their leaders to undermine democratic processes once they attain power. Authoritarian regimes in the Middle East used this argument to justify repressing Islamic political parties from taking part in elections. In Algeria, the Islamic Salvation Front (FIS) was poised to win elections in 1992, but this result was nullified by the government based on fears of how the FIS would rule once they took power. Egypt allowed the Muslim Brotherhood to run in and win elections, but when it came to power it tried to entrench its rule indefinitely by undermining any democratic institutions.

A more optimistic view argues that participating in elections will have a moderating effect, with two possible dynamics likely to take hold. The first dynamic focuses on the role of electoral incentives. In this case, based on the 'median voter' model of Anthony Downs (1957), once parties have committed to taking part in elections, they must attract a plurality of voters. Having extremist policies will make it difficult to attract voters, forcing these parties to moderate their positions and adopt more centrist platforms (Kirchheimer, 1966). The very act of taking part in elections forces groups to moderate, recognize the state and reject violence in order gain political power (Schwedler, 2006). Moderation takes place after elections because extremist groups learn the rules of the game and become forced to make adjustments in order to win elections (Karakatsanis, 2008).

The second dynamic is based on the work of Robert Michels (1959). As he sees it, revolutionary parties that decide to take part in elections will have to set up a formal bureaucratic organization to launch public campaigns, raise and disburse funds and develop policies. This requires enormous amounts of time and energy, pulling attention away from plotting acts of violence. These new large formal organizations require practical leaders who can administer the party and provide services and convince voters that they can deliver on their promises. Thus the pressures to govern (e.g. ensure adequate sanitation) are more important than the pressures to reinforce passionate levels of radicalism.

Returning to the Sinn Fein example, it was its participation in conventional politics that eventually led to peace. For many years the IRA and Sinn Fein rejected British sovereignty in Northern Ireland, rejected the existing political institutions and were committed to using violence to achieve their goals. But a step towards moderation took place when Sinn Fein decided to engage in elections in 1981. This participation imposed some constraints on the party and forced the group to refine their aims and use the existing system. This was known as the 'Armalite and ballot box' strategy in which elections would be contested while the IRA maintained an armed struggle (McAllister, 2004). Though the IRA did not give up their arms, competing in elections even in a limited fashion forced the group to dilute its radicalism and appeal to a larger array of interests (Whiting, 2016). Sinn Fein also entered a power-sharing arrangement with its former rival, the Democratic Unionist Party, in 2006, and after years of refusing to recognize the Royal Ulster Constabulary, it now sits on the board of its successor, the Police Service of Northern Ireland (Morrison, 2015: 190).

But also critical to the politicization of Sinn Fein and eventual peace agreement with the IRA was the British government's tolerance of Sinn Fein. As noted before, many states respond to separatist threats with acts of repression rather than accommodation. States fear that any tolerance of these organizations will empower the separatist movements (Erk and Anderson, 2013). Turkey has mostly suppressed Kurdish nationalism and banned Kurdish parties. Though Spain has granted cultural recognition and autonomy for the Basques, it has banned many of their parties (Whiting, 2016).

In the following chapter, we examine how likely it is that violent groups will cease using violence. The scholarship on terrorism is mixed in terms of the prognosis for political groups that use violence eventually ceasing to use violence altogether. Abrahms (2008) claims that terrorist groups rarely transform into non-violent political parties. In contrast, Jones and Libicki (2008) argue that the most common end for terrorist groups was to take part in the political process and eventually stop engaging in violence. According to Chenoweth et al. (2009), of the 182 of 268 groups that have ended since 1968 without splintering, 114 did so through entering non-violent politics. Again, the discrepancies are likely due to the way that terrorist groups are conflated with insurgencies.

There are many insurgencies that have laid down arms once they were permitted to take part in the government in some way. This is especially true after a conflict has taken place and a peace accord has been implemented that allows the previous armed party to participate. The Farabundo Marti National Liberation Front (FMLN) is one of two major parties in El Salvador that emerged after years of right-wing repression. It was formed from five leftist guerrilla organizations on 10 October 1980. After the war ended, the FMLN's armed wings were demobilized and the party became a leftist political party in El Salvador. In 2009, one of its candidates, Mauricio Funes, won the presidential elections and the party also won a majority of the seats in the mayoral races and a plurality of seats in the National Assembly.

Box 11.2   Sandinistas National Liberation Front

The FSNL of Nicaragua formed in 1961 as a political movement made up of many different opposition organizations, responding to a repressive and unjust environment.[5] The movement would splinter various times and then reunify under one banner composed of five guerrilla organizations, eventually overthrowing the Somoza regime in 1979. The FSNL won the majority of votes in the first elections in 1979, but would soon have to contend with a right-wing paramilitary organization that was supported and trained by the US called the Contras. In 1990, after over a decade of fighting, the decision was made to hold elections. Though the Sandinistas lost the presidency to opposition candidate Violeta Chamorro that year, they still retained a plurality in the legislature. This same year, the fighting between the Sandinista guerrillas and the Contras finally ended. The Contras had to disarm and the Sandinistas army was reduced from 96,000 to 15,000, with the remaining to be incorporated into the military. Today the Sandinistas remain one of the leading parties in Nicaragua, and its leader, Daniel Ortega, has been in power since being re-elected for president in November 2011. Unfortunately, since taking over, the party has been marred by accusations of corruption and has lost much of its ideological commitment to helping the poor.

CONCLUSION

The idea that violent groups would engage in party politics or vice versa seems inimical to what characterizes each group. Violent groups often want to remain hidden and want to use violence in order to extract concessions from the state, challenge the democratic process and threaten civilians in democratic countries. These groups are sometimes very small organizations that want to avoid public notice until they carry out an attack. On the other hand, political parties are enormous bureaucratic organizations that are focused on mobilizing voters, engaging with citizens and winning elections by attracting broad levels of support. They are committed to democratic processes. But can we distinguish between the political and militant wings? In the case of Hezbollah, Australia, New Zealand, the UK and the European Union classify only its security wing as a terrorist organization. But most Western

---

[5]The party is named after Augusto Cesar Sandino who fought against US occupation of Nicaragua in the 1930s.

countries classify the entire organization as a terrorist group. Meanwhile, countries in the Arab world classify Hezbollah as a resistance movement.

A related question is how these groups should be dealt with. Hezbollah's and Hamas's provision of charities and social service networks have not made either organization give up their weapons. These networks only have served to de-legitimize the state. Because of this, critics argue that states need to uproot these social networks created by these groups that are still armed (Abuza, 2009). At the same time, if the ultimate aim is to encourage violent groups to understand that playing by the rules is a better alternative to violence, states may need to explore creating incentives for them to do so.

Summary Points

- Some violent non-state actors have political parties that are either associated with the larger movement or part of the same organization.
- Many violent groups moderate and want to engage in conventional politics.
- Many political parties with armed wings form in a fight to achieve independence.
- Many political parties with armed wings also form as part of a left-wing struggle to improve socio-economic conditions of the poor.
- Though Hezbollah and Hamas are contesting elections, neither group has disarmed.

Key Questions

1. Why do political parties sometimes choose to use violence?
2. Why do militant organizations decide to contest elections?
3. What are the important strategic considerations for parties with militant organizations to consider when they contest elections?
4. In what ways do parties with militant wings challenge the state?
5. Why have Hezbollah and Hamas been considered to be terrorist organizations? Do you agree with this classification? Why or why not?
6. Theory: What are rational explanations for why political parties turn to violence? What are constructivist explanations for why parties associated with militant wings may have difficulty disarming?

FURTHER READING

Altier, M.B., Martin, S. and Weinberg, L.B. (eds.) (2016) *Violence, Elections, and Party Politics* (Routledge). Analyses terror groups that participate in elections and offers in-depth chapters on ETA and Hamas.

Azani, E. (2016) *Hezbollah: the Story of the Party of God: from Revolution to Institutionalization* (Springer). Provides a good overview of how Hezbollah has transformed itself and what limits there are to this.

Bhasin, T. and Hallward, M.C. (2013) 'Hamas as a political party: democratization in the Palestinian territories', *Terrorism and Political Violence* 25 (1): 75–93. Explains what political development has taken place in the Palestinian territories and assesses how well institutionalized the party is.

Schwedler, J. (2006) *Faith in Moderation: Islamist Parties in Jordan and Yemen* (Cambridge University Press). Overview of Islamist parties in the Middle East; looks at the more moderate parties in Jordan and Yemen.

Weinberg, L., Pedahzur, A. and Perliger, A. (2008) *Political Parties and Terrorist Groups* (2nd ed.) (Routledge). Essential overview of political parties that are connected to terrorist groups.

12

COUNTER-STRATEGIES TO VIOLENT GROUPS

Key Terms

- Counter-narratives
- Decapitation
- Deradicalization
- Exclusive approach
- Inclusive approach
- Mano Dura
- Money laundering
- Targeted killings

Dealing with violent groups is a major challenge for states not only in conflict zones but supposed zones of peace as well. And it is no longer states that are the targets of threats, but civilians. How do we best deal with these threats, given that traditional tools at a state's disposal may not be effective? While the first half of the chapter will examine approaches that focus on long-term approaches for prevention, the second half will explore the effectiveness of strategies for dealing with violent groups after they have emerged. Before looking at the best counter-strategies and avenues of institutional reform, it is important to explore how violent groups typically end.

HOW DO VIOLENT GROUPS END?

In general, it is very hard to end groups that are economically motivated. Criminal groups and gangs sometimes fall apart when their leadership has been killed off or arrested, but they tend to be very resilient even after this has happened (Mallory, 2011: 44). More and more criminal groups are being negotiated with to rein in their leadership, but new groups have emerged in their absence. Private military companies dissolve when the business is no longer lucrative. Paramilitaries can often be negotiated with to exit, if the terms are favourable to them.

Surprisingly, most terrorist groups do not last long. On average, 90% of terrorist groups last less than one year, and more than 50% of the ones remaining disappear within ten years (Rapoport, 2004). Most terrorist groups are one-hit wonders. In contrast, insurgencies tend to last much longer, on average, 14 years (Jones and Libicki, 2008). Insurgencies tend to last longer because they are much more powerful and capable than terrorist groups. Defeating an insurgency may require military action and winning over the hearts and minds of the population. Insurgencies end 50% of the time by a negotiated settlement with the government. About 25% of the time, the insurgency achieved a victory, while 19% of the time the state defeated the group militarily (Jones and Libicki, 2008). There is no study on rebel/marauder groups since their tenure tends to be limited to resource-fuelled wars.[1]

There are several factors that impact whether or not a group may end. The structure is the first factor. Groups that are cellular with flatter structures are more difficult to eliminate. The aims of the group also matter. Economically charged groups can last a long time since there is always a large pool of individuals willing to participate. These groups do not require much in terms of maintaining the motivation of recruits. Politically charged groups that are motivated by ethno-nationalist causes have the longest lifespan because they tend to generate more genuine support. Religious groups also appear to be very resilient compared to right- and left-wing groups. About 62% of terrorist groups have ended since 1968, but only 32% of religious groups have ended (Jones and Libicki, 2008). Larger groups that have multiple bases are also more likely to survive. Groups of 10,000 members or more have won major concessions 25% of the time, while this is rare for smaller groups (Jones and Libicki, 2008). Though the climate of a country that a violent group is based in does not matter, it does matter if a group is based in a landlocked country, because the lack of access to international waters is an obstacle to the movement of assets (Gaibulloev and Sandler, 2013).

There are several ways in which politically charged groups end (see Cronin, 2006): the leader has been captured or killed (for more on this, see later in the chapter on decapitation); the group has been forcefully eliminated (also see later in the chapter); the group has lost popular support; the group cannot transition to the next generation and falls apart; the group has achieved its aims; the group has made a transition. All of these factors may cause a splintering of the group as well.

Groups often fall apart due to complete loss of support. Groups that lose support have more difficulty with funding, recruitment and finding sanctuaries to operate out of. Their operations are more likely to be disrupted when support is lost. This usually happens when a group miscalculates and repulses the population with their tactics. Basques in Spain were repelled by the actions of ETA. Abu Nidal lost support from Libya, which led to its disappearance. There is evidence that groups that have more casualties per attack reduce their longevity (Blomberg et al., 2009).

Groups can also fall apart because the next generation has different views or have effectively been aged out. The cadres no longer have the same ideological fervency and vigour as before. Left-wing and anarchist groups have a more difficult time making the generational shift. In this case, the group simply burns out. They can no longer continue to commit to the organization's goals and the group starts to lose cohesion. Individual members may want to take fewer risks, and desertions and defections are common (Ross and Gurr, 1989). This may also

---

[1]Rebel groups are often conflated with insurgencies in the literature.

be due to power and ideological struggles among generational leaders, as well as personality clashes (Gvineria, 2009). Power struggles and differences of opinion can lead to splintering. The more violent the organization's tactics, the more likely it is that the organization will splinter (Asal et al., 2012). Repressive state policies also lead to group splintering, as members diverge regarding how to respond (Asal et al., 2012).

Groups sometimes lay down their arms because they have achieved their objectives. It is more likely that an insurgency would meet its goals than a terror organization. Few terrorist groups have ended because they accomplished their aims. A study demonstrated that only 10% of terrorist groups since 1968 have ended because they attained their policy demands (Jones and Libicki, 2008). It is important to note that violent groups did not accomplish their goals due to terrorism (Chenoweth et al., 2009: 197). Religious groups rarely achieve their objectives and no religious group has achieved its goals since 1968 (Jones and Libicki, 2008). The Irgun organization, a Jewish terrorist group, is one exception that was founded in 1931; it disbanded after the state of Israel was created.

The chances of violent groups making a transition on their own are reasonably high (see Chapter 11). Groups can decide that it makes more sense to denounce violence. Members may push to become engaged in the political process, act as political parties and negotiate with the government. A RAND study found that of the 404 terrorist groups that have ended since 1968, 268 decided to renounce violence (Chenoweth et al., 2009: 185). A study of terrorist groups showed that 43% of groups ended because they transformed into non-violent politics due to government pressures (Jones and Libicki, 2008). This strategy may require negotiations. Negotiations have taken place in the case of the PIRA with the 1998 Good Friday Agreement and the LTTE, which negotiated with the Norwegian and Sri Lankan governments in 2002. The Official Irish Republican Army transformed into the Workers' Party. Many Sri Lankan violent groups laid down their arms after an agreement in 1987, choosing to engage in elections. As Chapter 11 illustrated, some groups may decide to engage in an electoral strategy.

———————— Case Study   Will the Islamic State End? ————————

Though the IS has dominated the headlines, it is a group that is waning in power. The biggest problem for the IS is that it does not have a sustainable endgame. Its ideology is too extreme and unappealing to the masses. Moreover, it is surrounded by enemies (Byman, 2015). It has made grandiose claims about its ambitions and the strength of its fighters, claiming that it was willing to lose thousands of fighters in battle. But in the battle for Kobani in Syria in 2014, the IS fighters fled quickly after losing a few hundred men. By 2016, the IS had lost 40% of its territory overall and 65% of its territory in Iraq. Though the IS holds some territory in Syria, it is comparatively less integrated into the Sunni population there. There are many other Sunni groups that Syrian Sunnis can pledge allegiance to. It mostly lays claim to Raqqa in Syria and its base of Mosul in Iraq.

Several groups in the region have also been effective in taking on the IS. The Kurds in the north have been successful in pushing the group back, and somehow pro-government Shiite forces in Iraq have also pushed it out of the Diyala province in the Tikrit area of northern Iraq. The IS has also been dislodged from the cities of Ramadi and has suffered other losses in the Anbar province at the end of 2015.

In contrast to previous assessments that the IS had highly trained fighters, opposition commanders have recently been observing that they don't actually fight well and surrender quickly when surrounded (Mueller and Stewart, 2016). More troublesome for the organization is that their most effective fighters have to be imported from Chechnya (Rich and Conduit, 2015). Most of the fighters it has now are poorly disciplined.

By late 2014, there were also major problems with its government services. It was unable to supply quality services, such as keeping the water potable and providing functioning schools. The IS also had a failed venture to create its own currency, and now has to rely on US dollars. The economy of the IS may be strong for an insurgency, but it is very small compared to its neighbouring states. It has become increasingly corrupt and its institutions are fragile and vulnerable (Mueller and Stewart, 2016).

Part of the problem for the IS was that it employed a campaign that used too much indiscriminate violence. Scholars have argued that insurgencies that target civilians too much never win (Abrahms and Gottfried, 2016; Fortna, 2015). Though it was alarming that it was attracting recruits from Western countries, it was not attracting high-level recruits. And the trend is that fewer and fewer are coming from Europe and the US. The IS may be just an ordinary insurgency that was unduly given too much attention, due to its spectacular brutality. It may be there was little substance behind the IS and it could be obsolete sooner rather than later.

DEALING WITH VIOLENT NON-STATE ACTORS

Chapters 3–5 examined the global, state, organizational and individual factors that explain the rise and facility of violent non-state actors. But what level of analysis is the best approach to end the violence? The primary global strategy is to tackle the lack of transparency in the global financial system. We offer an analysis of this in Box 12.1 on money laundering. This covers both economic and politically violent non-state actors. Global strategies are best suited to undermine groups that already exist. At the state level, there are many preventive approaches that can pre-empt the emergence of violent groups, such as administrative reform, security reform, judicial and prison reform. At the organizational level, there are also many ways to address violent groups once they have emerged. These include both exclusive and inclusive approaches, which are detailed in the counter-strategies section. Finally, at the individual level, we focus on deradicalization strategies in our case study.

PREVENTIVE MEASURES

INSTITUTIONAL REFORMS TO COUNTER NON-STATE GROUPS

Institutions are important for dealing with violent groups. When there are institutional weaknesses this can facilitate organized crime and insurgencies. Here we focus on the needs for administrative, judicial, security and prison reform. Institutional strength/reform is critical to preventing violent groups from becoming too powerful.

ADMINISTRATIVE REFORM

In dealing with non-state actors, the state itself needs to be stronger. By the administration we are referring to the institutions that are charged with administering the policies of the state.[2] Administrative institutions are therefore important because without them, citizens are denied access to public goods, which is a key element of the state's responsibility to provide for its citizens and satisfy their expectations. Administrative institutions 'make a difference when it comes to the legitimacy of the regime and policy outcomes' (Hydén et al., 2003: 3). Administrative institutions that provide services help the state to appear effective in the eyes of its citizens. And the more effective the state is, the more citizens may support and offer allegiance to the state instead of to non-state actors.

There are several ways in which the administration can ensure that it is strong enough to combat violent non-state actors. One is through maintaining low levels of administrative corruption. Corruption impacts violent non-state groups in several ways. Corruption permits these groups to operate carte blanche. When they can bribe officials, they have free movement to operate. This holds for both politically motivated and economically motivated non-state groups (Buscaglia, 2003, 2008). In particular, administrative institutions with higher levels of political intervention in the appointment, dismissal and promotion process and poor pay are correlated with higher levels of organized criminal activity (Buscaglia, 2003). A well-trained administrative sector is better able to ensure that financial regulations that organized criminal groups try to circumvent are more consistently enforced.[3] States with stronger administrative institutions are better able to prevent illicit activities and are better at monitoring money-laundering activities.

Box 12.1   Money Laundering

Money laundering is a core activity of organized crime. Money laundering is so important for the drug trade that the amount of money laundering taking place has been used as a proxy to measure the extent of drug trafficking. Money laundering takes place when illegal money is separated from its source, the origins are concealed and then it is transferred into legally incontestable forms. It is possible that as much as one trillion dollars is laundered. The International Monetary Fund claims that the number stands at half a trillion, or 2%–5% of the global GDP, whereas the United Nations Office on Drugs and Crime claims that it stands at about 2.7% (UNODC, 2011).

---

[2]For more on the importance of administrative institutions and its functions, see Goldsmith (1999). He writes that 'societies need a capable administration to keep order, collect revenue, and carry out programs' (p. 531).

[3]When institutions such as the banking system are more transparent with higher standards of regulatory enforcement, it also decreases organized crime. It is also helpful for businesses to have access to financial services within a regulatory framework (Buscaglia, 2003). Anti-money laundering legislation is also important.

Criminals and other violent groups thrive from a corrupt financial sector. Governments may also have a lax attitude about money laundering and may prefer to attract funds regardless of the source. Money laundering poses a threat to the global community for various reasons. Not only does it lead to great levels of bank instability, but it also helps to fund violent non-state actors (Nagle, 2003: 1699).

One of the major obstacles to fighting organized crime and other organized politically violent groups is offshore banking. About half of the world's money flows through offshore banks. Criminals can launder over $500 billion each year in illegal profits (Mair, 2005). Such large sums can enable organized criminal groups in particular to exercise control over major banks. This problem is acute in the Caribbean, but also in southeast Asia, parts of Europe and the US as well. Money can be deposited in secrecy. These countries may also have rules to protect assets, provide economic citizenship, tax exemption and may license banks that don't physically have to be in the country.

Countries in the Caribbean have been particularly reluctant to deal with money laundering. These small island countries may refuse to cooperate with international money-laundering regulations and offer low supervision of financial transactions. The Cayman Islands has only 300,000 people but over 550 banks. Only 17 of these banks are physically located on the islands (Thachuk, 2001a).

Anti-money laundering strategies are important in the fight against funding violent non-state actors. A National Money Laundering Strategy aims to deal with this problem by targeting the illegal proceeds from organized crime and other violent political groups. The National Money Laundering Strategy designates high-risk money-laundering zones. Targeting the money supply undermines these groups in conducting their operations. Assets can be seized (Thachuk, 2001a: 754). Some countries in Latin America have created financial information units to analyse, treat and provide information relevant to preventing the laundering of funds (Nagle, 2003: 1700).

Mutual legal assistance allows for the exchange between states of evidence and information in criminal and related matters. Financial and banking records can be exchanged which helps facilitate international cooperation in preventing groups from accessing their funds (Thachuk, 2001a: 754). Money laundering can also be affected by asset forfeiture to ensure that the proceeds of illegal funds do not re-enter the market (Nagle, 2003).

When institutions such as the banking system are more transparent, with higher standards of regulatory enforcement, it also decreases organized crime. It is also helpful for businesses to have access to financial services within a regulatory framework (Buscaglia, 2003).

For politically motivated actors corruption is a source of grievance that propels people to support these groups. When there are massive levels of administrative corruption, there are also issues with service delivery. Money that would be needed for education and healthcare gets diverted, affecting human capital and social welfare. Corruption affects citizens the most on a daily basis. They may be frequently harassed to pay bribes. These daily irritants erode trust in government. Once faith is lost in the government, these individuals may become involved in paying bribes to cross borders with contraband at the behest of politically and economically motivated groups. Research has shown that many individuals joined politically motivated violent groups due to frustrations with corruption, such as has been the case of those joining the Taliban in Afghanistan (Chayes, 2015). Marauding rebels have also been motivated to form due to high levels of government corruption (Collier and Hoeffler, 2002).

JUDICIAL REFORM

Scholars have argued that insurgencies have developed in countries with dysfunctional justice systems and persistent inequalities (Aguirre, 2006: 4). While the elites enjoy the rule of law and the protection of property rights, the urban and rural poor are excluded. The laws are not effective across an entire territory, and in most cases the poor are left to fend for themselves (O'Donnell, 1998, 2004). When the law is applied, it is unjust (Koonings and Kruijt, 2004: 8). People also take the law into their own hands in order to protect themselves, and in some cases are forced to engage in 'unorthodox criminal enterprise that victimizes others' (Fernández-Kelly and Shefner, 2006: 35–6). Death squads, paramilitaries, PSCs and insurgencies have all overstepped the boundaries of legality with impunity (Koonings and Kruijt, 2004: 7). Organized criminal groups have also thrived in societies with weak judicial institutions (Bibes, 2001). Therefore, to deal effectively with crime, government must strengthen their judicial institutions.

The World Bank claims that organized crime persists due to high rates of impunity (Fajnzylber et al., 1998: 31). Criminals who commit crimes once are more likely to commit crimes again, with low frequency of punishment (Davis, 1988). Therefore, it is critical that judicial institutions convict criminals when crimes are committed and offer adequate punishment. If the judicial institutions are not autonomous, upright and accountable, judges may be easily bought off and organized crime will persist.

In Colombia, weak judicial institutions have enabled organized crime to persist. Judicial decisions are heavily influenced by political considerations, intimidation and bribery (Buscaglia and van Dijk, 2003: 256). Criminals have gone unpunished and the justice system was unable to produce any results. The conviction rate was only 5%. Criminal organizations operated with impunity. Laws were even rewritten to suit the needs of drug kingpin Pablo Escobar due to his intimidation strategy of 'plomo o plata' (bullet or bribe). Being a judge was a dangerous job in Colombia, with some 350 judges killed during the height of Escobar's Medellin cartel (Thachuk, 2001a). As a result, sentences were reduced and criminals who surrendered to authorities were offered benefits.

SECURITY REFORM

One of the biggest problems for enabling violent non-state actors is corruption in the security sector, more specifically the military and the police. Corruption in the security forces is a problem because it facilitates an environment where violent non-state actors can thrive. Police are paid to provide information on planned raids, when arrests will occur and how investigations will proceed.

There is also tremendous corruption in regulating the borders, both for the movement of people and illegal goods that fund these groups. Borders are exploited by violent non-state actors, and many states are too weak to control and monitor this. Bribes can be given to a commanding officer to ignore a shipment of drugs or arms passing through international borders.

Studies show that organized crime levels are highest in countries where the police are poorly trained (Buscaglia, 2003: 12). The largest return on expenditure invested in criminal justice systems may lie in the training of specialized personnel.

When countries create special anti-organized crime units and introduce more training, significant reductions in organized crime have been observed. Deterrence is higher with more convictions per crime committed. In many countries with an ineffective police force, victims lack confidence in state institutions and so citizens rarely report crimes (Buscaglia, 2003: 10). In states where crime has become more entrenched, the state and the people may be less disposed to use whatever capacity they have to fight it.

Georgia represents an interesting case of police reform. In Georgia in the early 1990s, the police were so weak that they were unable to keep order on the streets of the capital, let alone in the separatist areas of Abkhazia, Ajaria and South Ossetia (Fairbanks, 2001). Armed groups and criminal networks were able to base themselves there and act with impunity. Law enforcement capabilities were non-existent and large sections of Georgian territory were captive to organized crime. When Mikheil Saakashvili came to power in 2004, sweeping reform of the nation's police agency, at that time considered the most corrupt institution in the country, were enacted. Saakashvili fired the vast majority of the country's policemen and then gave the remainder a significant raise in pay and better training. This caused bribe-taking virtually to disappear from the police force, and by 2011 the police had become one of the most trusted organizations in Georgia (Nasuti, 2012).

PRISON REFORM

Heavy-handed policies have led to extreme overcrowding in prisons. Unfortunately, far from being able to keep citizens safe, prisons are a breeding ground for turning criminals into radicals and vice versa. In some cases, they have helped to improve the organizational skills of gangs. In 1994, the French police aggressively pursued the Armed Islamic Group of Algeria (GIA) networks, and many were put in prison. In prison, GIA prisoners had a captive audience for their ideology and they developed relationships where this ideology could be inculcated.

Prison impacted the radicalization of those involved in the Madrid terrorist attacks in 2004. One of the ringleaders, Hamid Ahmidan, was a drug dealer in the 1990s. After time in a Spanish prison, he became completely radicalized. In spite of this religious revival, he continued to engage in the drug trade. At a raid on his safe house, thousands of ecstasy tablets were seized. His earnings and links were important for executing the attack in Madrid.

Prisons are also breeding grounds for resentment and activism. They are not institutions of reform but are vocational centres for crime. Prison radicalization had taken place in the case of Saudi prisoners as well. Over 25% of the 639 jihad militants who participated in a deradicalization programme had prior crime histories, with half arrested for drug offences (Boucek, 2008). Most of the jihadists actually knew very little about Islam. Prisoners also help keep demands alive for politically charged groups. ETA always had a policy of not allowing prisoners to apply for a reduced sentence or to be released upon good behaviour. They needed these prisoners to help maintain the grievances for the regime.

Penal policies in Italy and Germany – such as allowing convicted terrorists reduced sentences and other concessions, even including daytime furloughs from prison to hold a normal job – had a significant impact in affecting the long-term reduction in terrorist violence in those countries. Though prison reform is costly and unpopular, the current policies of allowing prisons to foment grievances are more costly for states in the long run. Prisons need to be reformed to ensure the rehabilitation of those arrested.

COUNTER-STRATEGIES

STRATEGIES TO DEAL WITH VIOLENT GROUPS

Counter-strategies are approaches to dealing with violent groups once they have already emerged. With these approaches, the organization itself is targeted. The most common way of dealing with a violent group is to take an exclusive approach, notably using repression. Using a repressive approach on its own for politically motivated groups can backfire for many reasons. Repressive measures can radicalize the violent group further. It may also lead to massive retaliation by economic groups. Studies of terrorist groups in both Germany and Italy found that the state's excessive use of violence was a reason to justify their own violence (Della Porta, 1995: 158). The use of the military to combat crime can also cause citizens' trust in these institutions to wane. In the case of Russia's strategy with dealing with the Chechen insurgency, the brutal tactics of the Russians spawned a more fervent movement, with greater reliance on suicide terrorism since 2002. Repression can also export a problem somewhere else. The heavy-handed response of the Russians facilitated the spread of the conflict to Dagestan and Ingushetia. The instability caused by various terror groups in Southern Thailand has been blamed on the heavy-handed tactics of former leader Thaksin Shinawatra. After taking office in 2001, he was so repressive that he destroyed the human intelligence network in Southern Thailand. He also disbanded the key institutions that offered administration and support for the south (Abuza, 2011).

When repressive tactics have been used on gangs, the results have not been positive. In Central America, murder rates have mostly increased as a result of 'Mano Dura' (strong hand) programmes. This has especially been the case in El Salvador. In 2003, the year that the Mano Dura programmes were implemented, homicide rates were 36 out of 100,000; by 2006, the number reached 65. Mexico has also seen rising violence. The war against the cartels, which started in 2006, has seen homicide rates skyrocket. From 2007 to 2014, over 164,000 homicides took place. In 2011, 27,000 people were killed. While there is no question that organized crime and criminal gangs must be dealt with, a singularly repressive strategy may not work. Crackdowns in Venezuela have led to spiralling murder rates. In 2015, the Venezuelan government deployed massive security forces in Venezuela's poorest and most violent neighbourhoods in order to weaken the power of organized crime and criminal gangs. The results have been about 100 more murders per month, including more extrajudicial killings by police. The crackdown forced criminal groups to become more organized and violent.

However, using repression has worked in some instances in which the group was incredibly weak. The US government used sustained pressure on Las Fuerzas Armadas de Liberación Nacional (FALN) and Los Macheteros, two Puerto Rican nationalist groups pursuing independence from the US. There have also been some cases of success in dealing with an insurgency. The Turkish government responded to the PKK insurgency with a tough counter-insurgency campaign involving the Turkish army and intelligence services. Turkey also pressed Iraq and Syria, the main sponsors of the PKK, to stop providing the group a sanctuary and surrender high-level PKK members, even threatening Syria with military action in 1998. Many of the members were killed, especially important members of the leadership who recruited and fundraised and trained new cadres. However, it is important to note that the Turkish government also became less repressive of Kurdish rights. Currently tensions with the Kurds have intensified again.

Part of an exclusive approach is to use targeted killings or captures. Targeted killings are supposed to reduce command and control, impede communication and force members underground. They keep members of violent groups on their toes, restricting their freedom of movement. They also reduce operational control and create power vacuums which may instigate feuds that may diminish the capabilities of the organization. Within this line of reasoning there are two potential types of targets: the head of the organization and the middlemen. Tackling the heads of organizations is referred to as a 'decapitation' strategy. The success of this strategy, however, is dependent on how powerful the leader is, whether there are viable successors and how much the leader has created a cult of personality. For groups with a strong value base, or politically motivated groups, replacing leaders should in theory be more difficult (Price, 2012).

Many scholars have noted that decapitation is not effective. One study claimed that it has only been effective in 17% of all cases (Jordan, 2009: 753). The issue is that the leader may have been preventing more large-scale violence, lone-actor violence and recklessness of other members. As will be explained in greater detail, splinter organizations may be more violent.

Other scholars have claimed that decapitation can work when it takes place early in the organization's life. This is particularly true for politically motivated groups. A terrorist group or insurgency that has had the leader eliminated during the first year of the group's existence will be eight times more likely to end than a non-decapitated group. These effects decrease by 50% within ten years, and have no impact after 20 years (Price, 2012). The groups most likely to be affected by decapitation are terrorist groups, compared to insurgencies. It is notable that the US claims to have killed an inordinate number of very high-level al-Qaeda leaders, with no major consequences.

There are examples, however, where a decapitation strategy has worked. This strategy worked in the case of several politically minded groups such as the Shining Path, the PKK, the Real Irish Republican Army (RIRA) and Aum Shinrikyo. The leader of the Shining Path, Abimael Guzmán, was captured on 12 September 1992. From jail, he repudiated his initial claims and told his followers to put down their weapons. The leader of the PKK, Abdullah Öcalan, was taken into custody in Kenya in February 1999. From jail, he renounced violence and the group renamed itself the Kurdistan Freedom and Democracy Congress (KADEK). Aum Shinrikyo's leader, Shoko Asahara, was arrested in May 1995. The group's membership decreased from 45,000 worldwide to fewer than 1,000. In all of these cases, it is important to note that the leader was arrested but not killed. Some scholars have argued that the arrest is more compelling than killing the leader (Jackson, 2007). There is a logical explanation for why a decapitation strategy may work for tackling a politically motivated organization. Values-based organizations have a more difficult time replacing their leaders. The leader is important to articulating a vision. They tend to be more charismatic because they must attract and motivate individuals not based on greed, but on an ideological agenda.

When it comes to dealing with economically motivated groups, the decapitation strategy is not likely to succeed in ending the greater problem. It may temporarily affect the group, but new groups will form and most often new leaders will rise. In the case of the Medellin cartel in Colombia, the killing of its leader, Pablo Escobar, in 1993 led to a massive splintering of smaller cartels. By 1996, 3,000 'baby' cartels (cartelitos) had appeared. One school of thought argues that for economically minded groups, the best strategy may be to take out or deal with the middlemen. For example, organized crime groups are complex networks where there are many different important members. There are members that serve as a bridge for the group, responsible for connecting the legal with the illegal, such as police and governors who have been bought off by the cartels. In these instances, the answer lies with security and political reform (see the section on preventive measures).

There are also many different exclusive measures that do not use force. States can impose travel sanctions for leaders of these groups. Preventing travel is more useful then expelling group members because when they have been expelled, they can engage in mutual learning with foreign violent groups. After five Israeli soldiers were killed in 1992, Israeli Prime Minister Itzak Rabin sent 415 Islamic Palestinian activists to Lebanon. While in Lebanon, they established close ties with Hezbollah (Hoffman and McCormick, 2004: 266). Under Hezbollah's tutelage, the group learned how to use car bombs and suicide attacks. Like Hezbollah, Hamas developed the same procedures for finding a candidate for suicide operations, training and preparing the individual psychologically, writing a farewell letter and making a videotape before the mission (Mishal and Sela, 2006). The leadership void left by the expulsion of the activists was filled by more violent young followers who wanted to increase the threat level against Israel.

States can also freeze the foreign assets of these groups' leaders. Leaders of these groups can go on most-wanted lists and be blacklisted. Groups can be named and shamed. The international community can set up a war criminal tribunal to prosecute the leaders of violent groups. Furthermore, economic sanctions against other states that may be offering support for violent groups can be implemented.

Another strategy for dealing with violent groups is to focus on controlling and containing them. This calls for reducing their freedom of movement and their ability to communicate with members of the group. This method requires having strong intelligence measures and strict surveillance of violent groups and their members. This is easier to accomplish with groups that are concentrated in one particular area.

Another strategy is to marginalize and isolate violent groups. This aims to reduce the influence of groups. This may be more pertinent for politically active groups that actually have some sort of political agenda. In this case, the group is isolated by public discourse and isolated physically as well. This is mostly a war of ideas; the strategy assumes that reacting to the group with violent provocations will be counterproductive. The state must aim to gain popular support, win the war of words and delegitimize the group. Groups that are not entirely popular to begin with may be easy to marginalize.[4]

---

[4]Here it is the group itself that is targeted, not individuals, such as in the deradicalization strategy.

The Saudi government has engaged in a war of ideas against extremist Muslim groups. They have co-opted former critics of the regime and used highly credible individuals to undermine the support for radicals (see the case study on deradicalization). This was not difficult to do after jihadists killed many Muslims in different attacks. These groups were easy to portray as dangerous thugs to the Saudi people who were outraged by the violence against innocent people. Saudi Arabia also pressured groups like Hamas to denounce the violence against Muslims. The Saudi government also published confessions of captured jihadists which revealed how brutal their mindsets were and how ignorant they were about Islam (Byman, 2008).

Another exclusive strategy is to focus on creating a split within the group. This has been done with many economically motivated groups by luring members to confess and spill information, but this has led to the creation of splinter groups that are even more violent, as the case of Colombian cartelitos has illustrated. This may pose a bigger threat to politically motivated groups. This strategy may entail trying to separate the moderates from the extreme elements of the organization. States can offer secret deals to key figures in these groups and involve them in the political process. Certain members of these groups can be encouraged to leave or to transform the group into a political movement, or to splinter off to create a political movement. The problem, though, is again that this strategy can establish radical fringe groups that may be more extreme and violent than the former group. The moderates of the organization may have been critical to managing the level of violence of the group. This has happened often with terrorist groups and insurgencies.

Another exclusive strategy is to induce individual members of the groups to cooperate with authorities. This is an option for politically and economically motivated groups, but makes the assumption that many of their members are rational and self-interested. As economically motivated groups are motivated by greed, making an offer they can't refuse has been a viable option. Inducements can also be offered to members of politically motivated groups to disarm and take a post in the government, which has happened in the case of insurgencies in the Philippines. This approach can also involve intimidating and threatening members and their families, or a mix of carrots and sticks. The strategy works better with economically motivated actors, but it is also feasible to lure politically motivated actors whose resolve has grown weak.

The second way of dealing with violent groups is to try an 'inclusive' approach. Inclusive approaches include finding ways to negotiate and engage in dialogue and dissemination. The state may also train and build capacity, mediate between conflicting groups and provide more direct services.

One form of inclusiveness is to engage in mediation. Mediation entails using external actors to negotiate between different actors. This can take place with both politically charged actors and economic ones (Wennmann, 2014). Negotiation has been used in the case of El Salvador with the major gangs, to come up with some sort of agreement about how to lessen the violence. This approach requires that negotiators have contacts within these groups and that the negotiators offer a clear list of the costs and benefits of negotiation, and knowledge of the best available solutions. Long-term engagement may be necessary. Insurgencies are more easily integrated into a peace deal than warlords or terrorists. They are more capable of transforming into political movements. Terrorist groups and warlords can be involved when they want to make a transformation into a non-violent political position, but using negotiation methods is more applicable to groups with a defined and legitimate constituency.

In the Philippines government, the power of the Muslim insurgencies, which had de facto control over parts of the southern Philippines, forced the government to forge peace deals. In August 1996, the Filipino government and the MNLF finalized an agreement for autonomy and the MNLF transitioned into a political pressure group rather than an insurgent organization. This came after almost a decade of negotiations and agreements, starting with MNLF's agreement to accept a semi-autonomous status in 1987.

Agreements have been ongoing between the government and the other notable Filipino insurgency, the MILF, but the most significant peace agreements took place in 2014, and have led to a new autonomous entity, Bangsamoro. Under the ongoing agreement, there would be more Muslim self-rule in southern Philippines in exchange for a deactivation of its forces. MILF would have to give up their arms and a regional peace force would be deployed. Agreements were also made possible by the fact that most of the cadres were now well into their retirement age and its founder, Hashim Salamat, had died of a heart attack in 2003.

In a shocking policy turn in 2012, the government in El Salvador decided to engage in negotiated talks with the leadership of the MS-13 and 18th Street Gangs. The gangs agreed to a truce in exchange for transferring the gangs to less restrictive prisons and offering some other concessions to them. This pact led a reduction in homicide rates, with murders decreasing by 45% from 2011 to 2012, though when the pact ended, murders increased again (Agius and Wolff, 2015).

Co-optation and integration is another inclusive strategy. Violent groups and their leaders can be co-opted and integrated into non-violent politics. For example, for insurgencies with political agendas, power sharing can take place, particularly at the local level so that these armed groups can disarm and focus on day-to-day politics (Jarstad and Sisk, 2008). MNLF leaders received financial incentives and were incorporated into the government payroll in various administrative positions. Co-optation may be easier to implement with groups that have a clear agenda that can be worked with, rather than a broad but dogmatic agenda. As part of an integration strategy, it is important to socialize these actors to accept new norms. Members of armed groups have to understand the problems associated with their previous violent strategy.

In some cases, as part of a co-optation strategy, amnesty is given. This can happen for politically and economically motivated groups. Though it is questionable to not pursue justice for those who have perpetrated violence (especially for the victims), the rationale is that providing incentives to leaders and members of these groups will force them to stop engaging in violence and prevent further violence. Amnesty is part of a larger political deal and cannot be applied to everyone, which would lead to an impunity gap. This approach may work when a violent group has been engaging in violence for a long time, and has not achieved their objectives and may want to have a different life. By doing so, these individuals have to respect new norms of non-violence, but this makes the assumption that politically charged groups can be persuaded to pursue a deal. Amnesty was offered to the terror group the Red Brigades in Italy in 1979 and 1982. Amnesty was also offered to members of the Shining Path. Amnesty is a successful strategy to induce members and leaders of a group to give up arms when they are aware that they are facing defeat (Art and Richardson, 2007). For economically charged groups, it is not uncommon for these members to take plea deals in exchange for some form of immunity or a favourable punishment deal.

An inclusive strategy may also be focused on reaching out to disenfranchised groups that may be vulnerable to joining violent organizations (for more on this, see the case study in this chapter on deradicalization). Survey data has revealed that for many Muslims living in non-Muslim countries, racism and discrimination are major threats to their communities that need to be addressed (Choudhury and Fenwick, 2011). Many Muslims living in non-Muslim countries feel hostility towards them. Reaching out to these communities and making sure that they feel welcome and integrated is another important step in preventing the type of alienation that may lead to having sympathy for militants. In the Netherlands, a comprehensive and inclusive approach is taken to tackling extremism. Policies are aimed at preventing radicalization and other social problems, such as segregation and disenfranchisement (Demant and Graaf, 2010).

─────────────── Case Study   Deradicalization ───────────────

Deradicalization programmes are a way for extremists to understand compromise, practise non-violence and adopt more moderate views. A deradicalization approach must first understand the ideological appeal of violent ideologies at the individual level. Individuals who are insecure and feel insignificant, with poor career prospects may be particularly vulnerable to joining radical groups. These radical groups help lost individuals feel significant and offer them a solid structure (Doosje et al., 2016).

There is a cognitive component of exposing extremists to opposing views to justify the use of violence and to also provide some form of motivation based on material support, job training and assisting families of detained individuals. This usually pertains to politically motivated groups. Extremists can be left-wing, right-wing, anarchist, religious, or possibly something else. However, these programmes can also be applied to gang members who need to understand the importance of non-violence and breaking out of a gang and also need motivational support. For many militants and criminals, jail conditions are often very difficult, but far more challenging is finding employment and re-joining mainstream society. Because conditions outside are so difficult, it is important for deradicalization programmes to provide this additional support (Blaydes and Rubin, 2008). These programmes also understand the need to relocate individuals and place them in social environments that are more supportive of non-violence.

Some authors have argued that for deradicalization to take place, the best approach is to provide 'counter-narratives' (Braddock and Horgan, 2016). Just as violent groups can generate persuasive narratives, counter-narratives can be disseminated to contradict radicalizing themes. However, to do so effectively, there are several important strategies. First, it is important for the counter-narrative to be disseminated by someone who is well respected in the community. In the case of Islamic extremism, authors argue that it is critical to involve the Muslim community in constructing and disseminating counter-narratives as much as possible (Corman and Schiefelbein, 2008). Individuals who may agree with some of the major themes of an ideology in principle but disagree with the use of violence may also be useful in a deradicalization process. Second, counter-narratives need to reveal the contradictions in the violent ideologies. Again, in the case of Islamic extremism, it is important for members of the Muslim community to identify what aspects of Islam are at odds with extremist strategies and actions (Braddock and Horgan, 2016).

For Islamic militants, there have been encouraging reports of attempts to de-radicalize militants (Striegher, 2013). Indonesia has won over hearts and minds of some of the former members of Jemaah Islamiyah through deradicalization programmes that typically last several

(Continued)

(Continued)

months. Former militants are enlisted to persuade detained terror suspects and those vul-nerable to joining violent groups to renounce extremism and cooperate with the government (Salam and Abdullahi, 2014). To lure individuals to take part in these programmes, incentives are offered such as reduced sentences and financial assistance to those participating and their families as well. Ex-militants communicate that acts of violence are unacceptable and un-Is-lamic. They also try to convey the idea that the authorities are not un-Islamic.

After militants bombed a compound in Riyadh, Saudi Arabia, in May 2003, the government began a deradicalization programme. Saudi Arabia reduced prison sentences of jailed militants if they agreed to undergo intensive classroom sessions, involving religious debates, re-edu-cation and psychological counselling (Boucek, 2008). It aimed to re-educate individuals who committed minor terrorism-related offences. Anyone who committed an actual act of terror was not allowed to enter the programme. The Saudi programme also offered those who com-pleted the re-education help with finding jobs, housing and a car. The government also officially encourages single detainees to marry and have children since they are less likely to pursue violence (Boucek, 2008). Financial and healthcare assistance is provided to the families of the detainees. The programme also offers follow-up psychological examinations (Boucek, 2008).

Egypt and Yemen had similar programmes, but also included those who had committed true acts of terror. Egypt's' programme began in 1997 after the imprisoned terrorist leader of the Islamic Group (IG) renounced the use of terror and violence (Blaydes and Rubin, 2008). The IG argued that the Koran did not support ideological extremism. As a result of these efforts, there have been no terrorist attacks committed by the IG (Ashour, 2010). The al-Jihad organization, which had strong ties to al-Qaeda, was able to de-radicalize as well under the leadership of its former commander, Dr Sayyid Imam al-Sharif. He wrote a book to explain his views and toured Egyptian prisons to encourage prisoners to relinquish their extremism. IG leaders also partici-pated in these meetings to help provide support for the case to de-radicalize.

There are several programmes that not only work on deradicalization of Islamic militants, but on right-wing extremists as well. A programme titled Exit Norway relies on mobilizing parents to remove their children from the influence of extremist organizations. The parents' networks have been successful in getting about 90% of their children to relinquish the use of violence. Exit Sweden does not exclusively seek out extremist youths and their families, but works with direct requests by members who want to disengage to provide safe houses. German programmes involve civil society groups, NGOs and government agencies that work to screen and monitor participants. An interesting study in Germany showed that for many right-wing radicals, involve-ment in deradicalization programmes was voluntary. The majority of those who got involved did so by contacting the organization themselves (Grunenberg and Van Donselaar, 2006). This suggests that publicizing the availability of deradicalization programmes could be useful.

CONCLUSION

There are several key strategies to reducing the threats from violent non-state actors. At the global level, the international community collectively needs to come up with a more comprehensive plan to fight money laundering to cut off sources of funding. At the state level, institutional reform is critical. This is not only a form of prevention but also serves to undermine violent groups that are taking advantage of the state's weakness. It is therefore important to reduce administrative corruption and ensure administrative services. States need to earmark more funds for healthcare, education and overall development. States also need to lessen judicial corruption and ensure the rule of law. They need to also reduce police corruption, train law enforcement and improve domestic security. Part of this plan may entail also focusing on small arms collection. Another important priority is to focus on prison reform. States also need to foster civil society, community engagement and integration of disenfranchised groups and individuals. At the organizational level, groups can be targeted in many different ways, but offering counter-narratives to the group's ideology can be helpful. Offering alternative sources of livelihood has also proven to be important. At the individual level, deradicalization programmes can target individuals who are vulnerable and help them understand the contradiction in extremist ideologies and the use of violence. Dealing with any group requires going beyond a merely repressive approach and tackling some of the deeper political, social and economic causes that explain the group's formation (Alonso, 2011).

Summary Points

- Organized criminal groups are the most ubiquitous and difficult to eliminate. Terrorist groups usually do not last very long compared to insurgencies.
- Groups last longer when they have flatter hierarchies.
- There are various components of institutional form that help to prevent the emergence of violent groups, such as administrative, judicial, security and prison reform.
- Preventing money laundering will weaken all types of violent non-state actors.
- There are many exclusive approaches to dealing with violent groups, but taking a comprehensive approach – which also includes inclusive measures – is a more effective long-term strategy.

Key Questions

1. Why are administrative and judicial reform so important in tackling organized crime?
2. In what ways might prison reform be important for preventing both political and criminal groups from strengthening?
3. What are the pros and cons of repressive strategies? Why do they fail to work when applied in isolation?
4. What are the strategies of an inclusive approach? What are the benefits of an inclusive approach to dealing with violent non-state actors? What might be the potential challenges of doing so?
5. What is meant by 'deradicalization'? In what ways can states tackle extremism through educational programmes? Do you think these might be effective?
6. Theory: What are the ways that realists might conceive a response to violent non-state actors? What is the logic behind this response? How might this contrast with liberals and constructivists?

FURTHER READING

Altier, M.B., Thoroughgood, C.N. and Horgan, J.G. (2014) 'Turning away from terrorism: lessons from psychology, sociology, and criminology', *Journal of Peace Research*, 51 (5): 647–61. Multidisciplinary approach to explain how to get individuals to stop using violence.

Choudhury, T. and Fenwick, H. (2011) 'The impact of counter-terrorism measures on Muslim communities', *International Review of Law, Computers & Technology*, 25 (3): 151–81. Extensive overview on how Muslim communities have been affected by counter-terror measures.

Connable, B. and Libicki, M.C., 2010. *How Insurgencies End* (vol. 965) (Rand Corporation). Extensive overview of how insurgencies might end.

Cronin, A.K. (2009) *How Terrorism Ends: Understanding the Decline and Demise of Terrorist Campaigns* (Princeton University Press).

Cronin, A.K. (2012) *Ending Terrorism: Lessons for Defeating al-Qaeda* (Routledge). Both books by Cronin offer interesting lessons for how terrorism ends, with the former offering an overview of terrorist groups and the latter focusing on how to defeat al-Qaeda.

Doosje, B., Moghaddam, F.M., Kruglanski, A.W., de Wolf, A., Mann, L. and Feddes, A.R. (2016) 'Terrorism, radicalization and de-radicalization', *Current Opinion in Psychology*, 11: 79–84. Overview of radicalization and de-radicalization.

Ganor, B. (2011) *The Counter-Terrorism Puzzle: a Guide for Decision Makers* (Transaction Publishers). Clear overview of various counter-terror measures; helps readers understand the trade-offs that decision makers face in pursuing an effective counter-terror policy.

Kenney, M. (2003) 'From Pablo to Osama: counter-terrorism lessons from the war on drugs', *Survival*, 45 (3): 187–206. Interesting analysis of the policies of leadership interdiction.

CONCLUSION

The concept of security has changed over time. In the past, security was conceived as the ability to protect the state from external threats. Today, security encompasses a much wider definition, taking into account human safety and well-being. This is all the more important given that threats to security no longer only endanger states, but citizens living in these states as well. Interstate conflict has become a rarity, while civil conflicts and unconventional forms of violence have become the norm. Some studies claim that due to unconventional forms of violence, the civilian death toll in conflicts could be as high as 90% (European Union, 2003). Though the 90% figure has been disputed as an inflated projection, there is no doubt that civilians constitute a larger percentage of the casualties than ever before. Norms that prevented violence against civilians have dissipated; citizens are the new targets.

Additionally, though the state is still prominent, the main threats emanate from violent non-state actors. Given the growing prominence of violent non-state groups, it is more critical than ever that our understanding of global politics encompasses a clear grasp of what violent non-state actors are and what impact they have. We continue to theorize about security as if states and violent non-states are one and the same. Though we can certainly draw some similarities, it is important to clarify their differences.

Part of the challenge in doing so is that violent non-state actors are constantly evolving and mutating. Politically motivated actors now have economic motives as well, and vice versa. Criminal groups can ally with political groups, while political groups are deeply involved in organized crime. Groups are becoming more networked and diffuse. Roles are fungible and interchangeable. Groups are better connected and can communicate with a bigger audience. Groups are linking up, allying and transforming.

There are many factors that help explain why violent non-state actors are more prominent, more powerful and more lethal. Globalization has elevated the power of violent non-state groups, facilitating these linkages and transformations. The proliferation of small arms and the erosion of the state have also levelled the playing field. Networks that can take advantage of vulnerable individuals have been another important factor.

States have often responded to these groups by assuming that they are just like states, or organized and motivated like violent groups of the past. But repressive strategies that may have worked before are now backfiring. Thus, there are many important tasks ahead in having a firm grasp of insecurity and the response to it. The first is to define what the actual threats are to security compared to what security threats were in the past. How has conflict and violence changed? Given that security threats are emanating from a host of different non-state actors, we need to understand what violent non-state actors are and how they differ from each other. This helps us to better comprehend what impact violent non-state groups have on state and society. We also need to know why and how they emerged in the first place and how they are evolving. This helps us come up with a clear and effective strategy and appropriate response.

But misunderstandings about unconventional violence still abound. For example, terrorism is the type of violence that garners the most media attention. It is not surprising, given that terrorist activity increased by 80% in 2014 – its highest recorded level, though it decreased slightly in 2015. Since 2000, the number of people who have died from terrorist activity has increased nine-fold. And the number of countries being afflicted by acts of terrorism is spreading. In 2014, 11 countries had over 500 deaths due to terrorism, while in 2013 only five did.

In spite of this alarming trend, terrorism does not constitute a major threat to those living in Western countries. Though many Westerners fear extremist Islamic organizations, there are fewer than four people per year killed by an extremist Islamic terrorist organization in the UK, while in Canada and Australia, the number is two in the last decade (Mueller and Stewart, 2016). Including all of the terrible terrorist attacks that have taken place in Europe in 2015 and 2016, far more people died in terrorist attacks during the 1970s and 1980s perpetrated by non-religious groups.

Moreover, it is still homicides that are more deadly than terrorist attacks. There are 13 times the number of homicide victims as terrorist victims. In 2014, there were 32,685 deaths due to terrorism, 7,512 of which were in Nigeria, one of the countries hardest hit by terrorism. In contrast, the number of homicides in Venezuela was as high of 28,000 in 2015. Brazil had over 50,000 homicides in 2012. The total death in the Mexican drug war could be as high as 120,000 and at the height of instability in Honduras, there were 19 murders per day in 2011, or 86 per 100,000 residents. Due to the rise of organized crime, Honduras has also seen a rise in massacres, with 95 taking place in 2015. Thus, terrorism has its biggest impact psychologically, not physically; other forms of violence are of greater concern. The book did not focus as much attention on this anomaly, but did try to offer a framework for understanding the different types of violent groups that exist beyond just terrorist groups and insurgencies, and how these actors may challenge traditional notions of security.

To do so, the book provided an overview of violent non-state actors in four parts. Part I offered an analysis of previous theories and paradigms of international security. Here we highlighted some of the weaknesses of previous approaches to security and the need for these approaches to update themselves to reflect today's realities. This was followed by a conceptualization of the different forms of violence taking place today and the ways in which these different types of violence represent a departure from the past. We also introduced who the violent non-state actors are that encompass global politics and what might be the best ways of conceptualizing these actors.

Part II provided an overview of the different levels of analysis to understand how violent non-state actors may emerge and thrive. We started with an examination of global factors, such as changes to the polarity of the system and the increasing interconnectedness of the world. Spurred on by improvements in technology and transportation, the world has become smaller but also more exposed to competing ideologies, views and values. Just as it is easier to communicate with loved ones, it is also easier to coordinate acts of violence.

We then turned to state-level factors and how they can explain why violent groups might emerge. The international relations literature (and in particular realism) has often made the assumption that the world is filled with sovereign states that only differed in terms of their military capabilities. However, many states are weak and unstable, with flawed institutions. This may provide motivation and opportunity for certain types of violent non-state actors. But we are still trying to understand what specific institutions matter. With regards to terrorism, it was previously argued by much of the literature that it is democracies that have mostly been targeted, but 78% of all terrorist attack deaths today take place in countries with weak democratic institutions: Iraq, Nigeria, Afghanistan, Pakistan and Syria. Western democracies, in contrast, are more likely to face lone-actor attacks. This means that the targets and perpetrators may be constantly changing.

We then turned to explore individual-level factors that help us to understand why individuals might join violent groups. For the most part, psychological approaches have been heavily criticized, but this does not mean that these approaches should be completely abandoned. New research is demonstrating that psychological factors may be more important than previously thought. Additionally, social psychological approaches that emphasize the importance of networks and the need to belong still offer a great deal of explanatory power.

Part III was divided into two parts, initially focusing on politically motivated actors such as insurgencies and terrorist groups, and then examining economically motivated actors such as warlords, criminals and PSCs. Distinguishing between the two politically motivated groups is very difficult. The actions of two of the most deadly insurgencies illustrate this complexity. Though most of the Western media's attention is on the IS, the group that has committed the most terrorist deaths is Boko Haram, with 6,644 deaths committed compared to IS with 6,073, though the IS still kills more on the battlefield (more than 20,000 killed) than through terrorist attacks. But both cases illustrate the changing tactics of violent groups. As the book explained, both groups are insurgencies because they hold territory and have to administer over this territory. But both groups also regularly engage in terrorist attacks.

Subsequent chapters demonstrated the power, structure and changing tactics of economically motivated groups. In particular, it is criminal groups that are the most ubiquitous and also the most damaging and destructive. But these groups are often overshadowed in security studies by terrorist groups and insurgencies. The fungible nature of political and economic groups also highlights the importance of tackling the source of these groups' funding to undermine their operations.

Part IV offered two chapters on how violent groups might moderate and end. Chapter 11 examined political parties with violent wings. There were many different formations that could take place, but ultimately any group that contested elections but was somehow associated with a violent group was considered. This provided a foundation for understanding the objective of the last chapter, which was focused on how violent groups end and moderate. The answer provided was a multi-pronged approach that shuns a repression-only strategy. Because they are far too complex to be dealt with solely by exercising repression, the chapter argued that a comprehensive strategy that tackles the global, state-level, organizational and individual factors that lead to the recruitment, formation and success of these violent groups must be understood.

Although there is no shortage of books on conflict, terrorism, crime and violence, to better understand the many threats to security, it is necessary to take a multidisciplinary approach that utilizes new research in a variety of areas. Past approaches to security have been too narrow in focus, too state-focused and too limited to one discipline. To break ground in the field of international security, future studies need to continue to incorporate other disciplines and work to update the dominant paradigms of security. This will help us to better understand not only the threats that we face today but also the solutions.

What is the nature of global politics when you also take into account weak and unstable states with complex demographics?

REFERENCES

Aas, K.F. (2013) *Globalization and Crime*. London: SAGE.

Abadie, A. (2004) *Poverty, Political Freedom, and the Roots of Terrorism* (No. w10859). Cambridge, MA: National Bureau of Economic Research.

Abadinsky, H. (2012) *Organized Crime*. Hampshire: Cengage Learning.

Abrahms, M. (2004) 'Are terrorists really rational? The Palestinian example', *Orbis*, 48 (3): 533–49.

Abrahms, M. (2008) 'What terrorists really want: terrorist motives and counterterrorism strategy', *International Security*, 32 (4): 78–105.

Abrahms, M. and Gottfried, M.S. (2016) 'Does terrorism pay? An empirical analysis', *Terrorism and Political Violence*, 28 (1): 72–89.

Abuza, Z. (Winter, 2009) 'Jemaah Islamiyah adopts the Hezbollah model', *Middle East Quarterly*, 15–26.

Abuza, Z. (2011) *The Ongoing Insurgency in Southern Thailand: Trends in Violence, Counterinsurgency Preparations, and the Impact of National Politics*. Washington, DC: National Defense University Press.

Adams, J. (1986) *The Financing of Terrorism: How the Groups that are Terrorizing the World Get the Money to do it*. New York: Simon and Schuster.

Adams, T.K. (1999) 'The new mercenaries and the privatization of conflict', *Parameters*, 29 (2): 103.

Adamson, F.B. (2005) 'Globalisation, transnational political mobilisation, and networks of violence', *Cambridge Review of International Affairs*, 18 (1): 31–49.

Adamson, F.B. (2006) 'Crossing borders: international migration and national security', *International Security*, 31 (1): 165–99.

Agbiboa, D.E. (2013) 'Why Boko Haram exists: the relative deprivation perspective', *African Conflict & Peacebuilding Review*, 3 (1): 144–57.

Aghedo, I. and Osumah, O. (2012) 'The Boko Haram uprising: how should Nigeria respond?', *Third World Quarterly*, 33 (5): 853–69.

Agius, C. and Wolff, M. (2015) 'Gang truce in El Salvador', *ECPR Standing Group on Organized Crime*, 12 (3): 2–3.

Agnew, R. (2006) 'Storylines as a neglected cause of crime'. *Journal of Research in Crime and Delinquency*, 43 (2): 119–147.

Aguirre, M. (2006) 'Failed states or weak democracies? The state in Latin America', *OpenDemocracy.net*, 17. Transnational Institute, 17 January.

Akgündüz, Y., Van den Berg, M. and Hassink, W.H. (2015) 'The impact of refugee crises on host labor markets: the case of the Syrian refugee crisis in Turkey', *Institute for Study of Labour*, Discussion Paper Series 8841, 1–24.

Akhtar, S. (1999) 'The psychodynamic dimension of terrorism', *Psychiatric Annals*, 29 (6): 350–5.

Alao, A., Mackinlay, J. and Olonisakin, F. (1999) *Peacekeepers, Politicians, and Warlords: The Liberian Peace Process*. New York: United Nations University Press.

Albanese, J. and Reichel, P. (eds) (2013) *Transnational Organized Crime: An Overview from Six Continents*. Thousand Oaks, CA: SAGE.

Albertson, K. and Fox, C. (2011) *Crime and Economics: An Introduction*. Abingdon: Routledge.

Alex, P.S. (2004) 'Frameworks for conceptualising terrorism', *Terrorism and Political Violence*, 16 (2): 197–221.

Allen, C. (1999) 'Warfare, endemic violence and state collapse in Africa,' *Review of African Political Economy*, 26 (81): 367–384.

Alleyne, E. and Wood, J.L. (2010) 'Gang involvement: psychological and behavioral characteristics of gang members, peripheral youth, and non-gang youth', *Aggressive Behavior*, 36 (6): 423–36.

Alonso, R. (2011) 'Why do terrorists stop? Analyzing why ETA members abandon or continue with terrorism', *Studies in Conflict & Terrorism*, 34 (9): 696–716.

Altheide, D.L. (2007) 'The mass media and terrorism', *Discourse & Communication*, 1 (3): 287–308.

Altier, M.B., Martin, S. and Weinberg, L.B. (eds) (2016) *Violence, Elections, and Party Politics*. London and New York: Routledge.

Andreas, P. and Nadelmann, E. (2006) *Policing the Globe*. New York: Oxford University Press.

Angrist, J.D. (1995) 'The economic returns to schooling in the West Bank and Gaza Strip', *The American Economic Review*, 1065–87.

Antonio Ocampo, J. (2005) *The Inequality Predicament: Report on the World Social Situation 2005*. United Nations Department of Public Information.

Arjona, A. and Kalyvas, S.N. (2009) Rebelling against rebellion: comparing insurgent and counterinsurgent recruitment. Paper presented at Human Security and Ethnicity Workshop: Mobilisation for Political Violence. What Do We Know? at Centre for Research on Inequality, March (Vol. 4, pp. 436–55).

Arnson, C.J. (2000) 'Window on the past: a declassified history of death squads in El Salvador'. In B. Campbell and A. Brenner (eds), *Death Squads in Global Perspective: Murder with Deniability*. New York: Palgrave Macmillan, pp. 85–124.

Art, R.J. and Richardson, L. (2007) *Democracy and Counterterrorism: Lessons from the Past*. Washington, DC: US Institute of Peace Press.

Aryasinha, R. (2001) 'Terrorism, the LTTE and the conflict in Sri Lanka', *Conflict, Security & Development*, 1 (2): 25–50.

Asal, V., Brown, M. and Dalton, A. (2012) 'Why split? Organizational splits among ethnopolitical organizations in the Middle East', *Journal of Conflict Resolution*, 56 (1): 94–117.

Asal, V. and Rethemeyer, R.K. (2008) 'The nature of the beast: organizational structures and the lethality of terrorist attacks', *The Journal of Politics*, 70 (2): 437–49.

Ashour, O. (2010) 'De-radicalization of jihad? The impact of Egyptian Islamist revisionists on al-Qaeda', *Perspectives on Terrorism*, 2 (5): 15–19.

Atkinson, A.B. and Brandolini, A. (2006) 'From earnings dispersion to income inequality', in F. Farina and E. Savaglio (eds), *Inequality and Economic Integration*. London: Routledge, pp. 35–62.

Atran, S. (2003a) 'Genesis of suicide terrorism', *Science*, 299 (5612): 1534–9.

Atran, S. (2003b) *The Strategic Threat from Suicide Terror*. AEI Brookings Joint Center for Regulatory Studies, 1–20.

Avant, D.D. (2005) *The Market for Force: The Consequences of Privatizing Security*. Cambridge: Cambridge University Press.

Avant, D. and Sigelman, L. (2010) 'Private security and democracy: lessons from the US in Iraq', *Security Studies*, 19 (2): 230–65.

Ayoob, M. (1995) *The Third World Security Predicament: State Making, Regional Conflict, and the International System*. Boulder, CO: L. Rienner Publishers.

Azam, J.P. (2006) 'On thugs and heroes: why warlords victimize their own civilians', *Economics of Governance*, 7 (1): 53–73.

Bahcheli, T., Bartmann, B. and Srebrnik, H. (eds) (2004) *De Facto States: The Quest for Sovereignty*. Abingdon: Routledge.

Bailey, J. and Taylor, M.M. (2009) 'Evade, corrupt, or confront? Organized crime and the state in Brazil and Mexico', *Journal of Politics in Latin America*, 1 (2): 3–29.

Baldwin, David A. (1995) 'Security studies and the end of the Cold War', *World Politics* 48 (1): 117–41.

Bangerter, O. (2012) *31: Internal Control Codes of Conduct within Insurgent Armed Groups.* Geneva: Small Arms Survey. Available at: www.smallarmssurvey.org/fileadmin/docs/B-Occasional-papers/SAS-OP31-internal-control.pdf (accessed 25 October 2016).

Barbieri, K. and Reuveny, R. (2005) 'Economic globalization and civil war', *Journal of Politics*, 67 (4): 1228–47.

Barker, T. (2010) *Biker Gangs and Organized Crime.* New York: Routledge.

Barkey, K (1994) *Bandits and Bureaucrats: The Ottoman Route to State Centralization.* New York: Cornell University Press.

Barnett, A., Held, D. and Henderson, C. (eds) (2013) *Debating Globalization.* Cambridge: Polity.

Barros, C.P., Passos, J. and Gil-Alana, L.A. (2006) 'The timing of ETA terrorist attacks', *Journal of Policy Modeling*, 28 (3): 335–46.

Basile, M. (2004) 'Going to the source: why Al Qaeda's financial network is likely to withstand the current war on terrorist financing', *Studies in Conflict & Terrorism*, 27 (3): 169–185.

Baylis, J., Wirtz, J.J. and Gray, C.S. (eds) (2013) *Strategy in the Contemporary World.* Oxford: Oxford University Press.

Beaton, L. (1972) *The Reform of Power: A Proposal for An International Security System.* London: Chatto & Windus.

Beckett, I. (2005) 'The future of insurgency', *Small Wars & Insurgencies*,16 (1): 22–36.

Becker, J. (1981) 'Another final battle on the stage of history', *Studies in Conflict & Terrorism*, 5 (1–2): 89–105.

Becker, M. (2014) 'Explaining lone wolf target selection in the United States', *Studies in Conflict & Terrorism*, 37 (11): 959–78.

Berdal, M. (2003) 'How "new" are "new wars"? Global economic change and the study of civil war', *Global Governance*, 9 (4): 477–502.

Bergen, P. and Pandey, S. (2005) 'The madrassa myth', *New York Times* (14 June).

Berman, E. (2003) *Hamas, Taliban and the Jewish Underground: An Economist's View of Radical Religious Militias* (No. w10004). Cambridge, MA: National Bureau of Economic Research.

Berman, E. (2011) *Radical, Religious, and Violent: The New Economics of Terrorism.* Cambridge, MA: MIT Press.

Berrebi, C. (2003) 'Evidence about the link between education, poverty and terrorism among Palestinians', *Princeton University Industrial Relations Section Working Paper* (477).

Betancourt, T.S., Simmons, S., Borisova, I., Brewer, S.E., Iweala, U. and De La Soudière, M. (2008) 'High hopes, grim reality: reintegration and the education of former child soldiers in Sierra Leone', *Comparative Education Review*, 52 (4): 565.

Betts, A. and Collier, P. (2015) 'Help refugees help themselves: let displaced Syrians join the labor market', *Foreign Affairs*, 94: 84.

Bezemer, D.J. and Jong-A-Pin, R.M. (2007) *World on Fire? Democracy, Globalization and Ethnic Violence.* Groningen: University of Groningen.

Bhasin, T. and Hallward, M. C. (2013) 'Hamas as a political party: democratization in the Palestinian territories', *Terrorism and Political Violence*, 25 (1): 75–93.

Bibes, P. (2001) 'Transnational organized crime and terrorism. Colombia: a case study', *Journal of Contemporary Criminal Justice*, 17 (3): 243–58.

Binder, A., Geis, G. and Bruce Jr, D.D. (2001) *Juvenile Delinquency: Historical, Cultural & Legal Perspectives*, 3rd edition. Cincinnati, OH: Elsevier.

Blakkisrud, H. and Kolstø, P. (2011) 'From secessionist conflict toward a functioning state: processes of state- and nation-building in Transnistria', *Post-Soviet Affairs*, 27 (2): 178–210.

Blaydes, L. and Rubin, L. (2008) 'Ideological reorientation and counterterrorism: confronting militant Islam in Egypt', *Terrorism and Political Violence*, 20 (4): 461–79.

Blomberg, S.B., Engel, R.C. and Sawyer, R. (2009) 'On the duration and sustainability of transnational terrorist organizations', *Journal of Conflict Resolution*, 54 (2): 303–30.

Blomberg, S. B. and Hess, G. D. (2005) 'The Lexus and the olive branch: globalization, democratization and terrorism', World Bank Workshop on Security and Development. Available at: https://papers.ssrn.com/sol3/papers.cfm?abstract_id=904024 (accessed 25 October 2016).

Bloom, M. (2005) *Dying to Kill: the Allure of Suicide Terror*. New York: Columbia University Press.

Bloom, M. (2012) *Bombshell: Women and Terrorism*. Philadelphia, PA: University of Pennsylvania Press.

Boeri, D. (2014) Brutal gang violence reigns in El Salvador. *WBUR News*, 16 December. Available at: www.wbur.org/news/2014/12/16/el-salvador-gang-violence (accessed 6 February 2017).

Bolz, J. (1995) 'Chinese organized crime and illegal alien trafficking: humans as a commodity', *Asian Affairs: An American Review*, 22 (3): 147–58.

Borjas, G.J. (2013) 'The analytics of the wage effect of immigration'. *IZA Journal of Migration*, 2 (1): 1.

Bosmia, A.N., Griessenauer, C.J. and Tubbs, R.S. (2014) 'Yubitsume: ritualistic self-amputation of proximal digits among the Yakuza', *Journal of Injury and Violence Research*, 6 (2): 54–56.

Boucek, C. (2008) 'Counter-terrorism from within: assessing Saudi Arabia's religious rehabilitation and disengagement programme', *The RUSI Journal*, 153 (6): 60–5.

Bourne, A. (2015) 'Why ban Batasuna? Terrorism, political parties and democracy', *Comparative European Politics*, 13 (3): 325–44.

Bourne, M. (2007) *Arming Conflict: The Proliferation of Small Arms*. Palgrave Macmillan.

Boutwell, J. and Klare, M. (1998) 'Small arms and light weapons: controlling the real instruments of war', *Arms Control Today*, 28 (6): 15.

Bovenkerk, F., Siegel, D. and Zaitch, D. (2003) Organized crime and ethnic reputation manipulation', *Crime, Law and Social Change*, 39 (1): 23–38.

Braddock, K. and Horgan, J. (2016) 'Towards a guide for constructing and disseminating counter-narratives to reduce support for terrorism', *Studies in Conflict & Terrorism*, 39 (5): 381–404.

Brafman, O. and Beckstrom, R.A. (2006) *The Starfish and the Spider: The Unstoppable Power of Leaderless Organizations*. London: Penguin.

Brancati, D. (2006) 'Decentralization: fueling the fire or dampening the flames of ethnic conflict and secessionism?' *International Organization*, 60 (3): 651–85.

Breslow, J. (2015) 'The staggering death toll of Mexico's drug wars'. *Frontline*. Available at: www.pbs.org/wgbh/frontline/article/the-staggering-death-toll-of-mexicos-drug-war/ (accessed April 2016).

Breuil, B.C.O. and Rozema, R. (2009) 'Fatal imaginations: death squads in Davao City and Medellín compared', *Crime, Law and Social Change*, 52 (4): 405–24.

Brinkerhoff, J.M. (2008) 'Diaspora identity and the potential for violence: toward an identity-mobilization framework', *Identity: An International Journal of Theory and Research*, 8 (1): 67–88.

Brisard, J.C. and Martinez, D. (2014) *Islamic State: The Economy-based Terrorist Funding*. Thomson Reuters Accelus.

BBC (1984) BBC On This Day: Memories of the Brighton bomb. Available at: http://news.bbc.co.uk/onthisday/hi/witness/october/12/newsid_3665000/3665388.stm (accessed 25 January 2017).

Brody, R. (1985) *Contra Terror in Nicaragua: Report of a Fact-finding Mission, September 1984–January 1985*. Boston: South End Press.

Brookes. S. (1991) 'The murder of Rio's street kids', *Insight Magazine*. Available at: www.stephenbrookes.com/international/2006/4/18/the-murder-of-rios-street-kids.html (accessed 25 October 2016).

Bruneau, T., Dammert, L. and Skinner, E. (2011) *Maras: Gang Violence and Security in Central America*. Austin, TX: University of Texas Press.

Brynen, R. (2002) 'Diaspora populations and security issues in host countries'. Paper presented at the Metropolis Interconference Seminar: 'Immigrants and Homeland' in Dubrovnik, Croatia (Vol. 4, May).

Bunker, R.J. (ed.) (2014) *Networks, Terrorism and Global Insurgency*. Abingdon: Routledge.

Bunker, R.J. and Sullivan, J.P. (2013) *Studies in Gangs and Cartels*. Abingdon: Routledge.

Burnham, G. (2011) 'Suicide attacks – the rationale and consequences', *The Lancet*, 378 (9794): 855-857.

Bursik Jr, R.J. and Grasmick, H.G. (1993) 'Economic deprivation and neighbourhood crime rates, 1960–1980', *Law & Sociology Review*, 27: 263.

Burton, J.W. (1987) *Resolving Deep-rooted Conflict: a Handbook*. Lanham: MD: University Press of America.

Buscaglia, E. (2003) 'Controlling organized crime and corruption in the public sector', *Forum on Crime and Society*, 3 (1/2): December.

Buscaglia, E. (2008) 'The paradox of expected punishment: legal and economic factors determining success and failure in the fight against organized crime', *Review of Law & Economics*, 4 (1): 290–317.

Buscaglia, E. and van Dijk, J. (2003) 'Controlling organized crime and public sector corruption: results of the global trends study', *Forum on Crime and Society*, 3 (1 and 2).

Buzan, B. (1984) 'Peace, power, and security: contending concepts in the study of ', *Journal of Peace Research*, 21 (2): 109–25.

Buzan, B. (1991) 'New patterns of global security in the twenty-first century', *International Affairs (Royal Institute of International Affairs 1944–)*, 67 (3): 431–51.

Buzan, B. (1997) 'Rethinking security after the Cold War', *Cooperation and Conflict*, 32 (1): 5–28.

Buzan, B. (2008) *People, States & Fear: an Agenda for International Security Studies in the Post-Cold War Era*. Colchester: ECPR Press.

Buzan, B. and Hansen, L. (2009) *The Evolution of International Security Studies*. Cambridge: Cambridge University Press.

Byman, D. (1998) 'The logic of ethnic terrorism', *Studies in Conflict & Terrorism*, 21 (2): 149–69.

Byman, D. (2005) *Deadly Connections: States that Sponsor Terrorism*. Cambridge: Cambridge University Press.

Byman, D. (2008) 'Understanding proto-insurgencies', *The Journal of Strategic Studies*, 31 (2): 165–200.

Byman, D. (2015) *Al Qaeda, the Islamic State, and the Global Jihadist Movement: What Everyone Needs to Know*. New York: Oxford University Press.

Byman, D., Chalk, P., Hoffman, B., Rosenau, W. and Brannan, D. (2001) *Trends in Outside Support for Insurgent Movements*. Santa Monica, CA: Rand Corporation.

Calderón, G., Robles, G., Díaz-Cayeros, A. and Magaloni, B. (2015) 'The beheading of criminal organizations and the dynamics of violence in Mexico', *Journal of Conflict Resolution*, 59: 1348–76.

Callaway, R. and Harrelson-Stephens, J. (2006) 'Toward a theory of terrorism: human security as a determinant of terrorism', *Studies in Conflict & Terrorism*, 29 (7): 679–702.

Cameron, G. (1999) 'Multi-track microproliferation: lessons from Aum Shinrikyo and Al Qaida', *Studies in Conflict and Terrorism*, 22 (4): 277–309.

Canetti, D. and Pedahzur, A. (2002) 'The effects of contextual and psychological variables on extreme right-wing sentiments', *Social Behavior and Personality: An International Journal*, 30 (4): 317–34.

Caramante, A. (2014) 'Sao Paulo's overcrowded prisons stretched to the breaking point', *Insight Crime*, 8 October. Available at: www.insightcrime.org/news-analysis/sao-paulo-overcrowded-prisons-stretched-to-the-breaking-point (accessed 31 October 2016).

Carney, H. (2005) 'Prosecuting the lawless: human rights abuses and private military firms', *George Washington Law Review*, 74: 317.

Carpenter, A.C. (2010) 'Beyond drug wars: transforming factional conflict in Mexico', *Conflict Resolution Quarterly*, 27 (4): 401–21.

Carter, D.B. (2012) 'A blessing or a curse? State support for terrorist groups', *International Organization*, 66 (1): 129–51.

Castells, M. (2011) *The Rise of the Network Society: The Information Age: Economy, Society, and Culture* (Vol. 1). Oxford: John Wiley & Sons.

Cederman, L.E. (1997) *Emergent Actors in World Politics: How States and Nations Develop and Dissolve*. Princeton, NJ: Princeton University Press.

Cetina, K.K. (2005) 'Complex global microstructures: the new terrorist societies', *Theory, Culture & Society*, 22 (5): 213–34.

Chalk, P. (2008) 'The Tigers abroad: how the LTTE diaspora supports the conflict in Sri Lanka', *Georgetown Journal of International Affairs*, Summer/Fall: 97–104.

Chapin, W.D. (1996) 'The Turkish diaspora in Germany', *Diaspora: A Journal of Transnational Studies*, 5 (2): 275–301.

Charrad, M. (2001) *States and Women's Rights: the Making of Postcolonial Tunisia, Algeria, and Morocco*. Berkeley, CA: University of California Press.

Chayes, S. (2015) *Thieves of State: Why Corruption Threatens Global Security*. London and New York: WW Norton & Company.

Chebel d'Appollonia, A. (2016) *Migrant Mobilization and Securitization in the US and Europe: How Does It Feel to Be a Threat?* London: Palgrave Macmillan.

Cheloukhine, S. and Haberfeld, M.R. (2011) *Russian Organized Corruption Networks and Their International Trajectories*. New York: Springer Science & Business Media.

Chenoweth, E., and Lawrence, A. (2010) *Rethinking Violence: States and Non-State Actors in Conflict*. Cambridge, MA: MIT Press.

Chenoweth, E., Miller, N., McClellan, E., Frisch, H., Staniland, P. and Abrahms, M. (2009) 'What makes terrorists tick', *International Security*, 33 (4): 180–202.

Chester, C.R. (1976) 'Perceived relative deprivation as a cause of property crime', *Crime & Delinquency*, 22 (1): 17–30.

Chesterman, S. (2016) 'Dogs of war or jackals of terror? Foreign fighters and mercenaries in international law', *Foreign Fighters and Mercenaries in International Law*, 27 July.

Chesterman, S. and Fisher, A. (2009) *Private Security, Public Order: the Outsourcing of Public Services and Its Limits* (Vol. 2). Oxford: Oxford University Press.

Chesterman, S. and Lehnardt, C. (2007) *From Mercenaries to Market: The Rise and Regulation of Private Military Companies*. Oxford: Oxford University Press.

Choudhury, T. and Fenwick, H. (2011) 'The impact of counter-terrorism measures on Muslim communities', *International Review of Law, Computers & Technology*, 25 (3): 151–81.

Cilliers, J. and Mason, P. (1999) *Peace, Profit or Plunder? The Privatisation of Security in War-torn African Societies*. Pretoria: Institute for Security Studies.

Clunan, A. and Trinkunas, H.A. (2010) *Ungoverned Spaces: Alternatives to State Authority in an Era of Softened Sovereignty*. Stanford, CA: Stanford University Press.

Cleaver, H. (1998) 'The Zapatista Effect: the Internet and the rise of an alternative political fabric', *Journal of International Affairs*, 51 (2): 621–40.

Coate, R.A. and Thiel, M. (eds) (2010) *Identity Politics in the Age of Globalization*. Boulder, CO: FirstForumPress.

Cockayne, J. (2010) 'Chapter ten: crime, corruption and violent economies', *Adelphi Paper*, 50 (412–413): 189–218.

Cockburn, A. and Clair, J.S. (1998) *Whiteout: The CIA, Drugs, and the Press*. London: Verso.

Collier, P. (2000) 'Rebellion as a quasi-criminal activity', *Journal of Conflict Resolution*, 44 (6): 839–853.

Collier, P. and Hoeffler, A. (2002) 'On the incidence of civil war in Africa', *Journal of Conflict Resolution*, 46 (1): 13–28.

Collier, P. and Hoeffler, A. (2006) 'Grand extortion: coup risk and the military as a protection racket'. In *Second Workshop on Political Institutions, Development and a Domestic Civil Peace (PIDDCP): PRIO, Hausmannsgate*, 11 (April): 19–20.

Comas, J., Shrivastava, P. and Martin, E.C. (2015) 'Terrorism as formal organization, network, and social movement', *Journal of Management Inquiry*, 24 (1): 47–60.

Conlin, J. (2013) *The American Past: A Survey of American History, Volume II: Since* 1865. Hampshire: Cengage Learning.

Conly, C.H. (1993) *Street Gangs: Current Knowledge and Strategies*. Collingdale, PA: Diane Publishing.

Corman, S.R. and Schiefelbein, J.S. (2008) 'Communication and media strategy in the Islamist war of ideas', *Weapons of Mass Persuasion, Strategic Communication to Combat Violent Extremism*. New York: Peter Lang.

Corner, E. and Gill, P. (2015) 'A false dichotomy? Mental illness and lone-actor terrorism', *Law and Human Behavior*, 39 (1): 23.

Cornish, D.B. and Clarke, R.V. (eds) (2014) *The Reasoning Criminal: Rational Choice Perspectives on Offending*. Piscataway, NJ: Transaction Publishers.

Cornell, S.E. (2005) 'The interaction of narcotics and conflict', *Journal of Peace Research*, 42 (6): 751–60.

Cornell, S. E. (2006) 'The narcotics threat in Greater Central Asia: from crime-terror nexus to state infiltration?', *China and Eurasia Forum Quarterly*, 4 (1): 37–67.

Cragin, K., Chalk, P., Daly, S.A. and Jackson, B.A. (2007) *Sharing the Dragon's Teeth: Terrorist Groups and the Exchange of New Technologies* (Vol. 485). Santa Monica, CA: Rand Corporation.

Crawford, B. and Lipschutz, R.D. (eds) (1998) *The Myth of 'Ethnic Conflict': Politics, Economics, and 'Cultural' Violence*. Berkeley, CA: University of California. Available at: https://escholarship.org/uc/item/7hc733q3 (accessed 31 October 2016).

Crayton, J.W. (1983) 'Terrorism and the psychology of the self'. In L.Z. Freedman and Y. Alexander (eds), *Perspectives on Terrorism*. Wilmington, DE: Scholarly Resources, pp. 33–41.

Crenshaw, M. (1981) 'The causes of terrorism', *Comparative Politics*, 13 (4): 379–99.

Crenshaw, M. (ed.) (1983) *Terrorism, Legitimacy, and Power: The Consequences of Political Violence*. Middletown, CT: Wesleyan University Press.

Crenshaw, M. (1987) 'Theories of terrorism: instrumental and organizational approaches', *The Journal of Strategic Studies*, 10 (4): 13–31.

Crenshaw, M. (ed.) (2010) *Terrorism in Context*. Pennsylvania: Penn State Press.

Crenshaw, M. (2015) 'The strategic logic of terrorism', *Conflict After the Cold War: Arguments on Causes of War and Peace*, 33: 481.

Crenshaw, M. and Pimlott, J. (2015) *International Encyclopedia of Terrorism*. Oxford: Routledge.

Cronin, A.K. (2002/03) 'Behind the curve: globalization and international terrorism', *International Security* 27 (3): 30–58.

Cronin, A.K. (2009) *How Terrorism Ends: Understanding the Decline and Demise of Terrorist Campaigns*. Princeton, NJ: Princeton University Press.

Cronin, A.K. (2012) *Ending Terrorism: Lessons for Defeating al-Qaeda*. Oxford: Routledge.

Cronin, A.K. (2015) 'ISIS is not a terrorist group: why counterterrorism won't stop the latest jihadist threat', *Foreign Affairs*, 94: 87.

Crozier, B. (1960) *The Rebels: a Study of Post-War Insurrections*. London: Chatto and Windus.

Cruz, J.M. (2010) 'Central American maras: from youth street gangs to transnational protection rackets', *Global Crime*, 11 (4): 379–98.

Cruz, J.M. and Durán-Martinez, A. (2016) 'Hiding violence to deal with the state: criminal pacts in El Salvador and Medellin', *Journal of Peace Research*, 53 (2): 197–210.

Curry, G.D. (2015) 'The logic of defining gangs revisited'. In S.H. Decker and C.C. Pyrooz (eds), *The Handbook of Gangs*. Chichester: Wiley, pp.7–27.

Dalgaard-Nielsen, A. (2010) 'Violent radicalization in Europe: what we know and what we do not know', *Studies in Conflict & Terrorism*, 33 (9): 797–814.

Danzell, O.E. (2010) 'Political parties: when do they turn to terror?' *Journal of Conflict Resolution*, 55 (1): 85–105.

Dasgupta, S. (2009) 'Paramilitary groups: local alliances in counterinsurgency operations', *Brookings Counterinsurgency and Pakistan Series Paper* (6).

Davenport, C. and Gates, S. (2014) 'Four reasons why interstate conflict scholars don't read intrastate work and why they are wrong, part I', *Political Violence @ a Glance*, 21 January. Available at: https://politicalviolenceataglance.org/2014/01/21/four-reasons-why-interstate-conflict-scholars-dont-read-intrastate-work-and-why-they-are-wrong-part-1/ (accessed 31 October 2016).

David, S.R. (1991) 'Explaining third world alignment', *World Politics*, 43 (2): 233–56.

Davies, J.C. (1962) 'Toward a theory of revolution'. *American Sociological Review*: 5–19.

Davies, S. (2010) *Global Politics of Health*. Cambridge: Polity.

Davis, B., Mausbach, W., Klimke, M. and MacDougall, C. (eds) (2013) *Changing the World, Changing Oneself: Political Protest and Collective Identities in West Germany and the US in the 1960s and 1970s* (Vol. 3). New York and Oxford: Berghahn Books.

Davis, D.E. (2010) 'The political and economic origins of violence and insecurity in contemporary Latin America: past trajectories and future prospects', *Violent Democracies in Latin America*, 35–62.

Davis, M.L. (1988) 'Time and punishment: an intertemporal model of crime', *The Journal of Political Economy*, 383–90.

Davis, P.K. and Cragin, K. (2009) *Social Science for Counterterrorism: Putting the Pieces Together*. Sanata Monica, CA: Rand Corporation.

Dayton, B.W. and Kriesberg, L. (eds) (2009) *Conflict Transformation and Peacebuilding: Moving from Violence to Sustainable Peace*. Oxford: Routledge.

Dear, K.P. (2013) 'Beheading the Hydra? Does killing terrorist or insurgent leaders work?', *Defence Studies*, 13 (3): 293–337.

de Cataldo Neuberger, L. and Valentini, T. (1996) *Women and Terrorism*. New York: Palgrave Macmillan.

Decker, S.H., Bynum, T. and Weisel, D. (1998) 'A tale of two cities: gangs as organized crime groups', *Justice Quarterly*, 15 (3): 395–425.

Decker, S.H. and Curry, G.D. (2000) 'Addressing key features of gang membership: measuring the involvement of young members', *Journal of Criminal Justice*, 28 (6): 473–82.

Decker, S.H., Melde, C. and Pyrooz, D.C. (2013) 'What do we know about gangs and gang members and where do we go from here? *Justice Quarterly*, 30 (3): 369–402.

Decker, S.H. and Van Winkle, B. (1996) *Life in the Gang: Family, Friends, and Violence*. Cambridge: Cambridge University Press.

de la Calle, L. and Sánchez-Cuenca, I. (2012) 'Rebels without a territory: an analysis of nonterritorial conflicts in the world, 1970–1997', *Journal of Conflict Resolution*, 56 (4): 580–603.

Dell, M. (2015) 'Trafficking networks and the Mexican drug war', *The American Economic Review*, 105 (6): 1738–79.

della Porta, D. (1992) 'Institutional responses to terrorism: the Italian case', *Terrorism and Political Violence*, 4 (4): 151–70.

della Porta, D. (1995) 'Left-wing terrorism in Italy', *Terrorism in Context*, 105–59.

della Porta, D. and Diani, M. (2006) *Social Movements: An Introduction*. Malden, MA: Blackwell.

Demant, F. and Graaf, B.D. (2010) 'How to counter radical narratives: Dutch de-radicalization policy in the case of Moluccan and Islamic radicals', *Studies in Conflict & Terrorism*, 33 (5): 408–28.

De Mesquita, E.B. (2005) 'The quality of terror', *American Journal of Political Science*, 49 (3): 515–30.

Demmers, J. (2007) 'New wars and diasporas: suggestions for research and policy', *Journal of Peace, Conflict and Development*, 11.

Denov, M.S. (2010) *Child Soldiers: Sierra Leone's Revolutionary United Front*. Cambridge: Cambridge University Press.

Densley, J.A. and Stevens, A. (2014) '"We'll show you gang": the subterranean structuration of gang life in London', *Criminology and Criminal Justice*, DOI: 10.1177/1748895814522079

DeRouen, K.R. and Bercovitch, J. (2008) 'Enduring internal rivalries: new framework for the study of civil war', *Journal of Peace Research*, 45 (1): 55–74.

DeRouen Jr, K. and Newman, E. (2014) *Routledge Handbook of Civil Wars*. Oxford: Routledge.

Dishman, C. (2001) 'Terrorism, crime, and transformation', *Studies in Conflict and Terrorism*, 24 (1): 43–58.

Dishman, C. (2005) 'The leaderless nexus: when crime and terror converge', *Studies in Conflict & Terrorism*, 28 (3): 237–52.

Dixon, P. (2009) '"Hearts and Minds"? British counter-insurgency strategy in Northern Ireland', *The Journal of Strategic Studies*, 32 (3): 445–74.

Donnellan, M.B., Trzesniewski, K.H., Robins, R.W., Moffitt, T.E. and Caspi, A. (2005) 'Low self-esteem is related to aggression, antisocial behavior, and delinquency', *Psychological Science*, 16 (4): 328–35.

Donnelly, C. (2004, June) 'Terrorism in the southern Philippines: contextualising the Abu Sayyaf group as an Islamist secessionist organisation'. In *Conference Proceedings, 15th Biennial Conference of the Asian Studies Association of Australia in Canberra* (Vol. 29).

Doosje, B., Moghaddam, F.M., Kruglanski, A.W., de Wolf, A., Mann, L. and Feddes, A.R. (2016) 'Terrorism, radicalization and de-radicalization', *Current Opinion in Psychology*, 11: 79–84.

Downs, A. (1957) 'An economic theory of political action in a democracy', *The Journal of Political Economy*, 65 (2): 135–150.

Dudley, S.S. (2010) 'Drug trafficking organizations in Central America: transportistas, Mexican cartels and maras', *Shared Responsibility*, 9: 63–93.

Dudley, S.S. (2011) 'Central America besieged: cartels and maras country threat analysis', *Small Wars & Insurgencies*, 22 (5): 890–913.

Duffield, M. (1998) 'Post-modern conflict: warlords, post-adjustment states and private protection', *Civil Wars*, 1 (1): 65–102.

Dupont, A. (1999) 'Transnational crime, drugs, and security in East Asia', *Asian Survey*, 39 (3): 433–55.

Dustmann, C., Glitz, A. and Frattini, T. (2008) 'The labour market impact of immigration', *Oxford Review of Economic Policy*, 24 (3): 477–494.

Duyvesteyn, I. (2000) 'Contemporary war: ethnic conflict, resource conflict or something else?', *Civil Wars*, 3 (1): 92–116.

Egan, V. and Beadman, M. (2011) 'Personality and gang embeddedness', *Personality and Individual Differences*, 51 (6): 748–53.

Ehrlich, P.R. and Liu, J. (2002) 'Some roots of terrorism', *Population and Environment*, 24 (2): 183–92.

Eitle, D., Gunkel, S. and Van Gundy, K. (2004) 'Cumulative exposure to stressful life events and male gang membership', *Journal of Criminal Justice*, 32 (2): 95–111.

Elms, H. and Phillips, R.A. (2009) 'Private security companies and institutional legitimacy: corporate and stakeholder responsibility', *Business Ethics Quarterly*, 19 (03): 403–32.

Elsea, J.K., Schwartz, M. and Nakamura, K.H. (2008) *Private Security Contractors in Iraq: Background, Legal Status, and Other Issues*. Washington, DC: Library of Congress.

El-Tom, A. (2009) 'US envoy gration and his "cookies and honey" strategy for Sudan', *Sudan Tribune*. Available at: www.sudantribune.com/spip.php?article32918 (accessed 31 October 2016).

Enders, W. and Sandler, T. (2000) 'Is transnational terrorism becoming more threatening? A time-series investigation', *Journal of Conflict Resolution*, 44 (3): 307–32.

Engvall, J. (2006) 'The state under siege: the drug trade and organised crime in Tajikistan', *Europe-Asia Studies*, 58 (6): 827–54.

Ergil, D. (2000) 'Suicide terrorism in Turkey', *Civil Wars*, 3 (1): 37–54.

Erk, J. and Anderson, L.M. (2013) *The Paradox of Federalism: Does Self-rule Accommodate or Exacerbate Ethnic Divisions?* Oxford: Routledge.

Esbensen, F.A. and Weerman, F.M. (2005) 'Youth gangs and troublesome youth groups in the United States and the Netherlands: a cross-national comparison', *European Journal of Criminology*, 2 (1): 5–37.

Esbensen, F.A., Winfree, L.T., He, N. and Taylor, T.J. (2001) 'Youth gangs and definitional issues: when is a gang a gang, and why does it matter? *Crime & Delinquency*, 47 (1): 105–30.

Esteva, G. (1999) 'The Zapatistas and people's power', *Capital & Class*, 23 (2): 153–82.

Eubank, W. and Weinberg, L. (2001) 'Terrorism and democracy: perpetrators and victims', *Terrorism and Political Violence*, 13 (1): 155–64.

European Union (2003) *A Secure Europe in a Better World: European Security Strategy*. Paris: European Union Institute for Security Studies. Available at: www.iss.europa.eu/uploads/media/solanae.pdf (accessed 6 February 2017).

Ezrow, N.M. and Frantz, E. (2013) *Failed States and Institutional Decay: Understanding Instability and Poverty in the Developing World*. New York: Bloomsbury Publishing.

Fabick, S.D. (2004) 'Us and them: Reducing the risk of terrorism'. In C.E. Stout (ed.), *Psychology of Terrorism: Coping with the Continuing Threat, Condensed Edition*, London: Praeger, pp. 95–115.

Fairbanks, C.H. (2001) 'Disillusionment in the Caucasus and Central Asia', *Journal of Democracy*, 12 (4): 49–56.

Fajnzylber, P., Lederman, D. and Loayza, N. (1998) *Determinants of Crime Rates in Latin America and the World: An Empirical Assessment*. Washington, DC: World Bank Publications.

Fall, B. (2015) 'The theory and practice of insurgency and counterinsurgency', *Naval War College Review*, 17.

Farrell, T. (1996) 'Figuring out fighting organisations: the new organisational analysis in strategic studies', *The Journal of Strategic Studies*, 19 (1): 122–35.

Farrell, T. (2010) 'Improving in war: military adaptation and the British in Helmand Province, Afghanistan, 2006–2009', *The Journal of Strategic Studies*, 33 (4): 567–94.

Fearon, J.D. (2004) 'Why do some civil wars last so much longer than others? *Journal of Peace Research*, 41 (3): 275–301.

Fearon, J.D. and Laitin, D.D. (2003) 'Ethnicity, insurgency, and civil war', *American Political Science Review*, 97 (1): 75–90.

Fellman, P.V. and Wright, R. (2014) 'Modeling terrorist networks, complex systems at the mid-range', arXiv preprint arXiv:1405.6989.

Ferguson, J. (1987) *Papa Doc, Baby Doc: Haiti and the Duvaliers*. Oxford: Blackwell.

Fernández-Kelly, P. and Shefner, J. (2006) *Out of the Shadows: Political Action and the Informal Economy in Latin America*. Pennsylvania: Penn State Press.

Fields, R.M., Elbedour, S. and Hein, F.A. (2002) 'The Palestinian suicide bomber', *The Psychology of Terrorism*, 2, 193–223.

Fierke, K.M. (2009) 'Terrorism and trust in Northern Ireland', *Critical Studies on Terrorism*, 2 (3): 497–511.

Fierke, K.M. (2015) *Critical Approaches to International Security*. Oxford: John Wiley & Sons.

Filkins, D. (2010) 'With US aid, warlord builds Afghan empire', *The New York Times*, 5 June.

Finckenauer, J.O. (2012) *Mafia and Organized Crime: A Beginner's Guide*. London: Oneworld Publications.

Finckenauer, J.O. (2005) 'Problems of definition: what is organized crime?', *Trends in Organized Crime*, 8 (3): 63–83.

Finnemore, M. and Sikkink, K. (2001) 'Taking stock: the constructivist research program in and comparative politics', *Annual Review of Political Science*, 4 (1): 391–416.

Fleshman, M. (2001) 'Counting the costs of gun violence', *Africa Recovery*, 15 (4).

Forest, J.J. (2012) *Confronting the Terrorism of Boko Haram in Nigeria* (No. JSOU-12–5). Macdill Air Force Base, FL.: Jsou.

Forst, B., Greene, J.R. and Lynch, J.P. (eds) (2011) *Criminologists on Terrorism and Homeland Security*. Cambridge: Cambridge University Press.

Fortna, V.P. (2015) 'Do terrorists win? Rebels' use of terrorism and civil war outcomes', *International Organization*, 69 (03): 519–556.

Fotiadis, A. (2016) 'This racist backlash against refugees is the real crisis in Europe', *The Guardian*, 25 February. Available at: www.theguardian.com/commentisfree/2016/feb/25/racist-backlash-against-refugees-greece-real-crisis-europe (accessed 31 October 2016).

Francis, B., Humphreys, L., Kirby, S. and Soothill, K. (2013) *Understanding Criminal Careers in Organised Crime*. London: Home Office.

Franco, C. (2007, November) *The MS 13 and 18th Street Gangs: Emerging Transnational Gang Threats?* Congressional Research Service, Library of Congress.

Freeman, L. (2015) 'The African warlord revisited', *Small Wars & Insurgencies*, 26 (5): 790–810.

Friedman, T.L. (2006) *The World is Flat: the Globalized World in the Twenty-first Century*. London: Penguin.

Frisch, E. (2012) 'Insurgencies are organizations too: organizational structure and the effectiveness of insurgent strategy', *The Peace and Conflict Review*, 6: 1–23.

Fuller, A. (1991) *Return to the Darkest Days: Human Rights in Haiti since the Coup* (Vol. 2259). New York: Human Rights Watch.

Gaibulloev, K. and Sandler, T. (2013) 'Determinants of the demise of terrorist organizations', *Southern Economic Journal*, 79 (4): 774–92.

Galeotti, M. (2002) '"Brotherhoods" and "associates": Chechen networks of crime and resistance', *Low Intensity Conflict & Law Enforcement*, 11 (2–3): 340–52.

Gallimore, T. (2004) 'Unresolved trauma: fuel for the cycle of violence and terrorism'. In C.E. Stout (ed.), *The Psychology of Terrorism*. London: Praeger.

Galula, D. (2006) *Counterinsurgency Warfare: Theory and Practice*. Westport: Greenwood Publishing Group.

Gambetta, D. (2000) 'Mafia: the price of distrust'. In D. Ga,mbetta (ed.), *Trust: Making and Breaking Cooperative Relations*, electronic edition, New York: Basil Blackwell, pp. 158–75.

Gambetta, D. (1996) *The Sicilian Mafia: The Business of Private Protection*. Harvard: Harvard University Press.

Garry, J. (2014) 'Potentially voting across the divide in deeply divided places: ethnic catch-all voting in consociational Northern Ireland', *Political Studies*, 62 (1 suppl): 2–19.

Gates, S. (2002) 'Recruitment and allegiance: the microfoundations of rebellion', *Journal of Conflict Resolution*, 46 (1): 111–130.

Gberie, L. (2005) *A Dirty War in West Africa: the RUF and the Destruction of Sierra Leone*. Indiana: Indiana University Press.

Gelvin, J.L. (2008) 'Al-Qaeda and anarchism: a historian's reply to terrorology', *Terrorism and Political Violence*, 20 (4): 563–581.

Getmansky, A. (2013) 'You can't win if you don't fight the role of regime type in counterinsurgency outbreaks and outcomes', *Journal of Conflict Resolution*, 57 (4): 709–34.

Gill, P., Horgan, J. and Deckert, P. (2014) 'Bombing alone: tracing the motivations and antecedent behaviors of lone-actor terrorists', *Journal of Forensic Sciences*, 59 (2): 425–35.

Gill, P. and Young, J.K. (2011) 'Comparing role-specific terrorist profiles', available at SSRN 1782008.

Gissinger, R. and Gleditsch, N.P. (1999) 'Globalization and conflict: welfare, distribution, and political unrest', *Journal of World-systems Research*, 5 (2): 327–65.

Giustozzi, A. (2004) '"Good" state vs. "bad" warlords? A critique of state-building strategies in Afghanistan'. Crisis States Research Centre working papers series 1, 51. London: Crisis States Research Centre, London School of Economics and Political Science.

Gleditsch, K. S. (2007) 'Transnational dimensions of civil war', *Journal of Peace Research*, 44 (3): 293–309.

Global Research (2016) Muslims are the VICTIMS of 'between 82 and 97% of terrorism-related fatalities': US Government. Available at: www.globalresearch.ca/muslims-are-the-victims-of-between-82-and-97-of-terrorism-related-fatalities-us-government/5516565 (accessed 25 January 2016).

Global Terrorism Database (2015) www.start.umd.edu/gtd/ (accessed 25 January 2017).

Global Terrorism Index (n.d.) http://economicsandpeace.org/wp-content/uploads/2015/11/Global-Terrorism-Index-2015.pdf (accessed 25 January 2017).

Goldberg, P.K. and Pavcnik, N. (2007) *Distributional Effects of Globalization in Developing Countries* (No. w12885). Cambridge, MA: National Bureau of Economic Research.

Goldsmith, A.A. (1999) 'Africa's overgrown state reconsidered: bureaucracy and economic growth', *World Politics* 51 (4): 520–46.

Goodhand, J. (2000) 'From holy war to opium war? A case study of the opium economy in North-eastern Afghanistan', *Disasters*, 24 (2): 87–102.

Goodhand, J. (2001) *A synthesis report: Kyrgyzstan, Moldova, Nepal and Sri Lanka*. London: Conflict, Security & Development Group, Centre for Defence Studies, University of London.

Goodhand, J. (2004) 'From war economy to peace economy? Reconstruction and state building in Afghanistan' *Journal of International Affairs*, 58 (1): 155–174.

Goodwin, J. (2006) 'A theory of categorical terrorism', *Social Forces*, 84 (4): 2027–46.

Gottfredson, M.R. and Hirschi, T. (1990) *A General Theory of Crime*. Stanford, CA: Stanford University Press.

Grajales, J. (2011) 'The rifle and the title: paramilitary violence, land grab and land control in Colombia', *Journal of Peasant Studies*, 38 (4): 771–92.

Gray, D.H. and LaTour, K. (2010) 'Terrorist black holes: global regions shrouded in lawlessness', *Global Security Studies*, 1 (3): 154–63.

Grieco, J.M. (1988) 'Anarchy and the limits of cooperation: a realist critique of the newest liberal institutionalism', *International organization*, 42 (3): 485–507.

Griffin, J. (1 February 2013) *Private Contract Security Services to See Steady Global Demand*. Security InfoWatch. Available at: www.securityinfowatch.com/article/10862533/freedonia-group-report-forecasts-global-demand-for-contract-security-services-to-reach-244b-in-2016 (accessed 25 January 2016).

Grillo, I. (2012) *El Narco: Inside Mexico's Criminal Insurgency*. New York: Bloomsbury Publishing.

Gros, J.G. (1996) 'Towards a taxonomy of failed states in the New World Order: decaying Somalia, Liberia, Rwanda and Haiti', *Third World Quarterly*, 17 (3): 455–72.

Grunenberg, S. and Van Donselaar, J. (2006) 'Deradicalisering: lessen uit Duitsland, opties voor Nederland?'. In J. van Donselaar and P.R. Rodrigues (eds), *Monitor Racisme & Extremisme: zevende rapportage*. Amsterdam/Leiden: Anne Frank Stichting/Universiteit Leiden.

Grynkewich, A.G. (2008) 'Welfare as warfare: how violent non-state groups use social services to attack the state', *Studies in Conflict & Terrorism*, 31 (4): 350–70.

Gunaratna, R. (1998) 'Impact of the mobilized Tamil diaspora on the protracted conflict in Sri Lanka', *Negotiating Peace in Sri Lanka: Effort, Failures and Lessons*. London: International Alert.

Gunaratna, R. (2002) *Inside Al Qaeda: Global Network of Terror*. New York: Columbia University Press.

Gunaratna, R. and Oreg, A. (2010) 'Al Qaeda's organizational structure and its evolution', *Studies in Conflict & Terrorism*, 33 (12): 1043–78.

Gurney, K. (2014) 'Guatemala extortion generates $61 mn a year: govt'. *Insight Crime* (18 July). Available at: www.insightcrime.org/news-briefs/guatemala-extortion-generates-61-mn-a-year-govt (accessed 31 October 2016).

Gurr, T.R. (1988) 'War, revolution, and the growth of the coercive state', *Comparative Political Studies*, 21 (1): 45–65.

Gurr, T.R. (1993) 'Why minorities rebel: a global analysis of communal mobilization and conflict since 1945', *International Political Science Review*,14 (2): 161–201.

Gurr, T.R. (2000) *Peoples versus States: Minorities at Risk in the New Century*. Washington, DC: US Institute of Peace Press.

Gurr, T.R. (2015) *Why Men Rebel*. Oxford: Routledge.

Gvineria, G. (2009) 'How does terrorism end?'. In P.K. Davis and K. Cragin (eds), *Social Science for Counterterrorism*, Sanata Monica, CA: Rand Corporation, pp. 257–91.

Haas, N.E., de Keijser, J.W. and Bruinsma, G.J. (2014) 'Public support for vigilantism, confidence in police and police responsiveness', *Policing and Society*, 24 (2): 224–41.

Hacker, F.J. (1976) *Crusaders, Criminals, Crazies: Terror and Terrorism in our Time*. New York: Norton.

Hagedorn, J. (2007) *Gangs in the GLOBAL CITY: Alternatives to Traditional Criminology.* Champaign, IL: University of Illinois Press.

Hagedorn, J.M. (1998) 'Gang violence in the post-industrial era', *Crime and Justice,* 365–419.

Hagedorn, J.M. (2001) 'Globalization, gangs, and collaborative research', in *The Eurogang Paradox.* Springer Netherlands, pp. 41–58.

Hansen, S.J. (2006) 'Warlords and peace strategies: the case of Somalia', *Journal of Conflict Studies,* 23(2). Available at: https://journals.lib.unb.ca/index.php/JCS/article/view/217/375 (accessed 11 November 2016).

Harmon, C.C. (2001) 'Five strategies of terrorism', *Small Wars and Insurgencies,* 12 (3): 39–66.

Harris, A.W. (2010) 'Coming to terms with separatist insurgencies', *Negotiation Journal,* 26 (3): 327–56.

Hashim, A.S. (2013) *Iraq's Sunni Insurgency.* Oxford: Routledge.

Hazen, J.M. (2008) 'Risk and resilience: understanding the potential for violence', Chapter 8 in *Small Arms Survey 2008: Risk and Resilience,* pp. 245–73. Available at: www.small armssurvey.org/publications/by-type/yearbook/small-arms-survey-2008.html (accessed 25 January 2016).

Hegghammer, T. (2007) 'Saudi militants in Iraq: backgrounds and recruitment patterns', *Norwegian Defense Research Establishment,* 8.

Hehir, A. (2007) 'The myth of the failed state and the war on terror: a challenge to the conventional wisdom', *Journal of Intervention and Statebuilding,* 1 (3): 307–32.

Held, D. (2013) *Global Covenant: The Social Democratic Alternative to the Washington Consensus.* Oxford: John Wiley & Sons.

Held, D. and McGrew, A.G. (eds) (2007) *Globalization Theory: Approaches and Controversies* (Vol. 4). Cambridge: Polity.

Helsinki Watch Organization (1991) *Punished Peoples of the Soviet Union: The Continuing Legacy of Stalin's Deportations* (Vol. 1245). New York: Human Rights Watch.

Hills, A. (1997) 'Warlords, militia and conflict in contemporary Africa: a re-examination of terms', *Small Wars & Insurgencies,* 8 (1): 35–51.

Hinnebusch, R.A. and Ehteshami, A. (2002) *The Foreign Policies of Middle East States.* Boulder, CO: Lynne Rienner Publishers.

Hoffman, B. (1998–99) 'Revival of religious terrorism begs for broad US policy', *Rand Review,* 22 (2).

Hoffman, D. (2004) 'The civilian target in Sierra Leone and Liberia: political power, military strategy, and humanitarian intervention', *African Affairs,* 103 (411): 211–26.

Hoffman, B. (2006) *Inside Terrorism.* New York: Columbia University Press.

Hoffman, B. (2007) *The Radicalization of Diasporas and Terrorism: A Joint Conference by the RAND Corporation and the Center for Security Studies, ETH Zurich* (Vol. 229). Rand Corporation.

Hoffman, B. (2008) 'The myth of grass-roots terrorism: why Osama bin Laden still matters', *Foreign Affairs,* 133–138.

Hoffman, B. (2013) 'Al Qaeda's Uncertain Future', *Studies in Conflict & Terrorism,* 36 (8): 635–53.

Hoffman, B. and McCormick, G.H. (2004) 'Terrorism, signalling, and suicide attack', *Studies in Conflict & Terrorism,* 27 (4): 243–81.

Hopf, T. (1998) 'The promise of constructivism in theory', *International Security,* 23 (1): 171–200.

Holmqvist, C. (2005) *Private Security Companies.* Stockholm: Stockholm International Peace Research Institute.

Horgan, J. (2014) *The Psychology of Terrorism.* Revised and updated second edition. Oxford: Routledge.

Horgan, J. (2011) *Terrorism Studies: A Reader.* Oxford: Routledge.

Horgan, J. and Morrison, J.F. (2011) 'Here to stay? The rising threat of violent dissident Republicanism in Northern Ireland', *Terrorism and Political Violence,* 23 (4): 642–69.

Horowitz, D.L. (2014) 'Ethnic power sharing: three big problems', *Journal of Democracy*, 25 (2): 5–20.

Horowitz, D.L. (1989) 'Incentives and behaviour in the ethnic politics of Sri Lanka and Malaysia', *Third World Quarterly*, 11 (4): 18–35.

Howe, H.M. (1998) 'Private security forces and African stability: the case of executive outcomes', *The Journal of Modern African Studies*, 36 (2): 307–31.

Huber, J.D. and Powell, G.B. (1994) 'Congruence between citizens and policymakers in two visions of liberal democracy', *World Politics*, 46 (03): 291–326.

Huckerby, J. (2015) 'When women become terrorists', *New York Times*, 21 January. Available at: www.nytimes.com/2015/01/22/opinion/when-women-become-terrorists.html?_r=0 (accessed 31 October 2016).

Hudson, R.A. and Majeska, M. (1999, September) *The Sociology and Psychology of Terrorism: Who Becomes a Terrorist and Why?* Washington, DC: Library of Congress.

Huggins, M.K. (2000) 'Modernity and devolution: the making of police death squads in modern Brazil'. In B. Campbell and A. Brenner (eds), *Death Squads in Global Perspective*. New York: Palgrave Macmillan, pp. 203–28.

Human Rights Watch (2009) *'You Can Die Any Time': Death Squad Killings in Mindanao*. New York: Human Rights Watch. Available at: www.hrw.org/report/2009/04/06/you-can-die-any-time/death-squad-killings-mindanao (accessed 31 October 2016).

Human Rights Watch (2015) *World Report 2015: Colombia: Events of 2014*. Available at: www.hrw.org/world-report/2015/country-chapters/colombia (accessed 10 February 2017).

Humphreys, M. and Weinstein, J.M. (2008) 'Who fights? The determinants of participation in civil war', *American Journal of Political Science*, 52 (2): 436–55.

Hunsicker, A. (2006) *Understanding International Counter Terrorism: A Professional's Guide to the Operational Art*. Boca Raton, FL: Universal-Publishers.

Hutchinson, S. and O'Malley, P. (2007) 'A Crime-Terror Nexus? Thinking on some of the links between terrorism and criminality 1', *Studies in Conflict Terrorism*, 30 (12): 1095–1107.

Hydén, G. (1999) 'Top-down democratization in Tanzania', *Journal of Democracy*, 10 (4): 142–55.

Hydén, G. Court, J., Mease, K (2003) 'Civil Society and governance in 16 developing countries', *World Governance Survey Discussion Paper*, London.

Hyde-Price, A. (2009) 'Realist ethics and the "war on terror"', *Globalizations* 6 (1): 23–40.

International Review of the Red Cross (2009) Interviews with Peter Wallenstein, 91 (873): 7–19. Available at: www.icrc.org/eng/assets/files/other/irrc-873-interview.pdf (accessed 25 January 2017).

Isenberg, D. (2009) *Shadow Force: Private Security Contractors in Iraq*. Santa Barbara, CA: ABC-CLIO.

Jaber, H. (1997) *Hezbollah: Born with a Vengeance*. New York: Columbia University Press.

Jackson, R. (2006) 'The state and terrorist sanctuaries: a critical analysis', *British International Studies Association (BISA) Annual Conference* (pp. 18–20).

Jackson, R (2007) 'The core commitments of critical terrorism studies', *European Political Science* 6 (3): 244–51.

Jackson, R. (2008) 'The ghosts of state terror: knowledge, politics and terrorism studies', *Critical Studies on Terrorism*, 1 (3): 377–92.

Jarstad, A.K. and Sisk, T.D. (eds) (2008) *From War to Democracy: Dilemmas of Peacebuilding*. Cambridge: Cambridge University Press.

Jarvis, L. and Macdonald, S. (2015) 'What is cyberterrorism? Findings from a survey of researchers', *Terrorism and Political Violence*, 27 (4): 657–78.

Jasperse, M., Ward, C. and Jose, P.E. (2012) 'Identity, perceived religious discrimination, and psychological well-being in Muslim immigrant women', *Applied Psychology*, 61 (2): 250–71.

Jayasekara, S. (2007) *LTTE Fundraising and Money Transfer Operations*. Presented at the International Conference on Countering Terrorism, held in Colombo, Sri Lanka, 18–20 October.

Johnston, D. (2008) 'Lifting the veil on corporate terrorism: the use of the criminal code terrorism framework to hold multinational corporations accountable for complicity in human rights violations abroad', *U. Toronto Fac. L. Rev.*, 66: 137–187.

Jones, S.G. and Libicki, M.C. (2008) *How Terrorist Groups End: Lessons for Countering al Qa'ida.* Santa Monica, CA: Rand Corporation.

Jordan, J. (2009) 'When heads roll: assessing the effectiveness of leadership decapitation', *Security Studies*, 18 (4): 719–55.

Juergensmeyer, M. (2005) *Terror in the Mind of God: The Global Rise of Religious Violence.* Berkeley, CA: University of California Press.

Kaldor, M. (2013) *New and Old Wars: Organised Violence in a Global Era.* Oxford: John Wiley & Sons.

Kalyvas, S. N. (2005) 'Warfare in civil wars'. In I. Duyvesteyn and J. Angstrom (eds), *Rethinking the Nature of War.* Abingdon: Frank Cass, pp. 88–108.

Kalyvas, S.N. (2006) *The Logic of Violence in Civil War.* Cambridge: Cambridge University Press.

Kalyvas, S.N. (2015) 'How civil wars help explain organized crime – and how they do not', *Journal of Conflict Resolution*, 59 (8): 1517–40.

Kalyvas, S.N. and Kocher, M.A. (2007) 'How "free" is free riding in civil wars? Violence, insurgency, and the collective action problem', *World Politics*, 59 (2): 177–216.

Kan, P.R. (2012) *Cartels at War: Mexico's Drug-fueled Violence and the Threat to US National Security.* Lincoln, NE: Potomac Books, Inc.

Kaplan, D.E. and Dubro, A. (2012) *Yakuza: Japan's Criminal Underworld.* Berkeley, CA: University of California Press.

Karakatsanis, N.M. (2008) 'Political learning as a catalyst of moderation: lessons from democratic consolidation in Greece', *Democratisation*, 15 (2): 386–409.

Karklins, R. (2005) *The System Made Me Do It: Corruption in Post-communist Societies.* London and New York: ME Sharpe.

Karstedt, S. (2012) 'Contextualizing mass atrocity crimes: the dynamics of 'extremely violent societies', *European Journal of Criminology*, 9(5): 499–513.

Kass, I. and O'Neill, B.E. (1997) *The Deadly Embrace: The Impact of Israeli and Palestinian Rejectionism on the Peace Process.* Lanham, MD: University Press of America.

Kaufmann, C. (2007) 'A security dilemma: ethnic partitioning in Iraq', *Harvard International Review*, 28 (4): 44.

Kay, B.H. (1999) 'Violent opportunities: the rise and fall of "King Coca" and Shining Path', *Journal of Interamerican Studies and World Affairs*, 41 (3): 97–127.

Kearney, V. (2013) 'Security forces in the Troubles', BBC, February. Available at: www.bbc.co.uk/history/topics/troubles_security_forces (accessed 31 October 2016).

Keen, D. (1998) 'The economic functions of violence in civil wars (special issue)', *The Adelphi Papers*, 38 (320): 1–89.

Keen, D. (2012) 'Greed and grievance in civil war', *International Affairs*, 88 (4): 757–77.

Keen, D. (2000) *Incentives and Disincentives for Violence.* Boulder, CO: Lynne Rienner Publishers; International Development Research Centre. (pp. 19–42).

Kegley, C.W. and Blanton, S.L. (2015) *World Politics: Trend and Transformation, 2016–2017.* Toronto: Nelson Education.

Kelley, M. (2014) *Terrorism and the Growing Threat of Weapons of Mass Destruction: Al-Shabaab.* Hamburg: Anchor Academic Publishing.

Kennedy-Pipe, C. and McInnes, C. (1997) 'The British army in Northern Ireland 1969–1972: from policing to counter-terror', *The Journal of Strategic Studies*, 20 (2): 1–24.

Kenney, M. (2007) 'The architecture of drug trafficking: network forms of organization in the Colombian cocaine trade', *Global Crime*, 8 (3): 233–59.

Keohane, R.O. (1989) *International Institutions and State Power: Essays in International Relations Theory.* Boulder, CO: Westview Press.

King, M. and Taylor, D.M. (2011) 'The radicalization of home-grown jihadists: a review of theoretical models and social psychological evidence', *Terrorism and Political Violence*, 23 (4): 602–22.

Kinsey, C. (2007) 'Problematising the role of private security companies in small wars', *Small Wars and Insurgencies*, 18(4): 584–614.

Kiras, J.D. (2007) 'Irregular warfare: terrorism and insurgency', *Understanding Modern Warfare*, 224.

Kirchheimer, O. (1966) 'The transformation of the Western European party systems'. In J. LaPalombara and M. Wiener (eds), *Political Parties and Political Development*, Princeton, NJ: Princeton University Press, pp. 177–200.

Kirwin, M. (2006) 'The security dilemma and conflict in Côte d'Ivoire', *Nordic Journal of African Studies*, 15 (1): 42–52.

Kleemans, E.R. and Van de Bunt, H.G. (1999) 'The social embeddedness of organized crime', *Transnational Organized Crime*, 5 (1): 19–36.

Klein, M.W. and Maxson, C.L. (2010) *Street Gang Patterns and Policies*. Oxford University Press.

Kolhatkar, S. (2003) *In Afghanistan, US Replaces One Terrorist State with Another*. Silver City, NM and Washington, DC: Foreign Policy in Focus.

Kolstø, P. (2006) 'The sustainability and future of unrecognized quasi-states', *Journal of Peace Research*, 43 (6): 723–40.

Koonings, K. and Kruijt, D. (2004) *Armed Actors: Organised Violence and State Failure in Latin America*. London: Zed Books.

Krause, K. (2012) 'Hybrid violence: locating the use of force in postconflict settings', *Global Governance*, 18 (1): 39–56.

Krieger, H. (2001) *The Kosovo Conflict and International Law: An Analytical Documentation 1974–1999*. Cambridge: Cambridge University Press.

Krieger, T. and Meierrieks, D. (2011) 'What causes terrorism?', *Public Choice*, 147 (1–2): 3–27.

Krueger, A.B. and Laitin, D.D. (2008) 'Kto kogo? A cross-country study of the origins and targets of terrorism', *Terrorism, Economic Development, and Political Openness*, 148–73.

Krueger, A.B. and Malečková, J. (2003) 'Education, poverty and terrorism: is there a causal connection? *The Journal of Economic Perspectives*, 17 (4): 119–44.

Kruglanski, A.W. and Fishman, S. (2006) 'The psychology of terrorism: 'syndrome' versus 'tool' perspectives', *Terrorism and Political Violence*, 18 (2): 193–215.

Kukhianidze, A. (2009) 'Corruption and organized crime in Georgia before and after the "Rose Revolution"', *Central Asian Survey*, 28 (2): 215–234.

Kumaraswamy, P.R. and Copland, I. (eds) (2013) *South Asia: The Spectre of Terrorism*. Oxford: Routledge.

Kupatadze, A. (2012) 'Organized crime, political transitions and state formation'. In A. Kupatadze, *Organized Crime, Political Transitions and State Formation in Post-Soviet Eurasia*. Basingstoke: Palgrave Macmillan, pp. 181–93.

Kupchan, C.A. and Kupchan, C.A. (1995) 'The promise of collective security', *International Security*, 20 (1): 52–61.

LaFree, G. and Freilich, J.D. (2012) 'Editor's introduction: quantitative approaches to the study of terrorism', *Journal of Quantitative Criminology*, 28 (1): 1–5.

Lane. E. (2010) 'The rise of the UK's private security companies', *BBC News*, 2 November. Available at www.bbc.co.uk/news/business-11521579 (accessed 31 October 2016)

Langdon, L., Sarapu, A.J. and Wells, M. (2004) 'Targeting the leadership of terrorist and insurgent movements: historical lessons for contemporary policy makers', *Journal of Public and International Affairs-Princeton*, 15: 59–78.

Laqueur, W. (1996) 'Postmodern terrorism', *Foreign Affairs*, 75 (5): 24–36.

Laqueur, W. (1977) *A History of Terrorism*. Piscataway, NJ: Transaction Publishers.

Laqueur, W. (2003) *No End to War: Terrorism in the Twenty-first Century*. London: Bloomsbury Publishing.

Le Billon, P. (2001) 'The political ecology of war: natural resources and armed conflicts', *Political Geography*, 20 (5): 561–84.

Lebson, M. (2013) 'Why refugees rebel: towards a comprehensive theory of refugee militarization', *International Migration*, 51 (5): 133–48.

Leiken, R.S. (2005) 'Europe's angry Muslims', *Foreign Affairs*, 84 (4): 120–35.

Lerman, D. (2014) 'Islamic state's oil refining undercut by airstrikes', *Bloomberg*, 8 November. Available at: www.bloomberg.com/news/articles/2014-11-18/islamic-state-s-oil-refining-undercut-by-airstrikes-u-s- (accessed 31 October 2016).

Lezhnev, S. (2006) *Crafting Peace: Strategies to Deal with Warlords in Collapsing States*. Lanham, MD: Lexington Books.

Lia, B. and Skjolberg, K. (2004) Causes of terrorism: an expanded and updated review of the literature. *Forsvarets Forskningsinstitutts Rapportdatabase (Norwegian Defence Research Establishment)*.

Li, Q. (2005) 'Does democracy promote or reduce transnational terrorist incidents?' *Journal of Conflict Resolution*, 49 (2): 278–97.

Li, Q. and Schaub, D. (2004) 'Economic globalization and transnational terrorism: a pooled time-series analysis', *Journal of Conflict Resolution*, 48 (2): 230–58.

Lipset, S.M. (2000) 'The indispensability of political parties', *Journal of Democracy*, 11 (1): 48–55.

Lisanti, D. (2010) 'Do failed states really breed terrorists? An examination of terrorism in sub-saharan africa comparing statistical approaches with a fuzzy set qualitative comparative analysis'. In *CAPERS Workshop at NYU*, May, pp.1–26.

Lischer, S.K. (2006) *Dangerous Sanctuaries: Refugee Camps, Civil War, and the Dilemmas of Humanitarian Aid*. New York: Cornell University Press.

Longman, J. (2016) 'IS increases use of child soldiers, says US report', *BBC News*, 19 February. Available at: www.bbc.co.uk/news/world-middle-east-35608878 (accessed 31 October 2016).

Lynch, D. (2002) 'Separatist states and post-Soviet conflicts', *International Affairs*, 78 (4): 831–848.

Lynch, D. (2004) *Engaging Eurasia's Separatist States: Unresolved Conflicts and De Facto States*. Washington, DC: US Institute of Peace Press.

Lynn-Jones, S.M. (1998) 'Why the United States should spread democracy', *Discussion Paper* 98–07, Cambridge, MA: Center for Science and International Affairs, Harvard University.

Mackinlay, J. (2000) 'Defining warlords', *International Peacekeeping*, 7 (1): 48–62.

Mackinlay, J. (1998) 'War lords', *The RUSI Journal*, 143 (2): 24–32.

Mair, S. (2005) 'The new world of privatized violence', *New Trends in International Politics and Society*, 47–62.

Makarenko, T. (2004) 'The crime-terror continuum: tracing the interplay between transnational organised crime and terrorism', *Global Crime*, 6 (1): 129–145.

Makarenko, T. (2012) 'Foundations and evolution of the crime-terror nexus'. In F. Allum and S. Gilmour (eds), *Routledge Handbook of Transnational Organized Crime*, pp. 234– 249.

Mallory, S.L. (2011) *Understanding Organized Crime*. Burlington, MA: Jones & Bartlett Publishers.

Mannes, A. (2003) *Profiles in Terror: The Guide to Middle East Terrorist Organizations*. Lanham, MD: Rowman & Littlefield.

Manwaring, M. (2011) 'Security, stability and sovereignty challenges of politicized gangs and insurgents in the Americas', *Small Wars & Insurgencies*, 22 (5): 860–889.

Manwaring, M.G. (2005) 'Street Gangs: The New Urban Insurgency'. Dissertation submitted to Army War College Strategic Studies Inst Carlisle Barracks PA.

Marchal, R. (2007) 'Warlordism and terrorism: how to obscure an already confusing crisis? The case of Somalia', *International Affairs*, 83 (6): 1091–1106.

Marcus, A. (2009) *Blood and Belief: The PKK and the Kurdish Fight for Independence*. New York: NYU Press.

Markowitz, L.P. (2012) 'Tajikistan: authoritarian reaction in a post-war state', *Democratization*, 19 (1): 98–119.

Marten, K. (2012) *Warlords: Strong-arm Brokers in Weak States*. New York: Cornell University Press.

Mason, T.D. and Krane, D.A. (1989) 'The political economy of death squads: toward a theory of the impact of state-sanctioned terror', *International Studies Quarterly*, 33 (2): 175–98.

Mathieu, F. and Dearden, N. (2007) 'Corporate mercenaries: the threat of private military and security companies', *Review of African Political Economy*, 34 (114): 744–55.

Matthews, C. (2014) 'Fortune 5: the biggest organized crime groups in the world', *Fortune*, 14 September. Available at: http://fortune.com/2014/09/14/biggest-organized-crime-groups-in-the-world (accessed 31 October 2016).

Matusitz, J. (2013) *Terrorism and Communication*. Florida: SAGE Publications, University of Central Florida.

Mavin, D. (2015) 'Calculating the revenue from antiquities to Islamic State', *Wall Street Journal*, 11 February. Available at: www.wsj.com/articles/calculating-the-revenue-from-antiquities-to-islamic-state-1423657578 (accessed 31 October 2016).

Mazzei, J. (2009) *Death Squads or Self-Defense Forces? How Paramilitary Groups Emerge and Challenge Democracy in Latin America*. Chapel Hill, NC: University of North Carolina Press.

McAllister, I. (2004) '"The Armalite and the ballot box": Sinn Fein's electoral strategy in Northern Ireland', *Electoral Studies*, 23 (1): 123–142.

McCormick, E.M. (2003) *Enemy Aliens: Double Standards and Constitutional Freedoms in the War on Terrorism*. New York: The New Press.

McCormick, G.H. (2003) 'Terrorist decision making', *Annual Review of Political Science*, 6 (1): 473–507.

McCormick, G.H. and Giordano, F. (2007) 'Things come together: symbolic violence and guerrilla mobilisation', *Third World Quarterly*, 28 (2): 295–320.

McEvoy, J. (2014) *Power-sharing Executives: Governing in Bosnia, Macedonia, and Northern Ireland*. Philadelphia, PA: University of Pennsylvania Press.

McEvoy, J. and O'Leary, B. (eds) (2013) *Power Sharing in Deeply Divided Places*. Philadelphia, PA: University of Pennsylvania Press.

Mearsheimer, J.J. (1995) 'A realist reply', *International Security*, 20 (1): 82–93.

Menkhaus, K. (2006) 'Quasi-states, nation-building, and terrorist safe havens', *Journal of Conflict Studies*, 23 (2).

Merari, A. (1993) 'Terrorism as a strategy of insurgency', *Terrorism and Political Violence*, 5 (4): 213–51.

Merari, A. (1998) 'Attacks on civil aviation: trends and lessons', *Terrorism and Political Violence*, 10 (3): 9–26.

Merkl, P.H. (ed.) (1986) *Political Violence and Terror: Motifs and Motivations*. Berkeley, CA: University of California Press.

Merkl, P.H. (1995) 'Radical right parties in Europe and anti-foreign violence: a comparative essay', *Terrorism and Political Violence*, 7 (1): 96–118.

Metz, S. (1994) 'Insurgency after the Cold War', *Small Wars & Insurgencies*, 5 (1): 63–82.

Meyer, J.W. (2000) 'Globalization sources and effects on national states and societies', *International Sociology*, 15 (2): 233–248.

Michels, R. (1959) *Political Parties: A Sociological Study of the Ligarchical Tendencies of Modern Democracy*. New York: Dover.

Mickolus, E.F. and Simmons, S.L. (2002) *Terrorism, 1996–2001: A Chronology*. Westport, CT: Greenwood Press.

Midtbøen, A.H. (2014) 'The invisible second generation? Statistical discrimination and immigrant stereotypes in employment processes in Norway', *Journal of Ethnic and Migration Studies*, 40 (10): 1657–75.

Miller, L. (2006) 'The terrorist mind: a psychological and political analysis', *International Journal of Offender Therapy and Comparative Criminology*, 50 (2): 121–38.

Mingst, K.A. and Arreguín-Toft, I.M. (2013) *Essentials of International Relations* (6th international student edn). New York: Norton.

Miranda, R. and Ratliff, W.E. (1992) *The Civil War in Nicaragua: Inside the Sandinistas*. Piscataway, NJ: Transaction Publishers.

Mishal, S. and Rosenthal, M. (2005) 'Al Qaeda as a dune organization: toward a typology of Islamic terrorist organizations', *Studies in Conflict & Terrorism*, 28 (4): 275–93.

Mishal, S. and Sela, A. (2006) *The Palestinian Hamas: Vision, Violence, and Coexistence*. New York: Columbia University Press.

Mittelman, J. (2010) *Hyperconflict: Globalization and Insecurity*. Stanford, CA: Stanford University Press.

Mobley, B.W. (2012) *Terrorism and Counterintelligence: How Terrorist Groups Elude Detection*. New York: Columbia University Press.

Molzahn, C., Ríos, V. and Shirk, D.A. (2012) *Drug Violence in Mexico: Data and Analysis through 2011*. Trans-Border Institute, University of San Diego, San Diego.

Monteleone, C., Caruso, R., and Locatelli, A. (2014) 'Some insights on the link between terrorism, organised crime and "New wars"', *Understanding Terrorism*, 22: 237–54.

Morrison, J.F. (2015) 'Peace comes dropping slow'. In I. Tellidis and H. Toros (eds), *Researching Terrorism, Peace and Conflict Studies: Interaction, Synthesis and Opposition*. Abingdon: Routledge.

Morselli, C. (2009) *Inside Criminal Networks*. New York: Springer.

Mueller, J. (2013) *War and Ideas: Selected Essays*. Abingdon: Routledge.

Mueller, J and Stewart, M. (2016) 'Misoverestimating ISIS: comparisons with Al-Qaeda'. *Perspectives on Terrorism* 10 (4). Available at: www.terrorismanalysts.com/pt/index.php/pot/article/view/525 (accessed 11 November 2016).

Muir, J. (20 June 2016) 'Islamic State group: the full story', *BBC News*. Available at: www.bbc.co.uk/news/world-middle-east-35695648 (accessed 1 September 2016).

Mulaj, K. (2010) *Violent Non-state Actors in World Politics*. New York: Columbia University Press.

Muro, D. (2013) 'ETA: Basque nationalist and separatist organization', *The Wiley-Blackwell Encyclopedia of Social and Political Movements*. Oxford: Wiley-Blackwell.

Nacos, B. (2016) *Mass-mediated Terrorism: Mainstream and Digital Media in Terrorism and Counterterrorism*. Lanham, MD: Rowman & Littlefield.

Nadarajah, S. and Sriskandarajah, D. (2005) 'Liberation struggle or terrorism? The politics of naming the LTTE', *Third World Quarterly*, 26 (1): 87–100.

Nagle, L.E. (2003) 'The challenges of fighting global organized crime in Latin America', *Fordham International Law Journal*, 26.

Nakhle, C. (6 December 2015) 'ISIS sells its oil but who is buying it?' *Al Jazeera*. Available at: www.aljazeera.com/indepth/opinion/2015/12/isil-sells-oil-buying-151206055403374.html (accessed 31 October 2016).

Napoleoni, L. (2014) *The Islamist Phoenix: The Islamic State (ISIS) and the Redrawing of the Middle East*. New York: Seven Stories Press.

Nasuti, P. (2012) *The Determinants of Anti-Corruption Reform in the Republic of Georgia*. Available at: http://ec2-107-22-211-253.compute-1.amazonaws.com/sites/default/files/NASUTI%20Research%20Summary.pdf (accessed 30 January 2016).

Newland, K. and Plaza, S. (2013) 'What we know about diasporas and economic development'. Migration Policy Institute, Policy Brief, 5: 1–14.

Newman, E. (2007) 'Weak states, state failure, and terrorism', *Terrorism and Political Violence*, 19 (4): 463–88.

Nicholas, R.M., Barr, R.J. and Mollan, R.A. (1993) 'Paramilitary punishment in Northern Ireland: a macabre irony', *Journal of Trauma and Acute Care Surgery*, 34 (1): 90–5.

Nye, J.S. (2003) 'US power and strategy after Iraq', *Foreign Affairs*, 82 (4): 60–73.

Nye, J.S. (2004) *Soft Power: the Means to Success in World Politics*, New York: Public Affairs.

Nye, J.S. and Lynn-Jones, S.M. (1988) 'International security studies: a report of a conference on the state of the field', *International Security*, 12 (4): 5–27.

O'Brien, B. (1999) *The Long War: the IRA and Sinn Fein*. Syracuse University Press.

O'Brien, K.J. (1996) 'Rightful resistance', *World Politics*, 49 (1): 31–55.

O'Donnell, G. A. (1998) *Polyarchies and the (un) Rule of Law in Latin America*. Instituto Juan March de Estudios e Investigaciones.

O'Donnell, G.A. (2004) 'Why the rule of law matters', *Journal of Democracy*, 15 (4): 32–46.

Oehme III, C. G. (2008) 'Terrorists, insurgents, and criminals – growing nexus?' *Studies in Conflict & Terrorism*, 31 (1): 80–93.

O'Leary, B. (2005) 'Mission Accomplished? *Looking Back at the IRA*', *Field Day Review*, 1, 217–45.

O'Leary, B. (2007) 'IRA: Irish Republican Army (Oglaigh na hEireann)', *Terror, Insurgency and the State*. In M. Heiberg, B. O'Leary and J. Tirman (eds), *Terror, Insurgency, and the State: Ending Protracted Conflicts*. University of Pennsylvania Press, pp. 189–228.

Olesen, T. (2004) 'Globalising the Zapatistas: from Third World solidarity to global solidarity?', *Third World Quarterly*, 25 (1): 255–67.

Olzak, S. (2011) 'Does globalization breed ethnic discontent?', *Journal of Conflict Resolution*, 55 (1): 3–32.

Omeje, K. (2007) 'The diaspora and domestic insurgencies in Africa', *African Sociological Review*, 11 (2): 94–107.

O'Neill, B.E. (2001) *Insurgency & Terrorism: Inside Modern Revolutionary Warfare*. Washington, DC: Brassey's Inc.

O'Neill, W.G. (2002) 'Beyond the slogans: how can the UN respond to terrorism', *Responding to Terrorism: What Role for the United Nations*, International Peace Academy, 5–17.

Onuoha, F.C. (2014) *Why Do Youth Join Boko Haram?* Special Report. Washington, DC: US Institute for Peace.

Oots, K.L. (1989) 'Organizational perspectives on the formation and disintegration of terrorist groups', *Studies in Conflict & Terrorism*, 12(3): 139–152.

O'Rourke, L.A. (2009) 'What's special about female suicide terrorism?' *Security Studies*, 18 (4): 681–718.

Osorio, A.E.F (2013) *The First Chechen War*. Moscow: Higher School of Economics.

Palma, O. (2015) 'Transnational networks of insurgency and crime: explaining the spread of commercial insurgencies beyond state borders', *Small Wars & Insurgencies*, 26 (3): 476–96.

Pape, R. (2005) *Dying to Win: The Strategic Logic of Suicide Terrorism*. New York: Random House.

Patrick, S. (2006) 'Weak states and global threats: fact or fiction?' *Washington Quarterly*, 29 (2): 27–53.

Pearce, J. (1990) *Colombia: Inside the Labyrinth*. London: Latin America Bureau.

Pearlstein, R.M. (1991) *The Mind of the Political Terrorist*. Wilmington, DE: Scholarly Resources.

Pearson, G. and Hobbs, D. (2003) 'King pin? A case study of a middle market drug broker', *The Howard Journal of Criminal Justice*, 42 (4): 335–47.

Pedahzur, A. (2005) *Suicide Terrorism*. Cambridge: Polity.

Pedahzur, A. and Perliger, A. (2006) 'The changing nature of suicide attacks: a social network perspective'. *Social Forces*, 84 (4): 1987–2008.

Pegg, S. (1998) *De Facto States in the International System*. Institute of International Relations, University of British Columbia.

Penglase, B. (2009) 'States of insecurity: everyday emergencies, public secrets, and drug trafficker power in a Brazilian favela', *PoLAR: Political and Legal Anthropology Review*, 32 (1): 47–63.

Pennell, S., Melton, R. and Hoctor, D. (2001) *Assessment of a Multi-Agency Approach to Drug Involved Gang Members*. San Diego Association of Governments.

Pérouse de Montclos, M.A. (2003) 'A refugee diaspora: when the Somali go west'. In K. Koser (ed.), *New African Diaspora*. London: Routledge, pp. 37–55.

Peters, K. and Richards, P. (1998) '"Why we fight": voices of youth combatants in Sierra Leone', *Africa*, 68 (2): 183–210.

Petersen, R.D. (2001) *Resistance and Rebellion: Lessons from Eastern Europe*. Cambridge, Cambridge University Press.

Peterson, J.K., Skeem, J., Kennealy, P., Bray, B. and Zvonkovic, A. (2014) 'How often and how consistently do symptoms directly precede criminal behavior among offenders with mental illness?', *Law and Human Behavior*, 38 (5): 439.

Pezzin, L.E. (1995) 'Earnings prospects, matching effects, and the decision to terminate a criminal career', *Journal of Quantitative Criminology*, 11 (1): 29–50.

Pham, J.P. (2011) 'Foreign influences and shifting horizons: the ongoing evolution of al-Qaeda in the Islamic Maghreb', *Orbis*, 55 (2): 240–54.

Phillips, B.J. (2015) 'Enemies with benefits? Violent rivalry and terrorist group longevity', *Journal of Peace Research*, 52 (1): 62–75.

Phillips, D.L. (2008) 'Disarming, demobilizing, and reintegrating the Kurdistan Worker's Party', *American Foreign Policy Interests*, 30 (2): 70–87.

Phillips, P.J. (2011) 'Lone wolf terrorism', *Peace Economics, Peace Science and Public Policy*, 17: 1.

Piazza, J.A. (2006) 'Rooted in poverty? Terrorism, poor economic development, and social cleavages', *Terrorism and Political Violence*, 18 (1): 159–77.

Piazza, J.A. (2009) 'Is Islamist terrorism more dangerous? An empirical study of group ideology, organization, and goal structure', *Terrorism and Political Violence*, 21 (1): 62–88.

Piquero, A.R. (ed.) (2012) *Rational Choice and Criminal Behavior: Recent Research and Future Challenges*. Oxford: Routledge.

Popescu, N. (2006) '"Outsourcing"de facto statehood: Russia and the secessionist entities in Georgia and Moldova', *CEPS Policy Briefs*, (1–12): 1–8.

Posen, B.R. (1993) 'The security dilemma and ethnic conflict', *Survival*, 35 (1): 27–47.

Post, J.M. (1987) 'Rewarding fire with fire: effects of retaliation on terrorist group dynamics', *Studies in Conflict & Terrorism*, 10 (1): 23–35.

Post, J.M. (1990) 'Terrorist psycho-logic: terrorist behavior as a product of psychological forces'. In W. Reich (ed.), *Origins of Terrorism: Psychologies, Ideologies, Theologies, States of Mind*. New York: Cambridge University Press, pp. 25–40.

Post, J.M., Ali, F., Henderson, S.W., Shanfield, S., Victoroff, J. and Weine, S. (2009) 'The psychology of suicide terrorism', *Psychiatry*, 72 (1): 13–31.

Post, J., Sprinzak, E. and Denny, L. (2003) 'The terrorists in their own words: interviews with 35 incarcerated Middle Eastern terrorists', *Terrorism and Political Violence*, 15 (1): 171–84.

Price, B.C. (2012) 'Targeting top terrorists: how leadership decapitation contributes to counterterrorism', *International Security*, 36 (4): 9–46.

Rabasa, A. (2014) *Political Islam in Southeast Asia: Moderates, Radical and Terrorists* (No. 358). Oxford: Routledge.

Randall, V. and Svåsand, L. (2002) 'Party institutionalization in new democracies', *Party Politics*, 8 (1): 5–29.

Rapoport, D.C. (2001) 'The fourth wave: September 11 in the history of terrorism', *Current History*, 100 (650): 419–424.

Rapoport, D.C. (2004) 'The four waves of modern terrorism', *Attacking Terrorism: Elements of a Grand Strategy*. Washington, DC: Georgetown University Press, pp. 46–73.

Rasmussen, M.V. (2003) *A New Kind of War: Strategic Culture and the War on Terrorism*, Copendigen: Danish Institute for International Studies.

Reilly, B. and Reynolds, A. (1999) *Electoral Systems and Conflict in Divided Societies*. Washington, DC: National Academy Press.

Reinares, F. (2001) *European Democracies Against Terrorism: Governmental Policies and Intergovernmental Cooperation*. The Oñati Internationl Institute of the Sociology of Law, London: Ashgate.

Reinares, F. (2004) 'Who are the terrorists? Analyzing changes in sociological profile among members of ETA', *Studies in Conflict and Terrorism*, 27 (6): 465–88.

Reiner, I. (1992) *Gangs, Crime and Violence in Los Angeles: Findings and Proposals*. Office of Juvenile Justice and Deliquency prevantion.

Reno, W.S. (1993) 'Foreign firms and the financing of Charles Taylor's NPFL', *Liberian Studies Journal*, 28 (2): 175–88.

Reno, W. (1995) *Corruption and State Politics in Sierra Leone* (Vol. 229). Cambridge: Cambridge University Press.

Reno, W. (1997) 'War, markets, and the reconfiguration of West Africa's weak states', *Comparative Politics*, 24 (4): 493–510.

Reno, W. (1999) *Warlord Politics and African States*. Boulder, CO: Lynne Rienner Publishers.

Reno, W. (2000) 'Shadow States and the Political Economy of Civil Wars'. In M. Berdal and D.M. Malone (eds), *Greed and Grievance: Economic Agendas in Civil Wars*. Boulder, CO: Lynne Rienner, pp. 43–68.

Reynal-Querol, M. (2002) 'Ethnicity, political systems, and civil wars', *Journal of Conflict Resolution*, 46 (1): 29–54.

Ribando, C.M. (2007) Gangs in Central America (August). Library of Congress, Washington DC: Congressional Research Service.

Rich, B. and Conduit, D. (2015) 'The impact of jihadist foreign fighters on indigenous secular-nationalist causes: contrasting Chechnya and Syria', *Studies in Conflict & Terrorism*, 38 (2): 113–131.

Rich, P.B. (ed.) (1999) *Warlords in International Relations*. London: Macmillan.

Richani, N. (2010) 'State capacity in postconflict settings: explaining criminal violence in El Salvador and Guatemala', *Civil Wars*, 12 (4): 431–455.

Richards, A. (2014) 'Conceptualizing terrorism', *Studies in Conflict & Terrorism*, 37 (3): 213–36.

Richards, L. (2006) 'Corporate mercenaries: the threat of private military and security companies,' *War on Want*, 1–26.

Richmond, O.P. (2003) 'Realizing hegemony? Symbolic terrorism and the roots of conflict', *Studies in Conflict and Terrorism*, 26 (4): 289–309.

Rid, T. and Hecker, M. (2009) 'The terror fringe', *Policy Review*, 158, 3.

Risen, J. and Mazzetti, M. (2009) 'Blackwater guards tied to secret CIA raids', *The New York Times*, 10 December.

Ritzer, G. ed. (2008) *The Blackwell Companion to Globalization*. Oxford: John Wiley & Sons.

Ritzer, G. and Atalay, Z. (2010) *Readings in Globalization: Key Concepts and Major Debates*. Oxford: John Wiley & Sons.

Rizzo, M. (2003) 'Why do children join gangs?, *Journal of Gang Research*, 11 (1): 65–75.

Robb, J. (2007) *Brave New War: The Next Stage of Terrorism and the End of Globalization*. Oxford: John Wiley & Sons.

Roberts, K. (1990) 'Bullying and bargaining: the United States, Nicaragua, and conflict resolution in Central America', *International Security*, 15 (2): 67–102.

Robertson, R. (1992) *Globalization: Social Theory and Global Culture* (Vol. 16). London: SAGE.

Robinson, T.P. (2001) 'Twenty-first century warlords: diagnosis and treatment?', *Defence Studies*, 1 (1): 121–45.

Robison, K.K., Crenshaw, E.M. and Jenkins, J.C. (2006) 'Ideologies of violence: the social origins of Islamist and leftist transnational terrorism', *Social Forces*, 84 (4): 2009–26.

Rodgers, D. (1999) *Youth Gangs and Violence in Latin America and the Caribbean: A Literature Survey*. World Bank, Latin America and the Caribbean Region, Environmentally and Socially Sustainable Development SMU.

Rodgers, D. (2004) *Old Wine in New Bottles Or New Wine in Old? Conceptualising Violence and Governmentality in Contemporary Latin America*. London: Development Research Centre, Development Studies Institute.

Rodgers, D. (2006) 'Living in the shadow of death: gangs, violence and social order in urban Nicaragua, 1996–2002', *Journal of Latin American Studies*, 38 (2): 267–92.

Rodrik, D. (1997) 'Has globalization gone too far?' *California Management Review*, 39 (3): 29–53.

Rogers, P. (2012) 'Nigeria: the generic context of the Boko Haram violence', *Monthly Global Security Briefing*, Oxford Research Group, pp. 1–5.

Ross, J.I. (1993) 'Structural causes of oppositional political terrorism: towards a causal model', *Journal of Peace Research*, 30 (3): 317–29.

Ross, J.I. and Gurr, T.R. (1989) 'Why terrorism subsides: a comparative study of Canada and the United States', *Comparative Politics*, 21 (4): 405–426.

Rotberg, R.I. (2003) *State Failure and State Weakness in a Time of Terror*. Washington, DC: Brooking Institute Press.

Roth, M.P. and Sever, M. (2007) 'The Kurdish Workers Party (PKK) as criminal syndicate: funding terrorism through organized crime, a case study', *Studies in Conflict & Terrorism*, 30 (10): 901–20.

Rothchild, D. and Groth, A.J. (1995) 'Pathological dimensions of domestic and international ethnicity', *Political Science Quarterly*, 110 (1): 69–82.

Rotman, E. (2000) 'The globalization of criminal violence', *Cornell JL & Pub. Pol'y*, 10: 1.

Ruble, N.M. and Turner, W.L. (2000) 'A systemic analysis of the dynamics and organization of urban street gangs', *American Journal of Family Therapy*, 28 (2): 117–32.

Rudner, M. (2013) 'Al-Qaeda's twenty-year strategic plan: the current phase of global terror', *Studies in Conflict & Terrorism*, 36 (12): 953–80.

Russell, C.A. and Miller, B.H. (1977) 'Profile of a terrorist', *Studies in Conflict & Terrorism*, 1 (1): 17–34.

Russett, B., Layne, C., Spiro, D.E. and Doyle, M.W. (1995) 'The democratic peace', *International Security*, 19 (4): 164–184.

Sageman, M. (2004) *Understanding Terror Networks*. Philadelphia, PA: University of Pennsylvania Press.

Saideman, S.M., Lanoue, D.J., Campenni, M. and Stanton, S. (2002) 'Democratization, political institutions, and ethnic conflict: a pooled time-series analysis, 1985–1998', *Comparative Political Studies*, 35 (1): 103–29.

Salam, A. and Abdullahi, E.F. (2014) Indonesia's counter-terrorism policy, 2001–2009. International Conference on Law, Order and Criminal Justice, 19–20 November, International Institute of Islamic Thought and Civilization (ISTAC).

Salehyan, I. (2007) 'Transnational rebels: neighboring states as sanctuary for rebel groups', *World Politics*, 59 (2): 217–42.

Salehyan, I. (2008) 'The externalities of civil strife: refugees as a source of international conflict', *American Journal of Political Science*, 52 (4): 787–801.

Sanchez, M. (2006) 'Insecurity and violence as a new power relation in Latin America', *The Annals of the American Academy of Political and Social Science*, 606 (1): 178–95.

Sánchez -Cuenca, I. and de la Calle, L. (2009) 'Domestic terrorism: the hidden side of political violence', *Annual Review of Political Science*, 12, 31–49.

Sánchez-Jankowski, M. (1991) *Islands in the Street: Gangs and American Urban Society*. University of California Press.

Sánchez-Jankowski, M. (2003) 'Gangs and social change', *Theoretical Criminology*, 7 (2): 191–216.

Sartori, G. (2005) *Parties and Party Systems: A Framework for Analysis*. Colchester: ECPR press.

Sandler, T. and Enders, W. (2004) 'An economic perspective on transnational terrorism', *European Journal of Political Economy*, 20 (2): 301–16.

Sanford, V. (2003) *Buried Secrets: Truth and Human Rights in Guatemala*. Basingstoke: Palgrave Macmillan.

Sanín, F.G. and Giustozzi, A. (2010) 'Networks and armies: structuring rebellion in Colombia and Afghanistan', *Studies in Conflict & Terrorism*, 33 (9): 836–853.

Scahill, J. (2011) *Blackwater: The Rise of the World's Most Powerful Mercenary Army*. London: Profile Books.

Schaefer, R.W. (2010) *The Insurgency in Chechnya and the North Caucasus: From Gazavat to Jihad*. Santa Barbara, CA: ABC-CLIO.

Schinkel, W. (2010) *Aspects of Violence: A Critical Theory*. New York: Springer.

Schmid, A.P. (ed.) (2011) *The Routledge Handbook of Terrorism Research*. London: Routledge.

Schneckener, U. (2006) 'Fragile statehood, armed non-state actors and security governance', *Private Actors and Security Governance*, 4: 23–40.

Schneckener, U. (2007) Armed Non-State Actors and the Monopoly of Force. In A. Bailes, U. Schneckener and H. Wulf (eds), *Revisiting the State Monopoly on the Legitimate Use of Force*, pp. 10–18. Geneva Centre for Democratic Control of Armed Forces (DCAF), Policy Paper No. 24.

Schneider, G., Barbieri, K. and Gleditsch, N.P. (2003) 'Does globalization contribute to peace? A critical survey of the literature', *Globalization and Armed Conflict*, 3–29.

Schwedler, J. (2006) *Faith in Moderation: Islamist Parties in Jordan and Yemen*. Cambridge: Cambridge University Press.

Schwedler, J. (2011) 'Can Islamists become moderates? Rethinking the inclusion-moderation hypothesis', *World Politics*, 63 (2): 347–376.

Schweitzer, G.E. and Schweitzer, C.D. (2002) *A Faceless Enemy: The Origins of Modern Terrorism*. New York: Basic Books.

Security InfoWatch (n.d.) Global demand for security services is driven by rising urbanization, the real and perceived risks of crime and terrorism, and a belief that public safty measures are insufficient. Available at: www.freedoniagroup.com/industry-study/world-security-services-2978.htm (accessed 24 January 2017).

Sedgwick, M. (2007) 'Inspiration and the origins of global waves of terrorism', *Studies in Conflict & Terrorism*, 30 (2): 97–112.

Shapiro, G. (2003) 'Terror reigns supreme and the cycle of violence is seemingly endless in the triple frontier', *NYL Sch. J. Hum. Rts.*, 19, 895.

Shapiro, J.N. and Jung, D.F. (2014) 'The terrorist bureaucracy: inside the files of the Islamic State in Iraq', *Boston Globe*, 14 December.

Shapiro, J.N., and Weidmann, N.B. (2015) 'Is the phone mightier than the sword? Cellphones and insurgent violence in Iraq', *International Organization*, 69 (2): 247–74.

Shapiro, Y. (1991) *The Road to Power: Herut Party in Israel*. Albany, NY: SUNY Press.

Shaw, E.D. (1986) 'Political terrorists: dangers of diagnosis and an alternative to the psycho-pathology model', *International Journal of Law and Psychiatry*, 8 (3): 359–68.

Sheffer, G.G. (2006) 'Diasporas and terrorism'. In L. Richardson (ed), *The Roots of Terrorism*. London: Routledge, pp. 117–32.

Shelley, L. (1999) 'Identifying, counting and categorizing transnational criminal organizations', *Transnational Organized Crime*, 5 (1): 1–18.

Shelley, L.I. (2014) *Dirty Entanglements: Corruption, Crime, and Terrorism*. Cambridge: Cambridge University Press.

Shelley, L.I. and Melzer, S.A. (2008) 'The nexus of organized crime and terrorism: two case studies in cigarette smuggling', *International Journal of Comparative and Applied Criminal Justice*, 32 (1): 43–63.

Silke, A. (1998) 'Motives of paramilitary vigilantism in Northern Ireland', *Low Intensity Conflict & Law Enforcement*, 7 (2): 121–56.

Silke, A. (ed.) (2003) *Terrorists, Victims and Society: Psychological Perspectives on Terrorism and its Consequences*. Oxford: John Wiley & Sons.

Silke, A. and Taylor, M. (2000) 'War without end: comparing IRA and loyalist vigilantism in Northern Ireland', *The Howard Journal of Criminal Justice*, 39 (3): 249–66.

Simons, A. and Tucker, D. (2007) 'The misleading problem of failed states: a 'socio-geography' of terrorism in the post-9/11 era', *Third World Quarterly*, 28 (2): 387–401.

Singer, P.W. (2011) *Corporate Warriors: the Rise of the Privatized Military Industry*. Cornell, NY: Cornell University Press.

Singh, B.P. and Verma, A. (2015) 'Cyber terrorism – an international phenomena and an eminent threat', *IITM Journal of Management and IT*, 6 (1): 164–8.

Siqueira, K. (2005) 'Political and militant wings within dissident movements and organizations', *Journal of Conflict Resolution*, 49 (2): 218–36.

Sluka, J.A. (2000) *Death Squad: the Anthropology of State Terror*. Philadelphia, PA: University of Pennsylvania Press.

Small Arms and Light Weapons, Africa (2008) *A Resource Guide for Religions for Peace*, United Nations, 1–28.

Small Arms Survey (2012) *Small Arms Survey 2012: Moving Targets*. Research Notes, Cambridge: Cambridge University Press.

Small Arms Survey (October 2013) *Parts for Small and Light Weapons*. 35: 1–4.

Smetana, J.G., Campione-Barr, N. and Metzger, A. (2006) 'Adolescent development in interpersonal and societal contexts', *Annual Review of Psychology*, 57: 255–84.

Smillie, I. (2013) 'Blood diamonds and non-state actors', *Vanderbilt Journal of Transnational Law*, 46: 1003.

Smith, B.L. and Morgan, K.D. (1994) 'Terrorists right and left: empirical issues in profiling American terrorists', *Studies in Conflict & Terrorism*, 17 (1): 39–57.

Smith, C.F., Rush, J. and Burton, C.E. (2013) 'Street gangs, organized crime groups, and terrorists: differentiating criminal organizations', *Investigative Sciences Journal*, 5 (1).

Smith, C.J., Zhang, S.X. and Barberet, R. (eds) (2011) *Routledge Handbook of Criminology*. Oxford: Routledge.

Smith, M.L.R. and Neumann, P.R. (2005) 'Motorman's long journey: changing the strategic setting in Northern Ireland', *Contemporary British History*, 19 (4): 413–35.

Soibelman, M. (2004) 'Palestinian suicide bombers', *Journal of Investigative Psychology and Offender Profiling*, 1 (3): 175–90.

Soloman, E. and Jones, S. (2015) 'Isis Inc: Loot and taxes keep jihadi economy churning', *FT*, 14 December. Available at: www.ft.com/cms/s/2/aee89a00-9ff1-11e5-beba-5e33e2 b79e46.html?siteedition=uk#axzz4HOzOqMXu (accessed 24 January 2017).

Spaaij, R. and Hamm, M.S. (2015) 'Key issues and research agendas in lone wolf terrorism', *Studies in Conflict & Terrorism*, 38 (3): 167–78.

Speckhard, A. and Akhmedova, K. (2006) 'Black widows: the Chechen female suicide terrorists', *Female Suicide Bombers: Dying for Equality*, 84 (1): 63–80.

Spergel, I.A. (1995) *The Youth Gang Problem: A Community Approach*. New York: Oxford University Press, pp. 145–281.

Stace. T. (2016) 'A bit of numeracy can take the heat out of the asylum debate', *The Conversation* (18 May). Available at: https://theconversation.com/a-bit-of-numeracy-can-take-the-heat-out-of-the-asylum-debate-59369 (accessed 24 January 2017).

Starita, C.L. (2007) Exploitation of border security by MS-13 in aiding al Qaeda's agenda for domestic terrorism in the United States. ProQuest. Dissertation. START Database.

Steinberg, L. and Morris, A.S. (2001) 'Adolescent development', *Journal of Cognitive Education and Psychology*, 2 (1): 55–87.

Steinberg, M. (2008) 'PKK terrorists named "Drug Kingpins": nations move against narcoterrorism', *Executive Intelligence Review*, 48–52.

Stern, J. (2000) *The Ultimate Terrorists*. Cambridge, MA: Harvard University Press.

Stern, J. and Berger, J.M. (2015) *ISIS: The State of Terror*. London: HarperCollins.

Striegher, J.L. (2013) 'The deradicalisation of terrorists', *Salus Journal*, 1 (1): 19.

Strom, K., Hollywood, J., Pope, M., Weintraub, G., Daye, C. and Gemeinhardt, D. (2010) *Building on Clues: Examining Successes and Failures in Detecting US Terrorist Plots, 1999–2009*, Institute for Homeland Security Solutions.

Sullivan, J.P. (2006) 'Maras morphing: revisiting third generation gangs', *Global Crime*, 7 (3–4): 487–504.

Sullivan, J.P. and Bunker, R.J. (2002) 'Drug cartels, street gangs, and warlords', *Small Wars and Insurgencies*, 13 (2): 40–53.

Sullivan, J.P. and Elkus, A. (2008) 'State of siege: Mexico's criminal insurgency', *Small Wars Journal*, 12: 1–12.

Sung, H.E. (2004) 'State failure, economic failure, and predatory organized crime: a comparative analysis,' *Journal of Research in Crime and Delinquency*, 41 (2): 111–129.

Swanson, A. (2015) 'How the Islamic State makes its money', *Washington Post*, 18 November. Available at: www.washingtonpost.com/news/wonk/wp/2015/11/18/how-isis-makes-its-money/?utm_term=.6b2700d91893 (accessed 24 January 2017).

Taber, R. (1970) *The War of the Flea: A Study of Guerrilla Warfare Theory and Practice*. St Albans: Paladin.

Takeyh, R. and Gvosdev, N. (2002) 'Do terrorist networks need a home?', *Washington Quarterly*, 25 (3): 97–108.

Tankebe, J. (2009) 'Self-help, policing, and procedural justice: Ghanaian vigilantism and the rule of law', *Law & Society Review*, 43 (2): 245–70.

Tarrow, S. (2007) 'Inside insurgencies: politics and violence in an age of civil war', *Perspectives on Politics*, 5 (3): 587–600.

Taulbee, J. L. (2002) 'The privatization of security: modern conflict, globalization and weak states', *Civil Wars*, 5 (2): 1–24.

Thachuk, K.L. (2001a) 'The sinister underbelly: organized crime and terrorism'. In R. Kugler and E. Frost (eds), *The Global Century, Globalization and National Security*, Vol II. Washington, DC: National Defense University Press, pp. 743–60.

Thachuk, K. (2001b) 'Transnational threats: falling through the cracks?', *Low Intensity Conflict and Law Enforcement*, 10 (1): 47–67.

Thiranagama, S. (2014) 'Making Tigers from Tamils: long-distance nationalism and Sri Lankan Tamils in Toronto', *American Anthropologist*, 116 (2): 265–78.

Thomas, C. (2001) 'Global governance, development and human security: exploring the links', *Third World Quarterly*, 22 (2): 159–75.

Thomas, T.S. and Kiser, S.D. (2002) *Lords of the Silk Route: Violent Non-state Actors in Central Asia* (Vol. 43). Collingdale, PA: Diane Publishing.

Thomas, T.S., Kiser, S.D. and Casebeer, W.D. (2005) *Warlords Rising: Confronting Violent Non-state Actors*. Lanham, MD: Lexington Books.

Thornberry, T. P., Freeman-Gallant, A., Lizotte, A., Krohn, M. and Smith, C. (2003) 'Linked lives: the intergenerational transmission of antisocial behaviour', *Journal of Abnormal Child Psychology*, 31: 171–84.

Thornton, W. H. (2003) 'Cold War II: Islamic terrorism as power politics', *Antipode*, 35 (2): 205–11.

Tilly, C. (2003) *The Politics of Collective Violence*. Cambridge: Cambridge University Press.

Tishkov, V. (2004) *Chechnya: Life in a War-torn Society* (Vol. 6). Berkeley, CA: University of California Press.

Tonwe, D.A. and Eke, S.J. (2013) 'State fragility and violent uprisings in Nigeria: the case of Boko Haram', *African Security Review*, 22 (4): 232–43.

Trejo, G. and Ley, S. (2013) Votes, Drugs, and Violence, Subnational Democratization and the Onset of Inter-Cartel Wars in Mexico, 1995–2006. Unpublished Paper, Notre Dame University.

Turbiville Jr, G.H. (2010) 'Firefights, raids, and assassinations: tactical forms of cartel violence and their underpinnings', *Small Wars & Insurgencies*, 21 (1): 123–44.

Türkeş-Kılıç, S. (2015) 'Political party closures in European democratic order: comparing the justifications in DTP and Batasuna decisions', *Journal of European Public Policy*, 1–18.

Tyler, P. (4 March 2000) 'Russian vigilantes fight drug dealers', *New York Times*, World Edition. Available at: www.nytimes.com/2000/03/04/world/russian-vigilantes-fight-drug-dealers.html?pagewanted=all (accessed 24 January 2017).

UNODC (United Nations Office on Drugs and Crime (2011) 'Illicit money: how much is out there? Available at: www.unodc.org/unodc/en/frontpage/2011/October/illicit-money_-how-much-is-out-there.html (accessed on 24 January 2017).

Urdal, H. (2006) 'A clash of generations? Youth bulges and political violence', *International Studies Quarterly*, 50 (3): 607–29.

van Scherpenberg, J. (2000) *Transnationale Organisierte Kriminalität: Die Schattenseite der Globalisierung*. SWP.

Väyrynen, R. (ed.) (1991) *New Directions in Conflict Theory: Conflict Resolution and Conflict Transformation*. London: SAGE.

Venkatesh, S.A. and Levitt, S.D. (2000) '"Are we a family or a business?" History and disjuncture in the urban American street gang', *Theory and Society*, 29 (4): 427–62.

Victoroff, J. (2005) 'The mind of the terrorist: a review and critique of psychological approaches', *Journal of Conflict Resolution*, 49 (1): 3–42.

Vigil, J.D. (2010) *Barrio Gangs: Street Life and Identity in Southern California*. Austin, TX: University of Texas Press.

Vinci, A. (2007) 'Existential motivations in the Lord's Resistance Army's continuing conflict', *Studies in Conflict and Terrorism*, 30 (4): 337–351.

Von Hippel, K. (2002) 'The roots of terrorism: probing the myths', *The Political Quarterly*, 73 (s1): 25–39.

von Lampe, K. (2016) 'The ties that bind: a taxonomy of associational criminal structures'. In G.A. Antonopoules (ed.), *Illegal Entrepreneurship, Organized Crime and Social Control*. New York: Springer International Publishing pp. 19–35.

Vowell, P.R. and May, D.C. (2000) 'Another look at classic strain theory: poverty status, perceived blocked opportunity, and gang membership as predictors of adolescent violent behavior', *Sociological Inquiry*, 70 (1): 42–60.

Wacquant, L. (2008) 'The militarization of urban marginality: lessons from the Brazilian metropolis', *International Political Sociology*, 2 (1): 56–74.

Wade, S.J. and Reiter, D. (2007) 'Does democracy matter? Regime type and suicide terrorism', *Journal of Conflict Resolution*, 51 (2): 329–348.

Wæver, O. (1995) 'Securitization and Desecuritization'. In R. Lipschutz (eds), *On Security*. New York: Columbia University Press, pp. 46–86.

Wagenlehner, G. (1978) 'Motivation for political terrorism in West Germany'. In M.H. Livingstone (ed.), *International Terrorism in the Contemporary World*. Westport, CT: Greenwood Press, pp. 195–203.

Walt, S.M. (1991) 'The renaissance of security studies', *International Studies Quarterly*, 35 (2): 211–39.

Waltz, K.N. (1959) *Man, the State, and War: A Theoretical Analysis*. New York: Columbia University Press.

Waltz, K.N. (1988) 'The origins of war in neorealist theory', *The Journal of Interdisciplinary History*, 18 (4): 615–28.

Waltz, K.N. (1993) 'The emerging structure of international politics', *International Security*, 18 (2): 44–79.

Wardlaw, G. (1989) *Political Terrorism: Theory, Tactics and Counter-measures*. Cambridge: Cambridge University Press.

Warren, J.W. (2015) 'On defeating the Islamic State', *Parameters*, 45 (1): 129–133.

Waterman, S. (2013) 'Study: Americans fear terrorism attacks more than violent crime'. *Washington Times* (13 April). Available at: www.washingtontimes.com/news/2013/apr/15/americans-think-more-about-terror-crime-study (accessed 3 February 2017).

Webber, C. (2007) 'Revaluating relative deprivation theory', *Theoretical Criminology*, 11 (1): 97–120.

Weimann, G. (2005) 'The theater of terror: the psychology of terrorism and the mass media', *Journal of Aggression, Maltreatment & Trauma*, 9 (3–4): 379–390.

Weinberg, L. (1991) 'Turning to terror: the conditions under which political parties turn to terrorist activities', *Comparative Politics*, 423–38.

Weinberg, L. and Eubank, W.L. (1987) 'Italian women terrorists', *Terrorism: An International Journal*, 9 (3): 241–262.

Weinberg, L. and Pedahzur, A. (2004) *Religious Fundamentalism and Political Extremism*. (Vol. 3). Hove: Psychology Press.

Weinberg, L., Pedahzur, A. and Canetti-Nisim, D. (2003) 'The social and religious characteristics of suicide bombers and their victims', *Terrorism and Political Violence*, 15 (3): 139–53.

Weinberg, L., Pedahzur, A. and Perliger, A. (2008) *Political Parties and Terrorist Groups*, 2nd edn. Oxford: Routledge.

Weinstein, J.M. (2005) 'Resources and the information problem in rebel recruitment', *Journal of Conflict Resolution*, 49 (4): 598–624.

Wendt, A. (1992) 'Anarchy is what states make of it: the social construction of power politics', *International Organization*, 46 (2): 391–425.

Wendt, A. (1995) 'Constructing international politics', *International Security*, 20 (1): 71–81.

Wennmann, A. (2014) 'Negotiated exits from organized crime? Building peace in conflict and crime-affected contexts', *Negotiation Journal*, 30 (3): 255–73.

Whiting, M. (2016) 'Moderation without change: the strategic transformation of Sinn Fein and the IRA in Northern Ireland', *Government and Opposition*, 1–24.

Whitney, K.M. (1996) 'SIN, FRAPH, and the CIA: US covert action in Haiti', *Sw. JL & Trade Am.*, 3: 303.

Whittaker, D. (2013) *Terrorism: Understanding the Global Threat*. Oxford: Routledge.

Wickham-Crowley, T.P. (1990) 'Terror and guerrilla warfare in Latin America, 1956–1970', *Comparative Studies in Society and History*, 32 (2): 201–37.

Wiegand, K.E. (2009).' Reformation of a terrorist group: Hezbollah as a Lebanese political party', *Studies in Conflict & Terrorism*, 32 (8): 669–80.

Wiktorowicz, Q. (2004) 'Conceptualizing Islamic activism', *ISIM Newsletter*,14, p.1.

Wiktorowicz, Q. (2006) 'Anatomy of the Salafi movement', *Studies in Conflict & Terrorism*, 29 (3): 207–39.

Williams, P. D. (2008) 'Violent non-state actors and national and international security', *Interational Relations and Security Network*, 1–25.

Williams, P. D. (2009) *Criminals, Militias, and Insurgents: Organized Crime in Iraq*. Carlisle, PA: Strategic Studies Institute.

Williams, P. D. (2012) *Security Studies: An Introduction*. Oxford: Routledge.

Williams, P. (2014) *Russian Organized Crime*. Abingdon: Routledge.

Wilson, M.C. and Piazza, J.A. (2013) 'Autocracies and terrorism: conditioning effects of authoritarian regime type on terrorist attacks', *American Journal of Political Science*, 57 (4): 941–55.

Wimmer, A. (2002) *Nationalist Exclusion and Ethnic Conflict: Shadows of Modernity*. Cambridge: Cambridge University Press.

Wimmer, A., Cederman, L.E. and Min, B. (2009) 'Ethnic politics and armed conflict: a configurational analysis of a new global data set', *American Sociological Review*, 74 (2): 316–37.

Windle, J. and Briggs, D. (2015) 'Going solo: the social organization of drug dealing within a London street gang', *Journal of Youth Studies*, 18 (9): 1170–85.

Winkates, J. (2006) 'Suicide terrorism: martyrdom for organizational objectives', *Journal of Third World Studies*, 23 (1): 87.

Womer, S. and Bunker, R.J. (2010) 'Sureños gangs and Mexican cartel use of social networking sites', *Small Wars & Insurgencies*, 21 (1): 81–94.

Woodworth, P. (2001) *Dirty War, Clean Hands: ETA, the GAL and Spanish Democracy*. Cork: Cork University Press.

World Bank (2012) *Fighting Corruption in Public Services: Chronicling Georgia's Reforms*. Washington, DC: The World Bank.

Worrall, J., Mabon, S. and Clubb, G. (2015) *Hezbollah: From Islamic Resistance to Government*. Santa Barbara, CA: ABC-CLIO.

Wucker, M. (2004) 'Haiti: So many missteps', *World Policy Journal*, 21 (1): 41–49.

Young, J. (2003) 'Merton with energy, Katz with structure: the sociology of vindictiveness and the criminology of transgression', *Theoretical Criminology*, 7 (3): 388–414.

Zack-Williams, A.B. (2001) 'Child soldiers in the civil war in Sierra Leone', *Review of African Political Economy*, 28 (87): 73–82.

Zimmermann, E. (2011) 'Globalization and terrorism', *European Journal of Political Economy*, 27: S152–S161.

INDEX

18th Street Gang: 135, 141, 145, 196

Abu Nidal: 78, 89, 185
Abu-Sayaf: 34, 89
affiliates: 34, 102, 111, 114–6
African National Congress (ANC): 100, 167, 173
Aidid, Mohammed: 121, 123, 126, 128
Airmobile Special Forces Group (GAFE): 136
Al-Aqsa Martyrs Brigade: 4, 71, 75
Al-Baghdadi, Abu-Bakr: 115
alienation: 51, 53, 56, 80–2, 197
al-Qaeda: 7, 32, 46–7, 50, 63, 65–6, 68, 72, 74–5, 77, 79–81, 94, 198 and chapter 7
al-Qaeda in the Arabian Peninsula (AQAP): 114
al-Qaeda in Iraq (AQI): 114–6
al-Qaeda in the Islamic Maghreb (AQIM): 108, 110, 114
al-Shabaab: 89, 94, 96
al-Zarqawi, Abu Musab: 114–5
al-Zawahiri, Ayman: 113, 115
anarchy: 10–1, 15, 98
ANC see African National Congress
Anti-Terrorist Liberation Groups (GAL): 161
AQAP see al-Qaeda in the Arabian Peninsula
AQI see al-Qaeda in Iraq
AQIM see al-Qaeda in the Islamic Maghreb
ARENA see National Republican Alliance party
Armed Forces of National Liberation (FALN): 89, 192
Armed Islamic Group: 109, 191
Aryan Brotherhood: 140
Asahara, Shoko: 193
AUC see United Self Defence Forces of Colombia
Aum Shinrikyo: 46, 81, 89, 102, 108, 110, 193
authoritarian regimes: 62–4, 68–9, 112, 179

Baader Meinhof Gang see Red Army Faction
balance of power: 10, 12–3, 16–7, 21–2, 42, 175
Barzani, Masrour: 115
Basque Nationalist Party (PNV): 169, 174
bin Laden, Osama: 68, 102, 109, 112–4
Black Guerrillas: 140
Black Tigers: 103
Black Tigress: 103
Blackwater: 148, 151, 155–6
Black widows: 71, 74
Boko Haram: 56–8, 89, 94, 203
Bloody Sunday: 59
bombings: 58–9, 108–110, 112, 156, 172, 179, 188
    suicide bombings: 44, 177, 179, 58, 63, 74, 78, 105–6, 110, 116
bribes: 30, 68, 129, 133, 145, 188–91,
Buzan, Barry: 15, 19–20

Cali cartel: 137
cartelitos: 132–3, 142, 194–5
cartels: 7, 31–2, 35, 60, 69, 73, 134–8, 141–6, 155, 158, 192, 194
Castro, Fidel: 90
CCM see Chama Cha Mapinduzi
Cells: 25, 36, 46, 50, 52, 66, 87, 92, 107–15, 136, 138, 154, 171, 174, 185
    sleeper cells: 86, 102
Central Intelligence Agency (CIA): 144
Chama Cha Mapinduzi (CCM): 60
child soldiers: 93–4, 116, 118, 124
CIA see Central Intelligence Agency
civil liberties: 62
civil war: 31, 66, 176
    Chechnya: 48
    El Salvador: 141
    Guatemala: 141, 152
    Lebanon: 174
    Liberia: 48
    Sierra Leone: 48, 124
    Somalia: 121
    Syria: 171
    Tajikistan: 68, 129–30
Cold War: 4–5, 11–13, 15–19, 22, 26, 31, 42, 50, 66, 88, 144, 149–50, 161
collective security: 13–14
Comando Vermelho (CV): 24, 35–6
constructivism: 4, 13–15
contras: 68, 144, 148, 152, 156, 158, 161, 181
corruption: 6, 48, 58, 64, 67, 68–9, 86, 97, 136, 144, 181, 188–90, 198–9
    administrative corruption: 61, 188–9, 198
    security corruption 190
Cosa Nostra: 142
counter-insurgency: 29, 155, 193
counter-narratives: 184, 197, 199
crime-terror nexus: 24, 34, 91
CV see Comando Vermelho
cybercrime: 67
cyberterrorism: 46

Davao Death Squad (DDS): 153–5
D-Company: 24, 36, 50
DDS see Davao Death Squad
death squads: 8, 148–55, 157–8, 161, 190
decapitation: 107, 133, 138, 184–5, 193–4
de facto states: 21, 34, 52, 85, 91, 97–100, 102, 114
democide: 55, 68
democracy: 57, 62–3, 90, 97, 130, 151, 159,

Democratic League of Kosovo (LDK): 52
Democratic Peace Theory: 13–14
demonstration effect: 95
deradicalization: 184, 187, 191, 194–5, 197–8
détente: 19
diaspora (diasporic communities): 32, 41–2, 49, 51–3,
    94, 96
Downs, Anthony: 180
drug lord: 35, 64, 137, 141–2, 144, 158
drugs: 32, 34, 48, 51, 67–8, 95, 108–10, 119, 123–5,
    133, 135, 137, 142, 157–58, 190
    cocaine: 35, 124, 135, 158
    heroin: 68–9, 95, 137, 143
Duvalier, François: 150
DynCorp: 148, 152, 159

education: 17, 52, 72–4, 76, 77, 98–9, 119, 125, 133,
    168, 188, 199
    Brazil: 35, 62
    Gaza: 172
    Lebanon: 171
    Liberia: 124
    Nigeria: 57–8
    Northern Ireland: 56
    Peru: 61
    Sierra Leone: 122, 124
EOKA see National Organization of Cypriot
    Fighters: 177
El Chapo: 138
electoral systems: 59, 176
Egyptian Islamic Jihad: 89, 113
ELN see National Liberation Army
enforcer gangs: 133, 135–6, 140, 142
Escobar, Pablo: 137, 190, 194
ETA see Euskadi Ta Askatasuna
ethnicity
    ethnic cleansing: 156
    ethnic criminal groups: 48
    ethnic favouritism: 61
    ethnic fragmentation: 17
    ethnic groups: 60–1, 100, 103, 120, 168
    ethnic guerrilla group/insurgencies: 60, 65, 88, 93,
        96–7, 177
    ethnic networks/linkages: 52, 134
    ethnic identities: 48, 51, 58–9, 64, 122–4,
        138, 140
    ethnic political organizations: 96
    ethnic sectarian groups: 58, 81–2
    ethnic terrorism: 103
Euskadi Ta Askatasuna (ETA): 33, 74, 79, 81–2, 89, 96,
    110, 161, 169, 174, 177, 185, 191
Executive Outcomes: 8, 148, 160–1
exclusive approaches: 184, 192–3
extortion: 31, 33, 34, 52, 94, 129, 143, 156, 171,
EZLN see Zapatista National Liberation Army

failed states: 65–9, 150
FALN see Armed Forces of National Liberation
Farabundo Marti National Liberation Front
    (FMLN): 181
FARC see Revolutionary Armed Forces of Colombia
Fatah: 78, 81, 172, 179
FRELIMO see Mozambique Liberation Front
Front for the Advancement and Progress of Haiti
    (FRAPH): 151
FSNL see Sandinistas National Liberation Front

GAFE see Sandinistas National Liberation Front
GAL see Anti-Terrorist Liberation Groups
globalization: 5, 32, 41–53, 201
Good Friday Agreement: 169, 186
grey zone violence: 24, 26, 31
group processes: 71, 80
guerrilla warfare: 5, 19, 22, 24, 29–30, 72, 90, 99, 116, 173
guerrilla groups: 29–30, 64, 90, 93, 99, 112, 137,
    144–5, 156, 158, 173–4, 177, 181
Guevara, Che: 95
Guzmán, Abimael: 92, 193

Hamas: 8, 27, 34, 60, 74–5, 81, 105, 110, 167, 172,
    178–9, 182, 195
Haqqani Network: 89
Herut: 175
Hezbollah: 8, 16, 34, 52, 60, 68, 73, 75, 81, 106, 110,
    167, 170–5, 177–8, 181–2, 194
Hobbes, Thomas: 11
hostage taking: 106–7, 125, 145
human security: 3–4, 13, 20, 128,
hybrid groups: 32, 34, 37, 50, 94
hybrid wars: 5, 22, 25, 31–2

identity politics: 41, 45
Idris, Wafa: 74
IG see Islamic Group
IMU see Islamic Movement of Uzbekistan
Inclusive approach: 184, 187, 195, 197
Institutional Revolutionary Party (PRI): 89, 143
insurgencies: see chapter 6
    liberation insurgencies: 87–8
    religious insurgencies: 87–8
    revolutionary insurgencies: 87, 89
    separatist insurgencies: 87–8
international institutions: 13–4, 21
International Monetary Fund (IMF): 67
IRA see Irish Republican Army:
Irgun: 175, 186
Irish Republican Army (IRA): 32–4, 57, 59, 81, 82,
    95–6, 104, 108–110, 153, 169, 175, 180
irregular warfare: 29, 90
Islamic Group (IG): 198
Islamic Movement of Uzbekistan (IMU):
Islamic Salvation Front (FIS): 179
IS see Islamic State
ISI see Islamic State of Iraq
ISIL see Islamic State of Iraq and the Levant
Islamic State (IS): 27–8, 34–5, 46, 57, 67, 77, 89, 91,
    102, 114–6, 177, 179, 186–7, 203
Islamic State of Iraq (ISI): 115
Islamic State of Iraq and the Levant (ISIL): 115

Japanese Red Army: 89, 110
Jemaah Islamiyah: 89, 106, 109, 197

Kalishnikov culture: 118, 128
kidnappings: 31, 35–6, 58, 94, 98, 106–7, 116, 125,
    135, 156–7, 161, 177
Kissinger, Henry: 12
Kony, Joseph: 121
KRG see Kurdistan Regional Government
Ku Klux Klan: 28, 77, 80
Kurdistan Regional Government (KRG): 115
Kurdistan Worker's Party (PKK): 33, 52, 68, 75, 89, 92,
    95, 98–9, 193

LDK *see* Democratic League of Kosovo
left wing groups: 88, 104, 137, 144, 181
legislatures: 59–60, 97, 176, 181
liberalism: 13–14
liberation Tigers of Tamil Eelam (LTTE): 34, 52, 75, 89, 91–2, 94, 98–9, 103, 105–6, 176
Lord Resistance Army: 119
Los Zetas: 8, 136, 140, 142
looting: 30, 35, 94, 119–20, 123, 125–6, 129
LTTE *see* Liberation Tigers of Tamil Eelam

M-19: 145
M-23 Movement: 120
Machiavelli, Niccolò: 11
Madrid bombings: 36, 63, 66, 108, 110, 111, 191
Maras: 8, 49, 73, 133, 135, 143, 145–6
Mafia: 7, 48, 133–4, 143–4
  Chechen mafia: 140
  Italian mafia: 138, 143
  Russian mafia 60, 134, 138, 145
  Turkish mafia: 95
majoritarian systems: 176
Mano Dura: 141, 146, 184, 192
Mara Salvatrucha (MS-13): 145, 196
Matta-Ballesteros, Juan: 137
Medellin cartel: 36, 137, 145, 190, 194
media: 27–8, 43, 45–6, 63, 78, 85, 90, 92, 94, 104, 111, 113–6, 141, 159, 202–3
mercenaries: 135, 140, 149, 151, 155–6, 161
Michels, Robert: 180
MILF *see* Moro Islamic Liberation Front
MK *see* Umkhonto we Sizwe
mobile phones: 26, 47, 141
Mobutu, Joseph: 126
money laundering: 31–3, 47, 50, 52, 67, 133, 171, 183, 187–9, 198
Moroccan Islamic Combat Group: 108
Mozambique Liberation Front (FRELIMO): 167, 171, 173–4
MNLF *see* Moro National Liberation Front
Morgenthau, Hans: 11–12
Moro Islamic Liberation Front (MILF): 89, 96, 196
Moro National Liberation Front (MNLF): 96, 196
MS-13 *see* Mara Salvatrucha

narcissistic aggression: 71, 79, 81
Nasrallah, Hassan: 178
National Islamic Front: 68
National Liberation Army (ELN): 36
National Organization of Cypriot Fighters (EOKA): 177
National Patriotic Front of Liberia (NPFL): 122
National Republican Alliance party (ARENA): 154, 158
National Union for the Total Independence of Angola (UNITA): 68, 91, 160
NATO *see* North Atlantic Treaty Organization
Naxalites: 89
neo-realism *see* realism
networks: 5, 7, 14, 31, 43–4, 47, 50–2, 113, 116, 191, 194, 198, 201, 203
  associational networks: 140
  commercial networks: 127
  computer networks: 50, 109
  criminal networks: 45, 50, 82, 126, 133–4, 138, 146, 191
  ethnic networks: 93, 133

networks *cont.*
  global networks: 5
  terror networks: 7, 37, 78, 85–6, 102, 108–9, 112
  patronage/clientelistic networks: 61, 121
  social/personal networks: 71, 73, 81, 107, 122, 138–9
  social service networks: 182
  smuggling networks: 109
NGOs *see* non-governmental organizations
non-governmental organizations: 52, 98, 109, 113, 151, 156, 158, 171, 198
nuclear weapons: 10, 12, 17, 19
NPFL *see* National Patriotic Front of Liberia

Öcalan, Abdullah: 92, 193
OECD *see* Organization for Economic Co-operation and Development
omni-balancing: 16
Organization for Economic Co-operation and Development (OECD): 49

Palestinian Islamic Jihad (PIJ): 105
Palestinian Liberation Organization (PLO): 105–6, 179
Paramilitary groups: 6, 8, 87, 136, 144, 152, 156–8, 161
party systems: 59–60
PCC *see* Primeiro Comando da Capital
personality traits: 71, 76, 78–9
PFLP *see* Popular Front for the Liberation of Palestine
PIJ *see* Palestinian Islamic Jihad
PIRA *see* Provisional Republican Army
piracy: 48, 50, 65, 133,
PKK *see* Kurdistan Worker's Party
plausible deniability: 148, 159, 161
PLO *see* Palestinian Liberation Organization
PNV *see* Basque Nationalist Party
polarity: 5, 10, 12, 13, 17, 19, 41, 42, 53, 202
political rights: 173
Popular Front for the Liberation of Palestine (PFLP): 110
power sharing: 176
PRI *see* Institutional Revolutionary Party
Prima Linea: 173, 177
Primeiro Comando da Capital (PCC): 24, 36, 47, 145
prisons: 35, 46–7, 59, 92–3, 140, 142, 145–6, 161
prison reform: 187, 191, 199
proportional representation: 55, 60, 176
Provisional Republican Army (PIRA): 175
provocation effect: 95
public goods: 8, 36, 55, 60–1, 66, 121, 137, 144, 188

Rabin, Itzak: 194
ransom: 35, 94, 116
rational choice: 22, 77–8, 137, 172
Reagan, Ronald: 19, 158
realism: 11
Red Army Faction (Baader Meinhof Gang): 32, 73, 79, 81, 89, 104
Red Brigades: 81, 89, 106, 174–5, 196
refugees: 25, 30, 49, 52, 56, 65, 96, 124, 131, 179
relative deprivation: 55, 57, 76, 95
religion: 20, 89, 103, 105
resource wars: 118, 126
Revolutionary Armed Forces of Colombia (FARC): 32–3, 37, 88–9, 92–3, 95
Revolutionary United Front (RUF): 118, 122, 124, 160,
right wing groups: 28, 72–3, 76–77, 79, 103, 104, 152, 168, 18, 197–8

robbery: 36, 106, 120, 129, 133
RUF *see* Revolutionary United Front
rule of law: 65–6, 153, 156, 159, 190, 199

Saakashvili, Mikheil: 69, 191
safe havens: 96, 111, 113, 127
Salafists: 109, 114–5
Sandinistas National Liberation Front (FSNL): 60, 144,
    167, 181
Sankoh, Foday: 121
security dilemma: 12
security studies: 3–5, 16–19, 203
self-defence militias: 100
separatist groups: 58, 80–3, 87–8, 104, 140, 180, 191
Shining Path: 33, 61, 73, 89, 92–3, 95–6, 193, 196
Sinaloa Cartel: 138, 142–3
Sinn Fein: 167, 169, 175, 180
small arms: 17, 26, 42, 48, 128, 199, 201
sobels: 118, 120
splintering: 50, 142, 172, 174, 176, 180–1,
    185–6, 193–5
state capture: 55, 68, 116
state repression: 52, 55, 58–9
strategic approaches: 167, 172
strategic studies: 17–19
structuralist approaches: 167, 176
Suarez, Roberto: 137
Sudanese People's Liberation Movement: 159

Taliban: 32, 68, 89, 92–3, 112, 130, 189
targeted killings: 184, 193
Taylor, Charles: 48, 118, 121, 122, 124, 126–7, 129
Taylorland: 129
terrorism: *see* Chapter 7
    lone actor terrorism: 28
    religious terrorism: 103–4, 109
    suicide terrorism: 105–7, 110, 116, 177, 179,
        192, 194
Third World: 15
Thucydides: 11
Titan: 151–2
Tonton Macoutes: 150–1

Triads: 134, 138, 140,
trafficking:
    arms: 31, 36
    drug: 31–6, 65, 67–8, 94–5, 109–110, 119,
        134–41, 143–5, 156, 158, 188
    humans: 48
transformation: 24, 33, 195, 201
tri-border area: 41, 48, 52, 64, 171

Umkhonto we Sizwe (MK): 173
unemployment: 56–8, 76–7
UNITA *see* National Union for the Total Independence
    of Angola
United Self Defence Forces of Colombia (AUC): 8,
    156, 158
United Tajik Opposition (UTO): 68
UTO *see* United Tajik Opposition

Volontaires de la Sécurité Nationale *see* Tonton
    Macoutes
Vietnam War: 19
Vigilantism: 153
VSN *see* Tonton Macoutes

Waltz, Kenneth: 11–12, 20
war economies: 48, 119–20, 129
warlords: *see* Chapter 8
    Neo-warlord: 118, 131
warlord militia: 118–9, 122–5, 129–30
Weather Underground: 89
welfare states/systems: 19–20, 35, 44, 61, 65–6, 98,
    116, 137, 170–2, 179, 189
Wendt, Alexander: 15
women and terrorism: 74–5
World Bank: 69
World War II: 11, 13, 30, 88, 96

Yakuza: 134, 138–9
Yusuf, Mohammed: 58

Zapatista National Liberation Army (EZLN): 7,
    89–90, 95